MW00999585

SPEAKING FOR OTHERS

SPEAKING
FOR OTHERS

The Ethics of
Informal Political Representation

WENDY SALKIN

HARVARD UNIVERSITY PRESS

Cambridge, Massachusetts
London, England
2024

Library of Congress Cataloging-in-Publication Data

Names: Salkin, Wendy, 1985– author.
Title: Speaking for others : the ethics of informal political representation / Wendy Salkin.
Description: Cambridge, Massachusetts ; London, England :
Harvard University Press, 2024. | Includes index.
Identifiers: LCCN 2023049939 | ISBN 9780674238534 (cloth)
Subjects: LCSH: Political ethics—United States. | Representative government
and representation—United States. | Political leadership—Moral and ethical aspects—
United States. | Political participation—Moral and ethical aspects—United States. |
Community organization—Moral and ethical aspects—United States. | African
Americans—Politics and government. | Power (Social sciences)—United States.
Classification: LCC JK468.E7 S35 2024 | DDC 172/.20973—dc23/eng/20231120
LC record available at https://lccn.loc.gov/2023049939

For my parents,

Linda B. Celauro and Richard E. Salkin,

who took me to city council meetings as a kid.

The way in which groups of human beings are led to choose certain of their number as their spokesmen and leaders is at once the most elementary and the nicest problem of social growth.

—W. E. B. Du Bois, "The Evolution of Negro Leadership"

It is easy to be outraged at the plight of others, especially easy (perhaps) for a man who shares or has shared that plight, but it is not easy to act for them when they are unable to act for themselves. Many men claim to do so; other men question their good faith.

—Michael Walzer, "The Obligations of Oppressed Minorities"

Contents

PART TWO

Introduction

We care a great deal about our formal political representatives (FPRs)—our legislators, governors, judges, city council members, and others whom we ourselves elect or who are appointed by others we have elected. We scrutinize who they are, how they come into their positions, what powers they wield, whether their values reflect ours, whether they listen to us, whether their actions are responsive to our interests and preferences. We laud and criticize them by turn for their handling of weighty political affairs that directly affect our everyday lives. Sometimes, we knock doors in support of their reelection; other times, we collect signatures to recall them. It is therefore no surprise that formal political representation is a familiar topic of discussion not only among democratic theorists but in our day-to-day conversations with the people around us.

What is surprising is how little attention we pay, by comparison, to political actors who can be just as influential as our FPRs, and sometimes more so, who speak and act for us in a wide variety of political contexts, who shape the terms of our public debates, who lead social movements that change the courses of our lives, and who somehow have these powers despite having never been granted them through formal, systematized election or selection procedures. They are our informal political representatives (IPRs). And this book is about them.

Informal political representation is nothing new.[1] It has long played a role in the public expression of the values, interests, and preferences of groups, particularly of oppressed and unjustly marginalized groups.[2] Consider Booker T. Washington's "Atlanta Compromise," which had its origins in a speech before an audience of both Black and white southerners at the 1895 Cotton States and International Exposition, offering a number of public concessions on behalf of all Black Americans. "The wisest among my race," he said, "understand that the agitation of questions of social equality is the extremest folly." He even made a promise to white southerners on behalf of his informal constituency: "I pledge that in your effort to work out the great and intricate problem which God has laid at the doors of the South, you shall have at all times the patient, sympathetic help of my race."[3]

Informal political representation is an inevitable and ineradicable practice in almost all societies and, indeed, in any deliberative forum besides small face-to-face committees.[4] The phenomenon emerges even in fora some may have hoped were immune: "direct democracies often cede political power to arrogant loudmouths whom no one chose to represent them."[5] Indeed, it was the presumed inevitability of the practice that motivated W. E. B. Du Bois, a recurrent critic of Washington's informal political representation of Black Americans, to advocate for the training of the Talented Tenth. In his 1903 essay of the same name, Du Bois asks, "Do you think that if the leaders of thought among Negroes are not trained and educated thinkers, that they will have no leaders? On the contrary a hundred half-trained demagogues will still hold the places they so largely occupy now, and hundreds of vociferous busy-bodies will multiply."[6] Yet informal political representation is not just an inevitability we must learn to live with whether we like it or not. To the contrary, there is reason to favor and even to celebrate the practice. Below, I discuss both its value and dangers.

IPRs are everywhere. Some are nationally or even internationally recognized leaders of social movements. Rev. Dr. Martin Luther King Jr. informally represented Black Montgomerians during the Montgomery Bus Boycott, and Black Americans generally throughout the course of the civil rights movement. Me Too movement leader Tarana Burke informally represents survivors of sexual assault, abuse, and harassment.[7] Black Lives Matter informally represents Black communities throughout the United States and beyond.[8] Former Marjory Stoneman Douglas High School student Aalayah Eastmond informally represents not only fellow former classmates but American high schoolers generally, as when she testified before Congress, "We *are* the generation that will end gun violence."[9] Malala Yousafzai informally represents Pakistani schoolchildren before the United Nations, while Greta Thunberg stands before the United Nations to informally represent Generation Z.[10] These IPRs have in common that they have been serving as IPRs over time, developing relationships with their informal constituencies, and building social movements, the norms of which inform how they represent. Not all IPRs, however, are internationally recognized movement leaders. Some IPRs live in our hometowns. They are our neighbors and friends. But when they go to the city council meeting to give voice to the shared interests of the people living in our neighborhood, they become our representatives, too.[11] Even more surprisingly, you or I may be an IPR without knowing it.

What exactly is an IPR? That is a question to be answered over the course of this book. Succinctly, for now: An IPR is an individual or group who is treated by an audience as speaking or acting for others on matters apt for broad public discussion despite having been neither elected nor selected to do so by means of a systematized election or selection procedure.

This description gets at the core features of the phenomenon. Even so, understanding who falls within the ambit of the category *IPR* and why can be a messy business, as IPRs often simultaneously fill other familiar social roles—group leader, descriptive representative, symbolic representative, role model, moral exemplar, advocate, ally, influencer.[12] But one can also be an IPR without inhabiting any of these other nearby social roles. Our neighbor may speak for us at the council meeting without being our leader.[13] They just happen to be the neighbor who can make the meetings, so they end up attending on behalf of all of us. In fact, the status of IPR is conferred by audiences, so the role can come unbidden. Our neighbor may have gone to the council meeting intending to speak only in a personal capacity, but the council members treated their complaints as expressed on our behalf.[14] In so treating our neighbor, the council members made them our IPR. Many people who are far from being group leaders find themselves one day, to their considerable surprise, in the role of IPR.

In this book, I provide a systematic conceptual and normative account of informal political representation. My approach is to identify the core features of informal political representation and advance a normative theory concerning that practice, independent of its coincidence with other social roles. The theory advanced here may have implications for extant theories of these other social roles, but informal political representation merits careful examination in its own right.

Despite IPRs' ubiquity and significance to our political lives, the role of the IPR is conceptually puzzling, morally troubling, and markedly undertheorized. What scholarship there is on informal political representation and similar phenomena has been a beacon for me as I have developed the account set forth in these pages.[15] To develop the theory found here, I also draw broadly on and synthesize ideas and arguments from many fields, including philosophy, political science, Black political thought, bioethics, disability studies, feminist theory, law, and negotiation theory. Scholars and practitioners across these fields have touched on this topic or nearby variants, and this book is indebted to their ideas.

Group Representation

Although an IPR may represent either an individual or a group, I accord group representation special attention for two main reasons. First, as Alexander Bickel notes, "We have, since Madison, realized that people tend to act politically not so much as individuals as in groups."[16] As political actors generally, and all the more so as represented parties, we tend both to act and to be regarded as members of groups rather than as individuals. Second, it is within the context of group representation that the most difficult and pressing moral questions arise. Although a group's members will often be united by some points of commonality—perhaps shared values, interests, preferences, commitments, needs, or experiences—they will also inevitably diverge in other respects. As Iris Young puts the point, "It is impossible to find the essential attributes of constituents, the single common interest that overrides the diversity of their other interests, experiences, and opinions. Representation understood in this way is impossible. Yet representation is both necessary and desirable."[17] Given these points of divergence, a representative will often have to make difficult and sometimes divisive choices about how to represent a group.

Moreover, group representation itself is not a monolithic category. An IPR can represent a group of any sort, and any sort of group can be informally represented. Groups vary widely with respect to features like what make them groups, how they are organized, and whether members identify as group members. For instance, a group might comprise people who share a common desire or common grievance—who "are united and actuated by some common impulse of passion, or of interest"—or about whom a certain proposition is true.[18] Some groups have internal norms that dictate how an IPR is to receive authorization from the group, while others do not.[19] Some groups' members regard themselves as sharing solidaristic ties or objectives, while others do not know themselves to be members of the same group at all. Whereas for the former type of group an IPR may primarily be valuable insofar as they can help the group realize its shared objective, for the latter type of group an IPR may be valuable simply insofar as they make the group's members aware that they belong to the same group. So, IPRs fulfill different needs faced by different sorts of represented groups—what is beneficial or required for one type of group may be inapposite or even downright harmful for another. Many discussions of informal political representation focus on the representation of social groups, overlooking other types of groups whose members share no special affinities, common history, or outwardly obvious characteristics, and who in some cases do not even recognize that they are members of such a group.[20] Yet IPRs may provide distinctive goods to these overlooked groups too. Accordingly, what value an IPR offers to a given represented group depends on, among other things, the kind of group being represented, what the group needs from a representative (*purposive considerations*), and what sort of relationship is possible between the group and the IPR (*relational considerations*). Throughout this book, I illustrate my analysis with real-world examples of many different varieties of group informal political representation. To further appreciate the varieties of group representation, consider how different types of groups benefit from different aspects of informal political representation.

The Value of Informal Political Representation

To understand the value of informal political representation, we need to first consider the value of political representation generally. We simply cannot be in all the places where we might prefer that our voices are heard, or where our voices are needed if we are to have our values, interests, or preferences considered and perhaps also protected or satisfied. "Representation is necessary," Iris Young tells us, "because the web of modern social life often ties the actions of some people and institutions in one place to consequences in many other places and institutions. No person can be present at all the decisions or in all the decision-making bodies whose actions affect her life, because there are so many and they are so dispersed. Though her aspirations are often disappointed, she hopes that others will think about

her situation and represent it to the issue forum."[21] To Young's considerations, I add these: Even if we were able to be in all of those far apart and
hard-to-find places, would we be invited to speak? Were we invited to speak,
would we know what to say? And even if we knew what to say, would we
say it as well or as convincingly as another who might have said it for us?
For each of these questions, the answer may be "no."

So, political representation generally is not "at best a grudging concession to size or efficiency."[22] It allows for effective communication, coalition
building, information collection and transmission, perspective taking, and
the crystallization of ideas from what people may at first only "dimly per-
ceive" to be what they in fact value, want, or prefer.[23] Those who become
political representatives become responsible to and responsible for others—
the represented and audiences—in distinctive and powerful ways. Moreover,
political representation enables all of us to better understand our shared
social world and its inhabitants.

Still, you may ask: What's so good about informal political representation in particular? IPRs can provide distinctive political goods to the groups
for whom they speak or act—publicly voicing groups' otherwise neglected
interests; making overlooked groups visible to broader publics; making
groups visible to themselves as groups by stirring group consciousness in
the members of oppressed or marginalized pluralities; serving as communicative conduits between represented groups and their unresponsive lawmakers; and, through each of these, educating public audiences about the
represented group. Consider each of these in turn.

First, IPRs often voice groups' otherwise neglected interests. Some IPRs
supplement a group's existing FPRs, giving voice to interests their FPRs fail
to express; other IPRs are lone voices for groups altogether lacking FPRs.[24]
Groups' interests go unexpressed for a variety of reasons. Some interests are
misunderstood or belong to groups too small to receive FPRs' attention.
Other interests belong to groups excluded from the electorate, like the undocumented and disenfranchised.[25] Such groups rely on virtual or informal
political representation to have their interests expressed.[26] Still other political
interests enjoy no public discussion because discussing them is widely
understood to be career ending for elected officials—the so-called "third
rail" of politics.[27] For instance, the unpopularity of stigmatized groups makes
it risky for FPRs, seeking reelection or donor support, to take up their man-
tles.[28] Consider an example: Registered sex offenders face stringent resi-

dency restrictions. They may be prohibited from living within certain "specified distances of schools, parks, day-care centers, and other areas."[29] In recent years, lawyers, scholars, and activists have questioned whether these restrictions are needed and also whether they are legal.[30] Despite these concerns, legislators are loath to consider (let alone put forth) bills that would be seen as providing public benefits to sex offenders.[31] This means that, even if residency restrictions leave registered sex offenders with no-where to go, few elected representatives will take up the charge of repre-senting their interests, as this would leave those elected representatives open to the staunch reprisals of their constituencies. As Robin van der Wall, a North Carolina registrant and board member of the national advocacy group Reform Sex Offender Laws, puts the point, "Who wants to risk being called a pedophile-lover?"[32] IPRs may tread where formal analogues dare not.[33] In both his 2009 *A Place for Paedophiles* and a companion magazine article, documentarian Louis Theroux uses interview and observation to give voice to the values, interests, preferences, and perspectives of sex offenders indefinitely detained in Coalinga State Hospital in California.[34] Similarly, the advocacy group Texas Voices for Reason and Justice "advocates for more relaxed penalties for sex offenders."[35] Both Theroux and Texas Voices for Reason and Justice informally represent sex offenders—people whose in-terests receive little to no expression by FPRs. Though not immune to criticism for representing unpopular groups, IPRs need not choose between representation and reelection.[36]

Second, IPRs can make overlooked groups visible. They can make gov-ernments and broader publics aware that there are groups whose interests ought to be weighed among others in political decision-making, as Indig-enous rights activist Rigoberta Menchú did in speaking to the Guatemalan government on behalf of Indigenous communities.[37] Of course, making a group visible to a broader society can bring with it attendant perils. It makes a difference what is made visible, and to whom.[38] Accordingly, some groups develop norms that constrain what an IPR may disclose about the repre-sented group to an audience of outsiders.[39]

Third, IPRs can raise group consciousness and even contribute to group formation. Some groups' members have common interests but do not see it that way—either because they do not realize individually that they have such interests themselves or, despite each one realizing that much, do not recognize those interests to be shared. Not recognizing their interests in either of these ways, *shared unrecognized interest group* members are unlikely to regard themselves as members of any such group and may, further, fail to recognize that there is such a group. But the fact that they are members of the interest group does not depend on either self-identifying or being identified by others as group members. Rather, something internal to their circumstances dictates that they are group members. Just as they may over-look their own group membership, so too may it be overlooked by others. The working poor, gig workers, and other groups whose members share eco-nomic interests are paradigmatic examples of such groups, as are survivors of sexual assault at the hands of the same assailant. IPRs can make such groups visible to themselves by impressing on their members that there is such a group, that they are members, that they share politically salient in-terests with other group members, that they ought to regard themselves as group members, and perhaps also that they ought to regard themselves as having obligations to fellow group members—long the aim of labor organizers and feminist consciousness-raising groups.[40]

Fourth, IPRs often serve as communicative conduits—ferrying messages between the represented and lawmakers, the media, or the broader public.[41] Menchú's ability to speak both Spanish and K'iche' enables her to com-municate between government officials and Indigenous Guatemalans.[42] The Abahlali baseMjondolo Movement communicates between judiciaries and South African shack dwellers.[43] An IPR may even negotiate on a group's behalf, as King did in Montgomery, Alabama, when negotiating between bus boycotters, the bus company, and the city.[44]

Fifth, an IPR may educate an audience about a group, which may in-volve correcting existing misunderstandings that the audience has about that group. In some cases, an IPR may educate an audience by dispelling the belief that there is any such group: Some groups' members are united by the fact that a social identity has been ascribed to them from without. As is the case for shared unrecognized interest group members, what I will call *ascribed membership group members* do not, at least initially, see them-selves as belonging to the group. However, unlike shared unrecognized in-terest groups, for ascribed membership groups, there is in a real sense no such group "from the inside." It is not, at least in the first instance, by virtue of something internal to individual group members or their experiences or circumstances that they come to hold membership in the group. Rather, the group is brought into being by the ascription of a common identity, often ascribed on the basis of some perceived feature of those who become group members. Consider the group *people who "look Muslim."*[45] This group ascription is generated from without—perhaps based on the incorrect assumption that there is some one way Muslims look, along with increased attention brought to such identifications as a result of (among other things) restrictive travel policies, discriminatory national security policies, racism, and Islamophobia. The group label arises from, for instance, prejudicial policies that make it matter "how Muslim" a person is perceived to be by an onlooker. The group classification is generated by a mistake on the part of the classifier (an audience) that the classification is felicitous to that (or any) context. Ascribed membership group members need only have in common that they are so classified by some audience. As for their shared interests, the groups' members may in fact have in common only the view that the errant classification tracks nothing of relevance and the demand that the classification no longer be ascribed. An IPR for an ascribed membership group will aim not to make the group itself visible (for the audience has had no trouble "finding" the group) but rather to make known to the audience their own error—namely, attempting to pick out such a group in the first place. Whereas an IPR for a shared unrecognized interest group aims to impress on group members that there is a group and that they are group members, an IPR for an ascribed membership group aims to impress on audiences that there is no such group.

Although IPRs can represent groups of any sort, the difference they make in political life is most salient in contexts where the group being represented is oppressed or marginalized. IPRs are well situated to promote more just circumstances for the most downtrodden, to empower them, and to seek equal treatment on their behalf. In fact, informal political representation can be a political lifeline for oppressed and marginalized groups, which tend to lack the political power that would aid them in redressing their oppression or marginalization. In representative democracies, this lack of political power often manifests as exclusion from or inefficacy in FPR lawmaking bodies. As a result, the interests of such groups do not tend to be expressed nonaccidentally in, let alone satisfied by, the FPR institutions that shape their members' lives. (Sometimes, the values, interests, or preferences expressed in or satisfied by FPR institutions by happenstance align with these groups' interests. That it is by happenstance means that such institutions are not responsive to the groups' interests. It matters not just that our representative institutions express or satisfy our interests but that they do so because they are our interests.) IPRs can play a sui generis corrective role for these groups. Informal political representation can give oppressed and marginalized groups some say—however mediate, partial, and imperfect— in how things go for them. Although unelected, IPRs come to speak for these groups in many fora, at protests and on picket lines, from city council meetings to Congress.

As these different examples illustrate, what counts as valuable informal political representation for a particular group will depend at least in part on what sort of group it is. In addition to the valuable features just discussed, IPRs can also, by their actions, promote a variety of democratic values—including relational equality, political influence, political agency, community recognition, and trust—thereby making their societies more just (see Chapter 4).

The benefits discussed here may give the impression that informal political representation provides second-best solutions, to be pursued only when formal political representation fails. This is not so, for the following three reasons, as well as many more that will come to light over the course of the book. First, informal political representation does not solely correct for FPR mechanisms' shortcomings; it also counteracts and eases communicative difficulties that are inevitable features of modern political life in large-scale societies more generally, including overlooked groups, disorganized pluralities, misunderstood interests, and siloed political fora. Second, IPRs are not only valuable under conditions of injustice, although they are especially important when there is injustice. Third, in our unjust world, IPRs are valuable for both groups that are oppressed or marginalized and groups that are not. What changes in these different contexts is not whether such representation is valuable but rather the sources of its value. In this book, I focus especially on the corrective role informal political representation can play for oppressed and marginalized groups that lack adequate or any formal political representation.

The Dangers of Informal Political Representation

At the same time, informal political representation is perilous. In the absence of the traditional authorization and accountability mechanisms available in FPR contexts, IPRs can have outsized control over the public narratives of the groups they represent without the represented having much recourse to object or protest. One cannot, after all, impeach the unelected. Without institutional or procedural constraints, IPRs may wield their *power to influence* free from fear of reprisal or rebuke. The power to influence is the IPR's capacity, through their statements or actions, to shape an audience's doxastic attitudes about a represented group and its values, interests, or preferences.[46] So positioned, IPRs may gravely mischaracterize the represented. They may *occlude* the group altogether, diverting attention away from the represented group and its interests and toward themselves. Occlusion may take another, partial form: IPRs may prioritize some group members' interests over others and, in so doing, divert public attention away from interests not prioritized. This second form of occlusion may, in turn, contribute to the marginalization of some group members by other group members.[47] When the IPR is not a member of the represented group, they may also *displace* group members who might have been more appropriate for the role. Through each of these actions, the IPR may contribute to the disempowerment of those they represent.

To make matters worse, IPRs are often the only political actors working to advance the interests of oppressed and marginalized groups, meaning that these groups come to rely on their IPRs. Those who are represented solely by IPRs are left subject to the whims and idiosyncrasies of whoever takes up the torch on their behalf—or, in cases in which the IPR is unwittingly or unwillingly conscripted into their position by an audience, has the torch handed to them (see Chapter 2).[48] These circumstances, taken together, leave many represented groups, particularly marginalized and oppressed groups, at the mercy of their IPRs, rendering such relationships inegalitarian and, sometimes, oppressive (see Chapter 4). And although occasionally there are plausible mechanisms for informal authorization and accountability (see Chapter 3), we cannot and should not expect these mechanisms to provide all or even most of the protections that the formal analogues of these mechanisms might. Consider these perils in detail.

First, IPRs are not (and, often, cannot be) reliably subject to authorization or accountability mechanisms that might check their power to influence. This leaves IPRs free, for instance, to pursue their own political agendas and aspirations at the expense of the represented group's members' interests, to override or simply ignore represented groups' members' expressed interests, and to forgo short-term advances for longer-term possible gains even when represented group members would not choose to do so. IPRs' unchecked power is of special concern for groups that lack adequate or any formal political representation, as such groups rely more significantly on their IPRs for the public expression of their values, interests, and preferences. These circumstances jointly can and often do lead to inegalitarian and in some cases oppressive relationships between IPRs and represented group members, for which reason we need an account of the ethics of informal political representation. In addition to this procedural concern, there are several substantive concerns at issue, too:

Second, IPRs may misrepresent the group. Instead of correcting misunderstandings about a represented group or its interests, an IPR may be the source of misinformation. For instance, they may mislead an audience as to what a group's interests are. Consider an example. In 2015, Israeli Prime Minister Benjamin Netanyahu, presenting himself as "the emissary . . . of the entire Jewish people,"[49] described the impending Iran nuclear deal as "very dangerous" and "threaten[ing] all of us."[50] He suggested that his concerns were voiced not merely on behalf of Israelis, for whom he was and is an FPR, but also on behalf of "the Jewish people" as such.[51] Earlier that same year, essayist David Harris Gershon objected, "Netanyahu has repeatedly claimed, as Israel's Prime Minister, to speak on behalf of all Jews. And it's a claim he's been articulating with troubling frequency as he prepares to attack President Obama's Iran diplomacy before Congress. However, not only is his claim both preposterous and dangerous, it's not even true with regard to the issue of Iran. Indeed, 52 percent of American Jews embrace Obama's diplomatic efforts with Iran."[52] An IPR may thus mislead an audience as to whether the interests or concerns they express are indeed shared by those for whom they speak or act (see Chapter 5).

Third, IPRs will often face and cause discord when engaged in the necessary task of prioritizing some group members' values, interests, and preferences over others. Some amount of prioritization among competing group values, interests, and preferences is inevitable. No group is homogeneous in all respects. Although occasionally group members unite around just one single value, interest, or preference, more often individual group members have many different values, interests, or preferences. Even within fairly cohesive groups, internal contests and disagreements arise concerning which values, interests, or preferences ought to be considered, prioritized, or expressed to broader audiences. Part of the work of the IPR is to make difficult and sometimes divisive choices about how to represent a group—deciding, for instance, which interests to prioritize over others.

Yet such prioritization becomes a cause for concern when it reflects or reinforces objectionable power imbalances between subgroups within a represented group. Barbara Ransby discusses such a concern about the Southern Christian Leadership Conference (SCLC): "The founders of SCLC were concerned primarily, but not exclusively, about access to the ballot box and dignified treatment in public accommodations. But theirs was a world apart from the lives of destitute sharecroppers and their families who constituted a considerable portion of the South's black population—people who could barely afford the fare to ride on public transportation even after desegregation."[53] In this example, although the SCLC was widely regarded to represent Black southerners as such, its founders prioritized expressing the interests of a dominant subgroup (middle-class Black southerners) over the interests of a subordinated subgroup (destitute Black sharecroppers). The prioritization of dominant subgroup members' values, interests, or preferences over those of subordinated subgroup members raises two distinguishable concerns: (1) subordinated subgroup members' interests may remain unexpressed to and therefore unanswered by broader audiences who may otherwise have interceded, and (2) the prioritization of dominant subgroup members' interests may itself reinforce and deepen the power imbalance between the dominant and subordinated subgroups. I return to this criticism of the SCLC, as well as general concerns about intragroup interest prioritization, in Chapter 5.[54]

Concerns about power imbalances in heterogeneous groups are not unique challenges for informal political representation—such challenges arise in all kinds of group representation, formal and informal alike. In fact, informal political representation may be better equipped than formal political representation to handle the challenges of inegalitarian intragroup dynamics and unequal power distributions, in part because, although the number of FPRs permitted in, say, a legislative body is usually fixed (e.g., one hundred U.S. senators, 435 U.S. representatives), there are no such de jure limits on how many IPRs a particular group can have. There can instead be productive contestation and competition among IPRs concerning such questions as who is the group's rightful IPR (perhaps according to particular standards internal to the group), what ought to be said on the group's behalf, or whether the group should instead be conceived as two groups or

ten, each with different IPRs whose representation meets the more particular needs of their newly splintered constituencies (see Chapter 5). Informal political representation is, in this way, without limit: one IPR may
arise, then another, and another, and their approaches to representation
may shift and diverge as suits their search for new audiences and, in some
cases, their search for the group they represent (see Chapters 4 and 6).

Fifth, consider the danger of *occlusion*. One of the main benefits of informal political representation is that it brings valuable public attention to
represented groups and their values, interests, or preferences. In many cases,
IPRs use their positions and the attendant power to influence to secure
this public attention for the groups they represent. But not always. Some
IPRs instead garner public attention only for themselves or only for some
represented group members. Call this *occlusion*: an IPR intentionally or
negligently leads their audience to focus on (1) the IPR themself rather
than the group they represent, or (2) some group members at the expense
of other group members (see Chapters 4 and 5).

Sixth, consider *displacement*. Although there are not de jure limits on how
many IPRs a given group can have, there are likely to be some de facto limits
on how many IPRs will be given meaningful attention by a broader public.
When there are such de facto limits, the IPR who fills the role for a given
group may displace others who might have been more appropriate for the
role. A common version of this displacement concern is that a person who
is not a group member may fill the role of IPR for a given group, thereby
displacing group members who would arguably have been more suitable
candidates. This concern has often been raised against Bono, the lead singer
of the Irish rock band U2, an internationally recognized philanthropist, and
an IPR for sub-Saharan Africans on matters relating to HIV / AIDS prevention and treatment. As George Monbiot points out in his op-ed "Bono
Can't Help Africans by Stealing Their Voice," "Bono claims to be 'representing the poorest and most vulnerable people.' But talking to a wide range
of activists from both the poor and rich worlds . . . I have heard the same
complaint again and again: that Bono and others like him have seized
the political space which might otherwise have been occupied by the Africans about whom they are talking. Because Bono is seen by world leaders
as the representative of the poor, the poor are not invited to speak. This
works very well for everyone—except them."[55] The displacement concern
Monbiot raises here depends for its force on the unstated background

principle that, when possible, it is best if a group is represented by one of its own members (see Chapters 5 and 6).

Seventh, some argue that IPRs contribute to the disempowerment of already vulnerable groups. Bono has been a target of this criticism too. Max Bankole Jarrett, quoted in the 2009 article "Are Bono and Bob Geldof good for Africa?," expressed the disempowerment concern this way: "For most Africans it's a turnoff when Geldof/Bono are used to present a range of African issues. . . . It perpetuates everything these guys claim to be speaking out against—an Africa that is weak and incapable of picking itself up."[56] This peril, *disempowerment,* may seem to arise most naturally in cases in which the IPR is not a member of the group they represent. But concerns over disempowerment at the hands of a dominating or occluding IPR may arise even when the representative is a member of the represented group (see Chapters 5 and 6).[57]

In Chapter 4, I give more systematic consideration to the dangers of informal political representation introduced here, where skeptical challenges grounded in these concerns are schematized.

The Central Ethical Question and the Argument

The central ethical challenge faced by informal political representation, the one that motivates all of the arguments set forth in this book, is this: There is a tension at the very heart of the IPR's relationship to the represented group. On the one hand, IPRs offer valuable political goods to represented groups— publicly voicing groups' otherwise neglected interests; making overlooked groups visible to broader publics; making groups visible to themselves as groups by stirring group consciousness in the members of oppressed or marginalized pluralities; serving as communicative conduits between represented groups and their unresponsive lawmakers; and, through each of these, educating public audiences about the represented group as well as correcting public audiences' misunderstandings of the group. In fact, for many, there is a need, sometimes desperate, for informal political representation. Were it not for their IPRs, many groups—particularly marginalized and oppressed groups—might have no one to speak their piece in public. The valuable features of informal political representation to these represented groups helps us appreciate what is at stake in defending the practice from a variety of different forms of skepticism. On the other hand, there are dangers built into the practice, unmoored as it is from the protections and safe-guards available in FPR contexts. The substantive and procedural dangers of informal political representation are significant: in the absence of the traditional authorization and accountability mechanisms available in FPR contexts, unchecked IPRs can misrepresent the interests of repre-sented groups; contribute to intragroup marginalization by prioritizing some group members' interests over others; occlude represented groups; displace other possible IPRs; and, through each of these, contribute to the disempowerment of those they represent. These dangers give us reason to take skeptical concerns about the practice of informal political representation seriously. Without adequate response, these dangers seem to counsel against the continued practice of informal political representation. The question before us, then, is this: How may IPRs permissibly undertake activities cen-tral to their roles without thereby harming or wronging those they represent? That is the question I answer in this book.[58]

To answer that question, we first need to answer more basic questions about informal political representation: What is an IPR, and how does someone become one? In what senses do IPRs represent us? What kinds of power do IPRs have and how do they come to have those powers?

In Part I, I tackle these foundational conceptual questions. I provide a general theory of informal political representation that both introduces the different features of the phenomenon and explains how those features fit together. From this general theory, we glean a few key insights: IPRs, are ubiquitous and, although neither elected nor selected through systematized procedures, are politically powerful. In some cases, however, they are also objectionably burdened by the demands of their roles.

In Chapter 1, "Audience Conferral," I provide a general analytical frame-work for understanding what IPRs are and how they come about—one that is conceptually clear and portable. Informal political representation is a species of a more general phenomenon, *informal representation*. An indi-vidual or group emerges as an informal representative when and because they are treated by an audience as speaking or acting for another individual or group in a context—call this *audience conferral*.[59] Characterizing the phe-nomenon of informal representation this way shows just how easy it is for a party to end up informally representing a group.

After setting out my understanding of the concept of *speaking for,* I dis-tinguish informal political representation from formal political representation, provide a preliminary account of the phenomenon itself, explain audience conferral, and consider but reject some alternative accounts of IPR emergence. Above, I discussed the different types of groups that can be informally represented. In Chapter 1, I provide preliminary characterizations of the other two parties that make up the representative relationship: the audiences that confer on parties the status of IPR and, of course, the IPRs themselves.

While, in Chapter 1, I focus on how IPRs emerge, in Chapters 2 and 3, I turn my attention to their powers.

In Chapter 2, "Conscription and the Power to Influence," I grapple with two considerations that, when taken together, have surprising normative implications for our theory of informal political representation.

The first consideration is that, sometimes, people are conscripted into the role of IPR. A party is conscripted just in case they are treated by some audience as speaking or acting for some group (*audience conferral*), but either do not know that they are so treated or do not want to be so treated—that is, the IPR is *unwitting* or *unwilling*. After providing a characterization of the widespread but unexamined phenomenon of IPR conscription, I consider why audiences conscript IPRs—both their motivations for seeking out parties to serve in this role at all and their reasons for treating some parties rather than others as speaking or acting on behalf of groups. I then discuss the duties that accrue to audiences by virtue of their power to conscript IPRs.

The second consideration is that, whether voluntary or conscripted, IPRs can have tremendous power to influence how those they represent are regarded by various audiences. Recall that the *power to influence* is the IPR's capacity, through their statements or actions, to shape an audience's doxastic attitudes about a represented group and its values, interests, or preferences. The power to influence emerges when and because an audience treats someone as speaking or acting on behalf of a group. This means that some IPRs have the power to influence the audiences they find themselves before even if (1) the IPR has not been authorized by the group for whom the audience treats them as speaking or acting and (2) the IPR themself does not want to be or does not know they are in the position. A party may thus be an IPR for a group even when they are unwilling, unwitting, and not authorized by the represented group. I argue that when an IPR has the power to influence how at least one audience regards the represented group, that IPR has corresponding pro tanto duties to the represented group, even when neither the IPR nor the represented group wants that IPR to occupy the position. Specifically, I argue that IPRs owe it to parties who are more vulnerable than they are—which tend to be but are not always the groups they represent—to guide their actions to accord with, among other principles, the principles of *due care* and *loss prevention*.[60]

One may quite reasonably object that my argument makes the role of the conscripted IPR excessively burdensome—first, the party is conscripted into an unsought role by an audience, then they come to have pro tanto duties to the represented group as a result. I respond to this burdensomeness objection first in Chapter 2 itself, identifying a number of grounds on which IPRs may reasonably reject the ascription of the duties that would otherwise accrue to them by virtue of their ascension into the role of IPR. I develop and expand my response to this burdensomeness objection in Chapter 6, where I discuss the value of nondescriptive IPRs, who can and in some cases should informally represent people who are not like them precisely to ease burdens that would otherwise fall to those more likely to be conscripted into the role. Some readers will no doubt find this account of IPR conscription counterintuitive. Some may even be tempted to think that, somehow, the account itself confers power on audiences to say who speaks or acts for whom.[61] That would, however, misdescribe this project. My aim is not to endorse the fact that IPRs are sometimes conscripted into their roles by audiences. (To the contrary, I find this fact deeply worrisome, as will become clear over the course of the book.) Rather, my aim is to highlight and examine what I take to be an accurate, realistic description of how audiences actually bring about IPRs in societies like ours. In fact, I am not the first to notice the role of the audience in bringing about IPRs. In his January 23, 1963, speech to the African Students Association and the National Association for the Advancement of Colored People Campus Chapter of Michigan State University, "The Race Problem in America," Malcolm X made a distinction between two types of IPR status conferral: "Most of the so-called Negroes that you listen to on the race problem usually don't represent any following of Black people. Usually they are Negroes who have been put in that position by the white man himself. And when they speak they're not speaking for Black people, they're saying exactly what they know the white man who put them in that position wants to hear them say."[62] Those "put in that position by the white man himself," who "don't represent any following of Black people," have, in the parlance of this book, the IPR role *conferred* on them by a white audience, which makes them *de facto IPRs*. Yet they fail to have "any following of Black people," which means they have not received *group authorization* and are, therefore, not *authorized IPRs*.[63]

I share readers' discomfort with the fact that some audiences will put people into the role of de facto IPR on specious grounds—treating any woman they find as speaking for all women or any Black person as speaking for all Black people. But our discomfort with this fact should not lead us to overlook the power that audiences have to confer the status of IPR on unwitting or unwilling parties on specious or objectionable grounds. We need a concept of informal political representation that captures all cases, not just the "good" ones. We should certainly be concerned about audiences' conferral power. More than that, we should have a way of evaluating and critiquing audiences for IPR role conferral that harms or even wrongs its targets. Accordingly, Chapter 2 provides accounts of both the ethics of audience conferral and the grounds on which IPRs can reasonably reject the ascription of pro tanto duties that would otherwise accrue to them by virtue of their power to influence—including the ground that an audience's conferral was based on morally objectionable interests or views.

In Chapter 3, "Group Authorization," I add another consideration to the theoretical framework by discussing what it might mean for an IPR to have "a following" in the sense used by Malcolm X—that is, authorization from the group they represent. *Group authorization* obtains when a party is informally authorized or informally ratified by a given group to speak or act for that group in a context. I provide an account of informal authorization and informal ratification, illustrating these phenomena using the example of the Montgomery Bus Boycott. I argue that an IPR can come to have discretionary and normative powers with respect to those they represent, but only if the IPR has received informal authorization or informal ratification from them. As I go on to discuss in Chapter 4, group authorization can affect the strength and substance of an IPR's duties to those they represent.

The exercise of these two types of power—the de facto power to influence that comes from audience conferral and the discretionary and normative powers that come from group authorization—can have profound repercussions for represented groups, so understanding the nature of these powers and how IPRs come to have them is crucial for understanding the ethics of informal political representation.

In Part II, building on the theoretical framework developed in the first half of the book, I examine several closely connected moral questions that arise for people in the position of IPR: What responsibilities do IPRs have to those they represent, and how do they come to have these responsibilities? Must an IPR share characteristics, experiences, backgrounds, or even group membership in common with those they represent, or are there ever reasons to allow for or even to prefer dissimilar or nonmember IPRs? Ought IPRs always defer to the expressed interests of the groups they represent, or are there contexts in which they may or even should decide to represent the group in ways that diverge from the group's expressed interests?

In Chapter 4, "The Duties of Informal Political Representatives," I narrow the scope of consideration to some of the most common, most important, and most precarious cases of informal political representation: the informal political representation of oppressed and marginalized groups.

The dangers of informal political representation, particularly to oppressed and marginalized groups that rely on it, are considerable. Skeptics quite reasonably caution that IPRs can imperil the represented by being unauthorized, unaccountable, inaccurate, elitist, homogenizing, overpowering, concessive, overcommitting, occlusive, inegalitarian, and oppressive. Such dangers lead many to the conclusion that the informal political representation of oppressed and marginalized groups is morally irremediable. Schematizing these skeptical challenges and considering how they apply to IPRs of oppressed and marginalized groups helps us understand precisely what is (and is not) wrong with such representation.

In response to these skeptical challenges, I argue that, to represent permissibly, IPRs of oppressed or marginalized groups must satisfy two sets of duties: *democracy within* duties and *justice without* duties. These two duty sets are specifications of two general principles applicable to all of us: *non-contribution* (one should not treat others in a manner that would contribute to their oppression or marginalization) and *eradication* (one should work to undermine others' oppression or marginalization), respectively. These duties emerge from the distinctive context of such representation, in which the represented's considerable vulnerability meets IPRs' sometimes completely unconstrained power.[64] *Democracy within* duties concern how the representative should treat and relate to the represented. They comprise four deliberative social practices in which IPRs should engage to correct for inequality in their relationship with the oppressed or marginalized groups they represent: consulting the represented, being transparent with them, welcoming their criticism, tolerating their dissent. *Justice without* duties concern how, when, where, and before whom IPRs should speak or act on represented parties' behalf.

Chapter 4 emphasizes a critical and distinctive feature of the relationship between the IPR and those they represent: because the norms that shape the relationship between the IPR and the represented cannot be institutionalized or codified, they must be promoted through deliberative social practices that arise within the relationship.

Note the relationships between the arguments of Chapter 4 and the two chapters that precede it. First, group authorization (see Chapter 3) mitigates the demandingness of IPRs' *democracy within* duties. *Democracy within* duties are meant to correct for relational imbalances that are inevitable between IPRs and oppressed and marginalized groups and to thereby protect the represented from relational inequality. When, however, an IPR has received authorization from the group they represent, the threat of relational inequality is diminished and the corrective protection of *democracy within* duties is not needed to the same extent. So, group authorization can give IPRs more discretion to decide how to carry out their *democracy within* duties than they otherwise would have had. What this discretion means concretely for IPRs is explored at some length in Chapter 4.

Second, the normative principles that ground the arguments of Chapters 2 and 4—*due care* and *loss prevention,* and *noncontribution* and *eradication,* respectively—are not distinctive to contexts of informal political representation. They admit, however, of new complexities in representative contexts, where there are always at minimum three different parties (representative, represented, audience) who must be taken into consideration when attempting to understand how these principles can be satisfied. In these chapters, I show how this tripartite structure gives rise to novel and sometimes surprising prescriptions and prerogatives for IPRs.

In Chapter 5, "The Legitimate Complaints of the Represented," I provide a schema for thinking about one of the most important features of the ongoing deliberative relationship between the IPR and those they represent: the legitimate complaints of the represented. I examine a variety of legitimate complaints that represented parties might raise against their IPRs and consider what sorts of responses, if any, these complaints compel from IPRs. In so doing, I aim to vindicate what is truly to be found in the common though misleading objection, "You don't speak for us!" Chapter 5 thus develops the account of deliberative social practices discussed in Chapter 4.

In Chapter 6, "Descriptive and Nondescriptive Informal Political Representation," I consider whether—and if so, why—IPRs must be descriptively similar to or members of the groups they represent. I approach this question in two ways. First, I examine a variety of historical and contemporary arguments that have been advanced in favor of representation by people who share characteristics, experiences, or backgrounds in common with those they represent (*descriptive representation*) and representation by people who are members of the group they represent (*member representation*). Second, approaching the question from a different angle, I consider whether there are ever compelling reasons to allow for or even to prefer IPRs who are neither descriptively similar to nor themselves members of the groups they represent (*nondescriptive representatives*). As it turns out, in some cases there are compelling reasons to prefer representation by people who are neither members of the group they represent nor descriptively similar to members of the represented group.

In Chapter 7, "Expertise and Representative Deference," I turn to questions of whether, when, and why IPRs ought to defer to those they represent concerning matters about which the IPRs are experts. The chapter develops the argument of Chapter 4, where I argue that IPRs must promote egalitarian and nonoppressive relationships with those they represent by satisfying *democracy within* duties. A question left open is whether doing so requires the IPR to always defer to the represented about how to represent them. I conclude that, although it is often the case that IPRs should defer to those they represent—particularly when those they represent are marginalized or oppressed—this is not always so. In fact, in some cases we have compelling reasons to think that deference to the represented group's members is not best for the represented group. *Democracy within* duties admit of ample flexibility as to the manner of their satisfaction, and in some cases expertise may allow IPRs greater freedom to decide how to represent groups, particularly when the group members suffer from false consciousness or internalized damaging false beliefs about their circumstances. Finally, I examine and defuse the objection that this conclusion, when taken together with the claim that in some cases there are compelling reasons to prefer nondescriptive representatives (see Chapter 6), produces a normative theory of informal political representation that permits degrading forms of paternalism.

Although several of the chapters of this book can be read as standalone reflections on their particular topics, the book comprises one full conceptual and normative theory of informal political representation with an argument that spans all its pages. Accordingly, I have highlighted several threads connecting different parts of the book that are worth keeping in mind as you read: the burdensomeness of the IPR role and how to respond to this concern (Chapters 2 and 6); how group authorization can mitigate the demandingness of IPRs' *democracy within* duties (Chapters 3 and 4); the normative principles that ground relationships between represented groups and their IPRs (Chapters 2 and 4); the role of the represented's legitimate complaints in the deliberative social practices that comprise the IPR's *democracy within* duties (Chapters 4 and 5); the tensions between cultivating egalitarian social relations and acting in accordance with one's expertise (Chapters 4 and 7); and whether nondeferential representation by nondescriptive expert IPRs is impermissibly paternalistic (Chapters 6 and 7).

This book is just a first step in coming to understand the structure and stakes of a critically undertheorized yet remarkably widespread social role. There is much work left to be done. Although this is a project in political philosophy, the ideas and arguments in this book may bear on other areas of philosophy—for instance, discussions in social epistemology concerning epistemic deference, epistemic injustice, social trust, and standpoint epistemology; discussions in philosophy of language concerning group testimony; discussions in social ontology concerning the constitution of different social roles; and discussions in philosophy of science concerning citizen science—and many cognate disciplines.[65] I am hopeful that contributors to those debates will be invigorated by the arguments they find here to bring them to bear on those discussions. In the Conclusion, I describe some of my own future directions on this score and enumerate a wide variety of open theoretical and empirical questions about informal political representation ripe for the picking.

The Normatively Neutral Approach

My aim is to open up a new and different conversation about an important, everyday political phenomenon that touches all our lives but that has received scant philosophical attention. I provide a novel and systematic ethical theory of informal political representation and, by so doing, answer the central ethical challenge delineated above.

Here I will say just a word about my methodological approach, which may surprise some readers. It might seem natural to think of the role of IPR as normatively laden from the outset: that the role's inhabitant (1) must intend and volunteer to fill the role, (2) can relinquish or disavow the role at will, (3) cannot fill the role without the represented group's authorization to do so, and (4) accrues certain duties and permissions to the represented group when the first three commitments (1–3) obtain. The normatively laden approach has benefits. For one thing, it makes informal political representation look a lot like formal political representation, wherein FPRs (1′) intentionally vie for positions, (2′) can leave office at will, (3′) must be authorized directly by constituents (through an election) or indirectly (by being selected by another party that was elected by those constituents), and (4′) accrue certain duties and permissions to constituents when the first three commitments (1′–3′) obtain. In addition to treating informal political representation as similar to a phenomenon with which we are already familiar, however, the normatively laden approach is attractive because commitments 1–3 reflect intuitions that many readers have about roles and responsibilities more generally: Commitment 1 reflects the intuition that we cannot be thrust into roles for which we did not ask, and commitment 2 reflects the intuition that we can leave roles we no longer want. Commitment 3 reflects the intuition that represented parties should have some say (if not the final say) as to who speaks or acts for them. Commitment 4 reflects two intuitions: that we ought not be saddled with role-based obligations for roles we ourselves do not want, and that we ought not be granted permissions to speak and act on others' behalf without their authorization.

In contrast, the approach I adopt in this book, the *normatively neutral approach,* begins with a very simple observation: sometimes, a person finds themself in a situation in which the things they say, write, or do are imputed by an audience to others besides that person themself. The audience's treatment confers on that person the social role of IPR. In many cases, that social role will not come to much, may fade with time, may not be very consequential. But in some cases, the conferral of the social role will be very consequential, imbuing the IPR with the power to influence how the group they now represent is treated, regarded, or understood by the conferring audience—and the power to influence new conferring audiences as they come along. In few but important cases, audience conferral may be granted by more and more audiences and a group can end up with an IPR whose power to influence is considerable and wide ranging, as in the case of Booker T. Washington's informal political representation of Black Americans (see Chapter 1). Such cases are devalued or excluded altogether if we impose normative constraints (commitments 1–4) on the IPR role from the outset. Instead, my approach begins with an observation of a common, everyday social phenomenon and treats that observation as the starting point for all subsequent conceptual and normative analysis in the book.

I opt for the normatively neutral approach because it allows us to consider many important ethical questions that the normatively laden approach renders inaccessible from the outset. First, the observation that audiences confer the social role of IPR on others allows us to appreciate that people sometimes end up *conscripted* into the role of speaking or acting for others besides themselves without their knowledge (*unwitting representatives*) or consent (*unwilling representatives*), a situation that can both burden and harm the conscripted party (see Chapter 2). The normatively laden approach sets such conscripted parties outside the ambit of its concern: being thrust into a social role unwittingly or unwillingly is foreclosed by commitment 1.

Second, the normatively neutral approach recognizes that those on whom this social role is conferred can sometimes find themselves stuck in the role even when they are unwilling—a real-life experience for many people, particularly for members of marginalized and oppressed groups. Contemplating audiences' power to confer the social role of IPR and the IPR's inability to thereafter unilaterally relinquish or disavow it, in turn, opens up conceptual space to consider audiences' duties to refrain from conferring this consequential and burdensome social role (see Chapter 2). The normatively neutral approach both acknowledges that audiences often thrust people into the social role of IPR unbidden and allows us to criticize audiences that do so. The normatively laden approach is unable to accommodate this common and worrisome social dynamic in its account of informal political representation; commitment 2 of the normatively laden approach requires that an IPR can unilaterally disavow or relinquish the role.

Perhaps the most counterintuitive feature of the normatively neutral approach is that it contemplates the possibility that a person could be a representative without the authorization of the group they represent. Yet this feature is in fact a great strength of the normatively neutral approach, as it provides conceptual space for a distinction foreclosed by commitment 3 of the normatively laden approach. The normatively laden approach treats those who have received no group authorization as not representatives in any sense. But commitment 3 removes an important class of cases from consideration: groups that are typically represented by IPRs tend to have poorly defined memberships, can be quite large and widely dispersed, may be difficult to access or contact, and in some cases struggle to communicate at all (see Chapter 4). Such groups cannot, in the normal course of things, engage in authorization. In fact, authorization in informal contexts is relatively rare (see Chapter 3). Yet these groups commonly have and often need people who speak or act for them in a wide variety of contexts (see Chapter 1). The normatively neutral approach provides conceptual space for these cases and, by so doing, shows us that we need an ethical theory of informal political representation that can provide action guidance to those who are not or even could not be authorized but must nonetheless figure out how to represent well. I provide that ethical theory in this book.

Although the normatively neutral approach allows that people may end up in the social role of IPR without group authorization, it does not cast aside group authorization entirely. On this approach, there is a crucial distinction between (1) *de facto IPRs*: parties who are conferred the social role of IPR by an audience, and who may thereby come to have the de facto power to influence how the represented group is treated, regarded, and understood; and (2) *authorized IPRs*: parties who, in addition to receiving audience conferral, have also received group authorization to be an IPR for the group. IPRs who receive group authorization enjoy greater permissions than their unauthorized counterparts and can in some cases come to have normative powers vis-à-vis the represented group that has authorized them (see Chapter 3).

There is an overall unity to the conceptual and normative parts of this book. The normatively neutral approach starts with an observation about the world as it is: Audiences treat some parties as speaking or acting for others besides themselves, thereby conferring on those parties the social role of IPR. IPRs gain the power to influence, and their exercise of that power affects the lives and circumstances of represented group members who did not and perhaps could not authorize the IPRs. Using this new conceptual framework (see Chapter 1), I develop a systematic ethical theory of informal political representation in which I (1) delineate the duties and permissions people come to have just by virtue of being in the audience-conferred social role of *de facto IPR* (see Chapter 2); (2) explain how those duties and permissions change if one becomes an *authorized IPR* (see Chapter 3); and (3) consider how those duties and permissions change in response to particular features of some representative-represented relationships, including oppression and marginalization (see Chapter 4), the represented's legitimate complaints (see Chapter 5), descriptive similarity between representative and represented (see Chapter 6), and IPR expertise (see Chapter 7).

This is not a book about what a political representative is. My aim is neither to offer an analysis of the extant concept *political representative* nor to try to shoehorn the concept *IPR* into a particular, extant conception of *political representative*. Rather, this book is an attempt to add a new idea to conversations about political representation and to show how that idea enriches and expands our moral theories of political representation. The question is not whether IPRs are "real" representatives but what we are to make of them, morally, regardless of what we call them.

Informal Political Representation at the Confluence of Ideal and Nonideal Political Theory

The arguments in this book are concerned with how a profoundly important social and political practice ought to be developed and constrained so as to accord with some of our highest moral and political ideals. To develop a normative theory of informal political representation, I draw on normative ideals and principles that we should endorse not only in the world as it is but would endorse even in a more fully just (or even ideal) society. I embrace ideal theory throughout the book—for instance, discussing individuals' autonomy to accept, reject, or disavow a given social role, as well as the duties we have to others to show them due care and to prevent losses that may otherwise accrue to them by virtue of our behavior (see Chapter 2); examining the roles of authorization and ratification in giving others the power to represent us (see Chapter 3); arguing for the importance of pro-moting and maintaining egalitarian relations between parties with different amounts and types of power (see Chapter 4); and examining the roles of legitimate complaints in structuring our deliberative relationships with one another (see Chapter 5). I consider the sorts of principled grounds that could justify considering someone's social identity or group membership when assessing whether it is reasonable for them to speak or act on behalf of others (see Chapter 6). I discuss the importance of our freedom from the domination of others who think they know better than we do which decisions are best for us as well as limitations on that freedom (see Chapter 7). In these ways and others, throughout this book, I bring the lessons of ideal theory to bear on informal political representation.

At the same time, the book is a study of informal political representa-tion as it in fact arises in societies like ours. Although the theoretical frame-work provided in Part I can be applied and adapted to a wide range of cases of informal political representation, my motivation in this book is to use this framework to develop an account of the ethics of informal political representation of oppressed and marginalized groups. I pay particular at-tention to the informal political representation of oppressed and marginal-ized groups in our unjust world because especially difficult and important questions emerge in that context. Accordingly, most of the examples and normative arguments in the book are focused on the indispensable and vital role that IPRs can play in this particular context, where corrective work is needed against a backdrop of serious injustice. In these ways, this is a project in nonideal theory—an attempt to think about what is owed to those who represent and those who are represented in the imperfect and unjust world we share with one another.

This book is enriched by a wide variety of real-world examples, used both to develop the concept of informal political representation and to eluci-date otherwise hidden features of the normative questions at stake. I have chosen well-known historical and contemporary examples of highly visible IPRs to help make the phenomenon of informal political representation easily recognizable and to give us some common and familiar cases with which to test the theory. But this is a book about all of us. Each of us is implicated in the practice of informal political representation simply by virtue of being in community with one another. We ourselves are the con-ferring audiences who, for good or ill, treat the people around us as speaking and acting on behalf of others. We ourselves are the members of groups represented by IPRs. And, of course, we ourselves are those conferred the role of representative by various audiences in surprising contexts.

No doubt, you already have familiarity with informal political representation from your own observations. I have yet to meet anyone who does not have, from their own experience, examples of and intuitions about the phenomenon of informal political representation. Very often, the examples people share with me are not of highly visible or publicly recognizable IPRs, but instead examples from their personal lives. Some recall with fondness and admiration people in their hometowns who gladly and to great effect took up the mantle of IPR on behalf of a particular local community or group. (My father has often told me stories of Dorothy Schwartz, who lived in our hometown of Hackensack, New Jersey, and who, despite not being affiliated with any of the tenants' advocacy groups in town, regularly attended city council meetings to informally represent Hackensack tenants on issues including cost of living, rent increases, and rent control.[66]) Others understandably regard their own experiences with informal political representation less fondly, recounting their own sometimes uncomfortable, usually unwelcome experiences of being treated as speaking for a group to which they belong—*people of color, the queer community, immigrants, people of faith, women, neurodivergent people, first-generation students*—whether in passing conversation, at school, or at work. I encourage you to keep the examples of informal political representation emanating from your own observations and experiences in mind as you read this book.

PART ONE

1

Audience Conferral

As an informal political representative (IPR), Rev. Dr. Martin Luther King Jr. spoke and acted for Black Montgomerians from the pulpit, in political planning meetings, and in leaflets urging a bus boycott. He made demands on their behalf on the nightly news and in back rooms. He negotiated for them with the mayor of Montgomery, Alabama; city commissioners; and bus company representatives.[1] So positioned, King had significant power to influence the political negotiations that unfolded between boycotters, the city of Montgomery, and the bus company, and played a central role in shaping how Black Montgomerians' values, interests, and preferences were understood by the rest of Montgomery.

But, to hear King tell it, this is not what he had planned, at least not at first: "I neither started the protest nor suggested it. I simply responded to the call of the people for a spokesman." Then, on Thursday, December 8, 1955—the fourth day of the bus boycott—King and other members of the Montgomery Improvement Association (MIA) met with the "city fathers" to offer up a list of proposals on behalf of the Black Montgomerian community: "The mayor then turned to the Negro delegation and demanded: 'Who is the spokesman?' When all eyes turned toward me [King], the mayor said: 'All right, come forward and make your statement.'"[2]

Call this *audience conferral*. Audience conferral obtains when an audience (an individual or a group) treats one person or group as speaking or acting on behalf of another person or group in some context.[3] By King's own account, he became an IPR for Black Montgomerians at that news conference when and because "all eyes turned toward me" after Montgomery's mayor W. A. Gayle asked, "Who is the spokesman?"[4]

In this chapter, I advance the thesis that informal representatives emerge when and because they are treated by audiences to be speaking or acting for a given group in a given context (audience conferral). I do so as follows: First, I clarify how I understand the concept of *speaking for* and discuss the relationship between speaking for and speaking about. Second, I elaborate the distinction between informal political representation and the more familiar phenomenon of formal political representation. I discuss four different respects in which political representation may be more or less formal (authorization, accountability, group membership, and norms). Third, I provide a general characterization of informal representation and explain what makes some informal representation political. Fourth, I provide an account of the phenomenon of audience conferral and, fifth, I illustrate that account with a detailed examination of the example of Booker T. Washington. Sixth, I consider and set aside three alternatives to the audience conferral account of IPR emergence.

Speaking For and Speaking About

It is relatively easy to draw a conceptually tidy distinction between speaking for and speaking about. But the activities cannot always be separated out so easily in practice.[5] Often, they occur simultaneously.

Speaking for concerns the attribution of a statement or speech act. According to the *Oxford English Dictionary*, to speak for is "to make a speech or plea in place of or on behalf of (a person)."[6] *Speaking for* picks out the relationship between the party that said something (the representative) and the party to whom what was said is imputed (the represented) rather than the content of what was said. As will be shown throughout this book, speaking for can take a variety of forms, but, in every case, what the speaker says is attributed to another party as though that other party had said or would have said it themselves.

Speaking about, by contrast, mainly concerns the content of what is said rather than its source. To say that a particular assertion, for example, is about a particular subject matter is to say, at least, that the content of the assertion conveys some information concerning that subject matter.

That speaking for and speaking about are conceptually distinct does not mean that they always come apart in practice. An instance of speaking can be, at the same time, both an instance of speaking about and an instance of speaking for, as Linda Alcoff points out: "When one is speaking for others one may be describing their situation and thus also speaking about them. In fact, it may be impossible to speak for others without simultaneously conferring information about them. Similarly, when one is speaking about others, or simply trying to describe their situation or some aspect of it, one may also be speaking in place of them, that is, speaking for them."[7]

Speaking for and speaking about are related, then, in the following ways: First, an instance of speaking for is also always an instance of speaking about something. But that speaker need not be speaking about the other person or group for whom they are speaking. Rather, the speaker may be speaking about just about anything. Still, the source of what the speaker says is, mediately, the other person. For instance, I speak for you when I give your order to the deli clerk: corned beef on rye. Yet, in ordering corned beef on rye on your behalf, I have not spoken about you. (In fact, I did not tell the deli clerk that the two sandwiches I ordered were for two different people, which may explain the pitying look they gave me.) Second, an instance of speaking about is not always an instance of speaking for. But an instance of speaking about can become an instance of speaking for if some further conditions are satisfied. What further conditions need to be satisfied depends on the sense of *speaking for* that we have in mind.

So, what does it mean to speak for another? There are more and less capacious ways of understanding the concept of *speaking for*. I conceive of speaking for as picking out a spectrum of phenomena. My motivation for adopting this more inclusive account of speaking for is that it allows us to better understand the relationships between these connected communicative phenomena.

At one end of the spectrum, there is a narrow, restrictive sense of speaking for that is familiar from, for instance, law: one party, *A,* is authorized by another party, *B,* to, in effect, stand in for *B* in certain contexts and for certain purposes such that, in those contexts and for those purposes, *A*'s statements are imputed to *B* as *B*'s own statements. In these cases, it is also common for *A* to intend to fulfill this role. So, in such cases, for an instance of speaking about to become an instance of speaking for, the speaker must be authorized and the speaker often intends to speak for.

At the other end of the spectrum, there is a different, more permissive sense of speaking for nicely characterized by Alcoff: "when one is speaking about others, or simply trying to describe their situation or some aspect of it, one may also be speaking in place of them, that is, speaking for them."[8] On this view of speaking for, the activity may be undertaken unintentionally or without the authorization of the spoken-for party, or both. One speaks for another in this sense when one speaks *in their place*.[9] In these sorts of cases, we find parties who seem merely to be conveying information about a group or its members' lives and circumstances. They may start out speaking about a group by virtue of having some special knowledge about that group or out of sincere concern for the group's conditions and prospects. But they do not claim or intend to speak for others, nor do they regard themselves as speaking for others. They intend to serve only as informational conduits, interpreters, or informants. And the group about which they speak will not have authorized them to speak for the group— indeed, the group's members may not even know that this party is conveying information about the group.

What sometimes happens to these parties is that they come to be treated by some audience as doing something further—namely, standing in for the group. The audience's manner of treatment confers on the speaker a status that comes bundled with the power to influence how the group is understood—what values, interests, or preferences the group members are taken to have or what the group members' doxastic and conative attitudes are taken to be. The particular manners of treatment by which audiences can confer this status—including *ascription, credibility conferral, testimonial reliance,* and *invitation*—are detailed below. In these sorts of cases, for an instance of speaking about to become an instance of speaking for, the speaker must be treated by an audience as standing in for the group in at least one of the four manners mentioned here, where this manner of treatment confers on them the status *informal representative.* Note that it is the manner of treatment that constitutes the party as an informal representative for the group.[10]

Throughout this book, I discuss forms of *speaking for* that fall all along this spectrum. The theory provided in Part I of this book progresses from the permissive end of the speaking for spectrum to its restrictive end. In this chapter, I consider cases in which the audience's manner of treatment confers on a party a role (informal representative) that comes bundled with the power to influence, where it is necessary neither that the conferred-upon party intends to speak for the group nor that the group has authorized the party to do so. In Chapter 2, I consider in detail what difference it makes, both conceptually and normatively, that one party intends to speak for another—what is added when the party is both witting and willing. Finally, in Chapter 3, I consider what further difference it makes that the spoken-for group authorizes the speaker. As we move from one side of the *speaking for* spectrum to the other, we see that some questions arise and others fall away.

I provide this opening note to clarify that the concept of *speaking for* is used in more than one way, not to stake out a strongly held view on the matter of how the concept ought to be used. The aim of this book is to understand better the familiar but undertheorized social practice of informal political representation rather than to advance a novel account of the phenomenon of speaking for. Those who would prefer to think of speaking for as an activity that can be undertaken only intentionally and with the authorization of those being spoken for should reinterpret cases that do not meet their more restrictive account as cases in which a party is *treated as speaking for others* or *merely putatively speaks for others*. The central arguments of the book about the ethics of informal political representation will not be affected by this choice.[11]

Distinguishing Informal Political Representation from Formal Political Representation

Formal political representation picks out representation in which a representative comes to occupy their role as a direct or indirect but predictable result of a systematized election or selection procedure. Examples are numerous and varied: congresspersons elected by their districts, nongovernmental organizations' boards of directors elected by members of the organization, judges elected by voters or appointed by elected officials.[12] What unites such cases are the systematized processes by which representatives are chosen and the fact that the parties to be represented perform these processes, either directly or indirectly. By contrast, IPRs emerge by virtue of audience conferral alone. An audience can, but need not, comprise the group to be represented.

Often we treat informal political representation as a deviant case of formal political representation. But informal political representation is neither an addendum to, nor is it well captured by, even our best theories of formal political representation. Accordingly, we need an account of informal political representation that takes the practice on its own terms. Yet the long-standing familiarity of formal political representation as a topic in political philosophy and political theory makes it an ideal point of comparison.

Although sometimes superficially similar, IPRs differ from formal political representatives (FPRs) in foundational respects. It would therefore be an error to think that formal political representation is an ideal form of political representation of which informal political representation is a nonideal approximation. Yet the two phenomena have at least one fundamental feature in common: in both cases, one party speaks or acts for another party before an audience in some context. Instead of differing in kind, the two phenomena fall in far corners of a space of political representation, throughout which we find many different types.[13] A political representative can be more or less formal by virtue of several different features of their role, including authorization, group membership, accountability, and the norms that guide their relationship to the represented, as I elaborate below. Differences between IPRs and FPRs with respect to these four features explain why IPRs are not constrained in ways their formal analogues are.

The first feature of political representation that contributes to a representative's formality or informality is whether—and, if so, how—the representative can be authorized. Some representatives are not authorized in any way. Among political representatives who do receive authorization, the more systematized (by which I mean organized, reliable, and repeatable) the mechanism by which the representative is authorized, the more authorizationally formal the representative. Political representatives who emerge as a result of a systematized election or selection procedure are fully authorizationally formal. Such representatives are paradigmatic examples of FPRs. In between these extremes, there are more and less systematic authorization mechanisms. Informal authorization and informal ratification are sometimes possible but differ from formal authorization and ratification both because they lack systematicity and because neither is a precondition for emerging as an IPR.[14] When they obtain, informal authorization and ratification may affect the nature and scope of the IPRs' duties to the represented (see Chapters 3, 4, and 7).[15]

The second feature of political representation that contributes to a representative's formality or informality is group membership—in particular, whether the representative speaks or acts for a represented group the membership of which can be determined accurately. A group's membership can be determined accurately when (1) there are widely accepted and perhaps even institutionally codified norms specifying who is included in the group, and (2) either there is no contestation as to who is included or, if there is contestation, there is a norm by which contests are adjudicated.

The determinateness of a represented group's membership affects what sorts of authorization procedures the group can effect. Formal authorization procedures tend to be stable, in part, because groups that use them tend to have well-defined memberships, the compositions of which are determined by law or, in cases of nongovernmental but still corporately organized bodies, established procedures and bylaws.[16] Legislators represent the citizens of their districts, whose membership in the citizenry is determined by law. Outside of government, corporately organized bodies like the National Association for the Advancement of Colored People have established procedures for determining who counts as a group member.[17] As a result, it can generally be said with confidence who may take part in election or selection procedures for FPRs. When there are questions concerning who may participate, there are fora like courts in which to adjudicate them. By contrast, IPRs often represent groups whose memberships are not well defined and for which there are no established procedures for determining membership. (It is, of course, possible for a group with a well-defined membership to be represented informally.)

The third feature of political representation that contributes to a representative's formality or informality is whether the representative can be held accountable—and, if so, how. Political representatives are *formally accountable* if they are subject to systematized accountability mechanisms—that is, organized, reliable, repeatable mechanisms that are, at least in theory, effective at holding representatives responsible. Some formal accountability mechanisms are sanctioning mechanisms, like censure and impeachment, carried out by representative bodies of which the representative is a part. Other accountability mechanisms are removal mechanisms, which may also be sanctioning mechanisms. A paradigmatic removal mechanism is the periodic election, whereby a given incumbent is either retained in or removed from a representative body by the electorate.[18] Political representatives subject to no accountability mechanisms whatsoever are *unaccountable.* In between these extremes, some representatives are subject only to less systematic or wholly unsystematic accountability mechanisms like protest, disavowal, cancellation, or dissent. Informal accountability mechanisms like protest do not predictably trigger legally encoded outcomes for representatives and so tend to be less reliable. Such representatives are *informally accountable*.

One may object that the mechanisms I have identified as paradigmatic examples of organized, reliable, and repeatable mechanisms (censure, impeachment, elections), although organized and repeatable, are in fact not very reliable and, accordingly, formal and informal accountability mechanisms do not function as differently as I am suggesting. It is certainly true that some methods for holding representatives accountable do not in fact function well in existing FPR systems, but that does not mean that those methods would not be reliable under more ideal conditions. The distinction I mean to draw here is conceptual: accountability mechanisms as they would instantiate in ideal (or even simply more fully just) FPR contexts will by definition be more reliable than those that arise in ideal (or more fully just) IPR contexts because the informal contexts by definition lack the structures needed to ensure them reliability. It is possible to draw this conceptual distinction even if, under current conditions, neither formal nor informal accountability mechanisms are particularly reliable.[19]

Another feature that contributes to a political representative's formality or informality is whether and to what extent the norms that guide the relationship between the representative and the represented are institutionalized and codified. In more familiar, formal cases, representatives must obey norms codified in law, organizational bylaws, or rules, applied in like manner across like cases. In less formal or wholly informal cases, these institutional structures are precisely what's missing. In some cases of informal political representation, there may be no norms whatsoever to guide one's representative activity (aside from social and moral norms that apply generally), as when, in casual conversation with friends, one is suddenly treated as speaking for a social group of which one is a member.[20]

By contrast, in other informal cases, there may be widely shared and established norms concerning the representative's responsibilities to the represented. For instance, an IPR and those they represent may be embedded in a social movement with established norms, like the Movement for Black Lives.[21] Even so, because these established norms cannot be reliably enforced through the power of the state or of a corporate body, the norms are not fully analogous to institutionalized, codified norms. Whatever normative requirements IPRs must satisfy, therefore, cannot usually be enforced through institutions but must instead be promoted through deliberative social practices. Whether and to what extent these norms are enforceable will also inform the aforementioned accountability considerations.

Each of these four features—authorization, group membership, accountability, and norms—informs whether and to what extent a given political representative is formal or informal. Representatives can be formal in some respects but not in others. For instance, one representative may be fully formally authorized but not at all accountable, while for another representative the reverse may be true. That said, in extant political systems, these four features tend to covary such that, for instance, a political representative who is formally authorized is also more likely to be subject to systematized and institutionally reinforced accountability mechanisms.

Although the practices of informal political representation and formal political representation can be conceptually separated, they often overlap in interesting and complex ways in practice. For instance, representatives may transition from positions of relative informality to positions of relative formality (or vice versa) over time. Consider unions: they are formal in some respects and at some times, and informal in other respects and at other times. When a group is in the process of unionizing but lacks the internal structure to enact an organized, reliable, or repeatable procedure (like an election, removal, or sanction), although the group may have a representative at that point, that representative could be subject to only informal authorization or accountability mechanisms exercised by the group. Yet once the union has formed, matters are different: Established voting procedures that enable members to effectively and repeatably sanction or remove representatives render these representatives formally, rather than informally, accountable. Election procedures that enable members to choose their representatives render these representatives formally authorized. Or, instead of transitioning from one position to another, often an individual or group will serve as both an FPR and an IPR, sometimes at the same time, and sometimes for groups whose memberships overlap. Rev. Dr. Martin Luther King Jr. formally represented the MIA and the Southern Christian Leadership Conference while informally representing, among others, Black Montgomerians.[22] And Israeli Prime Minister Benjamin Netanyahu formally represents Israelis while informally representing Jews.

The distinctions discussed in this section are reproduced in table 1.1.

Table 1.1   Distinctions between Formal Political Representation and Informal Political
             Representation

	Formal	Informal
Authorization	The FPR speaks or acts for their constituency by virtue of a systematized (that is, organized, reliable, and repeatable) election or selection scheme. In democratic contexts, the representative must have been elected or selected (even if at some remove) either by their constituency or by another person who was elected by their constituency. Formal authorization procedures tend to be both stable and well established, and are required for an FPR to emerge.	Although the IPR may receive informal authorization or ratification (*group authorization*), neither is required for emerging as an IPR.
Group Membership	Widely accepted and possibly institutionally codified norms specify who is included in the represented group, and either membership is not contested or there is a norm by which such contests are adjudicated. These reliable and well-defined group membership criteria help clarify who may participate in representative authorization procedures.	IPRs tend to represent groups or pluralities whose memberships are not well defined and for which there are no established procedures for determining membership.
Accountability	Political representatives are formally accountable if they are subject to systematized (that is, organized, reliable, and repeatable) accountability mechanisms that are, at least in theory, effective at holding representatives responsible.	Accountability mechanisms, if available, are less likely to be systematized or effective than those available in formal contexts.
Norms	Representatives are beholden to norms codified in law, organizational bylaws, or rules, applied in like manner across like cases. These norms shape, guide, and constrain the relationship between representative and represented.	Either there are no norms guiding representatives or, even if there are widely shared and established norms, these norms cannot be reliably enforced through institutions. The norms must be promoted through deliberative social practices.

The Phenomenon of Informal Political Representation

Informal political representation is a subtype of the more general phenomenon of informal representation. Informal representation generally, like its formal counterpart, is a tripartite relationship between a representative, a represented party, and an audience. An informal representative is an individual or a group who is treated by an audience as speaking or acting for another individual or group in a given context, despite not having been elected or selected by means of a systematized election or selection procedure.[23] (Although much of the ensuing discussion focuses on individuals serving as informal representatives, the arguments advanced apply to group informal representatives too.) In the next section, I discuss how the audience's treatment confers the status of *informal representative* on a party. Call conditions in which a party is selected to inhabit a representative role not by means of a systematized election or selection procedure *authorizationally informal.* When authorizational informality obtains, such representatives must be selected another way. Informal representatives are selected by audiences. Call the fact that makes it the case that someone becomes a representative under conditions of authorizational informality *audience conferral.* An audience can be an individual or a group, and when the audience comprises the represented themselves, I will speak of *group conferral,* a type of audience conferral.[24] A person or group becomes an informal representative in a given context just in case authorizational informality and audience conferral obtain.

Two slightly more precise formulations may be helpful. First, a party, *R,* informally represents a group, *G,* in a context, *C,* just in case (1) some audience, *A,* treats *R* as speaking or acting for *G* in *C* (audience conferral), and (2) *R* was selected not by means of a systematized election or selection procedure (authorizational informality). Second, party *R* informally represents an individual member of *G* (*P*) in context *C* just in case audience conferral and authorizational informality obtain, and *P* is a member of *G* (membership).

Informal political representation is a species of a genus: informal representation. So, when is informal representation political? Informal representation is political when its subject matter is political. By *political* I mean: regarding matters apt for broad public discussion by virtue of their bearing on our collective coordination and decision-making.[25] This is a capacious definition of *political,* comprehending not merely governmental affairs but, in effect, all issues on which we ought to communicate publicly with one another if we are to live well together. Moreover, the set of matters apt for broad public discussion is not fixed but is instead "explicitly a matter for contest" and, so, can and does shift over time.[26] Although the definition does not restrict which specific matters bear on our collective coordination and decision-making, some categories of matters tend to recur across time and context, including (and especially) the distribution of power and resources, the laws that guide and constrain our activities, and the state.

That an issue is apt for broad public discussion does not mean that IPRs must in fact address a broad public or have its attention to count as IPRs; rather, it just means that the subject matters of their representations are apt for such broad public discussion.

So characterized, informal political representation may take place in a wide variety of public and private fora. The paradigmatic examples of informal political representation on which this book's arguments rest occur in traditional political or broadly public fora, addressed to state actors or public audiences: Aalayah Eastmond testified before the U.S. Congress as an IPR for American high schoolers. Greta Thunberg addressed the United Nations Climate Action Summit as an IPR for Generation Z, or, as she has put it, "we who have to live with the consequences" of climate change.[27] As an IPR for Black Montgomerians, King addressed the public at a news conference in Montgomery concerning segregated bus seating policies. As an IPR for Black Americans, Booker T. Washington addressed the assembled public at the 1895 Cotton States and International Exposition concerning how race relations ought to develop between Black and white Americans. Yet informal political representation can—and often does—occur out of public view. It was only after the press conference ended and the cameras were shut off that King's real political negotiation with Mayor Gayle and the Montgomery City Council began.[28]

This more expansive conception of what is political allows the theory to contemplate both paradigmatic and penumbral cases. Consider an example that illustrates how an instance of informal nonpolitical representation may develop into an instance of informal political representation. Imagine that you and some neighbors are around the dinner table. None of your neighbors is religious, but you are. The conversation turns to the practice of prayer. Your neighbors ask you not only about your own practice but about the practices of fellow congregants at your church. No one has elected or selected you to speak for your fellow congregants by means of a systematized election or selection procedure. Still, your neighbors treat you as speaking for them—the relevant manners of treatment are discussed below—and by so doing, they make you an informal representative for your fellow congregants. Nothing about the case, as described, makes it especially political. But then the conversation shifts; your neighbors ask about how your fellow congregants feel about the permissibility of prayer at town meetings.[29] Their question is not an idle one; one of your fellow congregants has recently been publicly advocating for the adoption of a prayer practice at town meetings. Dinner with neighbors is not usually what we have in mind when we think of traditional political fora. Yet here you are, called upon by your neighbors to be an informal representative concerning a subject matter apt for broad public discussion by virtue of its bearing on your collective coordination and decision-making in the town you all share together.[30]

I use a wide variety of examples of informal representation throughout the book—some uncontroversially political, others not. This mixture is intentional and meant to illustrate that we may be political actors in many fora in our own lives in ways that are not obvious to us. Doubtless some readers will prefer a narrower definition of the term *political* than the one provided here. Fortunately, the force of my arguments does not depend on a reader's agreement as to whether all the examples that I identify as political are, on their view, political.

By casting a wide net in terms of what falls within the ambit of informal political representation, I do not mean to suggest that all instances of informal political representation will be similar in terms of their significance. The forum in which an IPR emerges, the political power held by the audiences in that forum, and the size of the represented group's membership all affect the significance of the representation. The paradigmatic examples discussed above, and others like them, are of special significance; through their statements and actions, IPRs like Eastmond, King, Thunberg, and Washington have profound capacities to shape audiences' doxastic attitudes about a represented group and its values, interests, or preferences—to thereby affect the lives and circumstances of those they represent through what they say and do on their behalf. The same cannot be said of all IPRs. In fact, most IPRs are unlikely to have the amount and type of power to influence that Greta Thunberg has—invited to speak at the United Nations for an entire generation. Even so, each of us may well be an IPR at some point in the course of our everyday lives in the less obviously political or public fora we frequent. Recognizing IPR as a position that may be thrust upon any of us also helps us understand just how many and varied are its manifestations.

Audience Conferral

Audience conferral is the constitutive condition for the emergence of an informal representative of any sort, political or not—one becomes an informal representative when and because one is treated by an audience as speaking or acting for some group in a context.[31] Audience conferral is the fact that makes it the case that a party is an informal representative. But what does it mean for an audience to treat a given party as speaking or acting for some group in a context? When I say that "an audience treats a party as speaking or acting for some group in a context," I mean that the audience engages in one or more of a complex of actions with respect to the party in the context. It is through those actions—those manners of treatment— that the audience confers the status of informal representative on the party in that context. Four such audience actions are each individually sufficient to confer the status of informal representative: ascription, credibility conferral, testimonial reliance, and invitation (see table 1.2).

The conferral actions enumerated here are illustrative, not exhaustive. There may be other conferral actions that we would also want to counte-

Table 1.2   Audience Actions That Confer the Status of Informal Representative ("Conferral Actions")

Ascription	An audience ascribes a party's statements or actions to a group or its members: treating the statements or actions as though made or taken by the group or its members themselves.
Credibility Conferral	An audience treats a party as a credible source of information about a group or its members values, interests, or preferences.
Testimonial Reliance	An audience relies on a party's testimony when attempting to understand what a group's members want, value, or prefer.
Invitation	An audience invites a party to stand in for a group or its members when the group's members' interests are at stake in a given forum.

nance as ways that audiences treat parties as speaking or acting for groups in contexts.

When an audience treats a party as speaking or acting for a group in a context, that audience thereby confers the status of informal representative on that party, a status that comes bundled with the *power to influence*. The power to influence is an informal representative's capacity, through their statements or actions, to shape an audience's doxastic attitudes about a represented group and the represented group's values, interests, or preferences. How much power to influence an informal representative has depends on, among other things, the forum in which the informal representative emerges, the political power held by the conferring audience, and the size of the represented group's membership.

Several further key features of audience conferral are important to have in view from the outset. First, informal representative is a social role conferred on a party through the behavior of an audience. Audience conferral is the fact that makes it the case that a party is an informal representative: the audience's treatment of the party, which does not include a systematized election or selection procedure (authorizational informality), constitutes that party as an informal representative. For audience conferral to obtain, it is neither necessary nor sufficient that the conferring audience think that the party speaks or acts for a group—rather, they must treat the party in certain ways in order to constitute that party as an informal representative. Of course, an audience might believe that a given party speaks or acts for a group and then, on the basis of that belief, treat the party as speaking or acting for the group in one of the manners described above.[32] Yet the audience confers the status of informal representative by treating the party in one or more of the manners described, not by believing something about the party. Moreover, the audience need neither use nor even have the concept *informal representative* to confer the status upon a party. Rather, they need only engage in some of the manners of treatment (*ascription, credibility conferral, testimonial reliance, invitation*) by which the role is conferred. The manners of treatment themselves are ordinary, everyday, often unreflective actions, meaning that an audience need not intend to engage—nor need they even be aware that they are engaging—in the manners of treatment that confer the status of informal representative in order to do so. An audience can confer the status unwittingly.

Second, each instance of audience conferral is indexed to both a particular audience and a particular context. This means that audience A can confer the status of informal representative for group G on party R in context C without party R thereby becoming the informal representative for group G by the lights of any audience besides A or in a context besides C.

Third, and taking the first two points together, audience conferral is not a cognitive state by which an audience tries to detect or discover whether a given party is an informal representative. It is true that one audience, B, could notice that another audience, A, has conferred the status of informal representative on party R in context C. But this noticing itself does not constitute audience conferral: B may notice A's conferral of the status of informal representative on R in C without B thereby themself conferring the status of informal representative on R.

Fourth, this account accommodates heterogeneity as to types of informal representatives. For instance, a party who is conferred credibility by an audience but not invited to stand in for the group in a given forum may have a different type of power to influence than would a party who is invited to stand in for the group in a given forum but who is not conferred credibility. Some parties will be treated in more than one of the manners described in table 1.2, meaning that they may be granted a broader swath of powers to influence than would a party who is treated in only one of those manners.

Fifth, in some cases of audience conferral, the party on whom the status of informal representative is conferred may in fact also be speaking or acting for the group in the more restrictive senses discussed above—intentionally and with the authorization of the represented group. And it may further be the case that the reason the audience confers the status of informal representative on the party is that the audience (1) recognizes that the party intends to be speaking or acting for the group, or (2) knows that the group has authorized the party to speak or act for the group. Yet although these features of the case may explain why the audience has treated the party as speaking or acting for the group in one of the manners described, neither the party's own intention to speak for the group nor the group's authorization of the party is a precondition for audience conferral to obtain.

Sixth, in this section, I have been describing the emergence conditions of informal representatives quite generally rather than IPRs in particular. This is because although audiences confer the status of informal representative on a party, they do not thereby make it the case that the party on whom the status is conferred speaks or acts on matters apt for broad public discussion by virtue of those matters' bearing on collective coordination and decision-making. The audience confers the status of informal representative on a party through how they treat that party; the status may be further specified as political if the party on whom it is conferred is speaking or acting on a matter apt for broad public discussion by virtue of that matter's bearing on collective coordination and decision-making. Throughout the rest of this chapter, I will refer to *informal representation* when the point I make concerns the general phenomenon and *informal political representation* when the point is particular to this species of the phenomenon.

The Example of Booker T. Washington

To better understand audience conferral, return to Booker T. Washington's "Atlanta Compromise" speech. Earlier, I contended that, giving that speech, Washington spoke as an IPR of Black Americans. But that would be true only if audience conferral obtained. Had it? To answer this question, we need to consider how Washington's various audiences treated him and examine whether those manners of treatment constitute conferral actions capable of imbuing a party with the status of IPR.

Audiences come in all shapes and sizes. They may be large or include just one person. An audience might be the crowd at a political rally or a political pundit or just a private individual.[33] Audiences can comprise members of the group to be represented only, nonmembers only, or a mixture of both. In Washington's case, several different individual and group audiences each independently conferred the status of IPR for Black Americans on Washington through different conferral actions in different contexts at different times. With the key features of audience conferral just discussed in mind, we can examine in detail exactly how the different audiences Washington encountered in different contexts each conferred the status of IPR upon him:

1. *Exposition commissioners.* When planning the program for the 1895 Cotton States and International Exposition (the *context*), the exposition's white commissioners (a *group audience*) conferred

the status of IPR for Black Americans (the *represented group*) on Washington (the *representative*) by inviting him to give an address on behalf of Black Americans at the exposition (*conferral action: invitation*). The commissioners extended this invitation because of "the favorable impression [Washington] had made in speaking before a white conference in Atlanta in 1893," during which he "stress[ed] conservative themes about how blacks could use the exposition to showcase their accomplishments rather than push for political rights." (Note here that Washington's 1893 speech was political in the sense delineated above.) One may be tempted to think that he was invited to speak merely in an individual capacity, failing to fully satisfy the *invitation* condition described above. Yet Washington was in fact explicitly invited to stand in for Black Americans: commissioners did not merely seek out Washington individually. Rather, they first decided that "a black man could speak at the opening ceremonies and [then] invited Washington to be that speaker."[34] He was invited to be *the* Black speaker at the exposition, and through this invitation the audience of exposition commissioners conferred the status of IPR on Washington in this program planning context.

2. *Governor Bullock.* Immediately before the address at the exposition (the *context*), Georgia governor Rufus Bullock (an *individual audience*) conferred the status of IPR for Black Americans (the *represented group*) on Washington (the *representative*) by welcoming him to the stage in the following manner: "We have with us to-day a representative of Negro enterprise and Negro civilization."[35] Bullock's introduction comprised three conferral actions. First, the introduction served as an invitation (*conferral action*) for Washington to take the stage as a representative for Black Americans. Second, the content of the introduction—Bullock's description of Washington as "a representative of Negro enterprise and Negro civilization"—indicated that he would ascribe Washington's statements during the address to Black Americans as though the statements were made by the group or its members themselves (*conferral action: preemptive ascription*), thereby treating Washington as a credible source of information about Black Americans and their values, interests, and preferences (*conferral action: credibility conferral*).

Consider a few further features of audience conferral illustrated by the two cases. First, as presented, each of these cases is an example of *synchronic audience conferral*: each audience conferred the status of IPR for Black Americans on Washington in one context at one time. But audience conferral can be diachronic, meaning that an individual conferral action itself takes place over a period of time (call this *diachronic audience conferral*). To see this, consider the following:

3. *Exposition attendees.* Exposition attendees also treated Washington as speaking for Black Americans, thereby conferring on him the status of IPR. At the exposition (*context* E), Washington spoke before an audience of both Black and white southerners (an *audience of many individuals*). At the conclusion of the address, many in the audience reacted strongly and approvingly to the speech: "When he was finished . . . 'tears ran down the faces of many blacks in the audience. White southern women pulled flowers from the bosoms of their dresses and rained them on the black man on stage.' It was a revolutionary moment, a black man . . . declaring a new social policy for the South."[36] Was any of this audience conferral? If so, which part or parts?

Begin by considering audience members' mere presence at the address. Normally, mere presence at a public speech or address would not be sufficient to confer IPR status; one can, in general, go to hear a speaker without thereby performing any of the conferral actions described above nor engaging in any other manners of treatment that would indicate that one is treating the speaker as though they are speaking on behalf of parties besides themself. A crucial feature of this example, however, is that Washington was introduced by Bullock to the attendees as a representative for Black Americans, and it is reasonable to believe that at least some of those attendees received him under this description. As I will discuss below, there can be interaction effects between instances of audience conferral, whereby one audience's conferral of the status of IPR (here, Bullock's) can affect whether another audience (here, attendees at Washington's speech) in fact also confers the status of IPR.

Imagine that some attendees (the *A*s) were very receptive to Bullock's introduction. They heard him introduce Washington and it was at that moment (time $t1$), in that context (E), and because of that introduction that the As began treating Washington as a credible source of information about Black Americans and their values, interests, and preferences (*conferral action: credibility conferral*). The As' treatment conferred the status of IPR for Black Americans on Washington at $t1$ in context E. Their conferral of IPR status on Washington developed over the course of the address: As they listened ($t2$), the As went on to rely on Washington's testimony, attempting to understand what Black Americans wanted, valued, or preferred (*conferral action: testimonial reliance*). By the end ($t3$), they had ascribed Washington's statements to Black Americans (*conferral action: ascription*). Yet the initial moment of audience conferral was synchronic—it happened for the As at $t1$ in E.

That was not so for other attendees in the audience (the Bs). Like the As, the Bs heard Bullock's introduction at $t1$ in E. But the Bs had come to the exposition more skeptical of Washington, and so Bullock's introduction did not have the same effect on them as it had had on the As. Still, it was because of Bullock's endorsement that they stayed for the address at all. It was only after they heard the address (time $t3$) that the Bs began to ascribe Washington's statement to other Black Americans (*conferral action: ascription*), thereby conferring on him the status of IPR in E. Here the Bs' conferral of the status of IPR upon Washington is diachronic, developing over the course of his address.

Notice another diachronic aspect of this example: Insofar as we think it apt to characterize the As and the Bs as parts of a larger conferring audience, we may further say that this larger audience conferred IPR status on Washington diachronically (over the course of times $t1$ to $t3$) in E.

The foregoing is a stylization of the Washington example to illustrate the difference between *synchronic audience conferral* and *diachronic audience conferral* of the status of IPR. Even so, it reflects the historical events of the time: at the exposition (the *context*), many attendees present for Washington's speech (an *audience of many individuals*) conferred him credibility as a source of information about Black Americans; relied on his testimony to know what Black Americans wanted, valued, and preferred; and ascribed his statements to Black Americans as though made by the group or its members themselves. Through these audience conferral actions, Black and white attendees alike seem to have conferred the status of IPR on Washington.

Some cases of audience conferral have both synchronic and diachronic aspects, whereby one audience confers the status of IPR upon a party in a context at a time but then, like the *As* in the previous example, augments, deepens, or further entrenches the status through subsequent conferral actions. Consider the following:

4. *Presidents.* Arguably, the first time that Washington was conferred the status of IPR for Black Americans by a U.S. president was in 1901, when Theodore Roosevelt invited him to the White House for dinner.[37] "The dinner secured Washington's position as the leading black figure and spokesman in the United States."[38] At this point in time, and in this context, Washington (the *representative*) was conferred the status of IPR for Black Americans by President Roosevelt (the *audience*) through the invitation to dinner at the White House (*conferral action: invitation*). This is not, however, where things ended.

Over a course of years, in several different contexts and through several different conferral actions, President Roosevelt treated Washington as speaking and acting for Black Americans. These subsequent conferral actions reaffirmed the prior role conferral initiated through the invitation to dinner but also deepened and further concretized Washington's position as IPR for Black Americans.

After the 1901 dinner, "Washington became an advisor to Roosevelt on race politics and Southern politics in general."[39] So, Roosevelt's initial conferral action (the invitation to dinner) was succeeded by an invitation to stand in as the voice of Black Americans in an ongoing way. By inviting Washington to become his advisor, Roosevelt also conferred credibility on Washington and indicated his testimonial reliance on Washington as "the one person to be consulted concerning the Negro problems in America and race problems everywhere."[40]

Washington's relationship to the president did not end when Roosevelt's term ended. He was also treated as speaking for Black Americans by Roosevelt's successor, President William Howard Taft.[41] Taft's audience conferral provides an interesting wrinkle for thinking about how to individuate instances of audience conferral: Taft was a distinct individual from Roosevelt, so his conferral of the status of IPR on Washington can be characterized as a distinct, synchronic instance of audience conferral. However, Taft filled the same institutional role (U.S. president) as his immediate predecessor, so his conferral of the status of IPR on Washington might not unreasonably be considered a reaffirming conferral from the Office of the President.

First through invitation, and then through ascription, credibility conferral, and testimonial reliance, Presidents Roosevelt and Taft both conferred the status of IPR for Black Americans on Washington.

Audience conferral can also have both *backward-looking* and *forward-looking* effects. In his address, Washington said, "I pledge that in your effort to work out the great and intricate problem which God has laid at the doors of the South, you shall have at all times the patient, sympathetic help of my race."[42] Imagine that some of the parties considered in the third case above—attendees at Washington's address—ascribed Washington's pledge to Black southerners (*conferral action*). When so doing, they may also have both revised beliefs they had formed in the past about Black southerners' commitments (*backward-looking*) and developed expectations on the basis of the pledge about what Black southerners would want, value, or prefer going forward (*forward-looking*). Note that although these revised beliefs and developed expectations are possible effects of audience conferral, they do not themselves constitute audience conferral, which is effected by how an audience treats a party and not by what an audience thinks of a party.

Now consider the following:

5. *W. E. B. Du Bois.* Part of what makes the Washington example so valuable to our understanding of the IPR role is that even Du Bois, one of Washington's most impassioned and constant critics, treated Washington as speaking for Black Americans: "To-day he stands as the one recognized spokesman of his ten million fellows." Du Bois was openly critical of the manner by which Washington ascended into the role of IPR for Black Americans with respect to so many audiences in so many contexts. Du Bois objected vehemently to the substance of Washington's representative statements and actions and tried to get Washington to change the way he represented. Yet, all along, Du Bois both recognized that other audiences conferred and himself conferred the status of IPR on Washington.[43] Du Bois never

tried to undermine the *fact* of Washington's status as an IPR. This example, as much as any example in this book, shows the distinctive methodological advantage of the normatively neutral approach to the IPR role: one need not normatively endorse a party's emergence into the role of de facto IPR to acknowledge that they have been put into the role nor even to oneself place that party into the role through one's own (in Du Bois's case, quite reluctant) conferral.

Du Bois also wrote of other Black Americans' reluctant conferral of the status of IPR on Washington. Although they begrudgingly recognized Washington as their IPR in a de facto sense, they did not thereby authorize him to be so, instead "feeling . . . deep regret, sorrow, and apprehension at the wide currency and ascendancy which some of Mr. Washington's theories have gained."[44] *Group conferral* and *group authorization* are distinct: When the conferring audience comprises the group to be represented itself, that conferring audience may simultaneously confer the status of de facto informal representative and grant group authorization. But a group may confer the status of de facto informal representative on a party without either granting the party authorization or otherwise normatively endorsing that the party is in the role. (Conversely, it is possible for a group to contingently authorize a party without thereby conferring the status of informal representative on the party. Such a contingent authorization would have the following form: *Should an audience confer the status of informal representative on party R, R is authorized by the group to fulfill the role of informal representative.*)

Washington's example brings into vivid relief the central role of audiences in conferring the status of informal representative. Without audiences, there could be no informal representatives.[45] As can be seen from these examples, audience conferral can be realized in many different ways. Washington was conferred the status of IPR for Black Americans several times over, by a wide variety of audiences in several different contexts. Just as audience conferral can be realized in different ways, so too can it be revoked or disappear quite differently in synchronic and diachronic cases. In the first case above, the exposition's commissioners conferred the status of IPR for Black Americans on Washington for a discrete purpose in a discrete context: to speak for Black Americans at the exposition. When the exposition ended, Washington's status of IPR for Black Americans at the exposition ended. By contrast, Washington's role as IPR for Black Americans to the president of the United States persisted across presidencies and he remained in this role for many years.

Over three decades after he wrote "Of Mr. Booker T. Washington and Others," Du Bois revisited and expanded on his earlier thoughts on Washington's role as an IPR for Black Americans, in the process explaining just how many audiences had conferred the status on Washington over the course of his career:

> Thus by 1905, to upwards of 90,000,000 people and largely to the rest of the world, Mr. Washington was the one person to be consulted concerning the Negro problems in America and race problems everywhere. He was a sort of clearing house for information, speaking to the White people concerning Colored folk and speaking to Colored people concerning White folk. From 1905 to 1911 he was the chief political advisor on racial appointments to Presidents of the United States and to state officials. He was the recognized leader in Negro industrial development. He was the treasurer of funds, temporary and permanent, set aside by philanthropists for the help of the Negro race; he was the voice and visible representative of the Colored people.[46]

In this passage, we see all four of the audience actions that confer IPR status. Washington's statements were *ascribed* to Black Americans ("he was the voice . . . of the Colored people"). He was *conferred credibility* and his *testimony* concerning Black Americans' values, interests, and preferences was *relied upon* (as "the one person to be consulted concerning the Negro problems in America" he "was a sort of clearing house for information . . . concerning Colored folk"). He was *invited* to stand in for Black Americans as an entrusted decision-maker in a variety of fora in which their interests were at stake (as "the chief political advisor on racial appointments to Presidents" and "the treasurer of funds . . . set aside by philanthropists for the help of the Negro race").

But there is something further to notice about Du Bois's description: The examples of audience conferral we considered above concern audiences of one (first Bullock, and then Roosevelt, Taft, and Du Bois), small groups (the exposition's commissioners), and larger collections of individuals (exposition attendees). These examples illustrate how a particular individual audience might engage in the manners of treatment and behavior that confer the status of IPR for that single audience in a particular context. But, as Du Bois points out in this passage, these many different individual instances of audience conferral built up over time and informed one another: An invitation to speak for Black Americans at an 1895 exposition and an approving gubernatorial introduction provided Washington an influential platform for expressing accommodationist assurances before a receptive audience. Audience conferral begat audience conferral, and, six years later, Washington was dining with one president, which became advising two presidents, until it happened: "Thus by 1905, to upwards of 90,000,000 people and largely to the rest of the world, Mr. Washington was the one person to be consulted concerning the Negro problems in America and race problems everywhere. . . . [H]e was the voice and visible representative of the Colored people."[47] Out of individual instances of audience conferral, something collective emerged. Call this phenomenon *widespread collective audience conferral*.

Collective audience conferral (I return to the *widespread* aspect below) obtains when several different individual instances of audience conferral by distinct audiences jointly converge on a shared result: that the same party R is an informal representative for a group G across the many contexts and commonly to all of the audiences that individually conferred the status. Collective audience conferral obtains only if the following conditions are satisfied. First, two or more distinct audiences confer the status of informal representative on R in one or more contexts. Second, these audiences' conferrals inform or are informed by one another in some way. The purpose of this second condition is to note a distinction between (1) mere aggregation of distinct and separate instances of audience conferral whereby distinct audiences each independently confer the status of informal representative on R in some context(s) (call this *aggregative audience conferral*, which is not sufficient for collective audience conferral), and (2) distinct audiences conferring the status of informal representative on R in some context(s) because other audiences have done so (call this *derivative conferral*), which is the case for *collective audience conferral*. A clarification on this second condition: To say that one audience, B, confers the status of informal representative on R because another audience, A, has done so is not to say that B is aware of A's conferral, nor even of B's own conferral. Recall that audience conferral is a matter of the audience's treatment of R, not their attitudes toward R. For some collection of distinct audience conferrals to bring about collective audience conferral rather than mere aggregation of individual instances of audience conferral, it must simply be the case that part of the full explanation as to why B conferred informal representative status on R is that A did so.

To see the difference between mere aggregative audience conferral and collective audience conferral, return to the third case above, concerning the exposition attendees at Washington's address. The As in the audience conferred IPR status on Washington because Governor Bullock had. This meets the minimum conditions for collective audience conferral: Bullock's introduction of Washington informed the As' conferral and, when we explain why the As conferred IPR status on Washington, Bullock's conferral forms part of our explanation. By contrast, imagine that another individual audience, D, wandered into Washington's address midway through it. D missed Bullock's introduction and only conferred IPR status on Washington after hearing Washington himself state "I but convey to you . . . the sentiment of the masses of my race."[48] At the time ($t2$) that D conferred IPR status on Washington, D's conferral was not part of the as-yet nascent collective audience conferral of IPR status to which the exposition commissioners, Governor Bullock, and perhaps some of the other exposition attendees (the As, if their conferral had informed another audience's conferral at that point) had already contributed. This does not mean, however, that D's audience conferral could never contribute to the collective audience conferral that Du Bois described in the passage quoted above. Imagine that, at some later point, $t4$, D is recounting Washington's address to their friend, F, and tells F that Washington "represented the interests of Black Americans in a compelling way." As it happens, just that morning, F also read a newspaper article about the address in which Governor Bullock's introduction was quoted. As a result of D's and Bullock's antecedent instances of audience conferral, F confers the status of IPR on Washington. From $t4$, D's audience conferral becomes part of the growing, expanding network of audience conferrals wherein the previous instances of audience conferral inform the subsequent instances of audience conferral.

Many different individual instances of audience conferral converged on the shared and widespread result that Washington informally represented Black Americans across many contexts and by virtue of the mutually reinforcing conferrals of many different audiences. As each individual audience's conferral informed, interacted with, and mutually reinforced the other individual audiences' respective conferrals, Washington emerged as an IPR for Black Americans across contexts and across audiences.[49] This is an example of robust, complex, and widespread collective audience conferral. Of course, not all cases of collective audience conferral will have this character. In those more modest cases, there is still collective audience conferral; it is simply not widespread. Collective audience conferral will be evident, to varying degrees, in examples throughout this book: A particular individual audience might engage in manners of treatment that constitute the target of the treatment as an informal representative. Then, those single, individual instances of audience conferral will inform other audiences—perhaps, as in Washington's case, more and larger audiences—to bring about collective audience conferral.

Collective audience conferral picks out a phenomenon whereby several audiences' conferrals mutually reinforce one another and give rise to an informal representative who represents a given group across contexts and across audiences. But what if something quite different occurs? What if multiple audiences disagree with one another as to whether a given party, *R*, speaks or acts for some group, *G*? As mentioned, conferral is indexed to an audience and a context. If one audience treats you as speaking or acting for a given group in one context, then you become an informal representative for that group with respect to that audience in that context. It does not follow that you become an informal representative for that group with respect to any other audience. Three further considerations follow from this point.

First, as already discussed: that another audience confers the status of informal representative of group *G* on some party, *R*, does not require me to follow suit. It is possible for me to recognize another audience's conferral without myself conferring the role on *R*. Returning to the third case, the *B*s in the audience may well have recognized that Governor Bullock was treating Washington as speaking for Black Americans (thereby conferring on Washington the status of IPR) at time *t1* in context *E* through Bullock's introduction, but still themselves declined to do so.

Second, my disagreement with another audience concerning its conferral does not revoke that audience's conferral. I may criticize that audience for its conferral or try to discredit its conferral. Still, that audience can go on treating that party as speaking or acting for the group, even over my objections. Of course, as mentioned, there can be interaction effects between audiences; audiences can persuade or influence one another to treat or not treat a given party to speak or act for a given group. Consider the above examples. In the third case, Governor Bullock's role-conferring introduction may have informed some exposition attendees' subsequent conferral. In the fourth case, the fact that President Roosevelt had conferred the status of IPR on Washington may have given his successor, President Taft, reason to do so as well. Now consider another case. Imagine that, while white southerners treated Washington as speaking for Black southerners, Black southerners themselves did not treat him in that manner. Imagine further that Black southerners publicly and repeatedly denied that Washington spoke for them. The fact that conferral is indexed to a given audience means that white southerners' conferral cannot be automatically revoked by Black southerners' contestation.[50] But that is not to say that white southerners are immune to criticism for continuing to treat Washington as speaking for Black southerners even in the face of the latter's public and repeated contestation, but instead that such criticism is not by itself sufficient to revoke white southerners' audience conferral (as discussed in this chapter and in Chapter 2). Likewise, that white southerners treated Washington as speaking for Black southerners may have given Black southerners instrumental reason to treat Washington as speaking for them—a consideration I discuss as part of a phenomenon I call *IPR capture* (see Chapter 3).

Third, it is possible to create conditions that make another audience's conferral more likely without thereby oneself conferring the status of informal representative. Conferral can be effected only by an audience that itself treats a party as speaking or acting for a given group in a particular context. By contrast, almost any party can try to create conditions that make audience conferral more likely. For instance, a person who wants to be treated and regarded as a representative for some group, G, might claim "I speak for G"—attempting to create conditions that make it more likely that an audience will come to treat them as speaking for G. Or members of G, who already treat and regard a given party as speaking for them, may try to create conditions under which other audiences will do so too. This seems to have happened to King in Montgomery when he received "the call of the people for a spokesman."[51]

Some attempts to create conditions that make audience conferral more likely cannot, however, be effected by a party without that party thereby themself also becoming a conferring audience in the process. To see this, consider the following example. Montgomery's Mayor Gayle attempted to create conditions that made audience conferral more likely during the bus boycott:

> On Saturday, January 21, the city commission made a different attempt to stifle the boycott. Mayor Gayle met with three little-known black ministers who were not members of the MIA, the Reverends William K. Kind, Benjamin F. Mosely, and D. C. Rice, and announced to the press late that evening that a settlement had been reached. With the active complicity of the *Montgomery Advertiser,* the commissioners' erroneous story claimed that the "prominent Negro ministers" had agreed to a pla whereby ten front seats would be reserved exclusively for whites and ten rear ones for blacks. Saturday night, as the *Advertiser* went to press, the wire services began distributing the story on the reported settlement.[52]

Mayor Gayle acted as if Kind, Mosely, and Rice spoke and acted for Black Montgomerians—attempting to create conditions under which others would confer IPR status on these ministers—precisely to avoid having to continue negotiations with King, whom he had already identified as the most significant IPR of Black Montgomerians.[53] Yet he did so by himself treating Kind, Mosely, and Rice as though they spoke and acted for Black Montgomerians, which is exactly how an audience confers the status of IPR upon another. Gayle ended up in the position of conferring IPR status on two different parties for two different reasons: He treated King as speaking and acting for Black Montgomerians because others, including the Black Montgomerian community, did. His conferral of the role of IPR on King was a consequence of others' antecedent role conferral—as the mayor of Montgomery, he was put into a position by others of negotiating with the party who had widespread audience conferral. Differently, he treated Kind, Mosely, and Rice as speaking and acting for Black Montgomerians in order to try to persuade others to do so, in the hopes that he could create conditions under which others would confer the status of IPR on Kind, Mosely, and Rice in lieu of King so that he could revoke his own conferral of the status of IPR from King. Of course, an audience can simultaneously treat several different parties as speaking or acting for the same group. And, given the known context of Gayle's negotiations with King, it is reasonable to conclude that Gayle decided to simply *pretend* that Kind, Mosely, and Rice

spoke and acted for Black Montgomerians rather than that he sincerely believed that they were doing so in some other sense, independently of Gayle's pretense.[54] Nonetheless, his pretense conferred IPR status on them.

Distinguishing audience conferral from creating conditions that make
an audience's conferral more likely helps us understand the place and
importance of self-appointment within a complete theory of informal
political representation.[55] When a party makes a self-appointing claim ("I
am the emissary of . . . the entire Jewish People," say), that claim may produce subsequent conferral.[56] An audience, hearing the self-appointing claim,
may treat the self-appointing claimant to be speaking or acting for the group
for whom they claim to speak or act. Yet although self-appointing claims can
create conditions that make audience conferral more likely, they are not
themselves audience conferral. Audience conferral and authorizational informality are jointly sufficient to bring about an IPR, meaning that one need
not (and, indeed, cannot) appoint oneself as an IPR. So, while Washington
publicly expressed the intention to be an IPR ("I but convey to you . . . the
sentiment of the masses of my race"), his audiences made him one.[57]

Audience conferral can be much more clearly identified in some cases
than in others. The central example of this chapter involves a complex case
of audience conferral whereby many different audiences across a number of
contexts and a number of years jointly treated one party, Booker T. Washington, as speaking and acting for Black Americans. Yet even within this
example, there is ambiguity as to which audiences conferred IPR status on
Washington. We may have thought that, whenever the audience is one
person or a handful of people, audience conferral can be clearly identified—
the exposition commission's invitation to Washington to be the Black
speaker at the exposition.[58] However, even examples involving individual
audiences can be ambiguous. On December 16, 1898, President William
McKinley made an official visit to what was then called the "Tuskegee
Normal and Industrial Institute" and pronounced Washington to be "one
of the great leaders of his race."[59] This pronouncement alone does not provide dispositive information as to whether McKinley treated Washington as
speaking or acting for Black Americans. (Recall that there is a distinction
between the roles of leader and informal representative, although the same
parties often inhabit both roles simultaneously.) Even so, perhaps President
McKinley engaged in audience conferral—either during this visit or outside

of it. But reports of the visit emphasize McKinley's praise for the educational institution as "of inestimable value in sowing the seeds of good citizenship" and praise for Washington for his "genius," "perseverance," and "enthusiasm and enterprise" in establishing it.[60] The reports do not describe McKinley as turning to Washington to consult on race relations between Black and white Americans, a stark contrast from the clear examples of audience conferral found in the Roosevelt and Taft examples, where these two later presidents often turned to Washington for insight into Black American communities.

Similarly, where larger or more amorphous audiences are involved, identifying audience conferral may be more difficult. As the third case above illustrates, that exposition attendees received Washington favorably upon the conclusion of his "Atlanta Compromise" speech leaves open the possibility that, favorably disposed as they were, some or even all of them may not have treated him as speaking or acting for Black Americans.[61] They may simply have enjoyed his speech. And if the exposition attendees formed not just a collection of individuals but an internally cohesive group audience, we may ask: How many audience members at the speech had to treat Washington as speaking for Black Americans for it to be said that this group audience, as such, did so? Of course, we can simply acknowledge that some but not all members of an audience confer the status of informal representative on a given party. Because, unlike for formal representatives, there are no de jure limits as to how many informal representatives a given group can have, many different informal representatives may receive conferral of the status from the same large and amorphous audience, even if not from the very same audience members.

Uncertainty as to whether audience conferral has in fact obtained in a given case is to be expected, particularly considering how widely various its types and manifestations. This uncertainty should not lead us to conclude that we have misdescribed or underspecified the phenomenon of audience conferral. Rather, there is an opportunity here for further exploration—both theoretical and empirical—concerning the heterogeneity of audience conferral. Moreover, despite present uncertainties, there will be clear cases of audience conferral and paradigmatic examples of informal representation about which reasonable people could not disagree, including many provided in this book. We can rely on those clear cases and paradigmatic examples for our subsequent discussion.

Alternative Accounts of Informal Representative Emergence

Some readers may be hesitant to adopt the audience conferral account of informal representative emergence. That an audience, and not necessarily an audience comprising the represented group, makes it the case that a party is an informal representative for a group may strike them as counterintuitive. Indeed, conceiving of informal representation in this way has some unusual and, one may object, undesirable consequences. First, one can come to be an informal representative nonvoluntarily, although we might well have thought that the position of informal representative is, like its formal counterpart, undertaken only with the consent of the representative, the represented, or both. Second, groups represented by informal representatives may be saddled with representatives they would not choose but cannot shake.

Informal representative does not pick out a natural kind but a social role, so an account of how a party comes into this role will always be somewhat tentative and open to contestation. My aim in this section, therefore, is not to try to settle the matter of what it is to *really* be an informal representative. Rather, my aim is simply to set out some plausible alternative accounts and to offer some preliminary reasons to think that they do not provide as many theoretically useful tools as the audience conferral account. The overall aim of this book is to show the theoretical fecundity of the account I am advancing here.

One alternative account, the *standards of reasonableness* alternative, emphasizes that in some cases an audience will appear to be entirely mistaken in treating someone as speaking or acting for a group. These cases of epistemically faulty or otherwise defective conferral, it may be argued, should not be thought to bring about real informal representatives.

Another alternative account, the *no conferral needed* alternative, allows that a party may be an informal representative without audience conferral. Perhaps an audience should treat a party as speaking or acting for a given group. That they do not does not change the fact that that party is in fact an informal representative in accordance with some other standard or set of criteria.[62]

A third alternative account, the *putative informal representative* alternative, posits a distinction between legitimate, bona fide informal representatives and merely putative informal representatives. On this account, only parties who receive both audience conferral and authorization from the group they are treated as representing are real, legitimate, bona fide informal representatives. Those who receive only audience conferral but not group authorization are mere putative informal representatives.

Two preliminary notes about these alternatives: First, each of the *standards of reasonableness* and *putative informal representative* alternatives adds further necessary conditions to the emergence conditions for becoming an informal representative. The standards of reasonableness account requires not merely that a party be conferred the status of informal representative by an audience but that the conferral meets certain epistemic quality standards. The putative informal representative account requires that a party receive group authorization to be a legitimate, bona fide informal representative, and further denies that one could in fact be a "real" informal representative without receiving group authorization. By contrast, the *no conferral needed* alternative removes the conferral condition and replaces it with different emergence criteria.

Second, although contrasted with the audience conferral account, each alternative highlights a feature of informal representation I agree is important to informal representation—respectively, how audiences think about conferring the status of informal representative (insofar as they do think about it at all), the criteria by which people are treated as speaking or acting for others, and the importance of group authorization. The disagreements between us concern only whether these features are part of the initial emergence conditions for coming into the position of informal representative or whether they find their place elsewhere in the theory. Consider each of these alternatives in turn.

First, consider the standards of reasonableness alternative. Imagine that Ambor is one of the few Black students at an elite university in the United States. She is sitting in a political theory seminar with fourteen white classmates when the discussion turns to the experience of growing up Black in the United States. Suddenly, everyone turns to Ambor, expecting her to speak for Black students who grew up in the United States.[63] You may quite reasonably think her classmates (audience) are deeply mistaken in doing so. Ambor was born and raised in Jamaica and moved to the United States only recently for college—facts known to her classmates. Surely the audience of classmates has gotten something wrong.

Can we use a standard of reasonableness or responsiveness to the evidence to separate out successful from defective cases of audience conferral? On a standards of reasonableness view, not all cases in which an audience treats a party as speaking or acting for a group succeed in conferring the status of informal representative on the party. Rather, the audience only succeeds in conferring the status if they do so in a manner that is reasonable or responsive to the evidence available to them. Manners of treatment that arise out of epistemically faulty audience attitudes or beliefs fail to confer informal representative status.

On a standards of reasonableness account, despite her classmates treating Ambor as speaking for Black students who grew up in the United States, Ambor does not become an informal representative for this group because the audience's treatment arose from an epistemic error: the audience regarded Ambor to be a credible source of information concerning growing up Black in the United States despite their lack of evidence as to whether she had this information and the presence of evidence suggesting that she may not. A standards of reasonableness account excludes from the ambit of the concept *informal representative* parties who are treated as speaking or acting for a group due to an audience's epistemic error.

Why should we think that Ambor emerges as an informal representative for Black students who grew up in the United States even though the audience seems to be treating her as speaking or acting for this group on the basis of an epistemic error? When Ambor's classmates treat her as speaking for Black students who grew up in the United States, she gains the power to influence. To say that a representative has the power to influence how an audience regards the represented in a context is to say, at least, that (1) the representative is able to, through their statements or actions, directly affect the audience's doxastic attitudes about the represented group and the group's values, interests, or preferences in that context, and (2) part of the explanation as to how the representative does so is that the audience treats the representative as speaking or acting for the represented group. The power to influence is a de facto power that emerges when and because the audience confers the status of informal representative. It is an informal representative's capacity to guide, sway, inform, change, or otherwise impact a conferring audience's understanding of the represented group's members' ideals, values, interests, preferences, or doxastic attitudes.[64] That power to influence is, as I elaborate in Chapter 2, the core feature of being an informal representative. It is a power that can emerge even out of audience error.

By characterizing audience conferral this way, we develop a more nuanced understanding of the relationships of power that arise between the parties, even in cases originating in an audience's epistemic errors. Both the audience (Ambor's classmates) and the party bestowed the status of informal representative (Ambor) have power with respect to the represented group (Black students who grew up in the United States):

1. When Ambor's classmates turn to her, expecting her to speak for Black students who grew up in the United States, they invite her to do so and treat her as a credible source of information—two conferral actions. Ambor's classmates, the conferring audience, thereby exercise their power to confer on Ambor the status of informal representative.
2. When the status of informal representative is conferred, Ambor is imbued with the derivative power to influence (a) how the represented group (Black students who grew up in the United States) is understood by the audience (Ambor's classmates) and, possibly, as a result, (b) many conditions affecting the group's members' lives.

Ambor is conferred the status of de facto informal representative for Black students who grew up in the United States when and because her classmates turn to her—regardless of why her classmates may have done so. Ambor's classmates' conferral actions may have been undertaken on the basis of bad evidence or in a manner that is unreasonable. Indeed, because conferral obtains when and because an audience treats the conferred-upon party in certain ways and not because the audience forms certain doxastic attitudes toward the party, audiences may even exercise their conferral powers unwittingly.

Of course, it is worrisome (and, as we will see, objectionable) that a room full of white students can put a single Black student in the position of representing a group—and a group of which she is not a member, at that. That is the point. A benefit of the audience conferral account, and the normatively neutral approach from which it emerges, is that the account and the approach give us the resources to (1) explain how a party comes to be in the weighty and sometimes significant social role of informal representative, (2) criticize those audiences who burden parties with this role, and (3) distinguish between such explanation and criticism. The standards of reasonableness alternative lacks the resources to capture this distinction; by placing epistemic constraints on how audiences may confer the informal representative role, the alternative account excludes from the ambit of its concern precisely the most worrisome cases.

The audience conferral account provides us with the conceptual resources to distinguish between different apt criticisms of Ambor's classmates: not only are her classmates epistemically criticizable for being improperly responsive to the available evidence and for discounting Ambor's testimony concerning her upbringing; they are also criticizable for foisting on Ambor an unsought and probably burdensome social role. To treat audience conferral as the constitutive condition for the emergence of informal representatives is to take seriously the lived experience of those who find themselves conscripted into this role, sometimes by epistemically errant audiences. As Lauren McGuill reports, "Laito Zarkpah, a junior philosophy and political science major, expressed frustration with feeling as though she had to be a 'spokesperson' for the Black community: 'Feeling like you have to be the spokesperson for your people, that you speak for every single person that looks like you . . . gets really frustrating. . . . Sometimes I just want to be a student and being a Black student on campus, sometimes you're not afforded that luxury.'"[65]

Audiences treat parties as speaking or acting for groups all the time— sometimes on epistemically laudable grounds, but often not. Neither the reasonableness of the audience's conferral nor the quality of any evidence on which the conferral is based affects whether an audience thereby bestows the power to influence. And that power to influence is the central and defining feature of the informal representative position.

Standards of reasonableness do, however, have a place in the audience conferral account: they are part of the evaluative criteria for whether an audience ought to be criticized for its conferral. We can and should (1) evaluate instances of audience conferral for their reasonableness and for the quality of any evidence on which the conferral is based, and (2) criticize conferring audiences for putting parties into the position of informal representative on unreasonable grounds (see Chapter 2). A core motivating concern for criticizing audiences on these grounds is precisely that they are able to put unwilling and unwitting parties into a weighty and burdensome social role.

The underlying motivation of the audience conferral account is to acknowledge the power that audiences in fact have by identifying what lies at the core of being an informal representative (the power to influence) and who confers that power (audiences). If you are persuaded that (1) being an informal representative is fundamentally about having the power to influence how various audiences regard the values, interests, and preferences of a given group, and (2) one could come to have that power even when the audience conferral that gave rise to that power is epistemically criticizable, unreasonable, or not responsive to some available evidence, then you have good reason to prefer the audience conferral account of the emergence of informal representatives. It captures more of the cases in which the power to influence arises than any account that requires audience conferral to be reasonable or responsive to available evidence.

To be clear, in saying that the audience puts Ambor into the position of informal representative in this case, I do not claim that she comes to speak for Black students who grew up in the United States in the intentional or authorizational sense of *speaking for*. She speaks for that group, if at all, at the other end of the *speaking for* spectrum: not intentionally, and not with the authorization of the group. Still, she stands in for the group by the lights of her audience, and that burdensome social role has a name: *conscripted informal representative*. I revisit the Ambor example along with the idea of informal representative conscription in Chapter 2.

Next, consider the *no conferral needed* alternative. One may think that, although no audience treats a given party as speaking or acting for a group, G, party R may still be an informal representative for G. Perhaps an audience has a standard rule it normally uses to decide whom to treat as speaking or acting for groups—for instance, when a party says that they speak or act for a given group G, treat them as speaking or acting for G—but did not apply that rule to R.[66] Had the audience applied the rules, it would have conferred the status of informal representative on R. So, R is an informal representative. The audience in this case just failed to identify R as one.

That an audience has standard rules it otherwise uses to decide on whom to confer the status of informal representative should not have bearing on the instant case. We might say that the audience erred by not applying its standard rules and we may even say that, had the audience applied those rules, conferral would have obtained. But where the rule has not been applied and conferral does not obtain, no informal representative has emerged.

Absent an audience, it makes little sense to characterize a party as an informal representative. The party may be an informal representative hopeful or informal representative has-been, but absent some audience who treats the party as speaking or acting on behalf of another (the represented), there is no informal representation taking place.

Consider Sharon Kiraly, who asked the State Housing Committee of Connecticut to block construction of a condominium she believed would endanger pedestrians, adding "I speak for the elderly and handicapped crossing the road in that area."[67] Imagine the committee normally applies the rule described above. Had it done so in this case, the committee would have conferred on Kiraly the status of informal representative of the group for whom she claims to speak. As it happens (let us imagine), however, Kiraly's letter never reached the committee; they never applied their standard rule. On the *audience conferral* account, Kiraly fails to become an informal representative for this group.[68]

Perhaps you think that the audience conferral requirement renders the concept of informal representation too different from other everyday conceptions of representation. In other contexts, seemingly, we can have representatives even absent audience conferral. For example, if I give power of attorney to my sister, she represents me for legal purposes even before anyone else realizes it. If my sister concludes a contract for me and someone fails to acknowledge her as my representative, then that third party has simply gotten it wrong—my sister is my representative in this case, and the third party simply does not realize it. This power of attorney case is not, however, a counterexample. That an audience is required for the representative relation to obtain does not mean that we need three distinct individuals to inhabit the three roles that make up a representative relationship (representative, represented, and audience). An audience in some cases comprises the represented themselves. In this example, my sister does indeed have an audience: me. I have granted her authorization to represent me, thereby treating her as speaking and acting for me within the terms of the power of attorney. More generally, as stated in the Introduction, it is not my aim to argue that informal representatives are "real" representatives in accordance with extant conceptions of representation, but to try to extend our concept of representation to account for the social role that is the subject matter of this book.

Finally, consider the *putative informal representatives* alternative, which shares some crucial features with the audience conferral account, as will become even clearer when I discuss group authorization in Chapter 3.

Although I describe this account as an alternative by way of clarifying subtle differences between the views, they are not in fact so far apart.

On the putative informal representatives alternative, to be an informal representative for a group, G, requires not merely that a party, R, is treated by some audience as speaking or acting for G but, further, that R is informally authorized by G to speak or act for G and its members. On such an account, when an audience treats R as speaking or acting for G, though R has not received group authorization, the audience's treatment only has the effect of putting R in the position of mere putative informal representative, a kind of pseudorepresentative. Even merely putative representatives may unwillingly or unwittingly find themselves with new obligations to group G by virtue of their putative representative status. Should putative representative R succeed in garnering audience conferral of the role of informal representative for G despite not having group authorization, they have done so under false pretenses. When members of G say "R does not speak for us," the members of G are correct, because R is not authorized by G to speak for them. Still, R may incur certain obligations toward G, at least so long as audience conferral persists. But that does not mean that R really informally represents G.

This alternative account aims to drive a wedge between cases of merely putative informal representation, on the one hand, and cases of legitimate informal representation, on the other, requiring group authorization for the emergence of a "real" informal representative. I imagine that some readers will be tempted by this alternative. It offers an account of the emergence conditions for informal representatives that tracks the emergence conditions for formal representatives like legislators. Moreover, it preserves the widely shared intuition that groups should have a say in who represents them.

But it is important to have an account of informal representation that does not build group authorization into the emergence conditions for the phenomenon. Some groups would benefit from having informal representatives although these groups not only have not authorized any informal representatives but indeed could not authorize any informal representatives in a meaningful sense. Informal authorization is very difficult to achieve in practice, particularly because the groups that informal representatives tend to represent are usually not able to effect the sorts of mechanisms that would bring about that status (see Chapter 3). There is just no way that W. E. B. Du Bois or Booker T. Washington could have been authorized as IPRs for

Black Americans as such, nor former Marjory Stoneman Douglas High School student Aalayah Eastmond for high schoolers, nor Greta Thunberg for Generation Z. These IPRs could thus not have spoken or acted for these groups in the narrow, restrictive authorizational sense familiar from law. Nevertheless, it is important to have such parties give voice to the collective interests or aspirations of these groups. Fortunately, the authorizational sense is just one of a variety of different ways one may speak or act for another. Moreover, whether or not IPRs are authorized, they have the power to influence a wide variety of audiences just by virtue of the positions they inhabit in public conversations concerning the groups for whom they are treated as speaking or acting.

Still, the putative informal representatives alternative gets some things right. First, authorization is important to any theory of informal representation. Second, there is a normatively meaningful difference between a party who is merely treated as speaking or acting for a group (a *de facto informal representative*) and a party who is, in addition, authorized to speak or act for a group by the group itself (an *authorized informal representative*).

Fortunately, the audience conferral account can make sense of these two important considerations, just in a different way. Like the putative informal representatives alternative, the audience conferral account also treats informal group authorization as playing a legitimating role (see Chapter 3). Also like the putative informal representatives alternative, the audience conferral account is clear that, without informal group authorization, informal representatives by definition do not speak or act for represented groups in the authorizational sense discussed at the outset of this chapter—thereby preserving (and in fact highlighting) the normative significance of the difference between de facto informal representative status and authorized informal representative status.

As I will discuss now, and show throughout the rest of this book, the audience conferral account has some distinctive advantages all its own.

The Advantages of the Audience Conferral Account

The foregoing provides a preliminary characterization of both the general phenomenon of informal representation and the species of the phenomenon that is the focus of this book. I have set out the relationship between informal political representation and its formal counterpart and introduced the three parties essential to all informal representative relationships: the groups represented, the conferring audiences, and the informal representatives themselves.

As the survey of alternative accounts illustrates, there is more than one way to construct the concept of *informal representative.* My aim in considering these alternative accounts has been, chiefly, to clarify the commitments of the audience conferral account and to give the reader some reasons to think that the audience conferral account captures all of the cases we would want treated by a theory of informal representation.

An obvious concern to have about the audience conferral account is that it appears to bestow on audiences the sole power to say who is an informal representative for a given group. There are two aspects to this concern. First, the audience conferral account appears not to preserve space for a powerful normative thought that many readers likely have: members of a represented group themselves ought to have some say as to who represents them.

One way to preserve this powerful normative thought in an account of informal representation would be to build group authorization into the necessary conditions for informal representative emergence: for a party to be an informal representative for a group at all, that party must have received group authorization. On such an alternative (the *putative informal representatives* alternative), when the audience confers informal representative status on a party but the group does not grant authorization, the audience's conferral is mistaken or defective and the conferred-upon party does not thereby come to "really" represent the group the audience says they do. If one then wanted to build an ethical theory of informal political representation using this approach, one would naturally frame the project around the question: How can someone be authorized by a group and thereby become that group's informal representative?

But that is not the question that animates this project. The question that animates this project is, instead: Since the group authorization of informal representatives is often not possible, what is an informal representative and, absent authorization, how may they undertake activities central to their role without thereby harming or wronging those they represent?

To begin answering this question, I have looked to the example of Booker T. Washington. One of the most striking features of the Washington example is that even Black Americans who did not authorize Washington (including some who expressly disavowed him) acknowledged that he did in fact represent them in a real sense. He may not have represented their interests to the audiences before whom he spoke and acted, but he did sit in a position of representing them. In fact, the core thought common to both of Du Bois's essays on Washington is not that Washington was not an IPR because he was not authorized; the core thought is that Washington was indeed a representative, and a rather powerful one at that, even for those Black Americans who had not authorized him, precisely because white audiences had conferred the status on him.[69] The audience conferral account incorporates the observation that authorized parties are not the only parties who end up being treated as speaking or acting for others. By incorporating this observation, the account offers a more complete picture of how the phenomenon of informal representation actually manifests in societies like ours.

Yet the audience conferral account manages to preserve the force of the powerful normative thought that groups should have some say in who represents them in two ways. First, on the audience conferral account, if an audience confers informal representative status on a party (1) absent evidence that the party has been group-authorized or (2) with evidence that the party has been disavowed by the group, then that audience has conferred the status of informal representative impermissibly (see Chapter 2). The audience conferral account is thereby able to make sense of both the observation that Washington inhabited an influential representative role vis-à-vis Black Americans and the powerful normative thought that there was something criticizable about the manner by which he emerged into that role. In addition, the account acknowledges that some informal representatives are in fact authorized and provides a comprehensive picture of how such group authorization can be effected (see Chapter 3). This makes authorized informal representatives a subset of a broader group of informal representatives. But the account is realistic about the fact that group authorization is difficult, if not impossible, in many of the contexts in which informal representation tends to emerge.

Second, the audience conferral skeptic might say: If an audience can, whenever it wants to, make somebody an informal representative and use the informal representative for its own purposes, even when those purposes are diametrically opposed to the interests of the represented group, this allows for the possibility that groups can have representatives who do not give voice to the group's interests. But, of course, this is not a special problem generated by the audience conferral account of informal representation nor for informal representation as such. That a party is a representative in either a formal or informal capacity for a group does not guarantee that that party will represent the group's interests well or accurately. Yet, far from being set aside by the audience conferral account, the concern that representatives (and audience-conferred informal representatives among them) can and often do represent groups in ways that are opposed to groups' members' interests serves to lay the foundation for the normative theory in this book: I argue that authorized and nonauthorized informal representatives alike have responsibilities to those they represent to treat them in certain ways and to represent them in ways that advance the interests of the represented group (see Chapter 4) and responsibilities to respond to the legitimate complaints of the represented when they fail to engage in these manners of treatment or advance these interests (see Chapter 5).

Among the greatest advantages of the audience conferral account is that it makes conceptual space for a distinction between two social roles that, although connected, are distinct in several significant respects: the *de facto informal representative* and the *authorized informal representative*.

First, the roles are distinct in terms of who has the ability to confer each role upon a party and the different mechanisms by which each role is conferred. The status of de facto informal representative is conferred by audiences when and because they treat a party as speaking or acting for a group in the ways described (*ascription, credibility conferral, testimonial reliance, invitation*). Authorization by the represented group is not required for the conferral of this status. By contrast, the status of authorized informal representative can only be conferred by represented groups, which authorize or ratify the representative party by way of procedures canvassed in Chapter 3. (Of course, the two social roles are connected, and each can affect the other. For instance, that an audience confers the status of de facto informal representative on a given party may give a group some reason to consider whether to authorize that party. And, in the other direction, that a group has authorized a given party to represent them may give a nongroup audience reason to confer the status of de facto informal representative upon that party.)

Second, these two different subtypes of informal representatives have different sorts of powers with respect to those they represent. De facto informal representatives—who have not been (and who perhaps could not be) authorized by the group for whom they speak or act—have only the power to influence how audiences regard the values, interests, preferences, and doxastic attitudes of the represented group (see Chapter 2) and only speak for a group in the sense that an audience imputes their statements or actions to the group. However, because they have not been authorized or ratified by the group, they neither speak nor act for the group in the restrictive authorizational sense nor do they come to have discretionary or normative powers with respect to the represented group.

By contrast, an authorized informal representative has two types of power (see Chapter 3): first, as an informal representative, they have the power to influence the audience(s) that conferred them the status, and second, by virtue of their authorization, the informal representative is imbued with discretionary and normative powers with respect to the authorizing group. What discretionary and normative powers they come to have are specified through the type of group authorization that obtains. When we say of this informal representative that they *speak for* or *act for* the represented group, we use the more restrictive authorizational sense of these locutions characterized at the outset of this chapter—the sense of being an agent of a principal that is more familiar to us from contexts of formal representation.

I illustrate informal authorization with the example of King's authorization by the Black Montgomerian community during the Montgomery Bus Boycott in Chapter 3. But that example is a relatively rare case of clear and undeniable group authorization. In many if not most cases of informal representation, it is not just that informal representatives are not in fact authorized but that they could not be authorized by the group in a meaningful sense.[70] It would be an unsatisfying moral theory of informal political representation that could not help us understand what sorts of powers and responsibilities befall most informal representatives—those who are not authorized and, crucially, those who could not be authorized.

Third, the distinct powers attached to each of these social roles in turn give rise to distinct prerogatives and duties for their respective inhabitants. Separating out these two social roles puts us in the unique position to tackle the normative questions that are at the heart of this book—questions that cannot even be adequately formulated without recognizing and distinguishing the two different roles that give rise to them. In Chapters 2 and 3, I turn to a more sustained treatment of informal representatives' de facto, discretionary, and normative powers, how those powers come about, and how having those powers shapes the normative landscape for both informal representatives and the parties that confer those powers on them.

2

Conscription and the Power to Influence

Here we turn our attention from informal representation generally back to informal political representation specifically. Two considerations, taken together, have surprising normative implications for our theory of informal political representation. The first consideration is that sometimes informal political representatives (IPRs) are conscripted. An IPR is conscripted just in case they are treated by some audience as speaking or acting for some group, but either do not know that they are so treated or do not want to be so treated—that is, the party is *unwitting* or *unwilling*. The second consideration is that, whether voluntary or conscripted, IPRs can have great power to influence how those they represent are regarded by various audiences. The IPR's power to influence can, in turn, have profound effects on the lives, circumstances, and choices of the represented. This chapter explores these two considerations, their interactions, and their normative implications for both conferring audiences and IPRs.

The discussion in this chapter proceeds as follows: First, I provide a characterization of the widespread but underexamined phenomenon of IPR conscription. Second, I consider why audiences conscript IPRs—their motivations for seeking out parties on whom to confer the role at all as well as their reasons for conferring the role on some parties rather than others. Third, I discuss the duties that accrue to audiences themselves by virtue of their power to conscript IPRs and apply this account to the case of Ambor, who was introduced in Chapter 1. Fourth, I provide a characterization of the power to influence that IPRs, whether voluntary or conscripted, come to have when and because audience conferral obtains. Fifth, I discuss what pro tanto duties accrue to IPRs by virtue of their power to influence, examining both (1) how the principles of *due care* and *loss prevention* shape

IPRs' duties and (2) how their duties vary in both degree and kind depending on how much power the IPR has to influence how the represented are regarded by various audiences, whether the IPR knows or ought reasonably to have known that they are an IPR, how willing they are to be an IPR, and other relational ties that may bind the IPR and the represented.[1] I conclude with a discussion of the grounds on which IPRs can reasonably reject the ascription of pro tanto duties that would otherwise accrue to them by virtue of their power to influence.

The Conscription of the Informal Political Representative

Sometimes, IPRs are both witting and willing, as the examples of Rev. Dr. Martin Luther King Jr. and Booker T. Washington each illustrate (see Chapter 1). But not always. IPRs can also be conscripted. Consider a forum like a small town meeting. Several individuals come together to make decisions for a larger group. However, these individuals do not usually think of themselves as serving in any sort of representative role—that is, they unwittingly serve as IPRs for silent or absentee counterparts.[2] Were we to inform them of their roles as IPRs and apprise them of the duties I shall argue follow from that role, they might then become unwilling IPRs. We might ask how town meeting attendees would behave differently were they to realize that they informally represent others. Surely many would balk at the suggestion that they have duties to absent others just by virtue of having shown up. Yet it is simply part of our everyday moral situation that we end up speaking or acting for others—whether before the U.S. Congress, at the dinner table, or in the town meeting, sometimes in spite of ourselves.

The town meeting is not, of course, the only context in which IPR conscription occurs. And although it is possible for each of us to be conscripted into the role of IPR in the course of everyday life, conscription is far more likely for some than others. Ta-Nehisi Coates has publicly bristled at "being seen as a spokesperson for black America."[3] Yet Coates has been adorned with many titles: "a defining voice of our times," "the pre-eminent black public intellectual of his generation," "the laureate of black lives," "the neoliberal face of the black freedom struggle."[4] Each of these designations is an instance of some form of audience conferral, converging on the conclusion that Coates is an IPR for Black Americans.[5] In this role, Coates has significant power to influence how a wide variety of audiences regard Black

Americans' values, interests, and preferences. What he says is taken up by audiences and ascribed to other Black Americans as expressions of their own views, values, and commitments. Coates has this power independently of ever having intended to attain it: "Obviously I write," he says, "and I write for the public and I want my thoughts considered, I want my writing considered. But I didn't ask for a crown."[6] Coates was conscripted.

Representative conscription is an experience so common among members of subordinated groups that it has become fodder for satirical news sites, which publish skewering articles like "Aïsha Unceremoniously Elected Spokesperson for All Black Women" and "Aboriginal Coworker Asked to Speak on Behalf of 700,000 People in Passing Conversation."[7] As these examples attest, it is especially common for members of a society's dominant groups to treat members of subordinated groups as speaking or acting for the whole of the groups of which they are members, often based on the errant assumption that members of subordinated groups are doxastically or conatively homogeneous.[8] In some cases, like the case of Ambor (see Chapter 1), an audience may even misattribute group membership to a party and treat the presumed group member as speaking or acting for a group of which they are not a member.

Most theories of informal political representation—the few that there are—fail to accommodate conscripted IPRs.[9] In fact, several theorists have characterized IPRs as arising by virtue of their own volunteering. These voluntarist accounts focus on people or groups who take themselves to speak or act for others though neither elected nor selected to do so. Laura Montanaro discusses Oxfam's self-appointment as the IPR of the poor.[10] Michael Saward emphasizes representative claim-makers, who advance themselves as representatives by their own say-so.[11] Andrew Rehfeld emphasizes not the would-be representative's self-appointment but instead their averment that, yes, they have become a representative.[12] Voluntarist accounts have in common an assumption that, to become an IPR, one must choose to do so, whether by appointing oneself, making a representative claim, or accepting the position once it is conferred by an audience.[13]

But that's not always how it is. Although people often hold themselves forth as representatives for various groups, they become IPRs (as opposed to mere wannabes) only when and because they are selected by others through audience conferral. So, although some who emerge as IPRs do so willingly (*voluntary representatives*), others end up becoming IPRs, either in their own private lives or in more public political fora, against their own wishes (*unwilling representatives*) or even without their knowledge (*unwitting representatives*). Some choose to be representatives; others are conscripted.

Audiences thus have considerable and easy-to-abuse power to put various parties into the position of IPR against their will (*unwillingly*) or even without their knowledge (*unwittingly*). Given their power to conscript IPRs, we must now confront two questions about audiences: Why do audiences confer the status of IPR on various parties? And what responsibilities do audiences have by virtue of their power to do so?

Audience Motivations and Audience Reasons

It need hardly be stated that there is something worrisome and, in many cases, objectionable about representative conscription.[14] So, why does it happen? There are two ways of understanding this question. First, what motivates audiences to treat parties as speaking or acting for others at all? Second, given that audiences do so, for what reasons do they treat some parties rather than others as speaking or acting for others? Although answering these questions depends in part on empirical research concerning audiences, we can identify some broad categories of both audiences' motivations and audiences' reasons.

First, consider audiences' motivations. Audiences may be motivated by a wide variety of interests to treat parties as speaking or acting for given groups. Some audiences are motivated to learn about a given group's political interests or to include group members' perspectives in a deliberative decision-making or knowledge production process. Such *group-regarding* motivations can reflect an audience's sincere regard for a represented group. These are the sorts of motivations that underlie efforts to get community stakeholders involved in the production of global health research and to bring lay citizens together to discuss complex political questions in citizens' panels.[15] Such group-regarding motivations are not uniformly objectionable.

Other audience motivations, by contrast, are uniformly objectionable—for instance, conferring the status of IPR so as to publicly appear concerned for a group or to avoid more direct interactions with the group, or conferring the status on parties whose statements or actions will justify the audience's currently retrogressive relationship with the represented group. (On audiences conferring the status of IPR on parties whose statements or actions will justify extant retrogressive relationships with the represented group, recall here Malcolm X's concern that "Most of the so-called Negroes that you listen to on the race problem . . . have been put in that position by the white man himself. And . . . they're saying exactly what they know the white man who put them in that position wants to hear them say."[16]) Such *audience-regarding* motivations share the aim of conferring the status of IPR as a mere means to further the audience's ends, often absent regard for either the IPR or the represented, sometimes at the expense of both.

An audience's motivations may, of course, be mixed. A community organization may add members of previously absent groups to a citizens' panel both to add new perspectives to decision-making and to shore up its public image as inclusive. Moreover, an audience's motivations may not be known to the audience itself.

In this chapter, I argue that some audience motivations can by themselves ground a conscripted IPR's reasonable rejection of the ascription of any IPR duties that would otherwise have accrued to them. Those skeptical of the value of informal political representation generally may argue that there is no such thing as an unobjectionable audience motivation—all attempts to put someone in the position of IPR are objectionable. This argument strikes me as more plausible with respect to unwitting and unwilling IPRs than with respect to voluntary IPRs. As I will discuss, the role of IPR is burdensome and so there is an extremely high bar to imposing it on an unwitting or unwilling party. However, many IPRs, and indeed most of the IPRs discussed in this book, themselves aim to inhabit the role of IPR and, by so doing, accept the foreseeable burdens that come along with the position.

Second, for what reasons do audiences treat some parties rather than others as speaking or acting for a given group? This question targets the particular grounds on which audiences confer the status of IPR on particular parties—rather than the first, more general question concerning why audiences are motivated to confer the status of IPR on anyone at all. Consider some reasons why audiences may be inclined to treat some parties rather than others as speaking or acting for a given group.

Member representation and descriptive representation. An audience may treat a given party, *R*, as speaking or acting for a group because *R* is a group member or descriptively similar to group members in some respect, like Booker T. Washington or Ambor, as discussed in Chapter 1. Such IPRs are regarded as standing in as tokens of given types. Member representation and descriptive representation are the focuses of Chapter 6.

Epistemic authority. An audience may treat a given party as speaking or acting for a given group because that party has or is regarded as having authoritative knowledge about the group. W. E. B. Du Bois was an epistemic authority about Black Philadelphians living in the Seventh Ward at the time of his sociological study of that community.[17] His epistemic authority with respect to the lives, circumstances, and plight of this community gave audiences reason to seek him out, rather than others, when trying to understand the values, interests, and preferences of the Seventh Ward community.

Derivative conferral. An audience may treat a given party as speaking or acting for a group because some other audience already does (see Chapter 1).

Instrumental usefulness. An audience may treat a party as speaking or acting for a group because it is instrumentally useful to the audience to do so, as Montgomery mayor W. A. Gayle did when treating Revs. William K. Kind, Benjamin F. Mosely, and D. C. Rice as speaking and acting for Black Montgomerians in an effort to avoid continuing negotiations with Rev. Dr. Martin Luther King Jr. (see Chapter 1).[18]

These reasons are not mutually exclusive and may compound. For instance, an audience may treat a party as speaking or acting for a group because the audience regards that party to be an epistemic authority, and the audience may regard the party to be an epistemic authority by virtue of the party's group membership.

By identifying and distinguishing different audience motivations and reasons, we are better able to explain why audience conferral obtains and whom it befalls. These distinctions also help us evaluate what duties, if any, an audience's conferral generates for a conscripted IPR and to whom satisfaction of those duties is owed. First, however, we consider how an audience's power to conscript IPRs gives rise to corresponding duties for the audience itself.

The Duties of Conferring Audiences

Audiences have a great deal of power to say who speaks or acts for whom. To treat another as speaking or acting for a group is to empower them, but also thereby to burden them with power they may not want (recall Coates: "I didn't ask for a crown"). Because the potential for an audience's abuse of this power is considerable, the duties on audiences must be substantial. To what corresponding duties does such power give rise?

Begin with this general principle: each of us is responsible to identify when we confer on others statuses or powers that burden or constrain them. From this general principle we can specify at least three audience duties: (1) to recognize generally that one is an audience, which in turn helps one (2) to identify when one confers representative status, which in turn helps one (3) to assess whether doing so is reasonable and permissible.

First, consider *recognizing that one is an audience.* Audience conferral is neither rare nor remote: whenever one treats a person as speaking or acting for others in those others' steads, one is or is part of a conferring audience. Yet, it is neither easy nor obvious to recognize when one may be acting as an audience. In our everyday lives, few of us, I suspect, actively consider whether we are acting as an audience in a given interaction. Once we do so, we find that the world is full of unwitting audience members conferring the status of IPR willy-nilly. If we know only one postal employee or just two adoptive parents, we may quite reasonably go to them with our questions about postal employees or adoptive parents. On receiving their answers, we may then ascribe those answers, not always unreasonably, to other postal employees or other adoptive parents. The phenomenon itself is not unusual; thinking about it as creating IPRs is. The first responsibility each of us has, then, is simply to recognize that we may, individually or with others, be an audience. Recognizing that one is an audience includes recognizing that one has the capacity to confer the sometimes burdensome status of IPR on another.

Absent empirical study of how audience conferral instantiates in the world around us, it is difficult to say more, substantively, about what this duty requires of each of us. Even so, I shall hazard a conjecture: people who are themselves less likely to be treated as speaking or acting for a whole community (for instance, the members of a society's dominant groups) may also be less likely to recognize the practice of audience conferral as one in which they unreflectively but commonly engage.

Recognizing that one is an audience is prefatory—it puts one on alert that one has the capacity to confer the status of IPR. We want to recognize that we have this capacity in order to be better at identifying when we tend to exercise it.

Second, consider *identifying when one confers representative status.* Each of us is responsible to try to identify when we tend to treat people as speaking or acting for others and what motivates us to do so in those cases. We want to know when we tend to exercise this capacity and our motivations for doing so in order to assess whether, in those cases, we may.

Third, consider *assessing whether one may confer representative status on a given party.* Imagine that you have both recognized that you are an audience generally and identified a particular context in which you tend to confer representative status. Two considerations should inform your assessment of whether you may treat a particular party as speaking or acting for a given group. First, is it reasonable, as an epistemic matter, to treat this party as speaking or acting for this group? Second, is it morally permissible to treat this party as speaking or acting for this group? If your answer to either question is "no," then you ought not treat the party as speaking or acting for the group.

First, consider reasonableness: Is it reasonable to believe that the party has requisite knowledge or experience to speak or act for the group in the context at issue?

In some cases, this is easily answered. A lifetime of careful scholarly or journalistic investigation of the particular struggles faced by a given community would surely be adequate to make it reasonable to think that the researcher or journalist who conducted the investigation knows enough to speak or act for the group in the context at issue. No wonder, then, that Ida B. Wells-Barnett, who devoted her life's work to in-depth research of and reporting on Black American communities terrorized by white lynch mobs, was widely regarded as the IPR of these communities.[19] It is an understatement to say that it would be reasonable to believe that Wells-Barnett knew enough about the Black American communities terrorized by white lynch mobs to informally represent those communities to broader publics, as she did through both her writing and her speaking tours.[20]

Of course, knowing enough about a particular group may not be enough to make it reasonable for a given party to *be* an IPR for that group. As I discuss in Chapter 6, several different considerations bear on whether a given party ought to represent a group, particularly when the representing party is neither a group member nor descriptively similar to members of the group. But the question that concerns us here is not whether it is reasonable for Wells-Barnett to be an IPR for the communities whose plights she documented over the course of her lifetime but, rather, whether it is reasonable for an audience to believe that she knew enough about those communities to speak or act for them concerning matters related to their vulnerability at the hands of white lynch mobs.

In trickier cases, in which an audience is not sure whether it is reasonable to believe that the party in question has requisite knowledge or experience, that audience may be tempted to consider whether some other audience already treats the party in question as speaking or acting for the group in question (*derivative conferral*). Some caveats about derivative conferral are in order: First, that another audience treats a given party as speaking or acting for a given group does not by itself give one dispositive reason to do so, since that other audience's conferral may be epistemically or morally errant. By relying on their conferral, one may replicate their error. Second, we may worry that defaulting to extant IPRs can lead to entrenchment, preventing other IPRs with novel perspectives from emerging.

Second, consider permissibility: Suppose you conclude it reasonable to believe that a particular party has requisite knowledge or experience to speak or act for the group at issue. Is it permissible for you to treat this party as speaking or acting for that group? Several different considerations will aid you, the audience, in answering this question, including:

1. *Self-appointment.* Has this party claimed to speak or act for the group or do they seem amenable to doing so? You ought to ask this not because by doing so you will discover who is the "real" IPR, but so as to avoid burdening a reluctant or unwilling party with so weighty a role.
2. *Group authorization.* Have members of the group to be represented authorized this party to speak or act for them? You ought to ask this so as to avoid burdening the group with an IPR the group's members would not choose for themselves.
3. *Rebuttable presumption.* Sometimes, there is a rebuttable presumption against treating a party as speaking or acting for a group. These presumptions may be generated in a variety of ways, but here

consider just one. Recall the tendency for members of a society's dominant groups to assume, as a matter of course, that members of subordinated groups speak or act for those groups. When this tendency reflects an objectionable inability or unwillingness to regard members of the subordinated groups as individuals, as it often does, it should activate in an audience a rebuttable presumption that the subordinated group member ought not be treated as speaking or acting for the group.[21]

Bringing the above pieces together, here is a test for assessing whether audience conferral of the status of IPR is permissible in a given case (call this *the audience conferral permissibility test*): as an audience, you may not treat a given party, *R*, as speaking or acting for a given group in a context unless you have concluded that (1) it is reasonable to believe that *R* has requisite knowledge to speak or act for the group in the context (the *reasonableness condition*), (2) *R* is willing to speak or act for the group (the *self-appointment prong*), (3) *R* has or would have the authorization of the group for whom you would treat them as speaking or acting (the *group authorization prong*), and (4) there is no presumption against audience conferral to be rebutted or, if there is, the presumption has been successfully rebutted (the *rebuttable presumption prong*). Prongs 2–4 jointly constitute the *permissibility condition* of this test. These four conditions are difficult conditions to meet.

Even unwitting audiences have these duties, because these duties emerge from audiences' power to confer the status of IPR, and even unwitting audiences have that power. However, because unwitting audiences do not know they are so positioned, usually they will not be blameworthy for failing to meet their audience duties. Unwitting audiences may be blameworthy, however, for failing to consider whether they are audiences in the first place.

Return to the example of Ambor (see chapter 1). Ambor is the only Black student sitting in a political theory seminar with her fourteen white classmates. She is treated by her classmates as speaking for Black American students regarding what it is like to grow up Black in the United States despite the facts—known to her classmates—that she was born and raised in Jamaica and moved to the United States only recently for college.

Nothing about the original Ambor case makes it reasonable or permissible for her classmates to have treated her as speaking or acting for Black students who grew up in the United States. Moreover, given that Ambor is a member of a subordinated group and her audience comprises members of the society's dominant group, there is a rebuttable presumption against Ambor's classmates treating her as speaking or acting even for a group of which she is a member—Black students at the university.

When, if ever, might it be reasonable and permissible for Ambor's classmates to treat her as speaking or acting for other Black students at the university? Consider two variants of the Ambor case. In the first, Ambor is president of the university's Black Student Association (BSA). In the second, she writes a popular and intensively researched column for the college newspaper about the perspectives and experiences of Black students at the university. In each case, these facts are known to Ambor's classmates. Is it reasonable and permissible in either case for Ambor's classmates to treat her as speaking or acting for other Black students at the university?

First, consider reasonableness. In both variant cases, it seems reasonable for Ambor's classmates to believe that Ambor has requisite knowledge to speak or act for at least some fellow Black students at the university regarding matters that fall squarely within the scope of Ambor's respective mandates in each variant case. As BSA president, Ambor has regular interlocution with and, so, access to the diverse perspectives of those in her constituency: BSA members. Likewise, to write her column, Ambor must research the perspectives and experiences of Black students at the university.

Add to the second variant: Recently, Ambor's columns have been picked up by an influential media outlet as part of its well-regarded "Emerging Black Voices" series. In publishing Ambor's columns in this series, the media outlet (itself an audience) treats Ambor as speaking for Black students at the university. Imagine further that it is widely known on campus that Ambor's columns have been included in this distinguished series. On this variant, it seems plausible that, when Ambor's seminar classmates confer on her the status of IPR for Black American students, they are not merely tokenizing her as a presumed descriptive representative but are instead engaging in *derivative conferral*—conferring the status of IPR on Ambor in deference to the credential she has been granted as an emerging public voice for Black American students.

Second, consider permissibility. Is it permissible for Ambor's classmates to treat her as representing fellow Black students at the university? Relevant considerations include the following:

1. *Self-appointment.* Does Ambor take herself to speak or act for Black students at the university or is she amenable to doing so? In the first variant, Ambor accepted a nomination and ran for BSA president—giving her classmates some reason to believe that Ambor is willing to represent other Black students at the university. Even so, her constituency is the BSA's membership, not Black students at the university as such. In the second variant, Ambor's choice to write a public-facing column voicing the perspectives of fellow Black students may suggest that Ambor wants to serve as an IPR for fellow Black students. We may think Ambor's reasonable expectation to not be treated as speaking for Black American students at the university in the original scenario is diminished in both variants, since both evidence Ambor's willingness to represent Black students at the university in some respect. Diminished, but not quashed: that Ambor willingly represents others in one domain does not necessarily mean she wants to serve as a representative in other domains.

2. *Group authorization.* Have other Black students at the university authorized Ambor to represent them? In the first variant, Ambor is a formal political representative (FPR) for the BSA membership. She won an election to serve as BSA president—evidence that a majority of voting BSA members want her to represent them in this formal capacity. Whether it follows that most Black students at the university want Ambor to represent them in an informal capacity depends on (a) whether the majority of voting BSA members also constitutes a majority of Black students at the university, and (b) whether there is a widely accepted norm that BSA presidents also serve as IPRs for Black students on campus. In the second variant, that Ambor writes a column about the perspectives and experiences of Black students at the university does not give her classmates much information as to whether Black students at the university have informally authorized her to speak or act for them. However, her classmates could have other sources of evidence that she is informally authorized—perhaps Ambor's column receives widespread social media amplification and endorsement from Black students on campus.

3. *Rebuttable presumption.* The Ambor variants illustrate two different scenarios in which audience conferral of the status of IPR may be

permissible. In each variant, Ambor is certainly an epistemic authority, and plausibly self-appointing and group authorized. And,
provided that her classmates know the aforementioned details of her
BSA presidency or newspaper column, it becomes plausible to think
that Ambor's classmates in these variant cases are treating her as
speaking for Black students in recognition of her epistemic authority,
self-appointment, and group authorization. Yet the strength of
the rebuttable presumption, even in these variant cases, cannot be
overstated. We still have reason to worry that Ambor's classmates
treat her as speaking for other Black students on the basis of an errant
and objectionable assumption that all Black students either know
what other Black students think or think the same thing.[22]

Now contrast the Ambor case with the Wells-Barnett example. Was it
reasonable and permissible for Wells-Barnett's audiences during her British
speaking tour to treat her as speaking for Black American communities
terrorized by white lynch mobs? As discussed above, Wells-Barnett was
known to be an epistemic authority (arguably *the* epistemic authority) on
these communities—so the reasonableness condition was satisfied. But was
it permissible? We have ample evidence that Wells-Barnett took herself to
speak for these communities—including her acceptance of invitations to
do so, as well as her attestations that she did.[23] So, the *self-appointment prong*
of the permissibility condition is satisfied. Wells-Barnett also seems to have
been authorized by a wide variety of Black American communities, notwithstanding some concerns about her increased militancy later in her
career—an indication that she was granted *group authorization* for at least
part of her career.[24] Of course, the *rebuttable presumption prong* would also
need to be satisfied in this case, because Wells-Barnett was a Black American woman being treated as speaking for Black American communities by
various (primarily white) audiences. Although not all presumptions against
audience conferral can be rebutted in the same way, we have reason to accept
the following rule of thumb as an addendum to the *audience conferral permissibility test* in cases like Wells-Barnett's: when there is a rebuttable presumption against treating a given party as speaking or acting for a given
subordinated group by virtue of that party's descriptive similarity to or
membership in that group, that presumption can be rebutted by evidence
beyond a reasonable doubt that the party is themself willing to take on the

role of IPR for the group (*self-appointment*) and that the group authorizes that party to represent them (*group authorization*).

Focusing on the role of audiences in the emergence of IPRs makes salient normative features of informal political representation that are occluded if we build our theory with only the witting and willing in mind. Audiences can confer the status of IPR unreflectively, foisting a burdensome role on often unsuspecting parties. Although audience conferral is easy to do, it is difficult to justify: As a general matter, one ought to avoid burdening others without good reason and due consideration. The *audience conferral permissibility test* captures what counts as good reason and due consideration in the contexts of interest to us. The test is quite stringent, and its conditions—reasonableness and permissibility (the latter condition comprising three prongs: self-appointment, group authorization, and rebuttable presumption)—are difficult to satisfy, meaning that there is a high moral bar on treating a party as speaking or acting for a group in a context. So, at present, there is an appreciable distance between how promiscuously and thoughtlessly audiences confer IPR status and how sparingly and reflectively they ought to. Recognizing the gulf between the current practice of audience conferral and when it might be permissible helps us uncover novel normative considerations like these:

1. To treat someone as speaking or acting for another is to both empower and burden them. To avoid imposing such burdens without good reason and due consideration, audiences must actively consider whether they are treating parties as speaking or acting for others so that they may assess whether doing so is reasonable and permissible in a given case.

2. Because audience conferral is a manner of treatment that can be (and often is) undertaken unwittingly, avoiding its performance requires audiences to actively avoid forming and actively aim to revise sincere but misguided attitudes and habits that lead to unreflective conferral.

3. However, satisfying the above two prescriptions is difficult for those who do not recognize that they are audiences. So it is incumbent on each of us that we recognize that we often unreflectively inhabit the role of conferring audience. Coming to this realization is especially important for members of a society's dominant groups: as people who are less likely to be treated as speaking or acting for a

whole group, dominant group members are, I conjecture, also less likely to recognize when we ourselves treat others in this way.

4. Audience conferral burdens some parties more than others. For some, like members of a society's subordinated groups, audience conferral is an iterative experience. In addition to the burden of individual conferrals, iterative conferral can have an additional cumulative burdening effect. Recall Laito Zarkpah, discussed in Chapter 1, who said, "Feeling like you have to be the spokesperson for your people, that you speak for every single person that looks like you . . . gets really frustrating. . . . Sometimes I just want to be a student and being a Black student on campus, sometimes you're not afforded that luxury."[25] The risk of contributing to this cumulative burden generates for audiences an additional consideration: Even if my conferral would pass the *audience conferral permissibility test,* will it contribute to an objectionable cumulative burden to this party?

We are all audiences. All of us unreflectively make enormous and, sometimes, objectionable demands on others that they speak or act for groups—often, although not always, because they are members of those groups or at least descriptively similar in some respect to those group members. Each of us is implicated by this theory of informal political representation, whether we think we are or not. Part of what it is to take this account of informal political representation seriously is to recognize oneself as an audience and to seriously reflect on the power with which one is imbued by virtue of that fact.

The ethics of audience conferral are a central topic throughout this book. Later in this chapter, I discuss grounds on which conscripted IPRs may reasonably reject duties that might otherwise accrue to them by virtue of audience conferral. Conferring audiences, although powerful, cannot unilaterally make it the case that conscripted IPRs are required to fulfill the demands of the IPR role. In many cases, IPRs can, and perhaps should, disavow, reject, or simply ignore objectionable or unduly burdensome audience conferral. In Chapter 3, I discuss the complicating phenomenon of IPR capture, whereby an IPR is appointed by a powerful audience whose interests are not aligned with the group the IPR represents. In Chapter 6, I discuss the controversial role of the nondescriptive IPR—a party who emerges into the role of IPR despite being neither descriptively similar to nor a member of the group for whom they are treated as speaking or acting. We have reason, in some contexts, to prefer the emergence of nondescriptive IPRs precisely because, by taking up the role of IPR, these nondescriptive parties can alleviate the burdens otherwise faced by descriptively similar parties or parties who are themselves members of a subordinated group.

Conscription complicates our normative theory of informal political representation. In general, an audience brings about an IPR, that IPR gains power to influence, and the represented are often at the mercy of both. In cases of conscription, however, the IPR did not ask for the power to influence conferred by the audience and, in many cases, the audience did not realize they were installing an IPR. Where does all this leave the conscripted IPRs? Later I consider what pro tanto duties IPRs, whether voluntary or conscripted, have to those they come to represent, as well as their grounds for reasonably rejecting the ascription of these duties. First, however, I consider in greater detail what it means for an IPR of any sort to have the power to influence.

The Power to Influence

IPRs are frequently invited to sit at the table with powerful counterparts. These counterparts may control vast wealth, command public influence, or even wield state power. Booker T. Washington had the ear of President Theodore Roosevelt when proffering accommodationist policies and publicly de-emphasizing the importance of Black Americans' civic and political rights.[26] Throughout his life, Rev. Dr. Martin Luther King Jr. was received by elected officials (from Mayor W. A. Gayle of Montgomery, Alabama, to President Lyndon B. Johnson) and public audiences alike as one of the most significant IPRs of, first, Black Montgomerians, then, Black southerners, and, eventually, Black Americans more generally.[27] U2 front man Bono met with President George W. Bush at Bush's ranch in Texas, successfully urging the president to commit billions of dollars to AIDS eradication efforts in the poorest African countries.[28] Malala Yousafzai met with President Barack Obama at the White House to discuss drone strikes, democracy, education, and Pakistan's self-determination.[29] Kim Kardashian brought prisoners with her to the Oval Office to discuss prison reform with President Donald Trump.[30] Rigoberta Menchú and other Guatemalan civil society leaders met with Vice President Kamala Harris as part of the Biden-Harris administration's effort to "work more closely with nongovernmental organizations and activist groups, channeling aid money away from corrupt politicians."[31]

When an audience confers IPR status on a party, the audience thereby bestows on the IPR a de facto power with respect to the represented group and their circumstances—power created by the audience and bestowed on the IPR through audience conferral. This is the de facto power to influence. Recall: to say that a representative has the power to influence how the represented are regarded by an audience in a context is to say, at least, that (1) the representative is able to, through their statements or actions, directly affect the audience's doxastic attitudes about the represented group and the group's values, interests, or preferences in that context; and (2) part of the explanation as to how the representative does so is that the audience treats the representative as speaking or acting for the represented group.

In some cases, an IPR's power to influence will not come to much—perhaps because the audience does not really care what the IPR has to say (that is, the IPR has little power to influence) or because, although the audience really does care and the IPR really does influence the audience's understanding of the represented group, the audience itself is relatively inconsequential, at least within the context at issue. In other cases, the IPR's power to influence will be considerable.

When substantial, the IPR's power to influence enables them to predictably, directly, and seriously alter the circumstances, options, or outcomes for the represented. The deft word or deed of a skilled IPR may increase in number or desirability the opportunities available to the represented. But a clumsy or malicious IPR may instead gravely constrain the choices available to a represented group's members. Through their power to influence, the IPR can affect many aspects of the represented's lives, including the opportunities open to the represented, the resources available to them, or even the laws under which they live. These effects of the IPR's power to influence should be distinguished from the power itself.

Informal Political Representatives' Pro Tanto Duties

The fact that IPRs' statements or actions can predictably, directly, and seriously alter the circumstances, options, or outcomes for the represented affects how IPRs ought to comport themselves. It is by virtue of their power to influence and the foreseeable effects of that power that IPRs come to have pro tanto duties to comport themselves in some ways rather than others. This is true of all IPRs, whether voluntary or conscripted.

The substance of these pro tanto duties are context sensitive, depending for their specification on different features of the relationship between the audience, the represented group, and the IPR. In the next sections, I have three aims. First, I illustrate the structure of an IPR's pro tanto duties using the examples of the principles of *due care* and *loss prevention*. These examples are merely illustrative, not exhaustive. Second, I consider how different features of an IPR's role can affect both the degree and kind of pro tanto duties they have. Third, I argue that conscripted IPRs can reasonably reject pro tanto duties that would otherwise accrue to them by virtue of their representative status unless their grounds for reasonable rejection are outmatched by a represented group's dire need for their representation in particular.

The duties to be described here are distinctive of informal political representation in one key respect, in the way they accrue to the IPR: they are generated for the IPR by one party (the conferring audience), but to whom satisfaction of the duties is owed (audience, represented, or both) in a given case depends on which party (audience or represented) is vulnerable or disempowered vis-à-vis the other.[32] But the IPR's pro tanto duties are not distinctive in their substance; they are the sorts of duties anyone would have were their statements and actions to predictably, directly, and seriously alter another's circumstances, options, or outcomes. And, like other duties we have, the IPR's duties can be more or less demanding depending on a variety of considerations. In the IPR's case, these considerations include whether (1) the stakes are especially high for the relatively more vulnerable or subordinate party (perhaps because of the importance of the interests at stake in the representative's statements or actions), (2) the represented group is unable to effectively object to or disavow the representative's statements or actions, and (3) the representative's statements or actions are especially likely to impact the represented's or the audience's circumstances (perhaps because they are the only representative present in the context at issue).

Due Care and Loss Prevention

The IPR's power to influence sometimes manifests as a capacity to create expectations in an audience regarding what the represented group will do— expectations, for instance, concerning how the group's members will behave or react. This capacity to create expectations gives rise to corresponding pro tanto duties to take due care and to prevent significant losses that might predictably result from the IPR's representative activities.

The IPR may create these expectations by way of explicit statements expressing or actions indicating what the represented group will do, as when King said, "I closed my remarks by assuring the commissioners that we planned to conduct the protest on the highest level of dignity and restraint, and I avowed that our aim was not to put the bus company out of business, but to achieve justice for ourselves as well as for the white man."[33] Or instead these expectations may be created in a less intentional way—the IPR may make statements or take actions that an audience treats as evidence about the group's members' intentions, on the basis of which the audience may infer how the group is likely to act.

According to T. M. Scanlon's influential account of expectation setting, if one is in a position to create expectations in another about one's own behavior, then there are at least two constraints on one's behavior.[34] The first is *due care*: "One must exercise due care not to lead others to form reasonable but false expectations about what one will do when one has good reason to believe that they would suffer significant loss as a result of relying on these expectations." The second is *loss prevention*: "If one has intentionally or negligently led someone to expect that one is going to follow a certain course of action, X, and one has good reason to believe that the person will suffer significant loss as a result of this expectation if one does not follow X, then one must take reasonable steps to prevent that loss."[35]

Allow that these are at least some of the constraints by which we are bound when we are in the position to create expectations in another about what we ourselves will do.[36] Now, compare this bipartite case to the more complex tripartite cases at issue in the context of informal political representation.

Whose interests in not suffering a loss justifies adherence to these two principles in the tripartite IPR relationship? That is, who is susceptible to suffer a significant loss as a result of the expectations that the IPR might create in an audience?

When there are just two parties—you and me, say—and I can create expectations in you by virtue of what I say or do, then it is you who is susceptible to suffer a loss by virtue of which *due care* and *loss prevention* apply.

In the case of informal political representation, however, there are three further considerations that make a difference to our analysis. First, the IPR is put in their representative position by the conferring audience. Second, the IPR is treated as speaking or acting for another (the represented group). What the IPR conveys to the audience is treated by the audience as reflecting the values, interests, or preferences and, in some cases, the intentions of the represented group's members. The IPR ends up, in effect, mediating the relationship between the audience and represented group through what the IPR says or does. Third, although sometimes audiences have more power than the represented, in other cases the relations of power are reversed: for instance, in imperialist contexts, the audience might be those subject to colonial rule, and the represented might be citizens of the ruling country.

Given these three considerations, how should we think about what the IPR owes, respectively, to the audience before which they speak or act and to the represented for whom they speak or act?

First, consider IPRs' pro tanto duties to audiences. When and how do IPRs come to have responsibilities to exercise due care and to take reasonable steps to prevent significant losses an audience may otherwise incur?

In some cases, a party will hold themself forth to an audience as an IPR for the represented group—what Laura Montanaro calls "self-appointment."[37] If the audience treats the party as speaking or acting for a group because the party unambiguously invited or encouraged the audience's conferral, then the IPR owes it to the audience to exercise due care and to take reasonable steps to prevent significant losses that the audience may otherwise incur.

In other cases, however, parties do not hold themselves forth as IPRs for a given group but are instead conscripted into the role of IPR by an audience. Do conscripted IPRs ever have responsibilities to exercise due care or take reasonable steps to prevent losses faced by conferring audiences? The short answer to this question is that it depends on whether the audience is in a vulnerable or subordinate position vis-à-vis the representative, the represented, or both. Here's the long answer:

Many of the cases of audience conferral that we have so far considered involve audiences who are relatively more empowered than both the IPR and the represented group itself. Such audiences are not vulnerable to the represented group. In such cases, when the IPR is conscripted by the conferring audience, that IPR is not responsible to exercise due care or to take reasonable steps to prevent losses that the conscripting audience faces by virtue of its conferral of the status of IPR on the conscripted party. After all, the audience opted into their own reliance on the party they have put in the position of IPR. No one forced them to do this. Audiences confer the power to influence of their own volition and at their own peril. So, although an IPR may create expectations in the audience about what the represented group's members will do, the audience has assumed the risk of relying on those expectations. Of course, the IPR has a responsibility to the audience to take due care and prevent significant losses the audience might suffer as a result of an expectation raised by the IPR about what the IPR themself will do. But when the IPR is unwitting or unwilling, what care is due to the audience by the IPR and what reasonable steps the IPR must take to prevent loss are both diminished, if not completely quashed. After all, it was not really the conscripted IPR who led the audience to form their expectations—rather, it was, in effect, the audience itself by its conferral of the status of IPR on that party. Even if it turns out that the party they chose as an IPR is not a reliable source of information about the intentions of the represented group, through conferral the audience assumed the risk of significant loss. This assumption of the risk argument applies only to relatively more empowered audiences, who are not vulnerable to the represented group and who may therefore freely decide whether or not to treat a given party as speaking or acting for the represented group.

Yet not all cases of audience conferral involve empowered audiences. Some audiences are vulnerable to the represented group for whom they seek an IPR. Consider, for instance, an imperialist context in which the audience is subject to colonial rule. The audience treats a random citizen of the ruling country as speaking for the ruling country, and, accordingly, audience members modify their conduct to their own detriment in response to idle talk by the IPR of the intentions of the ruling country or its people. In this imperialist context (or comparable contexts of inequality), where the audience is vulnerable to the represented group, it would be unfair to put the risk on the audience for conferring IPR status on a citizen of the ruling country. This is true especially given that, in imperialist contexts, citizens of the ruling country historically had special powers even if they were not FPRs. For instance, civil disputes between citizens of the ruling country and any member of the colonized group were sometimes taken to be causes of armed conflict. What an unwitting IPR says in such contexts therefore has special weight, given that they could ask for military assistance from the imperial center in resolving any dispute with the colonized, although they might have no intention to do so. It would therefore be very risky for the disempowered audience to deny IPR status to the citizen of the ruling country, given the possible costs of failing to do so. And so, at least when the audience is relatively disempowered vis-à-vis the represented, and particularly when the audience is vulnerable to the decisions and actions of the represented, it would be unreasonable to think that the audience assumes the risk of their own reliance on the conscripted IPR.

Now, consider IPRs' pro tanto duties to represented groups. What do IPRs owe to relatively vulnerable or subordinated represented groups by virtue of the IPR's capacity to create expectations in the audience about the represented group? Here, we may extend the aforementioned two principles to accommodate the additional complexities introduced by tripartite relationships.

First, a modified principle of *due care*, adjusted for the tripartite representative relationship: the IPR must exercise due care not to lead the audience to form reasonable but false expectations about what the represented will do or what their interests are when the IPR has good reason to believe that the represented would suffer significant loss as a result of the audience's reliance on these expectations.[38] So modified, the principle makes clear that, in the context of informal political representation, the party who may be at risk of forming reasonable but false expectations (the audience) and the party who could foreseeably suffer a significant loss as a result of those expectations (the represented) may not be and often are not the same. Due care is owed to the party who stands to suffer a significant loss (often, although not always, the represented), and, as discussed, not necessarily to the party who forms reasonable but false expectations (often, although not always, the audience).

Next, a modified principle of *loss prevention*, again adjusted for the tripartite representative relationship: if an IPR has intentionally or negligently led an audience to expect that the represented are going to follow a certain course of action, X, and the IPR has good reason to believe that the represented group will suffer significant loss as a result of the audience's expectation if the represented group does not follow X, then the IPR must take reasonable steps to prevent that loss.[39]

When the represented are vulnerable or subordinate to the audience, although expectations are created in the audience, what significant losses may result will often be faced by the represented, as illustrated by the preliminary discussion of the dangers of informal political representation (see the Introduction). When significant losses are likely to be borne by the represented by virtue of the IPR's statements or actions—common when the represented are vulnerable or subordinate to the audience—IPRs must fulfill special duties of care to the represented, and it is their losses that the IPR must take reasonable steps to prevent.[40]

What might these principles require of an IPR? While "there is no obvious way to specify the exact nature and extent of the 'due care' it is reasonable to require," loss prevention is "slightly more specific"—it requires that the representative take "reasonable steps to prevent that loss," and what counts as reasonable will be a function of "the magnitude of the threatened loss" and "sensitivity to the degree of negligence involved in creating the expectation."[41] So, if for instance an IPR is nonnegligently unaware of their representative status (they are unwitting), then it would be unreasonable to expect them to take steps to prevent loss faced by the represented by virtue of expectations the IPR unwittingly creates in the audience even if the magnitude of the represented's threatened loss is quite high. By contrast, if an IPR knows or should reasonably have known they were creating expectations in a powerful audience (because they knew or should reasonably have known that the audience conferred on them the status of IPR), and the vulnerable represented group faces quite significant losses as a result of the creation of these expectations, then the IPR's pro tanto responsibility to prevent those losses will be more demanding even if the representative is reluctant or unwilling to serve in the role. I return to these considerations in greater detail in the next section.

Differences of Degree and Kind in Informal Political Representatives' Pro Tanto Duties

An IPR's pro tanto duties to the represented vary in both degree and kind depending on a number of features of their role, including (1) how much power they have to influence how the represented are regarded (the *power to influence*), (2) whether they know or ought reasonably to have known that they are an IPR (*wittingness*), (3) how willing they are to be an IPR (*willingness* and *unwillingness*), and (4) how other relationships between the IPR and the represented bear on the nature and scope of the IPR's duties (*other ties*).

First, consider the IPR's *power to influence*. An IPR's power to influence will vary dramatically in amount and kind from case to case, depending on a variety of considerations, including how influential an audience they face and the scope of their representative mandate. Few IPRs have as much power to influence as Washington or King. If your audience is just your neighbors at dinner, the sort of power you have as an IPR may be rather limited; but if your audience is, say, the U.S. Congress, matters are different. Or your audience, however large and influential, may regard the scope of your representative mandate to be limited. For instance, the representative mandate of the religious neighbor (see Chapter 1) was limited in two ways: they were treated as speaking only for fellow congregants at their church and they spoke only on the subject matter of whether prayer should be permitted at town meetings. An IPR with little power to influence has, if any, correspondingly weaker duties to the represented than an IPR who has much power to influence. Because one's IPR duties track one's power to influence, all else equal, the strength of one's duties varies as one's degree of power varies. Because the power to influence is conferred by others, it does not vanish simply because the power holder is reluctant or unwilling. So, even if one is nonvoluntarily an IPR, and even if one is harmed or even wronged by having been made an IPR, one may still have considerable power to influence how the represented are regarded by various audiences and to thereby affect the interests and constrain the choices of the represented. It is that fact—the fact that one has such power to influence—that gives rise to corresponding pro tanto duties to those one represents.

Second, consider the IPR's *wittingness*. Even unwitting IPRs can have duties to the represented, since even they may have the power to influence. However, because unwitting IPRs do not know they are so positioned, they are usually not blameworthy for failing to satisfy their duties to the represented—their lack of knowledge is, in most cases, exculpatory. So, blameworthiness for failure to satisfy one's IPR duties tracks one's wittingness. There is, however, a constructive knowledge caveat: unwitting IPRs may be blameworthy for failure to meet IPR duties in cases in which it would be reasonable to expect them to know that they are IPRs.

Third, consider the IPR's *willingness* or *unwillingness*. Many who emerge as IPRs welcome the role or may even have vied for it. Unlike conscripted IPRs, voluntary IPRs opt to take on what may end up being considerable responsibilities. Further, by publicly signaling their willingness to represent, voluntary IPRs may both make others feel comfortable leaving the representation to them and create expectations in others, including the represented, concerning how they will represent. Accordingly, both whether an IPR is willing and whether they publicly express that willingness affect the degree and kind of duties that IPR has to the represented.

An increase in the degree of willingness an IPR exhibits corresponds to an increase in the accompanying duties' strengths for several reasons:

Constructive Knowledge. A party who publicly announces their willingness or intention to represent a group should reasonably expect that their announcement may well elicit IPR status conferral from an audience. By openly and publicly attempting to create conditions that make audience conferral more likely (see Chapter 1), they accept the possibility that they will be conferred the role. If they are then conferred the role, they have constructive knowledge that the role has been conferred—that is, it is reasonable to expect them to know that it has, even if they do not in fact know.

Expectation. Moreover, a party who publicly expresses their willingness to represent a group may create expectations in audiences, represented groups, or even other potential IPRs that they will in fact aim to carry out the demands of the IPR role if it is conferred. Knowingly raising expectations in another gives us reason to satisfy those expectations. In fact, by publicly expressing their willingness to represent, the party may not merely create expectations in others but may further give others assurance as to whether and how they intend to carry out their representation—thereby giving rise to even stronger duties.

Exhibiting Apparent Authority. Finally, some parties will even hold themselves forth to audiences as authorized by the group they purport to represent although they are not in fact authorized—that is, they exhibit apparent authority. When such a party is conferred IPR status on this basis, they become responsible to disclose this status conferral to the group and to seek retrospective ratification. And even if they do receive informal ratification, they remain open to criticism for antecedently exhibiting apparent authority (see Chapter 3).

What about the reluctant or unwilling IPR? Like a willing IPR, a witting but unwilling IPR knows they have been conferred the status of IPR. Unlike a willing IPR, the witting but unwilling IPR neither intentionally raises expectations nor gives assurance to the represented concerning how they will represent. Still, an unwilling IPR may have either the duty to represent or the duty to actively disavow the role's conferral ("I am speaking for only myself"), provided one of two further conditions is met: (1) the unwilling IPR lacks grounds to reasonably reject the ascription of duties that would normally accrue to a party in their position, or (2) the IPR's rejection of the ascription of these duties would significantly burden the represented. (Note that disavowal of one's IPR role is not adequate for effecting its revocation; the conferring audience must revoke the role. This means that one does not automatically cease to be an IPR simply by uttering "I am speaking for only myself.") I consider grounds for reasonable rejection in the next section.

Fourth, along with power to influence, wittingness, and willingness, the pro tanto duties of an IPR may vary according to *other ties* the IPR may have to the represented group. An IPR's duties to the represented may be constrained, expanded, or otherwise shaped by other ties that bind the IPR to the represented. Consider some such ties and how they can interact with an IPR's duties:

FPR. The IPR for one group may contemporaneously be an FPR for another, as King was an IPR for Black Montgomerians while an FPR for the Montgomery Improvement Association. When both roles required the same action, King's duty to perform that action was overdetermined. If, however, King's two roles mandated conflicting courses of action, he would have needed to weigh these by an independent standard.[42]

Party Whose Work Takes a Particular Group as Its Subject. Often, a party whose work takes a particular group as its subject (an artist, an author, a researcher, or a journalist, for instance) is treated by an audience as speaking or acting for that group and then criticized for failing to satisfy their duties as an IPR. How should we think about parties in these roles?

On the one hand, we may think that, in cases like these, audience conferral intrudes on a particular, protected social role such a party inhabits and, so, that party has grounds to reasonably reject the ascription of duties that would otherwise accrue to them by virtue of their power to influence. James Baldwin gives voice to the rejection of the ascription of the duties of an IPR in his assessment of Richard Wright's conscription:

> As for this New Negro, it was Wright who became his most eloquent spokesman; and his work, from its beginning, is most clearly committed to the social struggle. Leaving aside the considerable question

of what relationship precisely the artist bears to the revolutionary, the reality of man as a social being is not his only reality and that artist is strangled who is forced to deal with human beings solely in social terms; and who has, moreover, as Wright had, the necessity thrust on him of being the representative of some thirteen million people. It is a false responsibility (since writers are not congressmen) and impossible, by its nature, of fulfillment. The unlucky shepherd soon finds that, so far from being able to feed the hungry sheep, he has lost the wherewithal for his own nourishment: having not been allowed— so fearful was his burden, so present his audience!—to recreate his own experience.[43]

But, why, you may ask, should we think that these are protected social roles? Why should the fact that a party opts to produce work that takes a particular group as its subject render them immune to or protected from audience conferral that befalls so many others? Here, it may be helpful to assess such cases using the *audience conferral permissibility test.*

Consider, first, *reasonableness.* The parties described here are often epistemic authorities regarding the groups that are the subjects of their work, and so it seems reasonable for various audiences to believe that these parties have requisite knowledge or experience to represent the groups, at least with regard to matters directly related to the contexts at issue in their work— satisfying the *reasonableness* criterion introduced above.

Consider, next, *permissibility,* evaluated in terms of *self-appointment, group authorization,* and *rebuttable presumption.* Although all three prongs must ultimately be evaluated with reference to the particular features of individual cases, a general question concerning *self-appointment* is worth highlighting: Is the decision to produce work that takes a particular group as its subject a form of self-appointment or, short of that, the implicit expression of willingness to accept the increased likelihood that an audience will treat one as speaking or acting for the group? (I am assuming here that the parties whose work takes particular groups as their subjects were not compelled to develop their projects in this way and, so, could have done otherwise.) While I will not answer this question here, I highlight it to show how my theory of informal political representation gives us tools for understanding with greater nuance and specificity how such complex social roles as artist, author, researcher, and journalist can interact in surprising ways with the role of IPR.[44]

Beneficiary. Some parties who are conferred the status of IPR will accept personal benefits (beyond the power to influence, if that is considered a benefit) that accrue to them by virtue of their status. How should this consideration inform our evaluation of the strength of their duties to the represented? Generally, an IPR who accepts personal benefits that are products of their IPR status will be, other things being equal, less well positioned to reject the ascription of duties that would accrue to them by virtue of their power to influence than other IPRs who do not accept such personal benefits. Imagine that Ambor's "Emerging Black Voices" column lands her a lucrative book deal and public acclaim. In this case, objections Ambor has to being treated as speaking or acting for Black students at the university must be balanced against the consideration that she accepts personal benefits (beyond her power to influence) from being so treated.

Note that some parties whose work takes a particular group as its subject will also benefit from their IPR status, so there will be interaction effects between these two categories.

General Moral Duties. It should go without saying that one cannot come to have duties to a represented group that contravene one's general moral duties. As an example, imagine that a party is conscripted by a media outlet to represent white supremacists, expected to give voice to white supremacists' core ideological commitments. The conscript has—and, indeed, can have—no responsibility to white supremacists to publicly give voice to their core ideological commitments, as no one can be required to act (and in fact we are prohibited from acting) in the service of perpetuating a morally reprehensible ideology.

Grounds for Reasonable Rejection

Above, I argued that IPRs come to have pro tanto duties to the represented just by virtue of having the power to influence how audiences regard the represented. Conscripted IPRs can, like their voluntary counterparts, come to have significant power to influence how various audiences regard the represented. Upon attaining such power to influence, conscripted IPRs, like their voluntary counterparts, come to have pro tanto duties to those they represent—duties that arise despite IPRs' unwittingness or unwillingness. Still, in many cases, conscripted IPRs will have grounds to reasonably reject the ascription of duties that would otherwise accrue to them by virtue of their power to influence. I conclude that a conscripted IPR must

1. aim to fulfill their duties as a representative only when
   (a) they have significant power to influence, and
   (b) either (i) they lack grounds to reasonably reject the ascription of duties that would otherwise accrue to them by virtue of their power to influence or (ii) their grounds to reasonably reject the ascription of the duties are outmatched by the represented group's need for their representation, in particular; and
2. disavow the role only when
   (a) they have significant power to influence, and
   (b) either (i) they lack grounds to reasonably reject the ascription of a duty to disavow that would otherwise accrue to them by virtue of their power to influence or (ii) their grounds to reasonably reject the ascription of a duty to disavow are outmatched by the represented group's need for them to disavow.

A conscripted IPR has grounds to reasonably reject the ascription of duties that would otherwise accrue to them by virtue of their power to influence at least when (1) the audience's motivations for seeking an IPR generally, or reasons for treating this conscripted party in particular as speaking or acting for a given group, are demeaning, degrading, or require the IPR to violate their self-respect, or (2) satisfying the duties would be unduly burdensome for the conscripted IPR. Now, consider in greater detail how these two points each ground a conscripted IPR's reasonable rejection of the ascription of duties that would otherwise accrue to them by virtue of their power to influence.

First, consider *audience motivations* and *audience reasons*. Some audience motivations and some audience reasons can, by themselves, ground a conscripted IPR's reasonable rejection of the ascription of any IPR duties that would otherwise have accrued to them. Forms of audience conferral that degrade or demean the conscript, or require the conscript to violate their self-respect, can ground reasonable rejection of the ascription of any representative duty or even the duty to disavow. In particular, if the audience's motivations or reasons are based on morally objectionable interests (like avoiding direct interactions with the represented group) or views (like the assumption that all members of the group are doxastically or conatively similar), then the conscripted party can reasonably reject the ascription of any representative duty or the duty to disavow simply on that ground. Put differently: A conscripted IPR need not serve in an unjust cause.

Next, consider *burdens on the conscript*. So, too, can a conscripted IPR in many cases reasonably reject the ascription of any representative duty or the duty to disavow on the ground that to have to fulfill these duties would be unduly burdensome. For instance, when members of a society's subordinated group are subjected to iterative IPR status conferral, that cumulative burden can affect their daily interactions in the world and prevent them from living their lives in accordance with their own individual wishes. Recall Laito Zarkpah once more: "I just want to be a student and being a Black student on campus, sometimes you're not afforded that luxury."

That a conscripted IPR has grounds to reasonably reject the ascription of duties that might otherwise accrue to them by virtue of their power to influence does not, however, end the inquiry. As the IPR relationship is tripartite, there is one further party's interests to consider before concluding that a conscripted IPR may reject the ascription of duties that would otherwise accrue to them.

One must also consider *burdens on the represented group*. Although, often, it will be too demeaning, degrading, or demanding for a conscripted IPR to be required to fulfill representative duties or the duty to disavow, the conscript's otherwise reasonable rejection of the ascription of representative duties or the duty to disavow may be outmatched in some (though few) cases by the represented group's urgent and weighty need for that conscript, in particular, to fulfill representative duties or to disavow. In such cases, two conditions (*need* and *uniqueness*) must be met.

Need. Although usually one does not need representation with the urgency one needs, say, rescue, in some cases—during escalating violence or hostage negotiations, for instance—a group may need a representative urgently to stave off injury, danger, death, or another outcome the represented cannot be asked to bear. That a group needs a representative, however, does not by itself explain why any particular party must be that representative. In many cases, the conscript will not be uniquely situated to represent the group. In these cases, the conscripted IPR's duties may begin and end with having to make a reasonable effort to disavow the role and point out others better situated or more willing to represent—although even this may be too demanding or demeaning.

But what if this conscript is the only option?

Uniqueness. If a conscripted IPR is in fact uniquely positioned by virtue of special knowledge, special access, or unusual ability to represent a group that has urgent and weighty need for representation, the conscripted IPR then has very good, if not dispositive, reason to fulfill representative duties when a nonunique conscript would not.

In sum, a conscripted IPR is not responsible to fulfill the duties that would otherwise accrue to them if doing so would be degrading, demeaning, or unduly burdensome, or would require the IPR to violate their self-respect, unless the represented's need for a representative is urgent and weighty and either (1) the conscript is uniquely situated to represent the group (in which case the conscript ought to aim to fulfill their representative duties) or (2) there is someone else better situated or more willing to represent (in which case the conscript ought to disavow). So, in some (though few) cases, conscription can give rise to nonvoluntary obligations, as in many other situations that make moral claims on us simply because we are in a particular place at a particular time. In other contexts, we find it natural to think that even acts that wrong or burden us can confer on us responsibilities to third parties, so we should think it possible that an audience's conscripting conferral, even if wrongful or burdensome, could in some (though few) cases render an IPR responsible to a represented group.

Conclusion

My aim so far has been to introduce an analytical framework for understanding the phenomenon of informal political representation. I first discussed core features of the phenomenon and explained why it is a proper subject of moral inquiry (see the Introduction and Chapter 1). I then, in this chapter, examined two powers and the corresponding duties to which those powers give rise: First, I examined the overlooked power that conferring audiences have to conscript IPRs and discussed the duties that accrue to audiences (that is, all of us) by virtue of that power to conscript. Second, I examined IPRs' power to influence, considered how this power to influence gives rise to corresponding pro tanto duties for IPRs, and discussed when and on what grounds IPRs can disavow the role or otherwise wholly reject the ascription of any duty that would otherwise accrue to them by virtue of their power to influence. Still, we have only begun to understand the moral situation of IPRs, their duties and prerogatives, their relationships and responsibilities. That is the work of the rest of this book. In Chapter 3, on group authorization, I consider what difference it makes to the IPR's moral situation that the represented group's members do in fact want that IPR to represent them.

3

Group Authorization

So far, the following picture of informal political representation has emerged: All that is required for a party to become an informal political representative (IPR) for a group in a context is the conferral of the status by an audience. This means that IPRs can emerge nonvoluntarily and without group authorization. Furthermore, IPRs come to have the power to influence just by virtue of audience conferral. And because audience conferral gives rise to the power to influence, voluntary and conscripted IPRs alike have a variety of pro tanto duties to the represented.

One may worry that this account cuts out the represented group in certain important respects. After all, shouldn't the members of a represented group have some say—even the final say—as to whether a party speaks or acts for them? Or is the complaint "You don't speak for us!"—made across time and context—in fact bloodless?[1]

Recall Malcolm X's distinction between what I am calling, respectively, *audience conferral* and *group authorization*: "Most of the so-called Negroes that you listen to on the race problem usually don't represent any following of Black people. Usually they are Negroes who have been put in that position by the white man himself. And when they speak they're not speaking for Black people, they're saying exactly what they know the white man who put them in that position wants to hear them say."[2] We may think of those "put in that position by the white man himself," who "don't represent any following of Black people," as having received audience conferral but not group authorization. To have group authorization is to have a "following" from among the represented themselves. (Recall that group authorization is distinct from group conferral, the latter of which is a species of audience conferral. I return to this distinction later in this chapter.)

Group authorization has many faces. At times, it is loud and public and spectacular: the pews of Holt Street Baptist Church in Montgomery, Alabama, filled to capacity with thousands of Black Montgomerians; the streets jammed with traffic by those who could not get to the church, everyone ready to boycott.[3] But not always. Group authorization can instead present itself as an absence: empty city buses where usually there were many riders.[4] Nowadays, group authorization can be especially subtle and its currency digital: reposts or upvotes expressing fleeting approbation.

In this chapter, I consider what more is added when the represented group itself authorizes its IPR. Although group authorization is not necessary for an IPR's emergence, group authorization plays a profoundly important role in informal political representation. Whereas audience conferral bestows on a party a de facto IPR status and the concomitant power to influence, group authorization grants them discretion as to the manner of their representative undertakings and, in some cases, bestows on them normative powers with respect to the authorizing group.

In table 3.1, I succinctly show the difference that audience conferral and group authorization, respectively, make to the relationship between IPR, represented group, and audience.

Table 3.1 shows how group authorization and audience conferral each make a unique and distinctive contribution to a given IPR's permissions, powers, and duties. In addition, there are a few further interaction effects between audience conferral and group authorization to keep in view. As was discussed in Chapter 1, a represented group's disavowal of an IPR cannot automatically revoke IPR status conferred by a different audience. Nor can a represented group's authorization of a given party automatically make it the case that a different audience confers de facto IPR status on that authorized party. However, groups and other audiences can, of course, persuade and influence one another. Imagine a nongroup audience initially confers IPR status for a group on a given party but subsequently learns that most of the group's members have not authorized that party to represent the group—in fact, a number of group members vociferously disavow the party. Although the group's members' disavowal cannot revoke the audience's conferral of de facto IPR status, the audience might be persuaded or influenced to revoke its conferral in deference to the group's members' disavowal. The audience is more likely to do so if its members are aware of their duties: one of the three factors an audience member must consider when assessing whether conferral

Table 3.1 Powers, Permissions, and Duties Bestowed through Audience Conferral and Group Authorization

	No Audience Conferral	Audience Conferral
No Group Authorization	A party not conferred de facto IPR status by an audience is not imbued with the de facto power to influence. A party not authorized by a group is not granted that group's permission to speak or act for the group, nor any of the discretionary or normative powers that can be bestowed on a party through such authorization.	Audience conferral imbues a party with the status of de facto IPR and the corresponding power to influence. The IPR's power to influence gives rise to pro tanto duties to the represented group. Without group authorization, the de facto IPR is not granted the group's permission to speak or act for the group, nor any of the discretionary or normative powers that can be bestowed on a party through such authorization.
Group Authorization	Group authorization grants the authorized party the group's permission to speak or act for the group, discretion as to the manner of their representation, and (depending on the specific terms of the group authorization) can further grant the party normative powers with respect to the group—all of which become active in the event that some audience (the group itself or otherwise) confers on that party de facto IPR status. Absent the conferral of de facto IPR status by the group or another audience, however, this authorization can grant the authorized party only dormant permissions, discretion, and normative powers. (Because group authorization and group conferral are distinct, a group may conditionally authorize a party without thereby itself conferring IPR status on that party.)	Audience conferral imbues a party with the status of de facto IPR and the corresponding power to influence. The IPR's power to influence gives rise to pro tanto duties to the represented group. Group authorization grants the authorized party the group's permission to speak or act for the group, discretion as to the manner of their representation, and (depending on the specific terms of the group authorization) can further grant the party normative powers with respect to the group. These permissions, discretion, and normative powers are activated by audience conferral. The IPR's discretion and normative powers each give rise to special further duties and prerogatives with respect to the authorizing represented group.

is permissible in a particular case is whether the group to be represented has itself authorized the party under consideration (see Chapter 2). When some group members disavow a party on whom the audience has conferred IPR status, that disavowal gives the audience reason to revoke its conferral. At the extreme, if the entire group disavows the party, that fact gives the conferring nongroup audience strong if not dispositive reason to revoke its conferral. Likewise, if a nongroup audience learns that a given group has authorized a party to be the group's representative, the group's authorization gives the nongroup audience reason to confer de facto IPR status on the authorized party in deference to the authorizing group.

In this chapter, I examine how group authorization affects the normative relationship between IPR and represented group. When group authorization obtains, what is permitted and required of the IPR, and what may the IPR reasonably expect of the represented? First, I examine similarities between the representative-represented relationship and principal-agent relationships. I consider what makes it the case that, in principal-agent relationships, agents are able to bind their principals to certain arrangements, agreements, or courses of action. What are the normative powers these agents have with respect to their principals, and how do they come to have them? I consider this question in order to understand what would have to obtain between an IPR and a represented group for an IPR to have normative powers with respect to the represented group. Second, I provide a general characterization of the two types of group authorization—*informal authorization* and *informal ratification*—with the help of an illustrative example: the Montgomery Bus Boycott. Third, I argue that, when group authorization obtains, IPRs come to have discretion as to the manner of their representation and, further, can come to have normative powers with respect to the represented group. Fourth, I consider what sort of discretion the IPR has and what normative powers the IPR may have and why these matter to IPRs' relationships to the represented and audiences, respectively. Fifth, I consider a complicating feature that is idealized away in earlier parts of the chapter: the widespread phenomenon of IPR capture.

Principals and Agents

Our target case is an authorized IPR who has normative power to commit the represented group to some course of action or state of affairs—where, for instance, the IPR (an agent or quasi-agent) may enter into an agreement on behalf of the represented (the principal). What would have to be the case for an IPR to be able to make commitments on the represented group's behalf?

In common law, the creation of an agency relationship requires the mutual consent of the prospective agent and the prospective principal.[5] Often, as in the case of a lawyer-client relationship, the agent (the lawyer) has normative power with respect to the principal (the client) by virtue of the principal's prior authorization or subsequent ratification of the agent.[6] So authorized or ratified, the agent may bind the principal to agreements, rendering the principal responsible to act in accordance with those agreements (barring excusing conditions). If the principal fails to meet the terms of the agreement, the agent will not be held accountable for the principal's failure to comply—the principal will.

Yet there are relationships recognized in law "that are less than fully consensual" but that nevertheless "trigger legal consequences equivalent to those of agency." Court-appointed counsel have normative powers vis-à-vis their clients even though the standard of mutual consent fails to be fully met in several ways: (1) counsel represents the client at the behest of the court, (2) counsel may represent the client over the client's objections, and (3) counsel may not withdraw from the relationship without the court's assent. Durable powers of attorney, whereby "the agent's power survives or is triggered by the principal's loss of mental competence," also trigger agency-like legal consequences while failing to be fully consensual. A principal's loss of competence renders the principal unable to end or amend the terms of the relationship they entered into with the agent prior to their loss of competence—the relationship at this point "then resembles a trust."[7]

Principal-agent relationships also vary widely in terms of what agents are authorized to do on behalf of their principals. For instance, some agents have authority to enter into contractual agreements or otherwise bind their principals to relationships with various third parties. Others, while lacking the authority to enter into contractual agreements on their principals' behalf, "nevertheless often have authority to negotiate or to transmit or receive information on their behalf."[8] As we will see, there are resemblances between the varieties of authority imbued in different sorts of legal agents and quasi-agents and the varieties of discretionary and normative powers imbued in different sorts of authorized IPRs.

Formal political representatives (FPRs) are also sometimes agents of their constituencies. They may make agreements on behalf of their constituencies.

But unlike the paradigmatic lawyer-client case, although a majority or plurality of the constituency authorized the FPR by voting for them, not everyone did. Still, our FPRs can bind us to certain agreements or certain outcomes even when we disagree with those agreements or outcomes (and even if we dislike who the FPR is) provided that the process by which they became an FPR is a fair one and one we would endorse upon reflection. That the entire constituency—even those who did not vote for this FPR— can be bound by agreements or outcomes made by the FPR on their behalf means (1) the FPR is not open to criticism for the fact of having made the agreement or rendering the outcome (although they may, of course, be criticizable for the substantive content of the agreement or outcome, or the manner by which it was reached), and (2) members of the constituency may in some cases be open to criticism for failing to comply with the agreement or outcome once it is in place.

When we think this is so, the justificatory grounds are often procedural: FPRs have normative power to commit the represented to certain courses of action or states of affairs at least partly because they have been authorized to do so by way of formal, systematized (that is, organized, reliable, and repeatable) authorization procedures. The constituency is bound because (1) the process by which the FPR came into their position was a fair one, whereby the constituency's members had an opportunity to have their say at the outset (*authorization*); (2) the constituency had standing to raise substantive complaints to their FPR in advance of the agreement (*deliberation*); (3) complaints to which the constituency may quite reasonably expect to receive their FPR's response (*deliberation*); and (4) the constituency will at some future point have an opportunity to hold their FPR accountable for the FPR's decisions by means of a different procedure, like a subsequent election (*accountability*).

Whatever else we think is required to ensure that the process by which the FPR came into their position is a fair one, we generally think that it must at least be the case that everyone who is a member of the constituency gets a say.[9]

Now consider informal political representation. For an IPR to have discretionary or normative powers with respect to the represented, there must be some mechanism by virtue of which the represented themselves could be said to have authorized the IPR. But the formal, systematically organized procedures that normatively ground other agency and agency-like relationships are, by and large, unavailable in IPR contexts. And audience conferral alone certainly cannot provide the normative foundation for an IPR to have discretionary or normative powers vis-à-vis a represented group. After all, the members of the represented group have in many cases had no say at all. Yet, as we shall see, group authorization is possible—not merely possible, it has happened before.

Group authorization comes in two varieties: *informal authorization* and *informal ratification*. Informal authorization and informal ratification can take as their objects either particular representative statements or actions or the representative themself. Group authorization obtains when a represented group grants upfront informal authorization or retrospective informal ratification to either a representative or their particular representative statements or actions.[10]

The group-authorized IPR has not merely the power to influence of a de facto IPR but (1) comes to have discretion as to the manner of their representation and, (2) can come to have normative powers with respect to the represented, the details of which depend on the particular terms of the informal authorization or ratification. They may be granted, for instance, the power to transmit or receive information between the represented and audiences; to negotiate on the represented's behalf; or even (though rarely) to make agreements on behalf of or otherwise commit the represented to particular courses of action, outcomes, or states of affairs. Such cases are rare but they do happen, as the Montgomery Bus Boycott illustrates.

Informal Authorization and Informal Ratification

An authorization procedure of any kind may put the power to authorize representatives in the hands of either the represented themselves or a proxy who selects the representative on the represented's behalf. Only when authorized by the represented group's members themselves can an IPR be granted discretion as to the manner of their representation or normative powers with respect to the represented group. Authorization by proxy— by, for instance, an existing group leader, a central governing body, or another sort of intermediary—will not do. The members of the informally represented group, just like the members of formally represented groups, have fundamental interests in having a say in who can serve as their agent or quasi-agent.

Informal authorization takes place prospectively. As in the contexts considered above, there are a variety of different ways that informal authorization may be effected. Consider three candidate models for informal authorization: group vote, tacit informal authorization, and provisional authorization. These models both illustrate how informal authorization might look and expose some of the difficulties faced by attempts to effect informal authorization in societies like ours.

Group Vote. Were it possible, a group vote would be an ideal way to authorize a de facto IPR for a variety of reasons, many of them similar to the reasons that voting is a promising way to authorize an FPR. First, the procedural fairness of a group vote can promote relations of equality between group members, thereby ameliorating otherwise unequal relationships between group members (as when some group members are marginalized by other group members). Second, group votes can promote egalitarian relationships between group members and their IPR, as group members are given an opportunity to say whether, how, and by whom they would like to be represented.

Countless difficulties, however, stand in the way of group votes for IPRs. First, as discussed, many informally represented groups have memberships that defy precision (see Chapter 1). The question who gets to vote, which turns on the question who is a group member, will therefore be difficult to answer. Second, even for groups whose memberships are well defined and about whose composition there is little disagreement, many will lack the means to effectively orchestrate a group vote. Third, even setting aside concerns about the feasibility of a group vote, there remains a conceptual question concerning whether a representative relationship that can support a group vote is in fact informal: if the group vote is systematized (that is, organized, reliable, and repeatable), the representative relationship within which this group vote is effected will be authorizationally formal, although it may still be informal in other respects.[11]

Tacit Informal Authorization. What about tacit authorization? On a tacit authorization model, an IPR is presumptively authorized until the represented group's members express their disapproval of the IPR. For an IPR to be disauthorized by a represented group, the target of the represented group's disapproval must be the IPR themself, rather than particular statements or actions the IPR makes or takes. A represented group may, of course, also raise legitimate complaints concerning particular statements or actions made or taken by the IPR, but these do not by themselves serve to disauthorize an IPR, although they are, of course, important for defining the contours of the representative-represented relationship in other respects (see Chapter 5).

For tacit informal authorization to be effective, the group must be aware of the IPR and have the ability to register disapproval of them. These conditions make tacit informal authorization an especially difficult model to effect. For many groups that are represented informally, group members commonly face conditions (like oppression, marginalization, or dispersion) that make it foreseeable that the group's members will in fact be unaware of their IPR or unable to effectively express disapproval. For such groups, the absence of any expression of disapproval of a given IPR may therefore not in fact be evidence of tacit authorization but may instead simply be evidence that the group's members are unaware that there is a party representing them or unable to express disapproval of that party.[12]

Provisional Authorization. A third possible route to informal authorization is provisional authorization. Suppose again a de facto IPR, conferred the status by an audience but not yet authorized by the group. Suppose further that the represented group's members know that they have this de facto IPR and have the capacity to register disapproval, but have not done so. This IPR has *provisional authorization.* Provisionally authorized IPRs are imbued with a limited set of discretionary and normative powers, able to be exercised under carefully circumscribed conditions in which they must consult with the represented group iteratively to receive instructions, as a delegate might.[13] The provisional IPR does not yet have the group's trust or wholehearted support. So, before they go out and speak or act on the group's behalf (for instance, calling a press conference or issuing a public statement), they must make reasonable efforts to consult known and accessible group members to make explicit both their plan and its justification.

From their position of provisional authorization, the IPR's powers and prerogatives may grow or diminish. If, for instance, the represented group's members express sustained disapproval of the IPR, not simply complaint against certain of their representative statements or actions, then provisional authorization is revoked. The IPR loses what limited discretionary and normative powers they had provisionally gained. If instead the represented group iteratively expresses approval of the IPR (call this *informal ratification*), this is evidence that the IPR has been granted more discretion in deciding how to represent the group. They become less delegate and more trustee.[14] As time goes by, the group's sustained and evident trust in the IPR can eventually lead the IPR to have full-fledged authorization, with all the powers and prerogatives appropriate to the role. Of course, the provisionally authorized IPR may remain in an indefinite provisional limbo.

Contrast the provisionally authorized IPR with the fully authorized IPR, who has consistently been speaking or acting for the represented group for a prolonged period, has group authorization, and has not received much disapproval of prior representative statements or actions. The fully authorized IPR need not be so explicit or even communicative with the represented, as the represented already know (or it is reasonable to expect that they know) what the IPR is doing and, based on past practice, why. Aberrations are, of course, possible. For instance, if the seasoned, fully authorized IPR unilaterally changes course in a manner that contravenes the represented group's members' settled ideological or other commitments— imagine that Rev. Dr. Martin Luther King Jr. came later in his career to disavow his commitment to nonviolent direct action, although those he represented had not—then the fully authorized IPR becomes provisionally authorized once more, and must reestablish their relationship with those they represent. Fully authorized IPRs become provisionally authorized if they unilaterally change course and begin to represent the group in a manner that contravenes the group's settled commitments, not if (1) the IPR's ideological or other commitments change along with the group's members' commitments or (2) the IPR successfully convinces the group's members to revise their commitments.

One might object that provisional authorization just reduplicates problems faced by a group vote. How could a group with a vague membership and limited ability to coordinate express approval or disapproval of its IPR reliably and iteratively? Although this is a reasonable concern, provisional authorization does not simply collapse into group vote. Whereas a group vote confers authorization at a time based on a particular instance of widespread approval, provisional authorization is built of iterative processes of approval and disapproval. Moreover, provisional authorization protects the group against IPRs who seek the group's authorization even before any approval or disapproval mechanism has been exercised by severely limiting the ab initio powers of the IPR.

Tacit Provisional Authorization. A fourth route to informal authorization combines the second and third models. As in the third model, the IPR is conferred fully authorized representative status, remains provisionally authorized, or is disauthorized entirely. As in the second model, the authorization is tacit—to be discerned from the absence of expressed disapproval. So, for instance, if the IPR, provisionally authorized at the outset, represents the group over a long enough period of time without being the target of protest or disavowal, they would then become fully authorized.

Informal authorization also resembles more familiar formal models of authorization in another respect—namely, insofar as there can be variation with respect to the scope of the authority granted by the authorizing party. The scope of an IPR's authorization to represent a given group may be delimited in a number of different ways, including the following:

1. *The subject matter of the representation.* An IPR may be authorized to represent the group on some topics but not others. For instance, the IPR may have the group's authorization to represent its members' views concerning a city's segregationist bus policies, but not on other forms of segregation faced by the group's members.
2. *The forum of the representation.* An IPR may be authorized to represent the group in some contexts but not others. For instance, an IPR may be authorized to speak on the group's behalf directly to local political officials, but not authorized to speak with the public or the press even if on the same underlying subject matter.
3. *The actions the IPR is authorized to take.* Like the agents of principals in other contexts, an IPR may be authorized to do some things for the represented but not others. For instance, an IPR may be authorized to express the represented group's members' expressly stated demands concerning the bus policy revisions under consideration, but not to commit the group to an agreement with local political officials concerning which revisions to implement.

Now consider what informal authorization looks like in practice. On Friday, December 2, 1955, Rev. Ralph Abernathy, Rev. Dr. Martin Luther King Jr., and E. D. Nixon decided amongst themselves that Black Montgomerian bus riders should undertake a boycott. Yet they acknowledged

this decision could not be made unilaterally—they needed community support. They called a "meeting of all the ministers and civic leaders."[15] Between forty and seventy community leaders "from every segment of Negro
life . . . physicians, schoolteachers, lawyers, businessmen, postal workers,
union leaders, and clergymen" attended. The meeting was conflictual, and
attendance dwindled to twenty or so, at which point, "despite the lack of
coherence in the meeting, . . . [i]t seemed to be the unanimous sense of the
group that the boycott should take place."[16] Agreeing to the boycott was
an authorizing act—not by the whole community but by those present at
the end of the meeting.

Abernathy and King then "mimeographed leaflets concerning . . . the
proposed boycott" and at least two hundred volunteers distributed them
door-to-door on Saturday morning—now include these volunteers among
informal authorizers.[17] Also on Saturday, further informal authorization
came: "one of the [taxi] committee members informed [King] that every
Negro taxi company in Montgomery had agreed to support the protest on
Monday morning."[18]

Still, boycott organizers did not know until Monday morning, the first
morning of the boycott, whether they had received widespread informal
authorization from the community.[19] By surveying buses, organizers came
to learn that they had. As King recalled his drive through the streets of
Montgomery,

> I jumped in my car and for almost an hour I cruised down every major
> street and examined every passing bus. . . . Instead of the 60 percent
> cooperation we had hoped for, it was becoming apparent that we had
> reached almost 100 percent. . . .
>
> All day long it continued. At the afternoon peak the buses were still
> as empty of Negro passengers as they had been in the morning. Stu-
> dents of Alabama State College, who usually kept the South Jackson
> bus crowded, were cheerfully walking or thumbing rides. Jobholders
> had either found other means of transportation or made their way on
> foot. While some rode in cabs or private cars, others used less conven-
> tional means. Men were seen riding mules to work, and more than one
> horse-drawn buggy drove the streets of Montgomery that day. During
> the rush hours the sidewalks were crowded with laborers and domestic

workers, many of them well past middle age, trudging patiently to their jobs and home again, sometimes as much as twelve miles.[20]

Call this *en masse consultation.*

Informal authorization occurred again at the meeting at Holt Street Baptist Church that evening, where "three to four thousand people who could not get into the church" stood outside "throughout the evening, listening . . . on the loudspeakers" and there was a five-block traffic jam leading to the church. Recognizing this informal authorization, King reflected, "By now my doubts concerning the continued success of our venture were dispelled. The question of calling off the protest was now academic. The enthusiasm of these thousands of people swept everything along like an onrushing tidal wave."[21] The community's participation was their authorizing act.

The Montgomery Bus Boycott is a case of informal authorization if anything is. Not all cases look like this, nor need they for informal authorization to occur. The Montgomery case far outstrips what could ever reasonably be required—near unanimity is a far higher authorizational standard than is ever required in either formal or informal contexts. An IPR might have a smaller following, informal authorization from only some parts of the represented group (the taxi companies, say). Broad consensus may sometimes only be discerned from the en masse responses of group members: the buses empty, the church pews full.

Informal ratification takes place retrospectively.[22] It may serve as the lone basis for group authorization or instead serve in a supplemental role to informal authorization. When it serves as the lone basis for group authorization, informal ratification looks like this: A party holds forth to an audience as having the authority to make commitments on a group's behalf (that is, they exhibit apparent authority)—call this party *the self-appointer.*[23] An audience, treating the self-appointer as having this authority, makes a commitment with the self-appointer that both audience and self-appointer treat as having been made on behalf of the represented group. At some later point, the group on behalf of which this commitment was purportedly made ratifies the commitment, the self-appointer, or both.

Informal ratification is built on the questionable background assumption that an IPR could permissibly hold forth as the duly authorized agent of the represented group absent an authorizational moment having occurred beforehand—an action that, if knowingly and successfully undertaken, deceives the audience and disregards the group's claim to be consulted. And even if the represented group subsequently ratifies the exhibition of apparent authority performed by the self-appointer (thereby granting the IPR provisional or full-fledged authorization), the IPR wrongs the represented in the first instance by misleadingly holding forth as a duly appointed agent of the represented group before that was the case.

If instead it is the audience's error—their presumption—that imbues the IPR's actions with apparent authority and the represented group ratifies on this basis, then informal ratification occurs without any underlying wrongdoing on the part of the IPR. I return to cases like this in the discussion of IPR capture later in this chapter.

Tacit ratification—an IPR speaking or acting for a group without subsequent group dissent—is possible but unlikely, particularly when the represented group is oppressed or marginalized. The absence of dissent may indicate not tacit ratification but instead the silencing effects of oppression or marginalization.

Now consider what informal ratification looks like in practice. The widespread and public support exhibited throughout Montgomery on Monday, December 5, 1955, not only authorized King's representative activities going forward but, perhaps, also ratified decisions that Abernathy, King, and Nixon made privately on December 2, like the decisions to call a community leaders' meeting and to distribute leaflets announcing the boycott. In fact, prior to these December 2 decisions, there was opposition to boycotting.[24] So, Abernathy, King, and Nixon's December 2 decision to propose a boycott given known opposition exhibited apparent authority (for which they were contemporaneously criticizable) perhaps retrospectively ratified by the evident widespread support shown on December 5. That these December 2 actions were subsequently ratified (if they were) does not mean they were not criticizable at the time they were undertaken.

Effects of Group Authorization: Discretionary and Normative Powers

Authorized IPRs have more discretion regarding the manner and scope of their representations than they otherwise would have had were they mere de facto IPRs. What this discretion allows for depends on the particulars of the group authorization—for instance, how the informal authorization or informal ratification was carried out and what, if any, were its express terms. IPRs with expanded discretion (1) will not be criticizable for representative actions that fall within the purview of this discretion, even if those actions would otherwise have been criticizable in the absence of group authorization; and, accordingly, (2) will have grounds to dismiss complaints regarding these actions that they would otherwise have had reason to heed, because group authorization permitted the otherwise criticizable behavior.

Additionally, group authorization is required for an IPR to have normative powers with respect to the represented, although only some types of group authorization can imbue IPRs with normative powers. Group authorization may, for instance, allow IPRs to negotiate, commit, or concede on the represented group's behalf.

Consider, first, *negotiation* and *commitment.* Imagine that an IPR is negotiating on the represented group's behalf with a counterpart (audience). The counterpart offers, "If you call off the boycott, we will allocate ten seats at the back of the bus to members of your group." Imagine, too, that the IPR accepts this offer and gives the counterpart assurance that, when this allocation is made, the group will end the boycott.

Had the IPR no group authorization, then an apt interpretation of this scenario would be that the de facto IPR was either merely predicting what the represented group's members were likely to do or was exhibiting apparent authority.

But what if the IPR instead had group authorization of the sort King had in Montgomery on December 5? Some forms of group authorization give the authorized IPR normative power to make promise-like assurances on the represented group's behalf—although less than promises, they are not mere predictions about what the group's members are likely to do. The authorized IPR may noncriticizably raise expectations in an audience that the represented group's members will go along with an agreement reached by the IPR and the audience. So, in the bus seat allocation example:

1. The authorized IPR's accepting the offer is not merely a prediction that the group's members are likely to end the boycott but an assurance that they will.
2. Moreover, once the agreement is set, the authorized IPR will not be open to criticism by the represented group for having entered into

this agreement on the group's behalf. This is not to suggest that the represented cannot criticize the IPR at all. The represented may still, of course, raise legitimate complaints about the content of the agreement or other attendant concerns (see Chapter 5). But these complaints are different in kind from the group's objecting to the fact that an IPR they authorized to make agreements on their behalf has made an agreement on their behalf.

3. Finally, group members who fail to cease boycotting after the bus seat allocation has been made may be open to criticism by the authorized IPR and fellow group members for their noncompliance.

Consider again the Montgomery Bus Boycott. On Thursday, December 8, 1955, King and other members of the Montgomery Improvement Association (MIA) met with the mayor of Montgomery and representatives from the bus company.[25] King presented a trio of requests on behalf of Black Montgomerians: "(1) a guarantee of courteous treatment; (2) passengers to be seated on a first-come, first-served basis, the Negroes seating from the back; and (3) employment of Negro bus operators on predominantly Negro routes," in exchange for which the bus boycott would be brought to an end.[26] For King and his fellow MIA members to be able to make this deal, however, King had to be viewed by the audience (Mayor W. A. Gayle, the bus company's representatives, and their respective associates) as having the support of the Black community of Montgomery. And, of course, they had ample evidence for this support, as the buses had, by the time of this meeting, been empty or nearly empty for the past three days.

But one does not have the normative power to commit another to an agreement simply by virtue of being viewed to have the ability to make a deal; the perception that one is able to make a deal on a group's behalf is compatible with that party's having mere apparent authority. To be able to make a bona fide agreement with Mayor Gayle and the Montgomery Bus Lines representatives, King and his colleagues needed to in fact have the normative power to commit the Black community of Montgomery to a subsequent course of action—one on which the city and the bus company could rely lest King come to be viewed as having no real backing from the Black community of Montgomery. A negotiating IPR needs to be able to credibly say, "The people I am representing will go along with the agreement I make"; otherwise, the IPR's negotiation counterparts (the audience) are unlikely to continue to negotiate with them. The IPR's negotiation counterparts must be able to rely on the IPR's attestations in order to be able to decide what to do.

In Chapter 2, I concluded that an IPR for a subordinated group has neither a duty of due care nor a duty of loss prevention to an empowered audience, since the empowered audience assumes the risk of relying on the IPR, except when the IPR intentionally holds themself forth as an IPR. But the IPR in this example—King—did just that. To make it all the way to the negotiating table, or even as far as organizing a boycott, an IPR will have had to accept the role of IPR (*willingness*), and so should quite reasonably expect that the audience (1) will form certain expectations on the basis of what the IPR says concerning what the represented group's members are likely to do, and (2) will want to be able to rely on the IPR's attestations when deciding how to proceed. When King negotiated with Mayor Gayle and the bus company representatives, he voluntarily and intentionally led Gayle and the bus company representatives to believe that, if they accepted the proposed offer, then Black Montgomerians were going to stop boycotting.

People "want to be given assurances, and they care about whether these assurances are genuine. One reason for caring is that they may rely on these assurances in deciding what to do."[27] This is as true for tripartite cases as it is for bipartite cases; tripartite cases are simply more complicated. In tripartite cases, negotiating counterparts have reason to want assurances that are genuine, assurances on which they can rely in deciding what to do, and IPRs have reason to want to be able to give assurances that are genuine on behalf of those who have granted them informal authorization or informal ratification. But, unlike the bipartite cases—where one party, *A*, can with confidence voluntarily and intentionally lead another party, *B*, to expect that *A* will do *X*, because *A* typically knows their own mind—the tripartite cases of informal political representation are trickier. Can IPRs really give assurances that are more than mere predictions about the represented's behavior or wishes about what the represented will do?

The IPR's ability to give negotiating counterparts assurances that are genuine depends on another party: the represented. And the IPR can only know the represented group's members' minds when members indicate that they intend to go along with agreements reached on their behalf—at least those agreements the represented group's members know in advance that the IPR intends to reach.[28] We may call such advanced indications from the

represented group's members *informal authorization*. When a group authorizes its IPR to make particular agreements with a negotiating counterpart on its behalf, that authorization gives the IPR reason to expect
that the represented group will follow through on those agreements, if they
are reached.

Accordingly, in many cases, IPRs ought only raise expectations in negotiating counterparts concerning what the represented will do when they
have received clear indication that the represented group will go along with
what the IPR agrees to on the group's behalf.[29] Hence, perhaps, King's ea-
gerness to know whether the buses were empty and his "jubilan[ce]" at
finding out that they were.[30]

When King proposed that the boycott would end when an agreeable bus-
loading arrangement was reached, he was not merely predicting that the
Black community of Montgomery would ride buses again if an agreement
was reached. Rather, he was committing Black Montgomerians to end the
boycott if an agreement was reached. Of course, his proposal depended on
a prediction: for King to be able to commit in good faith, he had to believe
that the Black community would in fact end the boycott if an agreement
was reached. And, provided that King's bus-loading and boycott-ending
proposal had group authorization, King would not have been open to criticism for having proposed the plan to his negotiation counterparts. Furthermore, had an agreement been reached between King and his interlocutors,
and had the bus-seating arrangement been implemented, then, absent special justification, the Black Montgomerian community would have been
responsible to cease boycotting unless negotiating partners (the city and the
bus company) consented to their not ending it. (I will say more in the
coming paragraphs about the strategic and democratic limits of this responsibility—it is not and could not be absolute.) Finally, absent special justification, had the represented group not ended the boycott although an agreement had been reached, its members would have been open to criticism by
King, who gave assurance on their behalf.

Moreover, if represented group members knowingly authorized the IPR
but now do not want the IPR to make a particular commitment, C, on
their behalf, then, to cancel any expectation in the IPR that they would go
along with C, the group's members ought to complain against the IPR's
committing to C. That is, if the IPR has received group authorization that
could reasonably be interpreted to permit the IPR to commit to C on the

group's behalf, then the represented group's members (knowing their subsequent silence might reasonably be understood to be tacit consent to the IPR's actions) have an affirmative duty to let the IPR know if the IPR ought not make the commitment. Otherwise, the represented are complicit in the IPR's expectation setting.

So, some robust yet rare forms of group authorization imbue an authorized IPR with the normative power to speak and act for the represented group as their agent (call this subset of authorized IPRs *informal political agents*), where this means that the IPR can commit the represented to an action, outcome, or state of affairs such that (1) the IPR is not merely predicting what the group members are likely to do, (2) the IPR will not be open to criticism for having so committed the group's members, and (3) represented group members may be open to criticism by the IPR or fellow group members if they fail to follow through. Regarding the second point: the represented can raise legitimate complaints about the content of the commitment or about the procedure by which the representative was authorized to make the commitment, but not about the fact of being so committed.

The represented's responsibilities to go along with the negotiations concluded by an IPR they have authorized in this manner cannot, however, be absolute. There are three reasons why this is so—two concern strategic considerations (call them *threat of defection* and *threat of rejection*) and the third concerns fundamental and inalienable democratic values (call these *rights to dissent*).

Threat of Defection. Often, mainstream democratic social movements get some of their power from the fact that there exist some factions that are more radical and so are unlikely to go along with the agreement negotiated by the IPRs of the mainstream movement. In the case at hand, the Black Power movement strengthened King's negotiating position by providing his negotiating counterparts (the Montgomery city commissioners and the bus company representatives) further reasons to negotiate with him: if city commissioners and the bus company did not yield to King's demands, they might face a defection of members of his movement to more radical movements. Yet, for this threat of defection to be credible, there must be some room for more radical dissenters to defect from the agreement that King negotiated. Accordingly, he only needed to deliver enough people willing to comply with the negotiated agreement that the bus companies would be back in business. There was no blanket obligation on every boycotter to suspend the boycott. Instead of a blanket duty to go along with the negotiation, King only needed enough boycotters to go along with the agreement to make the negotiation worthwhile to his negotiation counterparts.

Threat of Rejection. In labor union negotiations, the bargaining power of union representatives is typically strengthened by the need to take a negotiated contract back to the represented for ratification. The credible threat that the contract may be rejected by the represented is critical to getting a better deal. Similarly, the bargaining power of IPRs is strengthened by the credible threat that the represented may not go along with a negotiated agreement reached by the IPR and negotiating counterparts. So, even if the represented have authorized an IPR, this does not mean the represented thereby come to have a blanket responsibility to go along with anything for which the authorized IPR negotiates; such a blanket rule would undermine rather than strengthen the represented's negotiating position.

Rights to Dissent. Even absent the two strategic considerations just discussed, rights to dissent and contests between representatives of a social movement need to be preserved under any circumstance. So, represented group members' responsibilities to go along with their authorized IPR must leave open room for some practical rejection of deals made by the authorized IPR on behalf of the group.

Consider, next, *concession.* The power to concede is the capacity to alter a group's negotiating position simply by putting forth a proposal on the group's behalf—it is, in effect, the capacity to give something away. IPRs can have two different types of power to concede—one de facto and the other normative.

Insofar as a de facto IPR is able to make it the case that an audience believes that a represented group will accept less than they previously asked for, that IPR has a de facto power to concede (a particular type of power to influence). The IPR may have this power by virtue of appearing to the audience to have received group authorization, or they may have this power simply because the audience does not care to negotiate with the group more directly and decides by fiat to treat the IPR as the group's negotiator. The de facto power to concede does not give the represented group's members a normative reason to go along with the IPR's concession. It may, however, give them an instrumental reason to do so in some cases. I consider contexts in which this instrumental reason may arise in this chapter's final section, on the phenomenon of IPR capture.

Group authorization may sometimes give an IPR the normative power to concede on the represented group's behalf. The power to concede differs from the power to make binding agreements in that, whereas one can only reach agreement with another, one can (as a descriptive matter) make concessions unilaterally. When one offers a concession to one's negotiating counterpart, often one does so in order to remove a barrier to reaching an agreement with that counterpart. Concessions are risky because they show that one is willing to accept less than one asked for previously. The IPR's normative power to concede allows the IPR to say that the group will accept less than it had formerly asked for, where the IPR's so saying gives the represented group's members a normative reason to not reraise a request for options that have been conceded. This is another instantiation of the IPR's normative power to commit the represented group to certain courses of action, outcomes, or states of affairs. The strategic and democratic limitations discussed just above apply here, too. The normative reason that the represented have to not reraise a request for already conceded options can be outweighed by strategic considerations or the general right to dissent.

Return to the case of Booker T. Washington's "Atlanta Compromise." In this speech, Washington claimed to be "convey[ing] . . . the sentiment of the masses of [his] race" when he (1) publicly encouraged Black southerners to "cast down your bucket where you are," advising that "it is at the bottom of life we must begin, and not at the top"; (2) cautioned that "the agitation of questions of social equality is the extremest folly"; and (3) made the following pledge: "I pledge that in your effort to work out the great and intricate problem which God has laid at the doors of the South, you shall have at all times the patient, sympathetic help of my race."[31]

Washington's pledge was certainly concessive in a de facto sense, since (1) audience conferral obtained and (2) Washington was attempting to change the represented's negotiating position by asking for less:

1. *Audience conferral.* At this point in his career, Washington had been conferred de facto IPR status by, among others, white southerners, white northern philanthropists, as well as many Black Americans.[32] His many audiences treated him as speaking for Black Americans

through all four conferral actions—*ascription, credibility conferral, testimonial reliance,* and *invitation* (see Chapter 1). Accordingly, Washington enjoyed the power to influence generated by audience conferral.

2. *Asking for less.* In offering this series of public concessions, Washington attempted to change Black Americans' collective negotiating position by undermining requests that Black Americans may otherwise have made—for instance, the request that Black Americans' civil and political rights be acknowledged and protected.[33]

And the concessions were accepted by white conferring audiences, who did not hesitate to treat them as made on behalf of Black Americans quite generally: "The prevailing public opinion of the land has been but too willing to deliver the solution of a wearisome problem into his hands, and say, 'If that is all you and your race ask, take it.'"[34]

The speech may also have been concessive in a normative sense: If members of the represented group had authorized Washington to speak or act on their collective behalf at the Cotton States and International Exposition (and some had), then the fact that Washington made these concessions gave these authorizing group members a defeasible normative reason to go along with the concessions.[35] A side constraint is worth making explicit here, however: group members had reasons to go along with Washington's concessions only if the proposed concessions were permissible—this is so even if they had granted Washington blanket group authorization. If it was impermissible simpliciter for Washington to make the concessions he made in his "Atlanta Compromise" speech (because, for instance, one cannot promise to accept an outcome that would undermine one's civil and political rights), then Washington could not make these concessions on behalf of others either. And so, even if Washington had been authorized by many or even most Black southerners, they would not have had normative reasons to go along with the concessions Washington offered on their behalf, because they were not concessions that Washington (or anyone) had the normative power to make in the first place. More generally, even if an IPR has been imbued with the normative power to unilaterally commit the represented group's members to a particular agreement or state of affairs, the IPR has not been conferred a power to do things no one may do on anyone's behalf—their own or others'.

The substantive questions (1) whether Washington's "Atlanta Compromise" concessions were permissible under the circumstances, and (2) whether those Washington represented had reasons to go along with these concessions are complicated by a variety of considerations, and I will not attempt to dispositively resolve these questions here. I will, however, briefly explore three considerations that bear on resolving these two questions.

First, given the widespread resistance to ensuring or even in some cases acknowledging Black Americans' civil and political rights at the time of Washington's speech, the strategic defense of the concessions Washington offered in the "Atlanta Compromise" is that the civil and political empowerment of Black Americans had to advance in stages. The underlying strategy was that, as Black Americans gained economic power through the compromise, that economic power would give them leverage at some later date to contend for voting rights and other political powers.[36]

Second, under conditions of oppression or marginalization, IPRs for oppressed or marginalized groups, and the oppressed or marginalized groups themselves, may have reasons to publicly accept certain unjust compromises strategically while secretly rejecting them as purported final or principled settlements and working secretly to undermine them. Consider, as an example, Washington himself: even as he publicly disavowed attempts by Black Americans to struggle for the recognition and protection of their civil and political rights, he secretly funded voting rights cases like *Giles v. Harris,* which made it to the U.S. Supreme Court.[37] IPRs for oppressed or marginalized groups may be strategically bound by compromises to limit their public acts to what they have agreed to, but they are not so bound to limit their private acts.

Third, IPRs cannot bind authorizing groups indefinitely into the future—this prohibition is an inherent feature of democratic systems, whether formal or informal. Unjust compromises struck by an IPR for an oppressed group as a mere modus vivendi are subject to revision when circumstances change.

Informal Political Representative Capture: Group Conferral without Group Authorization

Having now considered group authorization, return to the distinction between *group conferral* and *group authorization* discussed in Chapter 1.

Attention to this distinction helps us understand a complicating feature of many representative relationships—*IPR capture*—and the instrumental reasons it can give a represented group to engage in group conferral but not group authorization.

Recall that although group conferral and group authorization may occur simultaneously, they are distinct phenomena. Group conferral picks out a subtype of audience conferral in which the group to be represented itself comprises the conferring audience. Group authorization picks out two procedures (informal authorization; informal ratification), through each of which a group may imbue a party with discretionary and normative powers with respect to the represented group—procedures and powers that are the subject matters of this chapter. Each phenomenon may occur without the other: A group can confer the status of de facto IPR on a party without thereby authorizing that party, as we saw in the Washington example (see Chapter 1). Conversely, a group may conditionally authorize a party without thereby conferring IPR status: The group authorizes the party such that, in the event that some audience confers the status of IPR, that party has already been imbued by the group with dormant discretionary and normative powers—powers that become active only if an audience confers IPR status. Notwithstanding this conceptual distinction, group conferral and group authorization may of course occur simultaneously.

As Malcolm X has pointed out, many IPRs are handpicked to fill the position by a dominant group or oppressor class but do not have group authorization from those for whom they are treated as speaking or acting.[38] The IPR is appointed by a powerful audience whose interests are not aligned (and may instead be at odds) with the interests of the group for whom the IPR is treated as speaking or acting. Critics quite reasonably worry that the audience's conferral was motivated by the audience's interests—perhaps an interest in selecting an IPR who is uncritical of the conferring audience's advantage ("saying exactly what they know the white man who put them in that position wants to hear them say") or simply an interest in precluding others more critical from entering the role.[39] Such IPRs are thought to (and in some cases do) champion the values, interests, or preferences of their conferring audiences, even when these do not align with the values, interests, or preferences of the dominated or oppressed groups they come to represent.

This, of course, describes Washington's ascendancy to the role of IPR for Black Americans: "Part of the reason [President Theodore Roosevelt] desired to work with Washington was because of Washington's policy of accommodation and because he did not clamor forcefully for advancing blacks politically or civically." Treated by two presidents "as the leading black figure and spokesman in the United States," Washington had considerable power to influence their thinking on race relations between Black and white Americans, not to mention their understanding of Black Americans' values, interests, and preferences.[40] Yet despite Black Americans' criticism of Washington's ascendancy as their IPR, they indeed conferred on him the status of de facto IPR: "Naturally the Negroes resented, at first bitterly, signs of compromise which surrendered their civil and political rights, even though this was to be exchanged for larger chances of economic development. The rich and dominating North, however, was not only weary of the race problem, but was investing largely in Southern enterprises, and welcomed any method of peaceful cooperation. Thus, by national opinion, the Negroes began to recognize Mr. Washington's leadership; and the voice of criticism was hushed."[41]

Contemporary examples are also available. For instance, Malala Yousafzai, an IPR for Pakistani schoolchildren, has faced similar criticisms. "Malala backlash," as it has been called, picks out a variety of complaints raised by Yousafzai's critics—that "her education campaign echoes Western agendas," that she is "more loyal to the West," that she is "peddling a western narrative."[42] She has been called "an 'American agent,' a 'traitor.'"[43] According to activist Fouzia Saeed, while teenage Yousafzai "represented the progressive side of Pakistani society, . . . everything changed when the West lapped her up individually and not as a representative of [Pakistan]. The hatred for the West transcended into hatred for Malala."[44] Even seventh grader Taiba Ikhlas cast aspersions at Yousafzai, saying, "Malala is working against Islam and Pakistan, and she has no right to come to Pakistan when she is only working against us."[45]

Sometimes, an IPR is handpicked, or captured, by a dominant or oppressor audience and treated as speaking or acting for a given group. The handpicked party may not have sought out the position (that is, they may have been conscripted), and the represented group's members may not have wanted that person (or anyone) to be their IPR. And yet, even if the represented group previously had little or no independent reason to confer de facto IPR status on this captured party, the very fact that the person has been handpicked by a powerful audience (and, so, has access to that audience) gives the represented group's members an instrumental reason to confer de facto IPR status. Even so, the group may have no reason whatsoever to—and in fact very good reason *not* to—authorize the party.

The complication of IPR capture also reinforces the importance of articulating IPR duties and clarifying to whom those duties are owed. When a dominant or oppressor audience confers de facto IPR status on a party, this conferral does not come packaged with duties to that audience to serve its interests. This is not to say that the captured IPR has no responsibilities whatsoever to the dominant or oppressor conferring audience. Even a captured IPR will no doubt have some general moral duties to such audiences. They will, however, owe neither due care nor loss prevention to an empowered audience who conscripts them. When empowered audiences conscript a given party to speak or act for a relatively disempowered group, the audience assumes the risk of their conferral (see Chapter 2). The captured IPR's role-based responsibilities are directed in such cases only to the members of the vulnerable represented group.

Conclusion

Group authorization imbues authorized IPRs with discretion as to the manner of their representation and can imbue them with normative powers to—among other things—transmit or receive information, negotiate, commit, or concede on behalf of those they represent. Few IPRs are informally authorized or ratified; even fewer are thereby imbued with these normative powers. Yet when group authorization generates discretionary powers for an IPR, the IPR comes to have new freedoms to represent in accordance with their considered judgment of what the represented need from them; and when group authorization generates normative powers for an IPR, the represented in some cases come to have reasons to act in accordance with assurances the IPR gives on their behalf.

PART TWO

4

The Duties of Informal
Political Representatives

We return now to the central ethical challenge of this book: Informal political representation can be dangerous. Skeptics quite reasonably caution that informal political representatives (IPRs) can imperil the represented by being, inter alia, unauthorized, unaccountable, inaccurate, elitist, homogenizing, overpowering, concessive, overcommitting, occlusive, inegalitarian, and oppressive.[1] Such dangers lead many to the conclusion that informal political representation is morally irremediable. Yet there are concrete concerns at stake in defending informal political representation from skepticism. Informal political representation is not merely an ineradicable feature of political life; it is a valuable form of political communication that provides distinctive and salient political goods to many, particularly marginalized and oppressed groups. IPRs increase the visibility of otherwise overlooked groups, give voice to interests not adequately expressed in formal political institutions, influence public discourse, galvanize group consciousness, and serve as conduits between the represented and lawmakers (see the Introduction). The practice serves as a powerful tool by which groups may develop political voice and exert political influence. In fact, many groups, particularly oppressed and marginalized groups, rely quite considerably on informal political representation to help them exert political influence on the circumstances that shape their members' lives and opportunities. Some groups need informal political representation to have any political voice at all. Yet oppressed and marginalized groups' reliance on and need for informal political representation only redoubles its dangers to these groups in particular. Corralled by no legally enforceable authorization or accountability mechanisms, IPRs may represent vulnerable groups with impunity.[2]

The tension between informal political representation's peril and promise generates a desideratum for a moral theory of informal political representation: the theory must be able to tell us how the practice of informal political representation should be constrained so as to make it morally permissible for people to serve as IPRs for those who most need them—oppressed and marginalized groups. Given the dangers that ground skeptics' concerns, on what conditions is the informal political representation of oppressed and marginalized groups morally permissible?

To answer this question, we need first to identify and distinguish the dangers of informal political representation that ground skeptics' concerns. Accordingly, I begin with the voices of informal political representation's most ardent skeptics, who do and ought to set the terms of debate.

I respond to these skeptical challenges by discussing some of the moral considerations to which IPRs of oppressed or marginalized groups must respond if they are to represent permissibly. Specifically, I argue that, to represent permissibly, IPRs for oppressed or marginalized groups must satisfy two sets of duties—*democracy within* duties and *justice without* duties.

Democracy within duties emerge from the distinctive context of informal political representation of oppressed or marginalized groups, where the represented's considerable vulnerability meets the IPRs' often unconstrained and sometimes completely unchecked power. These duties cannot simply be read off the duties that formal political representatives (FPRs) have to constituents, because institutional procedural protections are available in formal contexts that are, by definition, absent here. *Democracy within* duties require IPRs to structure their deliberative relationships with the represented in certain ways so as to correct for inequality inherent in those relationships. I detail the deliberative social practices IPRs must work to develop with the represented—*consultation, transparency, welcoming criticism,* and *tolerating dissent*—and consider difficulties IPRs face doing so in real-world contexts. Rarely will IPRs of oppressed or marginalized groups have group authorization. When they do, however, the threat of relational inequality between IPR and group diminishes and, so, the corrective protection of *democracy within* duties is not needed to the same extent. Group-authorized IPRs of oppressed or marginalized groups therefore have more discretion to decide how to satisfy their *democracy within* duties than they otherwise would have had. I discuss the concrete details of this discretion later in this chapter.

Justice without duties provide substantive guidance concerning how, when, where, and before which audiences IPRs should speak or act on represented parties' behalf. *Justice without* duties require IPRs to use their power to influence to undermine the oppression or marginalization the represented face.

IPRs' duties to oppressed or marginalized represented groups are neither surprising nor particularly distinctive. This is a virtue of my account: against skeptics who contend that informal political representation is morally unsalvageable, my account shows that we have the moral resources to respond to their challenges.

I then discuss the additional roles that *democracy within* and *justice without* duties may play in shaping relationships between IPRs, represented groups, and third parties. I also consider how informal political representation can improve political life more generally—in particular, how the political goods it offers the represented (political influence, political agency, community recognition, trust, and democratic equality) can contribute to making a society more just.

Finally, I discuss hard choices faced by IPRs caught in the crosshairs of conflicting duties. Sometimes *democracy within* and *justice without* duties seem to prescribe conflicting courses of action. Apparent conflicts between these seem to lead to hard cases and painful tradeoffs, and return us to a perennial question at the heart of political philosophy: Should we seek justice by *any* means necessary? I conclude that *democracy within* duties are never canceled, even when forgoing them would be instrumentally useful in bringing about valuable outcomes for the represented. Fortunately, because *democracy within* duties admit of ample flexibility as to the manner of their satisfaction, seeming tensions between *democracy within* and *justice without* are in most cases merely apparent.

Skeptical Challenges to Informal Political Representation

In this section, I make clear the ills of informal political representation by schematizing skeptical challenges and considering how these challenges apply to IPRs of oppressed or marginalized groups in particular. Clarifying and distinguishing these challenges helps us understand with systematicity and precision what exactly is (and is not) wrong with such representation. Once we understand the challenges, we can consider how IPRs for oppressed or marginalized groups must comport themselves so as to meet them.

I canvas four families of challenges—*procedural, epistemic, power,* and *relational imbalance.* This typology is not exhaustive but accounts for the most significant challenges. A further family of challenges, concerning the question whether representatives must be group members or otherwise descriptively similar to the represented group, is reserved for Chapter 6. The challenges canvassed here have application beyond contexts of oppression or marginalization: Procedural, epistemic, and power challenges apply to political representatives generally. Relational challenges arise for informal political representation in particular, although they also sometimes apply to FPRs in backsliding or defective democracies. Even so, these general challenges tend to be most severe and therefore most worrisome in contexts of oppression or marginalization, particularly because they are compound.

These skeptical challenges must be answered by any normative theory of informal political representation as a condition of its adequacy and completeness.

Procedural challenges concern a defining feature of informal political representation: IPRs emerge in the absence of formal selection, monitoring, and sanctioning mechanisms. We begin here because, first, these are the most obvious challenges to informal political representation and, second, they help explain why other skeptical challenges raise distinctive worries about IPRs, even when those challenges also apply to FPRs.

First, there is the concern that IPRs who receive no or only very weak group authorization are fully or mostly *unauthorized.* Recall Malcolm X: "Most of the so-called Negroes that you listen to on the race problem usually don't represent any following of Black people. Usually they are Negroes who have been put in that position by the white man himself."[3] He does not deny that the "so-called Negroes" to whom he refers are IPRs. Indeed, he acknowledges that these speakers have received audience conferral from "the white man himself." That is, he claims, part of the problem: They are IPRs who came into their positions in the wrong way—without group authorization.

Second, there is the complementary concern that IPRs are *unaccountable*: Absent formal procedural mechanisms, IPRs may with relative impunity make substantial decisions about how to represent.[4]

Some conclude from these procedural challenges that informal political representation cannot be made good because, absent reliable authorization or accountability mechanisms, political representation is illegitimate.[5]

Epistemic challenges target the ways representatives mischaracterize the represented. They apply to both FPRs and IPRs. Consider three.

First, representatives are sometimes *inaccurate*, mischaracterizing the represented's interests or circumstances. The editors of *Freedom's Journal,* the first Black newspaper in the United States, objected, "Men whom we equally love and admire have not hesitated to represent us disadvantageously, without becoming personally acquainted with the true state of things."[6] Of course, anyone can mischaracterize anyone else. To be a fitting criticism of a representative, the fact that the criticized party is a representative must at least partly explain why the mischaracterization was imputed to the represented.

Second, representatives are sometimes *elitist*. Representatives are often in more privileged social positions than those they represent.[7] So positioned, they sometimes fail to notice and consequently fail to give voice to the interests of constituents whose lives are not like theirs. Instead, "the interests of the constituents are presumed identical" to those of the representatives.[8] Recall (from the Introduction) the criticism that the Southern Christian Leadership Conference, whose leaders often informally represented Black southerners generally, was "concerned . . . about access to the ballot box and . . . public accommodations" while ignoring "destitute sharecroppers . . . people who could barely afford the fare to ride on public transportation."[9]

Third, representatives are sometimes *homogenizing*. As George Cook notes, "Rev. Sharpton does not speak for all African Americans and he doesn't speak for anyone I know on many issues."[10] Even when representatives may accurately express some group members' interests, they may fail to capture the whole, leading audiences to erroneously believe that the group is doxastically or conatively homogeneous.[11]

Such challenges are not unique to informal political representation of oppressed or marginalized groups, nor even to political representation as such—indeed, such challenges are apt for many types of joint activity and joint negotiation. Yet they take on particular salience in the informal political representation of oppressed or marginalized groups.

Power challenges target the effects of a representative's position on how others receive their statements or actions. Because representatives often have significant power to influence how audiences regard the represented, representatives can *overpower* those they represent. From their positions of greater power, representatives may make controversial claims, concessions, or attempted commitments on behalf of the represented, as Booker T. Washington did as "the one recognized spokesman of his ten million fellows."[12] W. E. B. Du Bois later generalized his concern about Washington to a concern about the informal political representation of oppressed or marginalized groups as such, calling the practice "an impossible assumption of power" and adding, "This is not democracy, it is tyranny and even granted a large measure of right in the tyrants' dicta, the situation is intolerable and full of danger."[13]

Representatives may be overpowering in a variety of specific ways. First, representatives can be *concessive*. Sometimes, representatives' statements or actions have what negotiation scholars call "anchoring effects" on audiences, making it difficult for the represented to subsequently take positions more demanding than or significantly different from those previously articulated by their representative.[14] Du Bois criticized Washington for his concessive anchoring: "the prevailing public opinion of the land has been but too willing to deliver the solution of a wearisome problem into his hands, and say, 'If that is all you and your race ask, take it.'"[15] Per Du Bois, white southerners' ready willingness to meet Washington's demands indicates that Washington ought to have asked for more but instead limited his informal constituents' options going forward.

Second, representatives can be *overcommitting*, holding forth as though able to make commitments that bind the represented although not so authorized. Consider this example, *Backdoor Deal*: In a closed-door meeting during the Montgomery Bus Boycott, Rev. Dr. Martin Luther King Jr. presented a list of requests on behalf of boycotters.[16] King gave both the city and the Montgomery Bus Lines representatives reason to believe boycotters would abide the terms of any agreement reached. Whether King had requisite authority or was criticizable as overcommitting depends, I have argued, on whether he had received group authorization from boycotters (see Chapter 3).

Third, representatives are sometimes *occlusive*—instead of bringing attention to the represented, they bring attention to only themselves.[17]

Consider, finally, *relational imbalance challenges*. Procedural, power, and epistemic challenges compound in particularly worrisome ways when the represented are marginalized or oppressed, creating objectionable relational imbalances between IPRs and their oppressed or marginalized constituencies.

First, three of the aforementioned features of IPRs' relationships to oppressed or marginalized groups may jointly render these relationships impermissibly *inegalitarian*:

1. IPRs have outsized power to influence how the represented are regarded by audiences (*overpowering*).
2. IPRs can use this power unfettered by fear of reprisal (*unaccountable*) or threat of removal (*unauthorized*)—when they are not authorized in the first place, they have little cause for concern about being disauthorized.
3. Without FPRs and excluded from the broader society, oppressed and marginalized groups often rely considerably on their IPRs (*reliance*).

These features, taken together, may leave the represented at the mercy of their IPR.

The different dimensions along which representation can be more or less formal (see Chapter 1) affect how inegalitarian or oppressive challenges take shape. When a represented group's membership is poorly defined and widely dispersed, for example, relational imbalance challenges may emphasize the group's inability to effectively authorize an IPR. By contrast, for a badly marginalized group that has no political voice independent of its IPR, the fact that the group cannot effectively register public dissent against an *occlusive* IPR may be especially salient.

Relational imbalances can arise between representatives and groups neither marginalized nor oppressed. Yet relational imbalances are particularly worrisome when the represented are oppressed or marginalized, because there is an especially close nexus between the represented group's oppression or marginalization and their need for (and consequent reliance on) an IPR.

In these cases, the IPR fills a particular corrective role for groups whose oppression or marginalization manifests, partly, as exclusion from FPR lawmaking bodies. By contrast, when the represented are neither marginalized nor oppressed, their informal political representation does not need to be corrective for exclusion from FPR lawmaking bodies. The relational imbalances that manifest between IPRs and groups neither marginalized nor oppressed are less worrisome, at least partly because there is no background assumption that the IPRs are meant to play a corrective role for these represented groups.

At this point, you may object that there is no special problem here. There is always cause for concern whenever any person is at the mercy of another. An IPR is just one of many upon whom oppressed and marginalized people must rely with little redress. They also find themselves at the mercy of, among others, their FPRs (should they have any), their landlords, their bosses, and the state. Why think this relationship requires special moral analysis? There are several reasons. As discussed, IPRs are often uniquely situated to use their powerful social position to correct for marginalization or oppression that leaves these groups at the mercy of so many others. It is one thing for your oppressors to be your oppressors; it is quite another for your purported defenders and advocates to be your oppressors too. Moreover, the oppressed and marginalized are at the mercy of IPRs in some distinctive ways: The representative's role consists partly in saying what the represented want. The representative is thereby imbued with power to attribute interests to the represented whether or not the description of those interests is accurate (*epistemic challenge*). Additionally, when the represented are oppressed or marginalized, it is difficult for them to reject, protest, or correct mistaken impressions (*overpowering, unaccountable challenges*), particularly if their representative is not inclined to announce complaints on their behalf: "Washington strove publicly and secretly to take over control of newspapers to advance his message and suppress dissent."[18]

Second, when powerful and unconstrained, IPRs of oppressed or marginalized groups can themselves *oppress* those they represent by (1) treating group members carelessly—by being, for instance, *inaccurate, elitist,* or *homogenizing;* or (2) taking attention for themselves rather than for the represented—that is, by being *occlusive.*[19]

Relational challenges capture the specific convergence of procedural, epistemic, and power challenges in contexts of informal political representation (and formal political representation in backsliding or defective democracies).

Table 4.1 summarizes these challenges.

Table 4.1   Skeptical Challenges to Informal Political Representation of Oppressed
or Marginalized Groups

Challenge Type	Subtypes	Applicability
Procedural: Targets the absence of procedural protections.	*Unauthorized:* Representatives who do not receive group authorization do not have authority to speak or act for the represented.	Representatives generally
	Unaccountable: Representatives cannot easily or reliably be held accountable.	
Epistemic: Targets mischaracterizations.	*Inaccurate:* Representative errs by misstating represented group's members' interests or circumstances.	Representatives generally
	Elitist: Privileged representatives fail to give voice to the varied experiences of less privileged represented group members.	
	Homogenizing: Representative leads audience to believe that represented group is doxastically or conatively homogeneous.	
Power: Targets effects of representative's position on reception of their statements or actions. (*Overpowering*)	*Concessive:* Representatives' statements or actions anchor audiences' beliefs about represented's interests and preferences.	Representatives generally
	Overcommitting: Representative exhibits apparent authority.	
	Occlusive: Representatives bring attention to themselves but not to represented.	
	↓	
Relational imbalance: Targets relational imbalances in representative relationships.	*Inegalitarian:* (1) the IPR's power to influence (*overpowering*), (2) the IPR's lack of accountability or authorization (*unaccountable; unauthorized*), and (3) the represented's *reliance* on the IPR jointly leave the represented at the mercy of their IPR.	IPRs and, sometimes, FPRs in backsliding or defective democracies.
	Oppressive: IPRs may compound represented's oppression through (1) careless treatment (*unaccountable; unauthorized; inaccurate; elitist; homogenizing*), or (2) receiving attention for themselves rather than the represented (*occlusive*).	

There's the rub: IPRs of oppressed or marginalized groups can be unauthorized, unaccountable, inaccurate, elitist, homogenizing, overpowering, concessive, overcommitting, occlusive, inegalitarian, and oppressive. Unsurprisingly, many of the challenges raised here apply more generally. Normative differences between IPRs of oppressed and marginalized groups and IPRs in general, and normative differences between IPRs and FPRs, are not so sharp, especially given that FPRs rarely if ever operate in perfect democracies or under ideal conditions. (Recall, too, that sometimes a party serves as both an FPR and an IPR, sometimes at the same time, and sometimes for groups whose memberships overlap.) These are weighty challenges, and they raise serious concerns about the permissibility of the practice of informal political representation, particularly when the represented are oppressed or marginalized. So, we ask again: On what conditions might such representation be morally permissible?

Noncontribution and Eradication

When morally evaluating political representatives of any sort, two considerations are paramount: whether representatives treat the represented as they ought (*relational considerations*) and whether representatives' actions advance the aims of the representation (*purposive considerations*). Representatives have duties to the represented that correspond to each type of consideration.

Relational duties guide representatives in their immediate treatment of the represented. Purposive duties guide representatives to use their positions to advance the specific substantive aims of the representation—for example, advocating for voting rights or protesting unjust detention conditions.[20] The respective grounds of relational and purposive duties and, consequently, their content differ depending on the specific type of political representation at issue. IPRs of oppressed or marginalized groups have *democracy within* duties (relational) and *justice without* duties (purposive)—characterized briefly in this section and in greater detail below.

How do *democracy within* and *justice without* duties get their substantive content? They are specifications of two general principles applicable to all of us:

Noncontribution: One should not treat others in a manner that would contribute to their oppression or marginalization.

Eradication: One should work to undermine others' oppression or marginalization.

Noncontribution is a relational principle: it constrains the sorts of relationships we may have with others. Eradication is a purposive principle: it orients the aims of the actions we take. These are quite general principles. Each of us is bound to act in accordance with these principles in general, in everyday life. IPRs are no different from the rest of us in this respect. Unlike the rest of us, however, IPRs often fill special roles in the lives of those they represent, particularly when those they represent are oppressed or marginalized: As we have seen, an IPR's statements and actions may raise expectations in audiences about how the represented will act and what they will accept (see Chapters 2 and 3). Their statements and actions may be imputed to the represented without the IPR's knowing or intending that result (see Chapter 2). And, often, the oppressed or marginalized represented group will be unable to oust their IPR (see Chapter 1). By attending to special features of this relationship, we can imbue these general principles with substantive content that helps us say what, exactly, IPRs owe oppressed or marginalized represented groups. I conclude that IPRs owe these groups fulfillment of *democracy within* duties and *justice without* duties—duty sets that specify noncontribution and eradication, respectively, within the contexts at issue here.

Democracy within duties are inward-facing, procedural requirements aimed at establishing relational equality between IPRs and oppressed or marginalized represented groups. As has been discussed above, scant procedural protections, outsized power, and represented groups' reliance on their IPRs often create conditions in which IPRs can oppress or marginalize those they represent. To temper these conditions, IPRs should promote an egalitarian relationship between themselves and the represented by promoting certain basic rights and interpersonal commitments within those relationships. As in all interpersonal relationships, the IPR should regard and treat the represented as their equals and refrain from dominating them.[21] To achieve these aims, IPRs should build deliberative social practices like consultation, transparency, welcoming criticism, and toleration of dissent into their relationships with the represented. By doing so, IPRs work to avoid becoming additional oppressors or marginalizers of those they represent. *Democracy within* duties satisfy noncontribution by undermining the inequality inherent in the immediate representative-represented relationship.

Justice without duties are outward-facing, substantive guidelines concerning how, when, where, and before whom IPRs should speak or act on represented parties' behalf. By virtue of their platforms, IPRs are often especially well situated to work toward eradicating represented groups' oppression or marginalization. IPRs should use their platforms for these ends, combatting injustices faced by the represented. *Justice without* duties satisfy eradication by furthering the represented's appeals to a broader public or the state.

Democracy within and *justice without* duties are crucial to understanding the role of IPRs of oppressed or marginalized groups but do not exhaust these IPRs' duties, nor are these duty sets the exclusive province of IPRs for these groups. First, IPRs generally have many further responsibilities to the represented by virtue of specific features of their relationships (see Chapter 2) and the terms of any group authorization they receive (see Chapter 3). Second, all IPRs have noncontribution and eradication responsibilities. Yet because there is not inequality inherent in the relationships between IPRs and nonoppressed, nonmarginalized groups, satisfying noncontribution and eradication will often not require the corrective actions required of IPRs of oppressed or marginalized groups. When IPRs become potential oppressors or marginalizers of those they represent, they have the responsibility to ameliorate this threat through corrective measures delineated later in this chapter. Third, IPRs for nonoppressed, nonmarginalized groups will sometimes have to perform the very actions that are corrective in contexts of oppression and marginalization (namely, *consultation, transparency, welcoming criticism, tolerating dissent*); however, because they are not representing oppressed or marginalized groups, what grounds their responsibilities to do so will differ. Fourth, in addition to their special roles, IPRs of oppressed or marginalized groups are also just people in the world—accordingly, in addition to their *democracy within* and *justice without* duties, they have the general moral duties all of us have as well as other, more specific duties that arise out of their other particular social roles, attachments, and commitments.

Democracy within and *justice without* duties answer the skeptical challenges. To show how, I now consider what would be an adequate response to each skeptical challenge, then use these responses as the parameters for building the positive account of *democracy within* and *justice without* duties that follows.

Responses to Skeptical Challenges

To understand why IPRs of oppressed or marginalized groups must satisfy *democracy within* and *justice without* duties, we first need to understand what would be morally wrong with such representation were they not to.

Some of the skeptical challenges (*inegalitarian* and *oppressive*) arise from the convergence of others. These challenges have a nested structure such that responding to *inegalitarian* or *oppressive* requires responding to the underlying challenges that give rise to them. Accordingly, we will start with these two challenges and work our way in.

Oppressive. IPRs are often especially well situated to oppress the represented, violating *noncontribution.*[22] There is no one action IPRs can take to avoid this result, as its causes vary. Instead, to avoid oppressing the represented, IPRs should attend to the features of their relationships to the represented that may contribute to this oppression and take counteracting steps, discussed in the subsequent sections of this chapter.

Inegalitarian. When a relationship type admits of impermissible inequality, that relationship type should be either proscribed or constrained to eliminate the inequality. If proscription is impossible or undesirable, corrective measures must be taken to reduce or, ideally, eliminate the inequality. Since IPRs are valuable to oppressed and marginalized groups, the aim is to constrain the relationship to eliminate inequality as far as possible rather than to quash these representative relationships altogether. That these measures are corrective means the party positioned as superior (the representative) cannot simply refrain from engaging in behaviors that would otherwise introduce inequalities into the relationship but must take active steps to undermine existing inequalities in their relationship with the party positioned as inferior (the represented).

As discussed, inequality between IPRs and oppressed or marginalized represented groups emerges from the convergence of three features of their relationships:

1. scant procedural protections (*unaccountable, unauthorized*),
2. power imbalances (*overpowering: concessive, overcommitting, occlusive*), and
3. the represented's *reliance* on a given representative.

To correct for the resultant relational inequality, IPRs must combat one or more of these features. To subvert item 1 or 2 on the above list, IPRs must make themselves answerable to the represented's complaints in ways to be described. Although it may be difficult for a given IPR to subvert item 3, in the next section I consider a potential remedy for *reliance.*

Procedural Challenges. *Unaccountable* and *unauthorized* target the scant procedural protections in IPR relationships. Although it would be unreasonable to expect informal political representation to offer all or even most of the institutional protections available in formal contexts, IPRs can protect the represented by engaging in deliberative social practices with the represented so that they can regularly collect feedback from the represented. These practices can temper the effects of the procedural lacuna.

Power Challenges. *Overpowering* and its specific manifestations (*concessive, overcommitting, occlusive*) target the fact that representatives' statements and actions often have outsized power to influence how things go for the represented. One would not want to curtail a representative's power to influence entirely, as doing so would undermine the representative's very purpose: to speak or act effectively for the represented in fora in which the represented cannot easily do so for themselves. But unconstrained power imperils the represented. So, it falls to IPRs to distribute this power by subjecting their actions to the represented's (1) advisement through *consultation,* and (2) scrutiny through *being transparent, welcoming criticism,* and *tolerating dissent.*

Epistemic Challenges. The prediction made by this account is that epistemic concerns will be mitigated when IPRs consult, represent transparently, welcome criticism, and tolerate dissent, since these practices will increase the amount and types of input representatives receive from the represented.

The aforementioned challenges, summarized in table 4.2, set the parameters within which the ensuing normative account must be constructed.

Democracy Within Duties

Democracy within duties guide IPRs in developing dialogical, deliberative social practices that can bolster egalitarian relations between the representative and the represented, thereby undermining the perils that rightly concern skeptics. Treating another as an equal requires, at least, showing that

Table 4.2 Responding to Skeptical Challenges to Informal Political Representation of
Oppressed or Marginalized Groups

Challenges	Subtypes	Corrective Measure
Relational Imbalance	Oppressive Inegalitarian	IPRs must undermine the other features of the relationship that jointly give rise to these challenges: *Procedural; Power.*
Procedural	Unaccountable Unauthorized	IPRs must establish, promote, and maintain deliberative social practices with the represented.
Power (*Overpowering*)	Concessive Overcommitting Occlusive	Through deliberative social practices, IPRs should distribute their power to influence by subjecting their activities to the represented's (1) advisement through consultation, and (2) scrutiny through being transparent, welcoming criticism, and tolerating dissent.
Epistemic	Inaccurate Elitist Homogenizing	Consultation, transparency, welcoming criticism, and tolerating dissent mitigate epistemic concerns by improving the inputs IPRs receive from the represented.

other party recognition respect, and it prohibits, at least, dominating that other party.[23] To show the represented recognition respect, the IPR should *consult* and *be transparent* with the represented. To avoid dominating the represented, the IPR must render themself vulnerable to the represented's complaints by at least *welcoming criticism* and *tolerating dissent.* These four deliberative social practices make up the *democracy within* duties. The practices further alleviate *epistemic challenges* by helping IPRs learn the represented's values, interests, and preferences—information essential for IPRs to represent accurately. Through the exercise of these practices, the IPR can also win the trust of the represented.

One cannot treat another as an equal without exhibiting recognition respect to them. To respect someone is to "judg[e] that the fact that he or she is a person places moral constraints on [your] behavior."[24] If our relationship is such that your behavior is aimed at affecting what I get, but you neither know nor ask what I want, you have not exhibited recognition respect toward me. Accordingly, represented group members are entitled that their IPR learns the group's members' values, interests, and preferences and treats these as either guidance or demands from the group about how to represent them. Whether the IPR ought to regard these as guidance or demands depends on several features of the representative-represented relationship, including (1) whether the group has authorized the IPR, (2) how much the group trusts their IPR (which might be gleaned from whether the IPR is group authorized), and (3) the substantive content of the group's expressed values, interests, and preferences themselves—for instance, whether group members have general values they would like the IPR to help satisfy but about whose manner of satisfaction they are openminded or whether they have particular interests that could be satisfied only in one or a few ways.

IPRs exhibit recognition respect toward, build trust with, and learn about the represented through *consulting* and *being transparent* with the represented.

First, consider *consultation.* Each of us has an interest in mattering to others. Part of what it is for you to exhibit respect to me is to both regard and treat me as though I matter to you. So, if you are my IPR and you tell me that you aim to represent me so as to improve my position in a broader society, but you never ask me what such improvement would look like to me or what I might need in order to feel myself an equal in the society, I am unlikely to believe you have my interests in mind. Part of regarding and treating me with respect is to care how things are for me—to regard both my personhood and preferences as restricting how you may represent me. This does not mean that you will do everything I say you ought to do, but that you will consider what I would like (my subjective interests) or what I might need (my objective interests) when deciding what to do for me and in my stead.[25] By consulting the represented, the IPR receives valuable information from the represented about their values, interests, and preferences and (thereby) exhibits recognition respect toward and builds trust with the represented. So, the IPR should consult the represented. What this looks like in practice will depend on a variety of different features of the relationship between a given IPR and the group they represent. The consultative requirement allows for ample flexibility in the time, place, frequency, and manner of its satisfaction.

Regular consultation ex ante (that is, before representation occurs) is especially valuable in nascent representative-represented relationships, when the IPR may not know the represented well. Ex ante consultation allows the IPR to receive information concerning what the represented need and want, shows the represented that the IPR values the represented group's members' visions of what their representation is for (an expression of recognition respect), and thereby helps promote trust between representative and represented. Because representative relationships depend deeply on trust, it is vital that representatives take steps that build relationships of trust with those they represent.[26]

The need for an IPR to consult ex ante diminishes as the IPR comes to know more and more about the heterogeneity and subtleties of group members' values, interests, and preferences. As mutual understanding between IPR and represented grows, the represented group's trust increases. Trust in one's representatives properly substitutes to a certain degree for direct participation by the represented.[27] The represented properly demand more participation and consultation when they do not trust their representatives but properly give them more leeway when, for good reasons, they trust their representatives. IPRs who already know that they have the trust and support of those they represent—perhaps because they have received group authorization—need to consult ex ante less or, in some cases, not at all.

What form of ex ante consultation will be most valuable will depend on particular features of the representative-represented relationship, the represented group itself, and whether the IPR is also a leader for the group. For groups whose members have a clear, coherent, unified, and easily articulable sense of what they need and want independently of and prior to the development of their relationship to a representative, consultation ex ante can be valuable in giving an IPR specific information as to how precisely the group wants to be represented. For groups whose interests are uncrystallized, ex ante consultation can allow an IPR to serve as an informational conduit or go-between within the group, representing different group members to one another, sharing between them one another's perspectives.[28]

There is, however, a wrinkle when the IPR is also the group's leader; this is not always the case, but the roles are sometimes simultaneously inhabited by one party. The political science literature on public opinion and democratic leadership suggests that, regarding specific policies, many people follow their leaders' views rather than having firm independent opinions about the policy that they want their leaders to follow.[29] People want their leaders to offer an inspiring vision of a path forward, with policies that will articulate and fulfill their less clearly defined but firmly held values and aspirations such as *justice* or *equality.* We should expect, then, that some represented groups with uncrystallized interests will want their leader-representatives to serve not merely as mouthpieces for already worked-out policies or initiatives that the group has independently developed but to set policy agendas rooted in the more general values the represented group's members share. This expectation gives IPRs who are also group leaders some leeway in filling out the details of the represented group's vision of what justice or equality, for example, requires. This does not necessarily mean these IPRs ought to consult ex ante less than they otherwise would. It does however suggest that, when the IPR is also a group leader and the represented group's interests are uncrystallized, it may be more valuable to elicit information concerning the represented's general values and aims than specific policy preferences. Furthermore, when there is sufficient warranted trust, the represented may find it irritating and unnecessary to be consulted constantly on specific points of policy and strategy after the represented group has entrusted their IPR with the complementary roles of leader and policy agenda setter.

Generally speaking, the less sure an IPR is as to whether and how much of the represented's support and trust they have, the more often they need to consult—both generally and, in particular, ex ante.

Consultation sometimes best takes place after a representative has already taken an action or made a statement that affects the represented. In many cases, consultation ex post will be more important to the representative relationship than consultation ex ante will be. No matter how much consultation ex ante is possible or desirable, IPRs will always need to make decisions in the moment using their own judgments about how to represent the group. They must try things out, experiment. This experimentation is, in fact, one of the great strengths of democracy.[30] But because the outcomes of decisions can never be guaranteed, all decisions made without consulting the represented are inherently risky. IPRs therefore need democratic mechanisms to help them collect and respond to feedback from those they represent. The more room opened in the representative-represented relationship for ex post revision and repair in responding to ex post feedback, the more leeway IPRs have to move boldly to secure goods for the represented that might otherwise slip away if the opportunity were not promptly grasped. If the IPR's chosen course of action fails, the IPR may lose the represented's trust or support and further lose group authorization (if they had it to begin with). That is a risk inherent in undertaking the role of IPR or any representative role. In every case, the IPR is obligated to consult ex post about the results of their decisions.

How can the IPR effectively consult the represented when they are hard to access, find, or identify? Several features of the IPR relationship to oppressed or marginalized groups seem to confound the consultative requirement, including group vagueness, group size, geographical dispersion, limited access, and communicative inability. These complications demand even more flexibility in how the consultation of represented groups takes place. Here I consider what consultation might look like given these further complications.

Group vagueness. Although FPRs tend to represent well-defined groups (citizens in their districts or dues payors in their associations), IPRs often represent groups whose memberships are not well defined and for which there are no established procedures for determining membership. IPRs therefore face difficulty knowing who to consult. Satisfying *consultation* does not, for instance, always require consulting a majority, since the IPR perhaps could not find out the group's size or exactly how preferences are distributed within the group. For example, since rape is underreported, IPRs for rape victims cannot know if, in consulting n rape victims, they have consulted a majority.[31] The consultative requirement should be evaluated by a best efforts standard: Has the IPR done their best to consult known and available group members, immediately or mediately, to understand their interests or receive their feedback?

Group size. Even when a group's membership is known and geographically proximate, IPRs cannot be expected to individually consult every member. Consider the Montgomery Bus Boycott. Over forty thousand Black people rode the Montgomery city buses.[32] It would have been unreasonable to expect boycott organizers to consult each rider individually. Instead, when planning, organizers consulted FPRs and IPRs from Black Montgomerian subcommunities as proxy for consulting all riders.[33] Call this *proxy consultation.* Proxy consultation can produce intermediate IPRs who communicate between individual group members and IPRs of the larger group. (One risks, of course, running into problems of cumulative error and other epistemic hazards when getting information mediately in this way, as anyone who has ever played a game of Telephone can attest.) Typically, an IPR who is also a group leader and not just an accidental recruit will have a circle of other leaders with whom they consult on strategies. An

IPR will have to make determined efforts to insure that that circle, which is itself composed of IPRs, draws from diverse sectors of the represented group and not just, say, friends of the IPR.

Sometimes IPRs can consult represented groups directly en masse (*en masse consultation*), as King illustrated by driving through the streets of Montgomery to find out how many riders participated in the boycott (see Chapter 3).[34] In other cases, *tacit consultation* may be possible—the absence of dissent from the represented after an IPR calls for a boycott provides some evidence that group members support the boycott. When a group's members are oppressed or marginalized, however, it can be difficult to disambiguate the absence of dissent from the silencing effects of that group's oppression or marginalization. For this reason, tacit consultation ought not be relied on heavily when the represented group is oppressed or marginalized.

Geographical dispersion. Geographically dispersed groups cannot be consulted in the same way as geographically proximate groups. Today, however, digital communication has eased some of these difficulties.[35] An IPR may, for instance, triangulate the interests of a large and dispersed group by consulting reliable digital fora (provided that these can be found).[36]

Limited access. Other groups are difficult to consult even independently of these complications. Known group members may be inaccessible when normal communication channels (email, phone, in-person contact) are blocked—common restrictions faced by prisoners. When one cannot consult the represented directly, *proxy consultation* is appropriate. IPRs should seek out reliable proxies—either those currently in contact with inaccessible represented parties (e.g., friends, family, lawyers) or, if no one is currently in contact with the inaccessible parties (imagine the represented group at issue is *disappeared persons*), parties formerly similarly situated to uncontactable parties.

Communicative inability. Sometimes, represented groups' members have in common a noncontingent inability to speak for themselves. They may lack knowledge about their political interests (e.g., very young children) or live with conditions that make both verbal and nonverbal communication challenging or impossible (e.g., people living with severe cognitive disabilities). Here, too, representatives should consult proxies or intermediate IPRs with more direct access to the group.

Next consider *transparency.* Representative power to influence manifests in many ways: the IPR can, for instance, call a press conference, take a private meeting, or state demands, often without the represented knowing why—or even that—the IPR is doing so. To correct for this, IPRs should, as feasible, let the represented know what they are doing and why.[37] Transparent disclosures take many forms in societies like ours: holding meetings with the represented, writing op-eds to publicly explain one's positions or decisions, and (perhaps) posting to social media platforms.[38]

Provided that the represented are not unavailable or inaccessible, it must be possible for the represented to receive reasons, justifications, and explanations from IPRs concerning why the representatives do what they do, and these explanations will, when necessary, involve appeal to the higher-order principles that motivate the IPRs to act as they do. Yet, as is the case for the consultative requirement, there must also be ample flexibility and context sensitivity concerning how much and what sort of transparency an IPR is required to practice. Again, the question of timing arises. In some cases, transparent disclosures undertaken prospectively will be ideal, allowing an IPR to receive group input before the IPR acts, as when King consulted proxies before announcing the boycott.[39] However, when it is impossible or counterproductive to disclose in advance, an IPR may satisfy transparency through retrospective disclosures.

The manner of disclosure required will also vary. Sometimes, being transparent is a passive responsibility: one should provide information when another requests it. At other times, transparency requires more—not just providing information when requested, but telling others there is information to be had (call this *active transparency*). Return to *Backdoor Deal*: Had King not published details of these closed-door negotiations with Montgomery city officials and the bus company, boycotters might never have known those negotiations had taken place.[40]

There must also be flexibility with respect to the content of an IPR's disclosures. Transparency sometimes conflicts with the strategic secrecy needed to prevent oppressors from undermining an IPR's plans. Accordingly, although IPRs must be transparent with those they represent about the values, aspirations, and goals they pursue on the represented's behalf, sometimes the IPR's planned or implemented strategies for advancing these will need to remain undisclosed. The IPR may also opt to consult along the way with their small circle of fellow IPRs on strategies that must remain opaque to outsiders until the last moment—a way of being transparent with proxies that is compatible with the strategic secrecy sometimes required in delicate circumstances.

There is also a feasibility constraint on being transparent. One can be transparent with only those one can access.

Transparency has expressive value. By being forthcoming concerning how they plan to represent and what guides them in so doing, IPRs express recognition respect to the represented. Transparent disclosures can signal an IPR's acknowledgment that the represented are central to their own representation.

Transparent disclosures also have epistemic value and, furthermore, are instrumental in ensuring that the representative relationship is deliberative and dialogical. Active transparency enables a two-way exchange of information. The IPR tells the represented their plans and aims, as well as reasons, explanations, and justifications for these. So informed, the represented are put in a stronger position to raise legitimate complaints, which complaints in turn give the IPR further information concerning the represented's values, interests, and preferences. Enabling the represented to raise legitimate complaints is itself a way of *welcoming criticism*, discussed below.

Absent such transparent disclosures, the represented are left at a discursive disadvantage: they are less well situated to raise legitimate complaints and, without being able to criticize their IPR, the inegalitarian conditions of their relationship deepen. The IPR is in general the more empowered party in representative relationships with oppressed or marginalized groups. When the represented are not well positioned to effectively raise legitimate complaint against the IPR (which requires, among other things, knowing what the IPR is doing and why), this epistemic disadvantage can reinforce the power differential between the IPR and the represented, and by so doing, create a situation in which the represented are subject to the whims or arbitrary will of the IPR, which is to say dominated by the IPR.[41]

Domination impedes the formation of egalitarian relationships. To avoid dominating the represented, IPRs must *welcome criticism* and *tolerate dissent*.

First, consider *welcoming criticism*. Even if one can consult those one represents, it will sometimes be impossible or imprudent to do so before acting. Accordingly, IPRs must also open communicative channels that allow the represented to raise complaint. Doing so enables IPRs to receive information from the represented and allows the represented to voluntarily come forward.

The IPR may actively welcome criticism by holding court in one forum or another—at a town meeting or on a digital platform.[42] IPRs may welcome criticism passively simply by remaining accessible. IPRs may even opt to hold open fora in which especially vulnerable represented parties can raise complaints privately or anonymously.

In addition to its epistemic value, welcoming criticism also supports the development of an egalitarian dialogical relationship between the IPR and those they represent. Given the IPR's outsized power to influence, there is a looming threat that the IPR can dominate the represented even if they are disposed not to. But equals do not dominate one another, so the IPR should actively undermine the threat of domination they pose by making themself vulnerable to the criticism and complaint of the represented.[43]

How can making oneself available to the criticism of another be a way of not dominating them? In the case of informal political representation, opening avenues for criticism and complaint can lower barriers that members of oppressed or marginalized groups would otherwise face when attempting to enter into conversation with their IPRs. That the represented are "entitled to participate" requires of the IPR that they make it possible for the represented to participate, and doing so when those who are entitled to participate are marginalized or oppressed can mean making special efforts to engage with the represented—creating conditions under which the represented can be heard. The represented under consideration in this chapter are already excluded from the broader society in which they live, so the place where they can have an "open discussion among equals" must be, at least in the first instance, with their corepresentees and with their IPRs.[44]

There are limits to the IPR's responsibility to stand open to criticism from the represented. The IPR is only required to stand open to reasonable criticism and only to the extent that it is compatible with maintaining their own self-respect (see Chapter 5).

Next, consider *tolerating dissent.* Recall that Booker T. Washington "strove publicly and secretly to take over control of newspapers to advance his message and suppress dissent, to prevent the hiring or facilitate the firing of his opposition."[45] In his critique of Washington, W. E. B. Du Bois cautioned that "the hushing of the criticism of honest opponents is a dangerous thing. It leads some of the best of the critics to unfortunate silence and paralysis of effort, and others to burst into speech so passionately and intemperately as to lose listeners."[46] It will come as no surprise that suppression of dissent is incompatible with an IPR's openness to criticism. In addition to creating channels for receiving complaint, the IPR must not block existing channels for complaint (by, say, disabling comments on their blog posts). But the obligation to not suppress dissent from the represented is not just derivative of the obligation to remain open to criticism. The IPR is obligated to not suppress dissent because the intentional or negligent suppression of dissent is itself a form of domination. An IPR who suppresses dissent abuses a power they have over the represented—namely, to control communication between the represented and broader audiences. Insofar as the IPR stanches the promulgation of the represented's critical attitudes and opinions regarding the IPR, they dominate the represented and may thereby become an additional oppressor of the represented.

Two further points about these four deliberative social practices are worth making explicit.

First, the stringency with which each of these practices must be maintained varies. Welcoming criticism and tolerating dissent are always required. And although each of these requirements may, of course, be satisfied in different ways in different contexts, there is not that much variation in terms of what it would mean to satisfy them. Generally, an IPR welcomes criticism by, among other things, making themselves available to be criticized by the represented, and tolerates dissent by not actively trying to suppress it. By contrast, what is required to satisfy consultation and transparency varies depending on a number of different particular features of the representative relationships at issue—including considerations like trust, strategy, and feasibility. Accordingly, these two social practices admit of a great deal more flexibility concerning the details of their satisfaction than welcoming criticism and tolerating dissent.

Second, there will be interactions among these four requirements that will inform how they may be satisfied. For instance, transparency is in part justified by the role it plays in welcoming criticism. So, one consideration that should inform an IPR's disclosures is whether those disclosures would put the represented in a good position to provide feedback. And, of course, part of what it is to welcome criticism is to create conditions in which that criticism can be expressed, which is why opportunities for consultation ex post are so important. Moreover, the infeasibility of satisfying one requirement can strengthen an IPR's obligation to satisfy another. Imagine that a represented group, undocumented persons in Texas, is hidden and it would be costly for group members to become publicly visible. This group's hiddenness can make consultation ex ante difficult. Accordingly, the IPR incurs a correspondingly stronger responsibility to enable retrospective criticism from group members by being transparent and welcoming criticism (particularly, in this case, by creating safe and perhaps anonymous avenues for legitimate complaint), since doing so can help members of the hidden group seek out the IPR who cannot find them.

Cultivating nonreliance. Even given these deliberative practices, sources of inequality persist in relationships between IPRs and those they represent, particularly when the represented are oppressed or marginalized. Of particular concern is the represented's *reliance* on their IPR. There are several reasons to worry about the represented's reliance on a given IPR; consider just two. First, we may worry that power corrupts. An IPR who is well motivated at the outset may, over time, develop an inflated sense of their own importance, purpose, or knowledge. If this occurs, well-intended deliberative social practices will not prevent such an IPR from falling prey to outsized confidence in their own judgment even when it conflicts with input from the represented. Second, even if the IPR does not succumb to overinflated confidence in their own judgment, we may still worry that the very fact that the represented rely on a given IPR contributes to a relational imbalance between the parties, as that reliance is unidirectional.[47] How can the represented's reliance be undermined or counteracted? Is there anything IPRs can do early on to tie their own hands?

Self-imposed term limits seem like nonstarters. First, if power corrupts, then we cannot count on IPRs to voluntarily step down. Second, if a good IPR is required to step down, the represented lose out on that IPR's knowledge, talent, and skill. Third, some IPRs may be stuck in the position of IPR despite a preference to step down or to have never been in the position at all (see Chapters 1 and 2).[48]

An alternative: Each IPR has a responsibility to promote nonreliance by cultivating competitors and replacements from early on, even if those competitors and replacements have the potential to become the IPR's rivals. Trained by the IPR, these protégés will be positioned to replace that IPR without requiring the IPR to voluntarily retreat from public life. Moreover, by training protégés, the IPR can shore up stores of institutional knowledge and skill that may otherwise be lost. Deepening the field of competent IPRs mitigates the represented's reliance on any particular IPR, undermining one cause of relational inequality. Additionally, cultivating competitors offers IPRs a way to prospectively hold themselves accountable by making sure they are not the only game in town.

Making informal political representation formal. In some cases, the challenges relevant to *democracy within* duties both can and ought to be addressed by working to make the informal political representation of an oppressed or marginalized group more formal. But not always.

Consider an example, *Union Formation*: A group of workers is acting collectively to improve members' working conditions. At some stage of their organizing, the workers may judge that particular roles—for instance, addressing shop-floor issues and communicating with the boss—should be assigned by means of an election procedure. In cases like *Union Formation*, it is both (1) helpful, and therefore desirable, to the represented group (here, the workers) for their representation to become more authorizationally formal; and, crucially, (2) feasible that this can take place. Such an example may give the misleading impression that it will always be the case that the challenges relevant to *democracy within* duties both can and ought to be addressed by working to make the informal political representation of an oppressed or marginalized group more formal. However, there will be cases of informal political representation where the aim of working toward formal political representation will be infeasible, undesirable, or both.

First, consider *infeasibility*. Some instances of informal political representation will be especially poorly suited to efforts at formalization. Consider, for instance, the Black Lives Matter movement, which informally represents Black Americans. Such a large, decentralized, and widely dispersed represented group will likely struggle to incorporate more formal authorization mechanisms like elections because the relevant constituency cannot be determined with ease or accuracy or, even if it could, it would be infeasible to carry out a vote.

Next, consider *undesirability*. Even when feasible, efforts to formalize currently informal political representation may be undesirable. The implementation (let alone the design) of formal, systematic structures can be costly, and in some cases, can leave the represented worse off than if their IPR relationship were left just as it is. Consider, as an example, one such cost: FPR institutions often limit the number of representatives a given constituency can have. This is not the case for informal political representation, where, in theory, a given constituency can have as many IPRs as can receive audience conferral. Accordingly, one notable cost of making informal political representation more formal is placing limits on how many representatives a given group can have. While it can be useful in certain contexts (like *Union Formation*) to impose limits on the numbers of representatives that emerge, such limits also have their costs. Having multiple or even numerous IPRs can, for instance, encourage productive contestation, as the many IPRs give voice to the competing perspectives of a large, heterogeneous group, thereby undermining the entrenchment of a few more established spokespersons, which can in turn cultivate nonreliance.

Moreover, some social movements are valuable precisely because they encourage the emergence of more and more varied IPRs. Consider the example of the Me Too movement. As its name suggests, the movement formed as sexual assault, abuse, and harassment survivors emerged to share their experiences additively. These parties spoke on their own behalf, publicly announcing wrongs they had endured. Yet we may not unreasonably think that many of these parties also became IPRs for the large and widely dispersed group of *sexual assault, abuse, and harassment survivors,* for many of whose members such public proclamation is unavailable or prohibitively risky. The numerous survivors who shared their experiences, by their sheer numbers, attested to the utter ordinariness and pervasiveness of sexual assault, abuse, and harassment—an outcome that could not as effectively have been achieved had there been formal constraints on the number of parties permitted to aver "Me too."

Accordingly, efforts to address the challenges relevant to *democracy within* by making informal political representation more formal in some respect will face at least these two constraints: feasibility and desirability. Only when it is both feasible and desirable to make an IPR relationship more formal in some respect have the IPR and the represented reason to do so. Moreover, we cannot consider whether the IPR and represented have reason to make their relationship more formal without considering specific respects in which the relationship should (or even could) be made more formal. As discussed in Chapter 1, representative relationships may be more or less formal in a variety of ways: authorization, group membership, account-ability, norms. While some groups and their IPRs will have reasons to seek more formal authorization mechanisms, others will instead have reasons to codify their norms, while still others will have reasons for neither.

There is one additional consideration: the different dimensions along which representation can be more or less formal (see Chapter 1) shape how *democracy within* duties should be discharged. For instance, IPRs who rep-resent groups poorly situated to effectively protest are not simply informally (rather than formally) accountable but are instead in fact closer to com-pletely unaccountable. Even if these IPRs are disposed to welcome criticism or tolerate dissent, the silencing circumstances faced by the groups they represent may make criticism or dissent impossible. Yet such IPRs must still promote a dialogical, deliberative relationship with the represented and, since welcoming criticism and tolerating dissent may be moot in such cases, these IPRs have correspondingly stronger duties to seek out group mem-bers to consult and with whom to be transparent.

Justice Without Duties

We now have a partial answer to the skeptics' challenges. For the informal political representation of oppressed or marginalized groups to be morally permissible, IPRs must, as feasible, consult, welcome criticism, be trans-parent, tolerate dissent, and cultivate nonreliance. These practices jointly constitute the inward-facing aspect of the IPR's duties—*democracy within*.

Still, some skeptical challenges remain unresolved. Consider, for instance, *concessive* criticisms. *Concessive* criticisms are complex. Partly, they target the representative's treatment of the represented—a relational concern to which *democracy within* duties respond. But they also concern whether the substantive content of IPRs' statements or actions leaves the represented foreseeably worse off because too much ground has been ceded—a purpo-sive concern to which *justice without* duties respond. An example: Du Bois criticized Washington not just for failing to consult Black southerners and suppressing their dissent (*relational concerns*) but also for publicly offering Black southerners' willingness to form amicable relations with white south-erners even if the latter did not recognize the former's civil and political rights (a *purposive concern*).[49] For Washington to have corrected course in light of these criticisms, he would have needed to not only consult and welcome criticism (*democracy within* duties) but, further, adjust the content of his "Atlanta Compromise" speech so as not to have made concessions that were, per Du Bois, objectionable.

All of which brings us to *justice without* duties.

Democracy within and *justice without* duties respond to concerns of different sorts. *Democracy within* duties respond to the concern that representative-represented relationships can be inegalitarian and oppressive by providing guidance concerning how IPRs should treat the represented.

Yet, to justify the informal political representation of oppressed and marginalized groups, it is insufficient to point out that the practice can be undertaken in a manner that is neither inegalitarian nor oppressive. Given its dangers, the practice must also offer something to the represented that could not come in its absence. Informal political representation must be justified at least partly by (1) the represented's need for it, and (2) benefits that may foreseeably accrue to the represented by virtue of it. The need for representation of some sort is not hard to see in the contexts at issue, where the represented's oppression or marginalization manifests partly as exclusion from FPR bodies. Still, these groups require informal political representation in particular only if it is valuable to them. Some of its valuable features were discussed in the Introduction. These features justify the practice to the extent that they serve *eradication*. Accordingly, *justice without* duties guide IPRs in performing their roles so as to undermine oppressive or marginalizing conditions represented groups face in their broader societies. In particular, *justice without* duties provide guidance concerning how, when, where, and before whom IPRs should speak or act on the represented parties' behalf so as to combat injustices faced by the represented. But what exactly does that mean?

We were able to identify generally applicable *democracy within* duties because those duties aim to correct for inequality inherent in all relationships between IPRs and the oppressed or marginalized groups they represent. But it is more difficult to identify generally applicable *justice without* duties, as different groups are oppressed or marginalized in different ways in different contexts. So, identifying substantive constraints on how a given representative should fulfill their purpose depends on the specific needs of the group they represent.

Justice without duties are specified in particular cases by considering questions like:

1. What ought this IPR say or do before this audience?
2. How may this IPR carry out this representation?
3. Before which audiences ought this IPR speak or act, when the IPR has discretion to choose?[50]
4. Who is (or is not) well situated to be an IPR for this group?[51]

Since *justice without* duties are context specific, my aim here is not to comprehensively enumerate each possible *justice without* duty. Rather, my aim is simply to identify some normative considerations that fall within the ambit of *justice without.* Some examples help illustrate how an IPR might think about the above questions.

Consider first: What ought the IPR say or do before their audiences? To answer, an IPR must consider specifying questions like *What is the nature of the represented's marginalization or oppression?* or *Who is the audience?* Consider two cases examining these questions, respectively:

1. *Complete Marginalization.* Imagine a group so marginalized that few know there is such a group. Here, all else equal, the IPR ought to at least direct attention to the fact of the group's existence, as when the group *children sexually abused by Catholic priests in Boston* was publicly identified.[52] A caveat: not all marginalized groups benefit from having attention directed to them. I return to this consideration in the discussion of *Avoidance,* below.
2. *Group Formation.* Next, imagine that members of a plurality do not know themselves to have shared interests, which keeps them from forming a group.[53] In this case, the plurality stands to the IPR as both audience and represented.[54] The IPR should represent the plurality to itself as a group to help the plurality's members come to understand themselves to be a group. Here, the IPR's work is prefatory: creating conditions under which plurality members will identify as group members and thereby recognize that their circumstances are shared.

Consider next that IPRs sometimes have discretion as to who their audiences are. When they do, before whom ought they speak or act? Different considerations bear on such a question, giving *justice without* duties further specificity:

3. *Scarcity.* A general constraint all representatives face is scarcity.[55] Representatives have only so much time and must assess which opportunities will best serve the represented. All else equal, to use their platforms effectively, IPRs should prioritize communicating with influential audiences that are not dogmatically unsympathetic toward either the represented or their values, interests, or preferences.

4. *Avoidance.* So, too, ought IPRs avoid certain audiences. Consider: A representative may rightly think law enforcement should not be alerted to the presence of a vulnerable group—the homeless, say—if it is foreseeable that the group's members will be harmed should notice be given to the prospective audience.[56] Furthermore, an IPR may have decisive reason to avoid an audience even when they would not harm and may even have helped the represented by representing before that audience. Imagine that an IPR for women is invited to speak before a male supremacist association. Stipulate that, were the IPR to accept the invitation, they would convince the association's members to condemn their founder's prolific rape apologist oeuvre and excise rape apology from the association's mission statement, a fact known to the IPR in advance. Accepting the invitation would satisfy *eradication* by undermining one of the association's oppressive core commitments. Even so, accepting the invitation may express an objectionable sort of regard for the organization, giving the IPR reason to reject the invitation.

Further Roles for *Democracy Within* Duties, *Justice Without* Duties, and Informal Political Representation

In my discussion of *democracy within* and *justice without* duties, I have so far placed special emphasis on the perspectives of IPRs themselves at least partly because IPRs are generally more difficult than FPRs for represented parties to hold accountable, and so IPRs must be self-evaluating and self-constraining.[57] Notwithstanding this special emphasis, *democracy within* and *justice without* duties also have other roles to play in the everyday practice of informal political representation. These duties clarify what sorts of complaints raised against IPRs are legitimate, thereby providing both structure and substantive content to the deliberative social practices that emerge between IPRs, the represented, and third parties with standing to raise complaint. Specifically, *democracy within* and *justice without* duties ground criticisms of errant IPRs. Since these duty sets are the norms in accordance with which IPRs ought to act to represent permissibly, they are also the norms in accordance with which IPRs ought to be criticized for failures, either by those they represent or by third parties who have standing to raise complaint against the IPRs. Critics may appeal to these duties when raising complaints against IPRs they regard to be errant. In this role, such duties ground legitimate complaints raised against IPRs (see Chapter 5).

These duties also provide IPRs with guidance as to which complaints they ought to heed and which they might instead be able to dismiss on the ground that the complaint corresponds to no duty satisfaction of which the IPR owes to the represented. In this role, such duties constrain what complaints give IPRs reason to correct or justify their actions. Accordingly, we may think of these duties as providing criteria by which IPRs themselves can evaluate the legitimacy of various complaints raised against them.

The practice of informal political representation itself also contributes to public life, more generally. By providing certain political goods to the represented—political influence, political agency, community recognition, trust, and democratic equality—informal political representation can contribute to making a society more just.

Political Influence. Each of us has an interest in influencing how things go in our political communities. Informal political representation enables represented parties to have mediated influence on their political communities.[58]

Political Agency. The ability to communicate one's political convictions to others freely and openly is a constitutive feature of having political agency. When one is silenced or simply ignored, that constitutive aim is undermined. As Ronald Dworkin points out, "Someone denied opportunity to bear witness to his concern for justice, as he understands what the concern requires, finds his political agency stultified not merely bounded."[59] When the freedom to bear witness to one's concern for justice is stunted, an IPR may serve as a proxy through which one's convictions are communicated to a broader public. The proxy message may even express concern regarding one's unjust exclusion from the political community.

One may object that informal political representation undermines, rather than supports, the individual political agency of oppressed or marginalized group members by treating them as group members first rather than individual political actors. Yet one's political agency is very often bound up with the political agency of others—as noted, "people tend to act politically not so much as individuals as in groups."[60]

Community Recognition. Informal political representation may promote one's recognition by the political community by which one has been marginalized. Community recognition has at least these two aspects: First, one is recognized by one's political community when one is regarded as belonging to that community. Being recognized as belonging to a political community is a way of being shown respect and consideration by one's political community. Second, one is recognized by one's political community when one's interests are "taken seriously by others," when one's views are considered and given weight, meaning at least that one's views are included in the public exchange of reasons.[61]

Members of oppressed or marginalized groups are commonly treated as not belonging to their political communities, and their interests are often overlooked—this is true even when their interests are incidentally satisfied in particular cases. In some cases, an IPR may bolster both sorts of community recognition simply by bringing awareness to the fact of the represented group's existence—the group *children detained by U.S. Immigration and Customs Enforcement* garnered widespread public support once the American public was made aware of it by various media outlets.[62] In other cases, the represented lack recognition not because they are unnoticed or unknown but because they are ignored by the broader community. In these cases, it can be more difficult for an IPR to aid the represented group in receiving either sort of recognition. IPRs with comparatively greater power to influence may have considerable leverage to pressure dominant groups to take the represented and their needs more seriously. Even IPRs without considerable power to influence can still amplify the represented groups' interests, making the group harder to ignore.

Trust. High levels of distrust in one's society can engender political apathy or political pessimism. Being a member of a society that does not recognize one's interests as mattering (a failure of recognition by one's political community) or that does not permit one the opportunity to express or communicate one's deeply held commitments (a failure of realization of one's political agency) can engender an individual's or group's justifiable distrust in that society. Having one's voice heard; having one's values, interests, and preferences taken seriously; having the sense that one's interests are understood by and matter to others; having the sense that one is thought to be a member of the political community—the promotion of each of these values may increase the trust a person has in their political community. IPRs can demand that those they represent receive due regard by the broader political community. When those demands are met, they give some evidence that these demands are not in vain and may undermine the represented's distrust. Of course, trust is not always required for a group to become politically engaged—in fact, deep and abiding distrust can sometimes catalyze political engagement, as when a group's members exercise their political agency to demand recognition by their broader political community: "Black lives matter." "Say her name." "Me too."

Democratic Equality. As Elizabeth Anderson states, "Democratic equality . . . denotes a kind of standing in civil society to make claims on others, that they respect one's rights, pay due regard to one's interests, and include one as a full participant in civil society, including those that inform democratic governance."[63] Without democratic equality, a society is unjust. What role should we expect informal political representation to play in bringing about democratic equality?

Members of oppressed and marginalized groups are not accorded the civic standing constitutive of democratic equality. Achieving democratic equality in a society requires undermining hindrances to this civic standing. Insofar as informal political representation can help represented group members achieve political influence, political agency, community recognition, and trust, the practice can undermine the muting and occlusive effects of a represented group's oppression or marginalization, thereby promoting democratic equality.

Of course, informal political representation is not by itself adequate for the realization of an individual's political agency. And we cannot know at the outset whether an IPR will in fact succeed in garnering community recognition for an oppressed or marginalized group. Nor, of course, is it guaranteed that a member of a represented group will be regarded as equal to others in their political community simply because someone who serves as that member's IPR in the political community says they ought to be. Even so, although informal political representation cannot guarantee the satisfaction of these democratic values, it can surely undermine hindrances to their realization.

Hard Cases

Democracy within duties satisfy *noncontribution* by undermining inequality inherent in the immediate relationship between the IPR and the represented. *Justice without* duties satisfy *eradication* by specifying how the IPR may use their platform to undermine the represented's marginalization or oppression. These duty sets answer skeptics' challenges—showing that there are morally permissible ways for IPRs to represent oppressed or marginalized groups. Still, there is a problem. There will be hard cases in which *democracy within* and *justice without* duties appear to be in conflict.

To see this, return to *Backdoor Deal.* On December 8, 1955, King and other Montgomery Improvement Association members met behind closed doors with Montgomery Mayor W. A. Gayle, city commissioners, and bus company representatives.[64] Imagine they had reached a provisional bus seating arrangement deemed desirable by the Montgomery Improvement Association, but the city needed to know contemporaneously whether Black bus riders would be on board with the arrangement.[65] If King took the deal back to riders to consult and be transparent with them, he would have satisfied *democracy within* duties, but at the expense of the deal itself. If instead King accepted the deal, he would have satisfied *justice without* duties, but at the expense of consulting and being transparent with his constituents.

What should King have done? To properly analyze this example, consider two variants. In the first, King is already group authorized; in the second, he is not.

Group authorization affects the stringency of *democracy within* duties. *Democracy within* duties are meant to correct for inequality inherent in the relationship between the IPR and the oppressed or marginalized groups they represent. However, when group authorization obtains, this relational inequality is diminished, so the collective protection of *democracy within* is not needed to the same extent. Group authorization gives IPRs more discretion regarding the manner and scope of their representations than they otherwise would have had. What this discretion allows for depends on the particulars of the group authorization—for instance, how it was carried out, the scope of authority granted, and what, if any, were its express terms. Some possible effects of group authorization include the following:

1. Representation that would be criticizable absent group authorization may not be so when group authorization obtains, even if the authorized IPR does not consult ex ante or act transparently. (The obligations to welcome criticism and tolerate dissent are never canceled.) Accordingly, authorized IPRs may have grounds to dismiss complaints that de facto IPRs would have had reason to heed because group authorization permits the authorized IPRs to take the action now being criticized by members of the authorizing group.
2. Group authorization allows authorized IPRs to hold forth as having authority to make commitments on the represented's behalf, contra the general prohibition expressed by *overcommitting.*
3. Rarely, group authorization may enable authorized IPRs to make binding commitments on the represented's behalf.

In the group authorization variant, King was not obligated to take the offer back to boycotters in advance of making a deal because, as an authorized IPR, he was empowered to enact specific experiments in pursuit of the values and aspirations endorsed by those he represented. When the represented authorized King, they also entrusted him with the details of how to go about promoting those values.

But what if King did not have group authorization? In this case, too, King ought to have accepted the deal. Sometimes there is good reason to secure urgently needed political goods, satisfying *justice without* duties, even when doing so seems to conflict with satisfying *democracy within* duties. The real question is how King's decision to accept the deal can be justified in this latter case.

One approach to justifying King's decision would be to treat *democracy within* and *justice without* duties as competing considerations to be weighed against each other. Place on one side of the scale all of King's reasons to bring the deal back to the boycotters: by consulting and being transparent, King would exhibit recognition respect to the represented, avoid exhibiting apparent authority, and make efforts to not represent their interests inaccurately, thereby correcting for the relational imbalance inherent in his relationship with the group he represents. These considerations reflect efforts to avoid contributing to the represented's oppression and marginalization (*noncontribution*). But then, on the other side of the scale, competing considerations of exigency in *eradicating* the unjust conditions the represented face in their broader community pile up: Black Montgomerians' circumstances had become untenable. King and the city were in the throes of urgent and tense private negotiations. The deal was on the table in that moment; it would not come again. As Rev. L. Roy Bennett put the point at the December 2, 1955, Montgomery community leaders' meeting, "This is no time to talk; it is time to act."[66] All of a sudden, *democracy within* duties seem almost beside the point—idealistic, lofty deliberative aspirations to be pursued only when they will not get in the way of real progress. More just circumstances for the represented should be pursued by any means necessary, *justice without* duties trump; *democracy within* considerations may be reserved for less consequential times.

The importance of *justice without* duties cannot be overstated: Oppression and marginalization are deep and pervasive violations of one's personhood. When present, they are fundamental moral considerations and so efforts to satisfy eradication ought not be compromised. The purpose of informal political representation in the contexts at issue is to help bring about the eradication of the oppressive and marginalizing conditions that the represented face in their broader society. *Justice without* duties reflect a commitment to achieving that purpose.

Yet the justificatory approach proposed here, whereby *democracy within* is to be weighed against *justice without,* will be deeply unsatisfying to the skeptics whose challenges we set out to answer. They are concerned that IPRs of oppressed or marginalized groups can, with impunity, abuse their power to influence, thereby relating to the represented not as equals but as oppressors.[67] To say that *democracy within* duties are to be satisfied only when not outweighed by *justice without* considerations is to treat IPRs' relational responsibilities to those they represent as waivable, cancelable, or merely advisory.

Yet *democracy within* duties are not any of these. *Democracy within* duties reflect an inviolable commitment to treat one another as equals. Eschewing *democracy within* duties reinforces objectionable relational imbalances between the IPR and those they represent—relational imbalances that may render the informal political representation of oppressed and marginalized groups unjustifiable by leaving already vulnerable represented groups subject to the arbitrary power of those who represent them (in addition to everyone else who already contributes to their marginalization or oppression). IPRs may not risk becoming the represented's oppressors even in order to undermine the represented's other oppressors.[68] In fact, the oppressed and marginalized have special, further claims against IPRs in particular that IPRs not violate *democracy within* duties precisely because of the inequality inherent in their relationship. That the represented are at the mercy of their IPRs gives those IPRs further reason to abide those relational demands outlined here as *democracy within* duties. That a person is oppressed or marginalized makes their individual claim to be treated in accordance with fundamental moral commitments no less strong. To do otherwise is to treat the oppressed or marginalized as objects or patients whose lives and circumstances must be managed rather than as agents whose claims to be treated as equals should be given the same weight as anyone else's. What's more, when conditions are unjust, those in dominant positions are responsible to take corrective measures to bring about conditions of relational equality. IPRs are in dominant positions vis-à-vis the represented. IPRs speak before the U.S. Congress, sit with the president, appear on television, say and do for the represented what the represented do not have platforms to say and do for themselves. This means IPRs for oppressed and marginalized groups have special, further responsibilities to correct for inequality inherent in their own representative-represented relationships. Doing so only when it suits IPRs' visions of what justice requires is as much a danger to the represented as many other violations of their agency are. Relational imbalances leave the represented at the mercy of their IPRs and *democracy within* duties correct for these imbalances.

Fortunately, IPRs need neither abandon their *justice without* duties in the interest of treating the represented as equals nor begrudgingly sacrifice *democracy within* duties when especially urgent, high-value goals are at stake. *Democracy within* and *justice without* duties are not competing considerations to be weighed against one another. IPRs need not (and should not) "balance" considerations of mutual respect or equality with considerations of effectiveness. This is the wrong way to conceptualize the relationship between these two duty sets. It is true that the two duty sets are directed at different aspects of the representative-represented relationship: inward-facing *democracy within* duties concern the IPR's immediate relationship to the represented; outward-facing *justice without* duties concern how the IPR should represent the group to bring about more just circumstances for them in the broader society of which they are a part. Yet both duty sets fundamentally provide guidance about how the IPR should approach their relationship to the represented—just different aspects of that relationship.

IPRs need not sacrifice their commitment to *democracy within* duties, even when the stakes are high. The deliberative social practices that constitute these duties already incorporate ample flexibility in dealing with conflicting values and demands. So, IPRs can engage in context-sensitive analysis of what would exhibit recognition respect to and equal treatment of the represented in a place at a time. Both consultation and transparency admit of flexibility as to the time, place, frequency, and manner of their satisfaction; consultative success is measured by a best efforts standard. Welcoming criticism is similarly flexible: what it means to be available to be criticized by the represented depends on many particular features of the representative-represented relationship. Although tolerating dissent is the least flexible of these practices, it is easily satisfied if the IPR simply forbears from actively suppressing dissent. Finally, as discussed, these practices interact in ways that inform how they may be satisfied. The flexibility built into *democracy within* duties enables IPRs to satisfy their requirements compatibly with achieving high-value *justice without* goals for the represented.

There will, of course, also be practical limitations on how well IPRs can satisfy their *democracy within* duties. Engaging in deliberative social practices with large, dispersed oppressed or marginalized groups will often be complicated, difficult, or infeasible. (It is worth noting that some of these deliberative social practices will be easier to satisfy than others. For instance, even when consultation and transparency are difficult, the IPR may still welcome criticism and tolerate dissent.) And, even when they are able to participate in these practices, however imperfectly, it may well still be impossible for IPRs to completely undermine the inequality inherent in their relationships with those they represent. But this should not worry us. Equality in a relationship is always a matter of degree, even though it is partially constituted by the parties to the relationship observing broad principles of treatment and interaction.

The moral situation of the IPR is therefore nuanced. Yet the question is not which duty set ought to trump another in a particular case. IPRs are called upon to contemporaneously satisfy both *democracy within* and *justice without* duties. The question, instead, is what satisfying both looks like in a particular case and how the IPR can justify their decisions to the represented. Fortunately, *democracy within* duties are not context-insensitive, rigid standards but instead general and flexible guidelines that inform how IPRs treat the oppressed or marginalized groups they represent. How these guidelines are to be satisfied in particular cases will of necessity be informed by both the outward-facing aims and practical limitations faced by the represented and their IPR.

In *Backdoor Deal*, the unauthorized King would never have been justified in forgoing his *democracy within* duties. This does not mean, however, that he would have had to take the deal back to boycotters in advance of agreeing to it. Consultation and transparency ex post, openness to the represented's criticism, and toleration of any dissent would have been adequate to discharge his *democracy within* duties in this case.

Given the considerable flexibility already built into the *democracy within* requirements themselves, circumstances would need to be truly exceptional to make the failure to satisfy even the very barest demands of *democracy within* duties justifiable. Even so, in practice, there will always be exceptions for dire circumstances or especially important external goals. An IPR may in some truly exceptional case be justified in falling short of their *democracy within* duties if, for instance, doing so were the only way to protect the group members' existential interests—for instance, protecting them from ongoing violence, injury, death, or other imminent harms. These compelling interests can in exceptional cases justify infringements on the represented's individual rights that would otherwise be respected by an IPR's adherence to *democracy within* duties. In exceptional cases like these, what is important for the vindication of the represented's individual rights are the other constraints placed on the pursuit of those compelling interests. Here we may find guidance from U.S. constitutional legal doctrine: Compelling state interests can justify the state's infringements on individual rights. However, to vindicate individual rights even while allowing for their exceptional infringement, there must be other constraints on the pursuit of these compelling state interests, like narrow tailoring requirements and duties of compensation for infringement. Such constraints serve an expressive function: "they express recognition of injury and reaffirmation of the underlying normative principles for how the relevant relationships are to be constituted."[69]

Similarly, an IPR may in some truly exceptional cases diverge from their *democracy within* duties in the interest of satisfying compelling *justice without* interests. These divergences must be (1) narrowly tailored to the compelling interests they are meant to serve, and (2) justifiable to the represented themselves. But such divergences, even if justified by compelling interests and narrowly tailored to satisfy those interests, may still seriously harm the relationship between the IPR and the represented, for which reason (3) subsequent repair may be required. So, IPRs must undertake divergences in ways that allow for (3a) recognition of any resultant injury to the relationship between the represented and the IPR and (3b) reaffirmation of the underlying normative principles fundamental for their relationship that have been temporarily deemphasized (namely, *democracy within* duties). Fortunately, just as IPRs have tools for promoting *democracy within* duties in their relationship to the represented, so, too, do they have tools for engaging in repair with the represented when they fail to satisfy the *democracy within* duties. For instance, IPRs may openly acknowledge their failure to satisfy *democracy within* duties, apologize, and attempt to make amends; they must leave themselves open to the legitimate complaints of the represented (see Chapter 5); and they may even aim to seek out informal ratification from the represented group for the decision they have made that violates *democracy within* duties (see Chapter 3). Despite such efforts, the IPR may still lose the trust of the group altogether. When trust is lost irrecoverably, the normative principles underlying the relationship may be reaffirmed only by means of the IPR's acknowledgment of their failure and the dissolution of the representative-represented relationship. Of course, resignation is tricky for an IPR, as some audience might continue to treat the party as the group's IPR despite the IPR's efforts to exit the role. Resignation requires of the outgoing IPR that they no longer purport to be group authorized (if they once were) and make efforts to encourage relevant audiences to revoke de facto IPR status.

Truly exceptional circumstances aside, supposed conflicts between *democracy within* and *justice without* duties may, then, be properly recast as features of informal political representation that inform when and why an IPR may adjust the time, place, frequency, or manner of their satisfaction of *democracy within* duties. We have considered several features of the representative-represented relationship that can impact these time, place, frequency, and manner considerations: feasibility, strategic secrecy, group authorization, exigency, trust. Whether the group trusts their IPR can be inferred from a variety of features of their relationship, including and especially whether the IPR has group authorization. Moreover, the mechanism of consultation ex post opens up discussion between the representative and the represented that allows for revision and repair, or, when the IPR's failure has been too great, replacement. Nonreliance will also make a difference: The manner in which an IPR must satisfy their *democracy within* duties will also be informed by whether or not the represented rely solely on one IPR for their communicative access to the broader society. The group may have other representatives (formal or informal) or direct access to relevant audiences. The underlying value of relational equality promoted by *democracy within* duties becomes no less important when nonreliance obtains. Rather, the group is simply not at the mercy of one single IPR to the same extent, and so one of the three features that gives rise to relational inequality between IPR and represented is subverted, allowing each individual IPR greater flexibility in the satisfaction of their *democracy within* duties. I reserve for Chapter 7 consideration of another feature that can impact the time, place, frequency, and manner in which *democracy within* duties may be satisfied—namely, the role of IPR expertise.

Conclusion

Informal political representation is a needed social practice in societies like ours. Yet it is a practice that can protect or oppress. It can improve the lives of oppressed and marginalized group members. Or it can crush them underfoot. Many groups, particularly oppressed or marginalized groups, rely on informal political representation to help them develop their political voice and exert political influence on the circumstances that shape their members' lives. Yet skeptics quite reasonably challenge the practice of informal political representation on a variety of grounds—chiefly, on grounds that the practice can create inegalitarian or oppressive relationships between the representative and the represented. Given these skeptical challenges, to represent permissibly, IPRs must treat the represented in certain ways that, taken together, make up the *democracy within* and *justice without* duties. *Democracy within* duties comprise four deliberative social practices IPRs must perform to treat the represented as their equals and to avoid dominating the represented: consultation, transparency, welcoming criticism, tolerating dissent. *Justice without* duties concern how, when, where, and before whom IPRs ought to represent oppressed or marginalized groups to broader audiences so as to bring about more just circumstances for those groups in the society by which they are currently oppressed or marginalized. Sometimes, *democracy within* duties and *justice without* duties appear to prescribe conflicting courses of action. But these conflicts are in all but the most exceptional circumstances merely apparent: Although *democracy within* duties are never canceled, they admit of ample flexibility, enabling IPRs to satisfy them compatibly with achieving *justice without* for the represented.

5

The Legitimate Complaints
of the Represented

W. E. B. Du Bois describes the singular importance of criticism to a well-functioning democracy this way: "Honest and earnest criticism from those whose interests are most nearly touched,—criticism of writers by readers, of government by those governed, of leaders by those led,—this is the soul of democracy and the safeguard of modern society."[1] Criticism is a needed and desirable feature of the representative-represented relationship. In fact, criticism is so important to this relationship that all four deliberative social practices that constitute the *democracy within* duties—consultation, transparency, welcoming criticism, tolerating dissent—share as a central aim creating conditions in which represented parties can voice their criticism of their informal political representatives (IPRs) (see Chapter 4). The IPR consults ex post to elicit feedback on the decisions they make and actions they take on behalf of the represented. The IPR is transparent so that the represented know what IPR decisions and actions to examine and, perhaps, criticize. Welcoming criticism and tolerating dissent are straightforwardly mechanisms for eliciting, rather than suppressing, criticism. Given the centrality of criticism to a well-functioning deliberative, democratic relationship, I devote the whole of this chapter to examining one of the most important elements of this criticism: the legitimate complaints of the represented. I begin by clarifying the force of just one complaint—an exceedingly common complaint, but one whose meaning is misunderstood.

Doubtless you have heard someone object, at one time or another, "You don't speak for us." Versions of this complaint are commonplace when a represented group or its members raise objection to their IPR. Consider again George Cook's objection: "Rev. Sharpton does not speak for all African

Americans and he doesn't speak for anyone I know on many issues."[2] Or consider this indirect exchange during the final stages of the U.S. negotiation of the nuclear deal with Iran in 2015: When, in a speech, Israeli Prime Minister Benjamin Netanyahu declared, "I feel that I am the emissary of all Israelis, even those who disagree with me, of the entire Jewish People,"[3] Senator Dianne Feinstein opined, "No, he doesn't speak for me on [the topic of Iran]. . . . I think it's a rather arrogant statement. I think the Jewish community is like any other community, there are different points of view."[4]

"You don't speak for us" and its variants have many different meanings and effects. Generally speaking, they express disagreement or disapproval, they register disavowal or dissent. Yet one feature common to all such complaints of this form is that they do not have the effect of unseating a de facto IPR—not, at least, when the complainant is different from the audience that conferred IPR status on that party. Complaints of this form are, when taken literally, false. After all, if an audience confers on Netanyahu the status of IPR for the entire Jewish community through ascription, credibility conferral, testimonial reliance, or invitation, then Netanyahu *does* speak for the entire Jewish community, at least from the perspective of the conferring audience; and so Feinstein's objection seems somehow inapposite. Yet Feinstein's objection is not that, as a descriptive matter, Netanyahu is not treated by many audiences as speaking or acting for the Jewish community. Of course he is. Rather, it is precisely the fact that Netanyahu has garnered such a reception that makes Feinstein and others concerned.

So, what is the force behind an objection like Feinstein's? It seems to be the following: "The views that Netanyahu espouses on behalf of the Jewish people are not my views, and I am a Jew." It matters to Feinstein and other Jews who disagree with Netanyahu's espoused positions to raise complaint against him precisely because he is a de facto IPR of Jews. Feinstein's complaint may be understood as an attempt to preempt an audience imputing Netanyahu's views on the Iran nuclear deal to her.

The relationship between IPR and represented should be understood as a dialogue, an ongoing exchange of ideas, reasons, explanations, and justifications. The legitimate complaints of the represented are at the center of this exchange. In this chapter, I distinguish, categorize, and examine a wide variety of different complaints so as to better understand their content, their force, and what insights they can give us into the deliberative relationship between the represented and their IPRs.

Perhaps you find yourself asking, "But why think that this is a special feature of the relationship between representative and represented? Of course, the represented will raise complaints against IPRs and audiences. But that is not a special feature of political representation. Represented parties, like all of us, raise complaints when and because they believe those complaints to be legitimate. And, when those complaints are legitimate, they are legitimate not because of their sources but because of their content. And, if that's right, then why devote so much attention to the represented's complaints? Couldn't anyone who reasonably disagreed with the IPR raise the same complaints?"

No. Although some complaints can be raised by anyone against anyone else, representative or not, just because the complaint itself is legitimate irrespective of its source, not all complaints are like this. Other complaints can be raised only by the represented themselves. Still other complaints can be raised only by the represented against their own IPR.[5]

In this chapter, I first briefly introduce and distinguish three genera of complaint—content complaints, procedural complaints, and power complaints—within which fall different species of complaint. Second, I provide a more extensive characterization of each species of complaint, illustrated with real-world historical and contemporary examples. By doing so, I identify complaints that could only sensibly be raised against someone in the position of IPR and that could only sensibly be raised by the represented themselves. Third, I argue that those complaints arise uniquely in representative-represented relationships because they arise from duties that IPRs have to those they represent but do not have to others. Fourth, I discuss what makes IPRs particularly susceptible to procedural and power complaints.[6] Fifth, I consider how much and what sorts of responses to these complaints the represented may expect from their IPRs. This chapter is an effort to vindicate what is truly to be found in the common though misleading objection, "You don't speak for us"—to understand what gives this objection its rhetorical force.

A Hartian note of clarification: The skeptical challenges schematized in Chapter 4 are put to the practice of informal political representation from the external point of view—that is, they are criticisms of various aspects of the practice as such, from the outside. Those challenges should be distinguished from the complaints at issue here—made by represented group members or third parties against particular IPRs. These latter complaints are often, although not always, complaints from the internal point of view—that is, from within the practice of informal political representation about a particular aspect of a particular representative-represented relationship.[7] That said, there is some conceptual overlap between the skeptical challenges of Chapter 4 and the complaints of the represented discussed here.

An Overview of Complaint Types

First, consider the varieties of complaints themselves. There are three genera of complaint—content complaints, procedural complaints, and power complaints. Some of these complaints take as their objects IPRs' statements or actions, while others take as their objects the IPRs themselves. Within these genera of complaint fall different species of complaints. The genera and species of complaints characterized here are intended to be illustrative, not exhaustive. There is ample room for both conceptual and empirical developments in this area of research. Before examining each species of complaint, consider roughly what each complaint expresses, as exhibited in table 5.1.

Let me set forth a few preliminary notes about these complaint types and their relationships to one another: First, a representative can be subject to more than one of these complaints at a time. But some of these complaints cannot be simultaneously satisfied, because they would require the IPR to pursue mutually exclusive courses of action. For instance, a reluctant IPR may be open to the missed-opportunity complaint. Should they overcome their reluctance and represent, they may then open themself up to one or more of the complaints concerning how they erred in their representations of the group. We may worry that IPRs are forced to make a tragic choice: they are damned if they do not represent, but damned if instead they represent in the wrong way, even if that manner of representation was unavoidable. However, this objection seems too quick. While these complaints are, in general, meant to be action guiding, they are not meant in every case to compel behavior changes in the IPR. Some complaints simply require response from the IPR. The IPR may, for instance, need to justify to the represented their decision to not revise their behavior in the way the complaint

Table 5.1 The Complaints of the Represented

Content Complaints

Bad consequences | "The audience responded poorly as a result of what you said / did, and you are to blame."

Misdescription | "That's not what we want." or
"That's not what we said." or
"That's not true of us."

Expressive wrong | "Your statement / action wrongs us by its very occurrence, by virtue of what it expresses."

Procedural Complaints

Wrong channels | "You did not come into the position of IPR in the right way."

Partiality | "Your loyalties are to us, the represented group members, and should not be compromised by attempts to appease outsiders or third parties."

In confidence | "There are some things that you do not say to anyone outside the group. Some statements and actions should be considered privileged—they should arise only within the group, among group members."

Heed the call | "You should willingly undertake the role of IPR for the group."

Failure to consult | "You should have consulted the group when deciding how to represent the group."

Power Complaints

Occlusion (two types) | "You are eclipsing the group. You garner audience attention not for the group's values, interests, or preferences, but only for yourself." or

"You are bringing attention to some group members' values, interests, or preferences at the expense of bringing attention to others'."

Displacement | "By being in the position of IPR for this group, you are displacing someone else who would have been more suitable for the role."

Concession | "Your statements have an anchoring effect on the audience, making it difficult for us to subsequently take more demanding or significantly different positions from those you have previously expressed on our behalf."

Missed opportunity | "You have been conferred the status of IPR for this group. You ought to have used your position to advance our goals and interests in a particular case. You have failed us by not doing so."

---

recommends. Other complaints simply require the IPR's due consideration. Still other complaints—if they do not correspond to a duty the IPR owes to the represented—may require of the IPR nothing at all.

Second, for some of the complaints (like misdescription, expressive-wrong, and the procedural complaints), members of the represented group could reasonably raise the complaint even if the IPR's speech or action (or failure to speak or act) has no effect on or even benefited the represented group. Others (like bad-consequences and the power complaints) are apt only when the IPR's speech or action (or failure to speak or act) brings about or is foreseeably likely to bring about some undesirable outcome for the group.

Third, some complaints will be apt only against voluntary IPRs, while others will have force against both voluntary and conscripted IPRs. For instance, it would be inapt for an audience to level the wrong-channels complaint against a conscripted IPR, who will not have had much say as to the manner of their ascent into the IPR role. But a voluntary IPR, who willingly holds themself forth as speaking or acting for a given group, may be an apt target for this complaint. Conversely, the conscripted IPR may be an especially apt target for the heed-the-call complaint, while it would be redundant to chide a voluntary IPR to heed the call when they already have. Moreover, these complaints will have more force against authorized IPRs than de facto IPRs, because the former (1) are in a standing contractual or quasi-contractual relationship with the represented group and so can be expected to know that the represented group expects something from them, and, presumably, (2) have accepted the authorized IPR role they inhabit (see Chapter 3). (It is possible for a nongroup audience and a represented group to both confer the status of IPR on a party, R, and for the group to authorize R, but for R to be unwitting or unwilling. In such cases, R may be susceptible to many of the complaints enumerated here but will have the ready response to all but the heed-the-call and missed-opportunity complaints that they did not want to be an IPR in the first place.)

By separating out the different sorts of complaints, we can see what is distinctive of the relationship between the IPR and the represented that positions the represented to raise complaints that others may not.

Now consider each complaint genus and its species in turn—their distinctive features, as well as when, how, and why they may be raised.

Content Complaints

Content complaints can reasonably be raised against any speaker or actor, regardless of whether or not that speaker or actor represents a given group. They immediately target the content of a statement or action and only mediately target the speaker or actor. We consider content complaints here primarily as a contrast class. First, whereas content complaints may be raised against representatives among others, both procedural and power complaints are apt only against representatives. Second, whereas content complaints may be raised by represented group members among others, for the most part both procedural and power complaints are apt only when raised by the represented themselves. (There are exceptions to this latter limitation, as when a concerned third party—an ally or activist, say—can reasonably raise the complaint on behalf of the represented group. Even so, the source of the legitimacy of the complaint is the represented group's members, whose interests are communicated by means of the complaint.) Accordingly, we consider just a few cursory characterizations of content complaints (*bad consequences, misdescription, expressive wrong*).

First consider the bad-consequences complaint. A group might reasonably complain that a statement or action led to an undesirable outcome for its members. However, this complaint is apt only if (1) the statement or action is directly causally responsible for the outcome, (2) the speaker or actor could reasonably have foreseen the outcome, and (3) the speaker or actor was morally responsible for the outcome. Direct causal links are not hard to establish if the speaker shouts "Attack!" and the audience does, or the speaker shouts "Fire!" and the audience runs out of the crowded theater, but most cases will be less direct than these. Yet even if a direct causal link can be established, it will often not be reasonable to expect that the speaker or actor could have foreseen the outcome. Finally, even assuming for the sake of argument that a direct causal link can be established and it is reasonable to expect the speaker or actor to anticipate the outcome, it will still often be the case that the speaker is not morally responsible for the outcome borne by the group. Consider an example: Imagine that Ida B. Wells-Barnett's public exposés on lynching in the American South were met with violent backlash against Black southerners undertaken as a direct response to their publication.[8] Imagine further that Wells-Barnett could have anticipated this outcome. Conditions 1 and 2 both obtained. Even so,

Wells-Barnett was not morally responsible for the result; the violent reactive audiences bore full and sole moral responsibility for their violence. In this case, Wells-Barnett might have responded to the complainant by denying that condition 3 had been satisfied: "Your complaint is with the audience, not with me." Only when conditions 1–3 are satisfied does the bad-consequences complaint become apt.

Next, consider the misdescription complaint. Any party might reasonably complain that a speaker has misdescribed a given group. Imagine that a speaker said, "Deep down in the confines of her soul where she hasn't even bothered to look, much less understand, a woman wants a man who exudes masculinity, who remains a steady rock in her current-filled stream of emotions and hormones."[9] Someone might object that the speaker has misdescribed the group *women* by making this claim about its members. A misdescription complaint targets (1) a false or misleading statement intentionally or negligently made by a speaker, who (2) knew or should reasonably have known the statement was errant.[10] A speaker might misdescribe a group by, for instance, attributing to the group's members attitudes they do not have or requests they have not made. One need not be a representative for one's statement to be the apt target of a misdescription complaint, and one need not be a member of the group being misdescribed to raise the complaint. Anyone can engage in mere misdescription, representative and nonrepresentative alike.

Although misdescription complaints apply quite generally, a special subset of them are apt only when a party is in a representative position or another position that lends heightened credibility to their statements as accurate characterizations of the group about which the statements are made. That is, the fact that they are in that position partly explains why their statements are regarded as accurate. Call these *misrepresentation complaints*. Imagine that the speaker of the above statement had antecedently been conferred the status of de facto IPR for women. So positioned, their audience tended to regard their statements about women's values, interests, and preferences to be particularly reliable—that is, the audience conferred credibility on them and relied on their testimony concerning the group. This heightened credibility and testimonial reliance gave them a special further responsibility of due diligence. Whereas misdescription complaints are apt if conditions 1 and 2 are both satisfied, for a misrepresentation complaint to be apt (and the ensuing special responsibility of due diligence to arise) it must further be the case that (3) the speaker is in a position that lends heightened credibility to their statements. Note that parties conscripted into a position that lends heightened credibility to their statements would not be blameworthy for failing to satisfy the special responsibility of due diligence (see Chapter 2).

Finally, consider the expressive-wrong complaint. Any party might reasonably complain that a speaker or actor wrongs a group just by what they express through their statements or actions, even absent bad consequences or misdescriptions. The statement or action, simply by its utterance or performance, wrongs the group by virtue of what it expresses. Consider, for instance, the proliferation of think pieces and listicles that give reasons why we should believe a woman would make a good president.[11] Suppose, not unreasonably, that these articles have no bad outcomes for the group about or in whose defense they are written—that is, women. Suppose further that they do not misdescribe women in any way. Still, a party may quite reasonably complain that the very fact of defending the view that a woman would make a good president wrongs women by its expression—perhaps because these articles appear to presume that this is the sort of thing that requires vigorous defense. Some actions, too, may wrong a group through what they express. For example, the acceptance of certain invitations may expressively wrong a group, as in the example (in Chapter 4) of an IPR for women accepting an invitation to speak before a male supremacist organization.[12] The represented group or third parties may quite reasonably object that, in accepting the invitation, the invitee wrongs the group by expressing an objectionable sort of regard for the inviting organization or event, regardless of the outcome of the ensuing speaking engagement.

Although content complaints are commonly raised against representatives, they are neither unique to nor apt only in contexts of representation. They are complaints apt against parties of any type and aptly raised by parties of any type. The same cannot be said for either procedural or power complaints.

Procedural Complaints

Procedural complaints concern how a party comes to be in the role of IPR, or how they are to comport themself once in the role. The five discussed here are illustrative of the category, not exhaustive: *wrong channels, partiality, in confidence, heed the call*, and *failure to consult*. These complaints, when expressed, reflect complainants' reasonable expectations as to how an IPR ought to enter the role or comport themselves once in the role.

Another Hartian note of caution: These procedural complaints should not be confused with the skeptical challenges concerning procedure discussed in Chapter 4. Those skeptical challenges charge that informal political representation is morally impermissible because it lacks the procedural protections and safeguards available in formal political representation. Quite differently, the procedural complaints at issue here are meant to be directed at particular IPRs because they have either failed to come into the role of IPR in the right way (presupposing that there is some procedure such that they could have come into the role in the right way) or they have failed to follow some procedure required of IPRs once IPRs are in their roles (again, presupposing that there are some such procedures).

First, consider the wrong-channels complaint. A group might reasonably complain that a party enters the role of IPR in the wrong way. For instance, the group may complain that a party wrongs the group when they encourage an audience to confer upon them IPR status by exhibiting apparent authority: acting as though they have received group authorization although they have not. This complaint is exemplified by the following critique leveled by Du Bois against Booker T. Washington: "Then came the new leader. Nearly all the former ones had become leaders by the silent suffrage of their fellows. . . . But Booker T. Washington arose as essentially the leader not of one race but of two,—a compromiser between the South, the North, and the Negro."[13] According to Du Bois, the IPR must arise through what he deems to be the proper channels—namely, through "the silent suffrage of their fellows" (group authorization). And although someone can, of course, become a de facto IPR through audience conferral alone, one may hold oneself forth as an authorized IPR only if group authorization has in fact obtained. So, to the extent that Washington presented himself as a group-authorized IPR for Black Americans before group authorization obtained, he was an apt target for the wrong-channels complaint because he pretended to an authority he did not enjoy. So, too, can we hear an echo of this complaint in Malcolm X's concern about the "so-called Negroes that you listen to on the race problem [who] don't represent any following of Black people."[14]

What would be an appropriate context in which to raise such a complaint? Recall that Montgomery Mayor W. A. Gayle strategically conferred on "three little-known black ministers who were not members" of the Montgomery Improvement Association the status of de facto IPR for Black Montgomerians, negotiating with them although they were not themselves involved in the Montgomery Bus Boycott and announcing in the local press that a bus seating agreement had been reached.[15] Had these three ministers encouraged in Gayle the belief that they were authorized by the group, the wrong-channels complaint would have been apt against them.

The wrong-channels complaint can also be apt in contexts in which group authorization is not the complainant's central concern. For instance, in some cases, it is thought that there is no correct channel. As Barry Malone writes about musician-activists Bono and Bob Geldof, "'For most Africans it's a turnoff when Geldof / Bono are used to present a range of African issues,' Max Bankole Jarrett, a Liberian living in Ethiopia responded to one story last month. 'It perpetuates everything these guys claim to be speaking out against—an Africa that is weak and incapable of picking itself up.'"[16] Per Jarrett, the elevation of Bono and Geldof to the position of de facto IPRs for Africans undermines a need Africans have to be self-representing (see Chapter 6). This complaint is apt against the two musicians insofar as they knowingly or negligently welcomed or otherwise gave the impression that they accepted the position of de facto IPR. If they did not, Bono and Geldof might avail themselves of a defense discussed above: complaint ought to be raised not against them but against the conferring audiences that have positioned them as de facto IPRs for Africans in the first place. (Note that, in addition to a wrong-channels complaint, there is also an expressive-wrong complaint embedded in Jarrett's statement. I shall not pursue that here.)

Second, consider the partiality complaint. In the foregoing quotation from Du Bois, he criticizes Washington for having divided loyalties as "a compromiser between the South, the North, and the Negro."[17] The partiality complaint arises from the view that IPRs owe special favor to those they represent, and that special favor should not be compromised by attending to other parties or their competing interests. A partiality complaint is apt when the IPR fails to show special favor, concern, or regard to those they represent or when the IPR shows willingness to compromise the represented's interests in an effort to appease or satisfy outsiders or third parties.[18]

Third, consider the in-confidence complaint. In some cases, group members expect that certain forms of communication or items of information will be treated as privileged and not expressed to anyone outside the group.

Rigoberta Menchú describes how this norm manifests in her community: "Indians have been very careful not to disclose any details of their communities, and the community does not allow them to talk about Indian things. I too must abide by this. . . . [W]e keep a lot of things to ourselves and the community doesn't like us telling its secrets. This applies to all our customs."[19] Although there may be many different justifications for this expectation, at least in Menchú's case, the commitment to intragroup confidence reflects interests in both defending and preserving the group's culture and customs from outside intervention and preventing a "false impression" by outsiders.[20] These interests, in turn, bespeak a background concern that nongroup audiences would misunderstand or react poorly to the privileged information. Accordingly, a group's members might reasonably complain that an IPR ought not speak to a particular audience in a particular manner or about a particular matter because those are reserved for group members only.

The in-confidence complaint is not a form of the bad-consequences complaint, as it does not depend for its force on the likelihood that a nongroup audience will misunderstand or react poorly to the IPR. Rather, because there is a norm internal to the group against this sort of communication, the wrong-making feature of such communication is to be found in the very act of the communication, independent of possible consequences. That said, an in-confidence complaint and a bad-consequences complaint might be raised in tandem about the same underlying representative action.

Fourth, consider the heed-the-call complaint. A group's members may implore a particular party to heed the call to represent that the party has attempted to reject. For reasons discussed in Chapter 2, this complaint is apt when the group desperately needs an IPR (*need*) and the group's desperate need is for one IPR in particular (*uniqueness*). Even when the complaint is apt, however, the called-upon party need not heed calls that are themselves—or would foreseeably eventuate in circumstances that are—degrading, demeaning, or unduly burdensome for the called-upon party, or that would require the called-upon party to violate their self-respect, although that party may have very good, if not dispositive, reason to heed the call if they are truly uniquely positioned to represent the group in need.

There are two variants of the heed-the-call complaint. First, the called-upon party may already be a conscripted de facto IPR. In this case, the party cannot revoke de facto IPR status conferred on them by the audience. When they reject the represented group's request to heed the call, they do not leave the de facto IPR role but instead reject the group's request to take on the role willingly. Second, the party may instead not yet be an IPR in any sense, but a group calls upon the party to be their own IPR, trying to persuade the called-upon party to willingly serve in the role. In this second case, if the called-upon party rejects the group's request, they may altogether deter the group from conferring de facto IPR status.

Fifth, consider the failure-to-consult complaint. Consulting the represented is valuable because it can improve input from the represented, exhibit recognition respect to the represented, and build trust between representative and represented. The failure-to-consult complaint can be apt when an IPR fails to consult known and accessible members of a represented group. However, an IPR may in some cases quite reasonably respond to this complaint not with a change to their behavior but instead with one of the excusing conditions contemplated in Chapter 4: that consultation was infeasible or not strategic, that they had requisite group authorization, that the represented were not uniquely reliant on them, or that exigency demanded acting before consultation. Furthermore, consultation ex post is more important than consultation ex ante, meaning that this complaint is more likely to be apt when an IPR fails to consult the represented after acting than when an IPR fails to consult beforehand. Finally, as the consultation requirement is extremely flexible and consultation faces many practical limitations, the applicability of this complaint is correspondingly limited.

Power Complaints

Like procedural complaints, power complaints may only reasonably be raised against an IPR and, usually, ought only to be raised by the represented themselves. There may be cases in which it would be appropriate for a concerned third party to raise a power complaint on behalf of the represented group. However, the source of the legitimacy of the complaint would still be the represented themselves. Note further that a complaint raised by a third party on the represented group's behalf may itself be an act of informal representation, itself the possible target of the represented's legitimate complaints. The complaints in this genus are united by a concern with how IPRs exercise their powers.

Contrast power complaints and procedural complaints: A procedural complaint can be raised irrespective of whether the target of the complaint (the IPR who failed to follow protocol) brought about an undesirable outcome for the represented group that issued the complaint. By contrast, a power complaint is apt only in cases in which an IPR's action or inaction brought about or was foreseeably likely to bring about some undesirable outcome for the represented. So, too, are power complaints distinguishable from content complaints. While content complaints may be raised against representative and nonrepresentative parties alike, power complaints are apt only when (1) their target has at least some of the representative powers described in Chapters 2 and 3, and (2) the exercise of those powers plays an essential role in the explanation of why an undesirable outcome occurred. Power complaints concern undesirable outcomes that, but for the complainee's status as an IPR, could not have come about. That the complainee is an IPR is an essential part of the explanation as to how the undesirable outcome occurred. Power complaints include *occlusion, displacement, concession,* and *missed-opportunity* complaints.

First, consider the occlusion complaint. Community recognition is a distinct political good (see Chapter 4). Often, and particularly when the represented are oppressed or marginalized, a key feature of the IPR's work is bringing public attention to the represented group's values, interests, and preferences, and in some cases to their very existence. But if the IPR instead intentionally or negligently (1) garners audience attention for themself rather than for the represented group, or (2) highlights the values, interests, or preferences of some group members at the expense of others, they may find themself subject to the occlusion complaint. Consider the two variants of this complaint.

Rarely will the IPR who has made it "all about themself" have a reasonable defense to the occlusion complaint. Narcissism and self-aggrandizement are vices for which there are no reasonable defenses, and in such cases the IPR's only reasonable response would be to revise their approach. Two caveats to note here: First, IPRs will not always have control over the amount and kind of attention they receive from an audience. IPRs are not criticizable simply for being the recipients of attention that would be better focused on the groups they represent. The occlusion complaint concerns cases in which an IPR intentionally or negligently leads the audience to focus on the IPR rather than the group. Second, there is at least one context in which the occlusion complaint will be inapt even though the IPR intentionally brings an audience's focus to themself—namely, when the IPR does so as a way of deflecting the negative attention of dangerous audiences away from group members. Such an IPR uses themself as a decoy or martyr to protect the group. As Rev. Dr. Martin Luther King Jr. wrote after several bus boycott leaders' homes and churches were bombed, "Then, in the grip of an emotion I could not control, I said, 'Lord, I hope no one will have to die as a result of our struggle for freedom in Montgomery. Certainly I don't want to die. But if anyone has to die, let it be me.'"[21]

A different sort of nuanced treatment is needed when the IPR highlights, prioritizes, or brings public attention to some group members' values, interests, or preferences at the expense of others'. Represented groups are often heterogeneous—their members' values, interests, and preferences diverge and are sometimes mutually incompatible. In some cases, part of what makes the group heterogeneous is that some group members are much worse off than other group members. Recall Barbara Ransby's reflection on the Southern Christian Leadership Conference: "The founders of SCLC were concerned primarily, but not exclusively, about access to the ballot box and dignified treatment in public accommodations. But theirs was a world apart from the lives of destitute sharecroppers and their families who constituted a considerable portion of the South's black population—people who could barely afford the fare to ride on public transportation even after desegregation."[22]

Often, the more vulnerable members of a represented group need informal political representation most immediately. The IPR who prioritizes the needs of the more vulnerable at the expense of the comparatively less vulnerable can quite reasonably appeal to the circumstances of the more vulnerable to justify their prioritization.

Of course, not all cases of intragroup prioritization will involve IPRs prioritizing the interests of the more vulnerable group members.[23] Imagine an IPR who aims to present a particular image of what the represented group is like that covers over or ignores variety within the group, occluding the interests of more vulnerable members of that group.[24] On first glance, it may seem that this sort of occlusion—hiving off the interests of more vulnerable group members in the interest of improving how the broader community receives the group as a whole—is always wrong because it sacrifices consideration of the most vulnerable group members' interests for the benefit of group members who are already better off. And, indeed, in many cases, occluding the interests of the most vulnerable is objectionable. But is it always?

Strategic considerations may in some cases justify the temporary occlusion of the interests of more vulnerable members of oppressed groups. But the occlusion must be strategic and only temporary, with the ultimate aim in view of including everyone, and with a clear plan to move in stages to that goal, on the understanding that each stage makes the next more viable. Of course, long-term strategies that occlude the most vulnerable group members' interests can at least temporarily harm these members and may in addition seem to express indifference to their special plights. Moreover, a planned long-term strategy may not, in the end, work out, and so may simply leave the most vulnerable badly (or even worse) off. So, it is especially important that the most vulnerable group members be not only considered but consulted when such long-term strategies requiring their occlusion are being contemplated.

We can test our intuitions about the propriety of strategic occlusion by thinking about real-world cases in which this sort of political strategy has been employed. A particularly complex case for thinking about strategic occlusion is the decision by well-funded LGBTQIA+ rights groups and impact litigation organizations in particular to prioritize marriage equality over a wide range of other LGBTQIA+ interests and issues.[25] Many members of LGBTQIA+ communities have objected that the prioritization of marriage, an institution which they had no interest in taking advantage of, occluded their interests.[26] And, indeed, the decision to focus on marriage equality before and in some cases to the exclusion of other interests shared by members of the LGBTQIA+ community was an explicit attempt to present community members as "normal" and nonthreatening, having the same mainstream aspirations to live in committed loving relationships as non-LGBTQIA+ people.[27] As William Eskridge has argued, "The recurrence of the same pattern in country after country suggests this paradox: law cannot move unless public opinion moves, but public attitudes can be influenced by changes in the law." He continues, "for gay rights, the impasse suggested by this paradox can be ameliorated or broken if the proponents of reform move step-by-step along a continuum of little reforms. There are a number of pragmatic reasons why such a step-by-step process can break the impasse over a period of time. Step-by-step change permits gradual adjustment of

anti-gay mindsets, slowly empowers gay rights advocates, and can discredit anti-gay arguments." According to Eskridge, "legal incrementalism
can contribute to gay equality" in a number of ways: (1) softening anti-gay
attitudes, (2) emboldening LGBTQIA+ people to come out and organize
politically, thereby garnering greater attention from "politicians and judges
to their arguments for equal legal entitlements," and (3) defanging "the
apocalyptic rhetoric of anti-gay groups" by showing that the "catastrophic
consequences" of which these groups warn ("rampant promiscuity and
public lewdness, predation against children, and erosion of families") simply
will not come to pass.[28] And, indeed, this prioritization / occlusion strategy
has been vindicated in years since insofar as it played a role in one of the
fastest changes in public opinion in American history, "outpac[ing] change
on other social dimensions like race and immigration status."[29] The effect
of prioritizing marriage in fact had demonstrable positive effects on acceptance
of LGBTQIA+ people more generally, opening the door to equal rights for
those who did not aspire to marriage.[30]

Notwithstanding these benefits, there is widespread and persistent concern among many scholars, lawyers, and LGBTQIA+ activists that the de-
prioritized interests, and particularly the interests of greatest concern to
the most vulnerable community members, will never become top priorities and in some cases have been directly negatively impacted by the strategies employed to secure marriage equality.[31] As Yuvraj Joshi points out,

> Prioritizing mainstream agendas does not necessarily drive other is-
> sues into oblivion, but it cannot help but align the catalogue of LGBT
> causes with the flow of capital and headlines. One might expect that
> there is value in addressing the most acceptable issues first—that these
> are a starting point rather than an end point. This raises the obvious
> concern that less acceptable issues might never be addressed. For
> organizations that strive to promote social justice for all but are forced
> to make strategic choices because of limited resources, their decisions
> should not be reduced to crude pragmatism. For example, it may be
> strategically unrealistic and incoherent to seek to adopt a mixture of
> more and less acceptable causes.[32]

As the marriage equality example illustrates, even when the decision to
strategically occlude the interests of a given group's most vulnerable mem-

bers renders benefits to the group as a whole, there are many serious lingering concerns about whether the associated costs ought to be borne primarily by those most vulnerable members. So, when a represented group's most vulnerable members complain that their IPR has occluded their interests to improve the reception and treatment of the group as a whole, that IPR must be able to justify their decision to those most vulnerable members. The IPR's justification must include at least clear articulations of (1) the ultimate goal to be achieved for the group as a whole, (2) the stage-by-stage plan by which the IPR intends to achieve the goal (including a reasonable explanation as to how the various stages are meant to bring about the goal), (3) why the IPR believes strategic occlusion to be required to achieve the goal, and (4) how the IPR plans to ensure that the strategic occlusion is only temporary. Additionally, as stated above, because a group's most vulnerable members stand to lose the most when their interests are occluded, an IPR may not strategically occlude their interests without consulting them. What this sort of consultation would look like in LGBTQIA+ communities is a topic of ongoing discussion, and one that is benefited by both critiques of extant consultation fora and proposals for new fora.[33]

Second, consider the displacement complaint. As George Monbiot writes, "Because Bono is seen by world leaders as the representative of the poor, the poor are not invited to speak."[34] Represented group members sometimes complain that a given party, by being their IPR, displaces others who would be more suitable for the role. This complaint depends for its force on the not unreasonable background assumption that, although there are not de jure limits on how many IPRs a given group can have, there are likely to be some de facto limits on how many IPRs will be given meaningful attention by a broader public. A common version of this complaint is that a nongroup member harms or wrongs the represented group by taking up the position that might otherwise be filled by a group member. Unlike other power complaints, this complaint concerns less how the power in question is being exercised than by whom. It is inapt against unwilling or unwitting conscripted IPRs, who did not aim to be conferred the status of IPR by an audience. These IPRs may respond to the complaint by telling the group to take up their complaint with the conferring audience. For those witting and willing, when the displacement concern is apt, their best course of action may be to make a reasonable effort to convince the conferring audience to revoke its conferral. I return to this complaint in greater detail in Chapter 6.

Third, consider the concession complaint. In Chapter 4, I concluded that an IPR's power to concede does not give us reason to reject the practice of informal political representation altogether. However, a particular IPR may be subject to the complaint that they have conceded too much in a particular case. When the IPR makes a request to an audience on the represented group's behalf, the IPR anchors the audience's expectations.[35] And even when that request is too modest, group members may find—to their disappointment, although not to their surprise—that the audience will not thereafter be moved to give more. As discussed, Du Bois has this very concern about Washington's "Atlanta Compromise" speech. Recall what Washington offers in that speech, conveyed as "the sentiment of the masses of [his] race." He claims that "the agitation of questions of social equality is the extremest folly" and pledges patience and sympathetic help toward white southerners.[36] To this Du Bois raises a concession complaint: "the prevailing public opinion of the land has been but too willing to deliver the solution of a wearisome problem into his hands, and say, 'If that is all you and your race ask, take it.'" In highlighting that white southerners have been "but too willing" to accede to Washington's requests, Du Bois suggests that Black southerners could have gotten more, and so Washington should have asked for more.[37] In anchoring Black southerners' requests, Washington made it difficult for others to successfully take more demanding or significantly different positions.[38]

Fourth, consider the missed-opportunity complaint. Some group members might complain that an IPR has failed to take an opportunity to represent and, in so failing, wronged the group by their omission. This complaint gets its force from the background purpose that the particular representation at issue is meant to serve. When, for instance, an IPR represents an oppressed or marginalized group, that IPR's aim is to work to eradicate the represented group's oppression or marginalization, and so the missed-opportunity complaint is apt when the IPR had but missed a clear opportunity to act in accordance with *eradication*. Yet, that this complaint is apt in a context does not mean the IPR ought to have taken the opportunity. After all, the opportunity may have required the IPR to compromise something of considerable value to them personally: their privacy, their self-respect, their safety, or even their life. Nothing in the foregoing account requires an IPR to lay down their life or compromise their safety, self-respect, or privacy for a group they represent— even a group they represent willingly.

The missed-opportunity complaint is distinct from the heed-the-call complaint. Whereas the heed-the-call complaint concerns a group's contention that a party ought to willingly serve in the position of their IPR, the missed-opportunity complaint concerns particular occasions on which an IPR could have represented the group but did not. It may be that both complaints would be apt regarding the same IPR for the same underlying omission.

Susceptibility and Responsiveness to Complaints

Although IPRs are, like all of us, susceptible to content complaints, these complaints (with the exception of misrepresentation complaints) do not target special features of the relationship between the IPR and those they represent. By contrast, both procedural and power complaints target concerns that arise out of distinctive features of the representative-represented relationship. These two complaint types are legitimate, when they are, because they track the needs and concerns that arise distinctively for the represented—people who, willingly or not, rely on others for the public expression of their values, interests, and preferences. Procedural and power complaints reflect reasonable expectations that represented parties have about how they should be treated by their representatives (*partiality, occlusion, concession*); concerns about whether they can trust their representatives (*in confidence, failure to consult*); their need to be represented (*heed the call, missed opportunity*); and who gets to be in the role of representative (*wrong channels, displacement*). Most of these complaints have greater force against voluntary IPRs than conscripted IPRs.

Even if an IPR is susceptible to the complaints discussed above, there are limits on when and how they must respond even to legitimate complaints. Imagine, for instance, that an IPR has decided to meet with a powerful elected official who has openly espoused bigoted attitudes toward the represented group. The represented group's members reasonably complain that their IPR ought not meet with the official because doing so would express an objectionable sort of regard for the elected official and implicit approbation of the official's bigoted attitudes. To this complaint, the group expects a response. Yet imagine also that the IPR's reasons for negotiating with this official must remain undisclosed, as they are part of a strategy, the disclosure of which would undermine the success of the negotiation.

Although the IPR must be transparent with the represented about the values, aspirations, and goals they plan to pursue on the represented's behalf, they need not disclose strategies the success of which depend on secrecy. The IPR must be able to take leave from being fully answerable to the represented, at least temporarily.

Moreover, an IPR cannot be expected to respond to complaints to such an extent that doing so significantly interferes with their ability to carry out their other life projects and responsibilities. It is not, for instance, a commitment of this account that an IPR must answer every reply they receive on a social media platform. Furthermore, in some cases, a high volume of legitimate complaints from the represented provides evidence that the IPR is not well suited to carry out the responsibilities of the role and so should, as discussed in Chapter 2, disavow the role. An attempt to abdicate is, in its own way, a reasonable response to a high volume of legitimate complaints. And if, as recommended in Chapter 4, the IPR has been cultivating competitors and replacements, there will be someone to step in.

Finally, even when complaints raised against an IPR are legitimate (that is, the complaints themselves are reasonable given how the IPR has acted), the complaints should also be raised for the right reasons. When they are not, the IPR's responsibility to be responsive to that complaint is diminished in one way, although not in another. Imagine that an IPR, by virtue of their social identity or social position, is more likely to be the target of complaints generally. Now imagine that a represented party has raised a complaint against that IPR that is reasonable given how the IPR has acted. But, let us add this: the represented party raised the complaint not because they want the IPR's behavior to change nor because they want the IPR to explain their actions but instead because the represented party wanted to frustrate, distract, or undermine the IPR owing to a prejudicial attitude toward the IPR (for instance, a belief that a particular woman IPR is not a competent IPR *because she is a woman*). In such a case, the IPR's responsibility to that particular complainant is quashed; she does not owe it to the complaining represented party to consider their legitimate complaint, since the complainant raised the complaint for the wrong reasons. The background principle operative here is that an IPR should not be expected to fulfill the position in a way that forces them to compromise their self-respect. Even so, provided that the complaint itself was legitimate in its substance, the IPR ought to consider the legitimate complaint despite its objectionable provenance.

Conclusion

In this chapter, I have both given structure to many legitimate complaints commonly raised against IPRs and provided analyses of and comparisons between these complaints. I have no doubt that there are many further legitimate complaints that will, once identified and characterized, fit well in the provided schema and continue to deepen our understanding of the ongoing deliberative exchange between representative and represented. In Chapter 6, I examine a widely endorsed principle that sometimes undergirds the complaint "You don't speak for us"—namely, the principle that, for a given context of representation, other things being equal, there is good reason to prefer group representation by descriptive representatives to group representation by those who are not descriptive representatives (*nondescriptive representatives*). Call this *the descriptive preference principle*.

6

Descriptive and Nondescriptive Informal Political Representation

A *descriptive representative* is a party who is similar to those they represent in at least one of a variety of respects.[1] The descriptive representative may have characteristics (visible or not), experiences, or backgrounds in common with the represented.[2] Sometimes, the descriptive representative will also be a member of the same social or affinity group as those they represent, although that need not be so.[3] Being a member of the same social or affinity group as another is itself a way of being descriptively similar to another. Call parties who are members of the same social or affinity group as those they represent *member representatives*—a subtype of descriptive representatives.

Defining *descriptive representative* so broadly may seem odd, as the definition is not limited in scope in a way that excludes a wide variety of highly specific, outlandish, or contingent ways of being descriptively similar—for instance, being born at 11:45 a.m. or sitting to the left of another. But the ensuing arguments do not depend on further limiting the scope of descriptive representative at this point. We can simply note that some ways of being descriptively similar tend to be more politically salient than others in societies like ours: being visibly pregnant is a politically salient way of being descriptively similar to another; having a mosquito bite is not. And, in keeping the definition quite general, we avoid prematurely excluding ways of being descriptively similar that may be politically irrelevant in some contexts but not in others. (Think here of left-handedness, which may seem at first glance to be politically irrelevant but is not always—for instance, in contexts that involve "decisions regarding the design of surgical instruments."[4])

Descriptive representation is widely regarded as having much to recommend it, particularly when those who are to be represented have systematically had their shared interests overlooked. We may characterize the favor that descriptive representation enjoys in terms of a principle that, at least on first glance, seems intuitively plausible:

> *Descriptive preference*: For a given context of representation, other things being equal, there is good reason to prefer group representation by descriptive representatives to group representation by those who are not descriptive representatives (*nondescriptive representatives*).

I include "for a given context of representation" for this reason: Without this clause, we may be drawn to cross-context comparisons as to whether a given group, G, has, say, good reason to prefer a nondescriptive formal political representative (FPR) over a descriptive informal political representative (IPR). And it may turn out that G has very good reason to prefer a nondescriptive FPR over a descriptive IPR—not because G would benefit from having a nondescriptive representative but instead because G has overwhelming reason to prefer an FPR, and this overwhelming reason crowds out any competing considerations concerning descriptive similarity. What we want, however, is to consider the difference that descriptive similarity in particular can make to political representation.

The descriptive preference principle strikes many as an attractive principle and seems to be motivated by commitments that, in our everyday lives, we quite reasonably endorse. It captures the spirit, if not the meaning, of the widespread and popular directive, "Let the people speak for themselves!"[5]

Representation theorists and others have defended versions of this principle, particularly as it applies to FPRs, on various grounds.[6] For instance, Jane Mansbridge argues that, at least "in the contexts of group mistrust, uncrystallized interests, a history suggesting inability to rule, and low de facto legitimacy," it can be crucial for representatives and those they represent to have shared experience if they are to meaningfully engage in democratic deliberation.[7] Melissa Williams argues that a group's self-representation (that is, representation by member representatives) is valuable at least because it promotes (1) the expression of perspectives that might not otherwise be given voice, and (2) the self-determination of groups whose interests have been historically downplayed or excluded.[8]

Some of the arguments advanced in favor of the descriptive preference principle are specific to contexts of formal political representation—particularly, representation in legislatures—where a limited number of seats is to be filled by a corresponding number of representatives.[9] Theories of descriptive representation focused on formal political contexts aim to answer questions of the following form: Given that there are one hundred seats (say) available in a given representative institution, what reasons do we have for thinking that at least some of those seats should be filled by descriptive representatives for groups historically excluded from the institution? The answers vary, but all share a background constraint: there are only so many seats, and we want to know what considerations ought to inform the fair distribution of those seats. In particular, we want to know whether one of the considerations ought to be the historical absence of descriptive representatives from certain historically excluded groups.

Informal political representation, however, is different. The legally codified numerical constraints that shape the terms of debate concerning descriptive representatives in FPR contexts are absent from informal political representation, where there can be as many IPRs as you please—indeed, as many as audiences will give the time of day. That there are not strict, legally codified, institutional constraints on how many IPRs there can be does not, however, mean that it will always be preferable for a given group to have more IPRs rather than fewer. As discussed, IPRs fulfill a wide variety of different functions with respect to those they represent.[10] Whether it will be valuable for a group to have many or few IPRs will depend partly on the role the IPR is meant to play for the group. For some representative functions, like voicing otherwise neglected interests or making a group visible to a broader audience, it will often be valuable to have many IPRs speaking before many audiences in the interest of expressing the group's values, interests, and preferences to more audiences more quickly. By contrast, there are other representative functions for which it would be better if there were fewer IPRs. When, for instance, an IPR is negotiating on behalf of those they represent, there is often neither institutional nor practical room for anyone else. In fact, when an IPR is negotiating on behalf of a group, it may even be the case that there is less room, not more, for multiple representatives than in a voting legislature where votes can be allocated.

Other arguments for the descriptive preference principle are generally applicable, if with modification, to both formal and informal political representation. For example, one may advance a general argument that, by virtue of their descriptive similarity to the members of a given group, a descriptive representative is epistemically better situated to represent that group than a nondescriptive representative would be. So, too, may one argue quite generally that a descriptive representative is more likely to be regarded by an audience as a credible source of information about a given group than a nondescriptive representative would be. Or one may argue quite generally that a given group's self-determination will be advanced by having a representative who is a group member but hindered by having a nonmember representative. Finally, one may argue that, even notwithstanding the absence of strict numerical limits on IPRs, there are de facto limits, and nondescriptive IPRs should be unpreferred lest they displace descriptive IPRs. If these arguments are compelling, they may support a general preference for descriptive representatives—one that applies to both FPRs and IPRs.

How compelling should we find these arguments, particularly as applied to IPRs? That is the motivating question for this chapter. I approach the question in two ways. First, I critically examine arguments commonly made in favor of the descriptive preference principle. My methodology is simple: I identify and distinguish several arguments that have been advanced in support of this principle, consider objections to each argument, point out some overlooked implications of each argument, and conclude by stating precisely which of these arguments can plausibly ground a considered preference for descriptive IPRs. It is not my aim to reject or undermine support for the descriptive preference principle, which, as we shall see, has much to be said in its favor. Rather, my aim is to deepen our understanding of the appeal of this principle while putting pressure on us to better understand the hidden commitments and limitations of the principle, particularly in contexts of informal political representation. Nor am I defending or rejecting the particular arguments for the descriptive preference principle that I examine. I make no final recommendation about how to prioritize or adjudicate between these different arguments for the descriptive preference principle. Rather, I am simply trying to provide some clarity, distinguishing between different arguments and examining them separately.

Second, I approach the question in a different manner: I consider whether there are ever compelling reasons to allow for or even to prefer informal political representation by parties who are not descriptive representatives (call these *nondescriptive IPRs*). Note that, although the account of nondescriptive

IPRs provided here may help us better understand and examine the phenomenon of allyship, I am not providing an account or treatment of allyship.[11]

My aim is to clear some ground for new and useful discussions about both the value and dangers of descriptive and nondescriptive representation, particularly in informal contexts.

Arguments for the Descriptive Preference Principle

In this section, I examine five different types of arguments advanced in support of the descriptive preference principle: *understanding* arguments, *credibility* arguments, *trust* arguments, *self-determination* arguments, and *displacement* arguments.

First, consider *understanding* arguments. One especially common argument in favor of the descriptive preference principle is that descriptive representatives will be better at representing a given group by virtue of having a better understanding of the group. Here is a sketch of such an argument:

1. A party who is descriptively similar to the members of a group in some respect is likely to understand that group's members better than those who are not descriptively similar.
2. Other things being equal, parties who understand a given group's members better will be better at the activity of representing that group by virtue of their superior epistemic position.
3. So, other things being equal, a party who is descriptively similar to the members of a group in some respect will be better at the activity of representing that group than those who are not descriptively similar.

The guiding thought here is that descriptive similarity is predicted to bring with it special understanding of the represented group—who its members are, what its members value, what its members want or need, and how best to give voice to each of these. This argument depends, partly, on the claim that, by virtue of one's social location, one may be more likely than others or even uniquely situated to have had certain kinds of experiences.[12] By *social location,* I mean the social role that one has (for instance, mother, student, worker) or the social identity one has (which may be informed by, for instance, one's race, gender, class, disability, language, geographical location, age, or intersections of these). Those experiences, in turn, give one epistemic privilege with respect to particular bodies of knowledge, sets of facts, perspectives, or even ways of knowing. On some views, one can access these epistemic goods only by way of those experiences.[13]

Some thinkers have advanced views even stronger than the one I have sketched above. As Melissa Williams discusses, underlying various historical "'point of view' arguments" in favor of women legislators was "the assumption that women's experience of social life, and hence their perspective on political concerns, was fundamentally different from men's"[14] and, because men are "restricted to the masculine stand-point of observation, to the thought, feelings, and biases of man,"[15] "men simply were not capable of representing women."[16] These point-of-view arguments for women legislators depended on the conviction that men were not epistemically well suited to the task of representing women in legislatures: "Men lack the experience that women have, and consequently women's perceptions, concerns, and needs are inaccessible to them. Clearly one person cannot represent another if the representative does not understand the interests of the represented."[17] Similar arguments for descriptive representation were raised by Black Americans during Reconstruction, like these, published in 1865 editorials in the *New Orleans Tribune,* the first Black daily newspaper in the United States: "'Who can better know our interest than we do? Who is more competent to discern what is good for us than we are?' 'There is no man in the world so perfectly identified with our own interest as to understand it better than we do ourselves.'"[18] The background thought common to these different calls for descriptive representation by women and Black Americans is nicely captured by a statement made at the State Convention of the Colored Men of Alabama on May 4, 1867: "'There is an eloquence in experience which can never be had elsewhere.'"[19]

Underlying these stronger understanding arguments is the background assumption that descriptive similarity is not merely preferable but indeed necessary for ensuring that a group receive adequate substantive representation.[20] That is, for a representative to know what interests a group's members have, that representative must be sufficiently like the members of that group.

In a similar vein, Michael Walzer has argued that oppressed people have special understandings of one another that all of them share and that none but them can readily share: "Their suffering is shared, and they come to know one another in a special way. They have an understanding among themselves . . . which no one outside the circle of oppression can readily share and which no one inside the circle can easily escape."[21]

I will not argue against the claim that there are certain kinds of understanding—particularly emanating from one's experiences—that are at least easier to acquire by virtue of one's social location. I will, however, raise four concerns about understanding arguments for the descriptive preference principle: incommunicable values, interests, preferences, and perspectives; essentialism; occluding difference; and burden. I will then vindicate some understanding arguments in view of these concerns.

Incommunicable Values, Interests, Preferences, and Perspectives. Among the chief aims of group representation is to communicate a given group's values, interests, preferences, and perspectives in fora that would not otherwise include them so that those values, interests, preferences, and perspectives can inform and shape public discussion, lawmaking, and other deliberative processes. Given this aim, understanding arguments favoring the descriptive preference principle are ambiguous between a moderate position that seems quite plausible and a strong position that, at least at first glance, seems to instead cast doubt on the entire enterprise of political representation. The strong position can be vindicated, however, by attending to the many and varied roles that representatives play in the lives of those they represent. (In saying that the strong position can be vindicated, I mean only that the strong position does not in fact cast doubt on the entire enterprise of political representation, not that it should be preferred over the moderate position.) Compare the moderate and strong positions:

1. *The moderate position.* Sometimes one can only come to know another's values, interests, preferences, and perspectives through either first-person access or through the testimony of another who has first-person access. One justification for preferring descriptive representatives, then, is that descriptive representatives are more likely to have first-person access to the values, interests, preferences, and perspectives of the members of the groups they represent and can testify to these before descriptively dissimilar audiences. In such fora, the descriptive representative is meant to be the conduit of these values, interests, preferences, and perspectives from the represented group to a descriptively dissimilar audience.

Others take up a stronger position, as illustrated by the aforementioned point-of-view arguments:

2. *The strong position.* First-person access is required not merely for discovering a given group's members' values, interests, preferences, and perspectives but for having access to these at all. On this view, one's social location or lived experience gives one the ability to access a body of knowledge or type of information that simply cannot be accessed by people who do not share that social location or who lack that lived experience. So no one (descriptively similar representative or otherwise) can effectively communicate the group's members' values, interests, preferences, or perspectives to descriptively dissimilar audiences—not because of any shortcomings in the representative's abilities but because descriptively dissimilar audiences simply cannot understand.[22]

Note that, in what follows, it is not my aim to adjudicate between the moderate and strong positions, and many of the points I make support both. In the rest of this subsection, I take for granted that the moderate position grounds a preference for descriptive representatives and focus only on whether the strong position does too.

Allow that there are bodies of knowledge that have the character described in the strong position. If it turns out that descriptive similarity is the only way to understand what it is like to be a group member or to know what group members want, value, or prefer, then no representative will be able to give voice effectively to a given group's values, interests, preferences, or perspectives to people who are not descriptively similar. The strong position, then, has a surprising result. Instead of grounding an understanding argument for favoring descriptively similar representatives, the strong position grounds a rather radical scope limitation for political representation: People who are not like us cannot come to understand what life is like for us; nor can they come to know what we value, want, or prefer. So, the strong position results in a limitation on the sorts of information a representative can successfully communicate to descriptively dissimilar audiences: the descriptive representative cannot effectively give voice to a group's values, interests, preferences, or perspectives to descriptively dissimilar audiences because those audiences would not be able to understand.

Does the strong position's limitation mean that political representation between parties occupying different social locations or lacking in shared experience is impossible? It does not. After all, giving voice to a group's values, interests, preferences, or perspectives to descriptively dissimilar audiences is only one among many of the activities in which political representatives engage. Even when their audience comprises descriptively dissimilar parties, descriptive representatives can still engage in many of the other activities constitutive of political representation. They may, for instance, credibly communicate to the descriptively dissimilar audience that the audience should not expect to be able to understand the group's values, interests, preferences, and perspectives and so should defer to the descriptive representative and the group's members as to how best to satisfy their values, interests, and preferences (provided, of course, that knowing when and how to defer to others does not require that the audience be able to access the sort of experiential knowledge that the strong position says they cannot).

Other common representative activities are probably also easier (or in some cases only possible) for descriptive representatives of groups whose values, interests, preferences, and perspectives cannot be communicated to descriptively dissimilar audiences. To see this, consider the strong position in the context of two other activities in which representatives commonly engage: negotiation and decision-making. Representatives often negotiate for and make decisions on behalf of the parties they represent. The matters about which the representative will need to negotiate or make decisions are often not known to the representative in advance of their arrival to the negotiation or decision-making forum, meaning that the representative will have to negotiate or decide for the represented group on matters about which the representative has not been able to consult the represented group in advance.[23] And even when the representative has advance notice of the matters on which they will be called to negotiate or decide, many practical difficulties stand in the way of effectively consulting represented groups (see Chapter 4).

Absent group consultation, representatives find themselves in the position of having to imagine or anticipate (as best as they are able) what the represented group's members would want or accept with respect to the negotiation or decision. The representative may have to imagine or anticipate many aspects of the represented group's members' preferences with respect to the negotiation or decision at issue. For instance: What would represented group members consider an optimal outcome? What would they minimally accept? Are there compromises group members would not accept under any circumstance? Is it important that a deal be struck today? Or are the represented willing and able to forgo immediate resolution if a better deal or decision might be reached later on?

There can be little doubt that a particular sort of descriptive similarity— namely, shared social location or sufficiently similar lived experience—can aid a representative enormously in imagining or anticipating the represented's preferences with respect to the negotiation or decision-making at issue. Of course, even representatives who share a social location with or have sufficiently similar lived experience to the represented can fail to imagine or anticipate accurately what the represented would want in a particular context of negotiation or decision-making. Furthermore, as I will discuss in the subsection "Occluding Difference," shared or sufficiently similar lived experience may make a representative overconfident that they are well positioned to imagine or anticipate what the represented would want. Shared experience does not guarantee that a given descriptive representative will imagine or anticipate well in such cases. Even so, it is reasonable to think that representatives who share a social location or sufficiently similar lived experience with those they represent will be better at imagining or anticipating the represented's preferences than would be those representatives who do not share a social location or lived experience with the represented.

We are now in a position to reexamine whether or not the epistemic circumstances described in the strong position in fact ground a considered preference for descriptive representatives. As it turns out, whether the strong position grounds a considered preference for descriptive representatives depends on what sort of representation is needed. When the representative task at hand is to convey information about a represented group's values, interests, preferences, or perspectives to a descriptively dissimilar audience but the information could not be understood by that audience, then we cannot appeal to the anticipated successful communication of that information to the descriptively dissimilar audience as grounds to prefer a descriptive representative. By stipulation, the information cannot be successfully communicated to that audience.[24]

However, the epistemic circumstances described in the strong position do ground a considered preference for representatives who share or have sufficiently similar lived experience over representatives who do not when the representative task at hand is one that requires representatives to anticipate or imagine what the represented would want—common features of negotiation and decision-making. Anticipating or imagining what a represented group's members would want requires (or is at least made significantly easier by) having relevant knowledge or information about the represented group's members' circumstances. Sometimes, as strong position adherents point out, the relevant knowledge or information can be accessed only by way of sharing a social location or having relevantly similar first-person experience. So, if (1) the representative task at hand is likely to require the representative to anticipate or imagine what the represented would want, and (2) as seems quite plausible, anticipating or imagining what the represented would want requires (or is made significantly easier by) having knowledge or information about the represented group's members' values, interests, preferences, or perspectives that is accessible only by way of shared social location or relevantly similar first-person experience, then there is good reason both (3) to favor representatives who share the social location or the relevantly similar first-person experience, and (4) to disfavor representatives who do not share the social location or relevantly similar first-person experience.

Essentialism. Another concern about understanding arguments for descriptive representation is that they can reinforce the "assumption that members of certain groups have an essential identity that all members of that group share and of which no others can partake."[25] Mansbridge suggests that these essentialist costs "can be mitigated by stressing the nonessentialist and contingent reasons for selecting certain groups for descriptive representation."[26] However, Mansbridge's proposal concerns FPR institutions like legislatures, where the aim is to include descriptive representatives in the institutions at least partly to correct for past exclusions.[27] Her "nonessentialist and contingent" justification for favoring descriptive representatives in historically exclusionary FPR institutions does not translate well to the context of informal political representation. IPRs are not vying for limited seats in historically exclusionary institutions. Far from being precluded from being IPRs, members of historically excluded groups are very likely to be conferred the status of IPR for groups of which they are members, as was made clear in the earlier discussions of IPR conscription in Chapters 1 and 2.

We have several reasons to be worried about the essentialist assumptions presupposed by adherents of understanding arguments. First, a common reason why people are conferred the status of IPR for a given group is precisely because they are descriptively similar in some respect to members of that group. When an audience's reason for conferring on a party the status of IPR for a given group is simply that party's descriptive similarity to the members of the group, we have reason to worry that a pernicious form of essentialism is afoot.[28] Second, when an audience regards the members of a represented group as sharing some essential identity, we have reason to worry that the audience regards members of the represented group to be epistemically fun_ble or indistinguishable—an objectionable form of epistemic objectification.[29] Third, the audience may then foist on the objectified party the responsibility to speak for the whole group, thereby conscripting them (see Chapter 2).[30] Fourth, descriptive IPRs are sometimes invited to be interlocutors with the conferring audience only on matters concerning the descriptively similar parties they represent.[31] Such representatives are instrumentalized—treated as mere means to the conferring audience's ends, regarded as knowledgeable concerning only matters that are in some way connected to their descriptive identity.

Occluding Difference. Understanding arguments in favor of descriptive representation also tend to occlude differences of two sorts. First, there is reason to be concerned that, when a given descriptive IPR gives voice to the values, interests, preferences, or perspectives of a represented group's members, an audience may regard that IPR as providing a comprehensive account of what the various members of the represented group want, value, prefer, or think. This is rarely, if ever, the case. However, because this is a general problem for group representation of any sort, I shall set it aside. (In fact, informal political representation fares better on this score than formal political representation, at least insofar as the lack of strict limits on the number of possible IPRs means that, for every combination of values, interests, preferences, or perspectives, there can in theory be a distinct IPR. Whether it is practical to have an IPR for every such combination depends on the representative function the represented group needs filled in a given context.)

Second, there is reason to be concerned that underappreciated differences in social position between descriptive IPRs and those they represent may lead audiences to regard these descriptive representatives as having better epistemic access to the interests of those they represent than they in fact do. As Jennifer Morton argues, the very circumstances that make it more likely for a given party to emerge as a descriptive representative—for instance, education in an elite institution or a high-paying job—can erode the epistemic ties that a given descriptive representative formerly had to the group they now represent.[32] However, those who come into the position of descriptive IPR do not always realize that their epistemic ties have been eroded.[33] Often, descriptive representatives do not regard themselves as any less well suited to speak or act on behalf of those with whom they share some (though now fewer) epistemic ties. As a Black legislator told Richard Fenno in an interview, "When I vote my conscience as a black man, I necessarily represent the black community. I don't have any trouble knowing what the black community thinks or wants."[34]

Burden. The background assumption that descriptive representatives are epistemically better suited to the task of representation than nondescriptive representatives can also unduly burden descriptively similar parties. That is, these epistemic arguments can generate assumptions not merely that descriptively similar representatives are better at representing groups whose members are like them but that, by virtue of their epistemic advantage, they ought to take on the burdens of serving in these representative roles.[35]

Correspondingly, this expectation can leave those who are not descriptively similar with the impression that they either need not or even ought not speak or act for groups whose members are not like them. Moreover, the tendency to expect descriptive representatives to speak or act for groups whose members are like them can reinforce complacency on the part of nondescriptive parties.[36] Nondescriptive parties may feel themselves free or even entitled to remain uninformed—the descriptive representatives will tell them what they need to know about the represented group, so why bother educating themselves?[37]

In sum, while shared experiences, backgrounds, or characteristics may well give parties special insights into what it is like for those with whom these features are shared, the decision to prefer such parties as representatives is not costless. Understanding arguments for the descriptive preference principle can amplify similarity and obscure difference, objectify and instrumentalize both representative and represented, and lead to burdensome expectations for descriptively similar parties. Moreover, arguments regarding understanding are often ambiguous as between (1) providing support for the descriptive preference principle and (2) undermining support for the feasibility of political representation to descriptively dissimilar audiences, generally.

Second, consider *credibility* arguments. Arguments for the descriptive preference principle based on better understanding aim to establish that descriptive representatives are epistemically better suited to represent a given group than nondescriptive representatives would be. By contrast, credibility arguments concern not whether descriptive representatives are in fact epistemically better suited but instead whether they are more likely to be regarded by an audience to be credible sources of information concerning the groups they represent than nondescriptive representatives would be. Credibility arguments have some intuitive appeal, particularly if the audience at issue finds the understanding arguments for the descriptive preference principle compelling—that is, if the audience members themselves believe that descriptive representatives are epistemically better suited to represent than nondescriptive representatives would be.

Consider two objections to credibility arguments for the descriptive preference principle: that descriptive similarity undercuts credibility and that it causes audiences to confer objectionable credibility excess.

Descriptive Similarity Undercuts Credibility. Sometimes, a descriptively similar representative will be regarded by their audience to be less credible than a nondescriptive representative would be. This sort of undercutting regard is particularly likely when the descriptive representative is the target of prejudicial attitudes held by members of the audience before which the descriptive representative speaks or acts. The audience's prejudicial attitudes may lead them to specifically discount representations made by a descriptively similar representative.[38] Imagine, for instance, that a given audience's members believe that women are prone to lying, not suited for serious discussions, or simply not very smart. A descriptive representative for women will have trouble being regarded as credible by the prejudiced audience, no matter how descriptively similar the representative is to the represented group. In this particular case, in fact, the representative's descriptive similarity (being a woman) along with the audience's prejudicial attitude (that women are prone to lying, not suited for serious discussions, or not very smart) seems likely to diminish the credibility the descriptive representative might otherwise have been granted were she not a woman or the audience not prejudiced.[39] I return to this objection in the next section of this chapter, "Nondescriptive Informal Political Representatives," where I discuss contexts of discounting.

<u>Objectionable Credibility Excess.</u> Suppose we grant both (1) that a descriptive representative is in general more likely than a nondescriptive representative to be regarded as a credible source of information about the group they represent, and (2) that this credibility conferral makes it likely that the descriptive representative will be more effective than a nondescriptive representative would have been at representing a given group. Even granting both 1 and 2, we may still quite reasonably be concerned that excessive credibility conferral is objectionable insofar as it harms or wrongs descriptive representatives themselves. As Emmalon Davis has argued, "a speaker who is overly esteemed in her capacity as a knower [can] be harmed qua subject and transmitter of knowledge in virtue of the inflated estimation."[40] This objection is most certainly apt when a party is foisted nonvoluntarily into the role of IPR.[41] You might think that this objection should not get as much purchase when a descriptive representative has intentionally and voluntarily opted into their representative role. People who run for elected office or voluntarily assume the role of IPR in order to represent those with whom they share descriptive similarities probably want audiences to confer credibility on them. Yet even voluntary descriptive representatives probably want to be regarded as credible for the right reasons (because they in fact understand the group's members interests, and not, for example, because they "look as if they would know") and in the right ways (valued as individuals who by virtue of their background or experience have special situated knowledge or even expertise, and not, for example, objectified or instrumentalized as mere tokens of a type).

Third, consider *trust* arguments. Another consideration one may offer in favor of the descriptive preference principle is that those who are represented are more likely to trust those who are like them (who look like them, who share experience with them, who grew up where they did, who suffer the same indignities or oppression), and there is value in that trust. As Mansbridge points out, "Representatives and [represented parties] who share membership in a subordinate group can also forge bonds of trust based specifically on the shared experience of subordination."[42]

Trust between representative and represented is valuable for several reasons. First, relationships of trust between IPRs and represented groups permit IPRs greater discretion concerning how to represent the group independently of consulting group members ex ante (see Chapter 4). Second, relationships of trust make the represented party more likely to communicate with the representative. Communication between representative and represented is valuable for all sorts of reasons—it can enhance deliberation between the representative and the represented (the exchange of information, of course, but also the exchange of reasons, ideas, and complaints) and make it easier for representatives to know what is expected of them. In support of this trust-yields-communication argument, Mansbridge points to Claudine Gay's 1996 research showing that "African American constituents in districts represented by an African American legislator are more likely to contact their representative than African American constituents in districts represented by a White legislator."[43] Third, in addition to the instrumental value of the represented trusting their representative, there may also be final value to this trusting relationship. For all these reasons, one may think that descriptive similarity in representative relationships is to be favored because it promotes trust between the representative and the represented.

Of course, we may worry that representatives will exploit the trust their constituents have in them. This is not, however, a concern about whether descriptive representation makes it easier for represented parties to trust their representatives but a concern about whether representatives ever take advantage of the trust afforded to them by those they represent.

I thus raise no concern about the trust argument for the descriptive preference principle. When descriptive similarity enhances the trust between representative and represented, other things being equal, descriptive representatives should be preferred.

Fourth, consider *self-determination* arguments. In *Where Do We Go from Here: Chaos or Community?* Rev. Dr. Martin Luther King Jr. advances a self-determination argument for Black self-representation:

> There is another mood, however, which represents a large number of Negroes. It is the feeling that Negroes must be their own spokesmen. . . . It is the psychological need for those who have had such a crushed

and bruised history to feel and know that they are men, that they have the organizational ability to map their own strategy and shape their own programs, that they can develop the programs to shape their own destinies, that they can be their own spokesmen. . . . [T]he Negro . . . has become more assertive in his search for identity and group solidarity; he wants to speak for himself.[44]

Similarly, in his 1968 book *Look Out, Whitey! Black Power's Gon' Get Your Mama!* Julius Lester advances a self-determination argument: "This right of self-determination has always been denied. It is a right which blacks have always fought for. The first black newspaper in America published its first edition on May 16, 1827. In its lead editorial, it stated, 'We wish to plead our own cause. Too long have others spoken for us.' That was the newspaper's *raison d'être:* 'We wish to plead our own cause.'"[45]

A widespread and foundational concern for groups whose members have historically been excluded from decision-making is that they be self-determining about what their interests are, how those interests are achieved, and, as expressed by both King and Lester, by whom those interests are given voice.

Self-determination arguments are fundamentally different from both understanding arguments and credibility arguments in at least three respects.

Motivating Concern. The first difference between understanding and credibility arguments, on the one hand, and self-determination arguments, on the other, are the concerns that motivate making such arguments.

Both understanding and credibility arguments assume the epistemic superiority of descriptive representatives. Understanding arguments are grounded in the view that one's shared social location or lived experience gives one better (or exclusive) access to knowledge, information, or understanding about those with whom one shares that social location or lived experience. Credibility arguments are grounded in the prediction that descriptive representatives will be regarded as epistemically better suited to the task of a particular group's representation than nondescriptive representatives will be. Both types of arguments defend the descriptive preference principle on epistemic grounds; they suggest that descriptive representation is to be valued insofar as it will provide epistemic goods to audiences, representatives, or represented parties, whether it is the transmission of better information about the represented group, the conferral of due credibility, or both.

By contrast, self-determination arguments concern a constitutive interest that represented groups have in being represented by a fellow group member. The interest is motivated by the recognition that such groups, whose members have historically been treated or regarded as incapable of self-governance, ought to be able to publicly assert their individual and collective agential capacities to be self-determining, self-ruling, and, to the point of this chapter, able to speak for themselves.

Contingency. Second, the ends at which understanding and credibility arguments aim could, in theory, be achieved by other means. By contrast, the ends at which self-determination arguments aim could not be achieved by other means.

Both understanding and credibility arguments concern the production of epistemic goods—better knowledge, information, or understanding about a group (understanding arguments) or more successful communication of these (credibility arguments). Likewise, these arguments share the epistemic superiority assumption: descriptive representatives are more likely than nondescriptive representatives to produce these epistemic goods. But things could, in theory, be otherwise. Should the strength of the epistemic superiority assumption be called into question (either in a particular context of representation or in general), the strength of the understanding and credibility arguments buttressed by that assumption will also falter. In some contexts, these epistemic goods might be achieved more easily by means of nondescriptive representation. I consider some such contexts in the next section of this chapter, "Nondescriptive Informal Political Representatives."

By contrast, self-determination arguments do not concern the production of some downstream epistemic good to be achieved by means of representation of one sort or another. Rather, self-determination arguments concern a represented group's members' shared aim of being self-determining. And although we could characterize being self-determining as an interest that these group members share, it is not just one interest among many to which any representative could give voice in a relevant public forum. (A nonmember representative could, of course, meaningfully utter the statement "Group *G* wants to be self-determining," but that utterance would not satisfy the represented group's interest in *being* self-determining. In fact, that a represented group has to have its interest in self-determination communicated by a nonmember representative is the very problem to be corrected by self-representation. Recall the Black newspaper declaring, "Too long have others spoken for us.") Being self-determining is an aim that is realized partly through the act of representation itself. As King and Lester point out, part of what it is for a group to be self-determining just *is* for that group to speak for itself rather than to be spoken for by a nonmember—or, in the parlance of this book, to have IPRs who are themselves fellow group members.[46]

Scope. The third difference between understanding and credibility arguments, on the one hand, and self-determination arguments, on the other, are their respective scopes. Generally, understanding and credibility arguments are broader in their scopes than are self-determination arguments: Understanding and credibility arguments are meant to provide support for preferring representatives who are descriptively similar *in some respect* to a given represented group's members, whether those representatives are themselves group members or not. By contrast, self-determination arguments provide strong support specifically for favoring member representation (that is, representation by fellow group members), particularly for groups that have historically been regarded as unable to self-govern, but not necessarily for the broader descriptive preference principle that is at issue.

A fifth type of argument for descriptive representation cites concerns about *displacement* (see Chapter 5). The legitimate complaint that a nonmember representative might displace a member representative is grounded in a concern related to the descriptive preference principle. As mentioned, unlike formal political representation, there are no strict, statutorily codified limits as to how many IPRs a given represented group can have. A represented group can, in theory, have as many IPRs as can receive audience conferral. So, arguments that favor the descriptive preference principle on grounds of proportional presence in legislatures or other formal representative fora are, on first glance, inapposite when considering informal political representation.

Even so, there are informal analogs to the formal concern about proportionality. First, for some representative functions, like negotiating, it is important that the group have one or just a few IPRs so that there is clarity and continuity between the IPR and their negotiating counterpart. Having many independent IPRs contemporaneously negotiating with a single counterpart on behalf of a given group would prove not only cacophonous but probably ineffective in many cases. Second, although difficult to specify, there are de facto limits on how many IPRs for a represented group will be given meaningful attention by the public or by the powerful political actors with whom these representatives sometimes negotiate.[47] When, for instance, President George W. Bush invited Bono to his Texas ranch as a nondescriptive IPR for Africans, Bono may have taken the place of a descriptive IPR.[48] As was discussed in Chapter 5, the concern is "that Bono and others like him have seized the political space which might otherwise have been occupied by the Africans about whom they are talking. Because Bono is seen by world leaders as the representative of the poor, the poor are not invited to speak."[49]

There is something intuitively compelling about the idea that nondescriptive IPRs ought not displace descriptive IPRs. But is this displacement concern, by itself, an independent argument in favor of the descriptive preference principle? It does not seem to be.

By itself, the displacement concern merely expresses the observation that there are practical limits on the number of IPR slots to be filled. What is needed is a normative argument that there is something wrong with nondescriptive IPRs displacing descriptive IPRs. One might argue, for instance, that displacement is objectionable insofar as it undermines the represented group's interest in being regarded as capable of self-governance and self-determination, as when the musician-activists Bono and Bob Geldof, rather than "African voices," are "used to present a range of African issues."[50]

So, the mere fact that nondescriptive IPRs will displace descriptive IPRs does not provide independent support for the descriptive preference principle. However, when displacement (1) is a reasonably foreseeable consequence of the emergence of nondescriptive IPRs, and (2) undermines other political goods to which a given represented group has claim (like self-determination), we ought to view displacement as a reason, though not by itself a dispositive reason, to support the descriptive preference principle in informal contexts.

We may also find an additional interpretation of the objection raised in the above two passages about Bono representing Africans. The objection is not (or not merely) that "Bono and others like him" displace potential descriptive IPRs, but that having Bono speak for Africans at all expresses a paternalistic attitude toward the group that is being represented. Does this mean that Bono ought not to have willingly served as a nondescriptive IPR for Africans in the context at issue or that he is criticizable for having done so? Answering this question depends on knowing some more about the context: The President's Emergency Plan for AIDS Relief (PEPFAR) is credited with saving twenty-five million lives in Africa. Former President Bush, who signed the legislation into law in 2003, has publicly informed Bono that "the truth of the matter is it never would have made it out of Congress had you not been engaged."[51] Bono had the ear of the president, while many others, including Africans who may otherwise have in theory been descriptive IPRs, did not. The fact that Bono had this access and power to influence while others did not (and perhaps could not have, even in Bono's absence) may mean that, even if he was acting paternalistically, he was not acting impermissibly given the known context. Arguably, the Bono / PEPFAR case took place within a context of *restricted access,* where the fact that a nondescriptive IPR but not a descriptive one has access to a given representative forum gives us reason to think that the nondescriptive IPR is permitted to represent in that forum. I turn to contexts of restricted access in the next section and return to considerations of paternalism at the end of Chapter 7.

The aforementioned arguments for the descriptive preference principle are not the only ones available. Instead, each argument separately gives reason to favor descriptive representation in informal political contexts, just as in formal political contexts.

At the same time, many of the arguments in support of descriptive representation have limitations and worrisome implications. Understanding arguments for descriptive representation can essentialize, objectify, and instrumentalize. They can obscure differences between members of the same represented group and burden descriptively similar parties with the expectation that they serve as IPRs. Credibility arguments seem not to hold when prejudicial attitudes lead audiences to discount the statements and actions of the descriptive IPRs before them. Excess credibility may also harm or wrong a descriptive IPR. Self-determination arguments provide strong support not for descriptive representation as such but for member representation in particular. And displacement is cause for concern only when informal political representation by nondescriptive representatives is a concern.

The aim of this first part of the chapter has been to examine these arguments and their implications for how we think about descriptive representation in IPR contexts, not to reject the descriptive preference principle itself. It matters how we argue for descriptive representation; better arguments improve our understanding and communication about why we want the representatives we do. In being able to articulate more clearly and more carefully when and why descriptive IPRs are preferable, we also put ourselves in a better position to consider cases in which this preference is outmatched by competing considerations.

Nondescriptive Informal Political Representatives

Despite the concerns just discussed regarding descriptive representation in informal political contexts, the alternative (*nondescriptive informal political representation*) might be worse, for the reasons just discussed. That a party who shares neither characteristic nor experience nor background with a given group's members speaks or acts for that group can be deeply worrying.

Yet nondescriptive informal political representation may be permissible in contexts in which (1) descriptive informal political representation is unavailable or inadvisable but (2) informal political representation of some sort would benefit the represented group or even be necessary for them to receive some political good.

In the same passage in which King advanced a self-determination argument for Black self-representation, he also discussed a context he viewed as one in which nondescriptive IPRs had formerly been appropriate:

> When the Negro was completely an underdog, he needed white spokesmen. Liberals played their parts in this period exceedingly well. In assault after assault, they led the intellectual revolt against racism, and took the initiative in founding the civil rights organizations. But now that the Negro has rejected his role as the underdog, he has become more assertive in his search for identity and group solidarity; he wants to speak for himself. This means that white liberals must be prepared to accept a transformation of their role. Whereas it was once a primary and spokesman role, it must now become a secondary and supportive role.[52]

Here, King supports the idea that nondescriptive IPRs can have a role to play in the public communication of the values, interests, preferences, and perspectives of a group's members when it would be difficult for descriptive IPRs to play this role effectively. He makes clear that the permissibility of nondescriptive informal political representation is context sensitive: white IPRs for Black Americans were appropriate when and because it was exceedingly costly or difficult for Black IPRs to serve in these roles. When the political context shifts and descriptive informal political representation becomes more feasible and less costly, both the need for and desirability of nondescriptive IPRs diminishes.

If the permissibility of nondescriptive informal political representation is context sensitive, then we must ask: Which contexts?

Consider five contexts in which there are compelling, though not necessarily dispositive, reasons to allow for nondescriptive IPRs: (1) in fora from which descriptive IPRs are excluded (*restricted access*), (2) when it would be objectionably burdensome for descriptive IPRs to represent (*burden*), (3) when it is reasonably foreseeable that a given audience is likely to regard a descriptive IPR to be less credible than a nondescriptive IPR as a source of information about a represented group (*discounting*), (4) when a represented group's members explicitly request representation by nondescriptive IPRs (*explicit request*), and (5) when serving as descriptive IPRs would require representatives to publicly disclose their relationship to or membership in the represented group in a manner that would render them vulnerable to serious harm (*risk of exposure*).

First, consider *restricted access*. Some fora are inaccessible to members of a given group or parties who are descriptively similar in some respect precisely because of the identity, social position, or descriptive similarity they have in common. Sometimes such fora are even intentionally designed to exclude those group members or descriptively similar parties, either as individuals or as members of the excluded group. But even in such fora, and perhaps especially in such fora, group members would benefit from the expression of their values, interests, preferences, and perspectives. As we saw in the Bono / PEPFAR example, in such cases, unless a nondescriptive IPR speaks the group's piece, the group will get no hearing in these inaccessible fora.

Women, for instance, do not have access to the men's locker rooms of the world, where their bodies and sexual habits are the subjects of disparagement, defamation, and worse (or so I am told). In a 2016 *Washington Post* op-ed titled "Many Men Talk Like Donald Trump in Private. And Only Other Men Can Stop Them," Shaun R. Harper writes, "Truth is, many men objectify women and say outrageously offensive things about their breasts, butts and other body parts in spaces we occupy with each other." Locker room talk, one imagines, grew out of the exclusionary nature of the forum—women are denigrated in locker rooms at least in part because it is a forum where the costs of denigration are lower than they might be in less restricted fora and because the likelihood of rebuke is lower. Surely women have interests in someone raising objections on their behalf. And, if women are to have someone speak for them in these spaces, it cannot be a woman—not because women lack the ability to speak for themselves simpliciter, but because they cannot be in the relevant fora to do so. As Harper writes,

> When men fail to challenge other men on troubling things they say about and do to women, we contribute to cultures that excuse sexual harassment, assault and other forms of gender violence. I know from my research that confronting male peers is difficult for a 14-year-old high school student-athlete who desperately wants his teammates to like and accept him. He needs his coach to step up and disrupt locker room banter. . . . But too many adult men fall short of this ourselves, especially when we are in 'men's only' spaces with guys whom we need to affirm our masculinities.[53]

If you find yourself generally compelled by the descriptive preference principle, think of this as your locker room caveat. This caveat, however, is just one example. Many are the places where we want our values, interests, preferences, and perspectives raised on our behalf, though we ourselves are not welcome.[54] Sometimes, the restricted forum is just a private home, as has been made salient by recent conversations about the responsibilities that white people have to talk to their white family members and white friends about racism and anti-Blackness experienced by Black Americans.[55] When white people have these conversations with their white friends and family members, they are giving voice to the values, interests, preferences, and perspectives of Black Americans who are not in the room. Sometimes these discussions will simply be instances of speaking about group members' experiences. However, instances of speaking about can and often do evolve into instances of *speaking for* (see Chapter 1).

Second, consider *burden*. It can be burdensome to have to speak or act for another—and especially burdensome if one is a member of a group disproportionately likely to be subject to audiences' expectations that the group have a descriptive representative.[56] The emotional and psychological harms of these expectations are numerous and varied.[57] Nor is this communicative labor evenly distributed among the population—it falls disproportionately on the shoulders of members of subordinated groups.[58] Worse yet, the communicative labor, even if performed, seems often to have little effect on the perspectives of dominant audience members. Reni Eddo-Lodge describes a scene in *The Color of Fear* by Lee Mun Wah: "I saw people of colour break down in tears as they struggled to convince a defiant white man that his words were enforcing and perpetuating a white racist standard on them. All the while he stared obliviously, completely confused by this pain, at best trivialising it, at worst ridiculing it." Eddo-Lodge adds her own experience of speaking with white people about race: "Their intent is often not to listen or learn, but to exert their power, to prove me wrong, to emotionally drain me, and to rebalance the status quo."[59] Michelle T. describes a similar experience: "As a WOC [woman of color], I've been explaining white privilege and white supremacy for far too long, and for free, especially online, and to basically no avail."[60] Both Eddo-Lodge and Michelle T. then express an intention to go on communicative strike. Eddo-Lodge writes, "I'm not talking to white people about race unless I absolutely have to. . . . I'm no longer dealing with people who don't want to hear it, wish to ridicule it and, frankly, don't deserve it."[61] Michelle T. writes, "I'm going on strike for my emotional labor henceforth and maybe forever."[62]

At the same time, oppressed and marginalized groups need their values, interests, preferences, and perspectives to be given voice in a wide variety of fora. So, it can be valuable to have nondescriptive IPRs take on some of this communicative labor, particularly in contexts where expectations of descriptive representation bring with them potential pernicious harms for a member of the group itself. Groups like White Nonsense Roundup (WNR) enlist white volunteers to "respond to racist trolls online at the request of people of color."[63] Michelle T. writes this of her decision to enlist WNR: "After a white dude follower commented something racist on a post I wrote about white supremacy, I tagged White Nonsense Roundup, and a volunteer rounded him up with incisive, straightforward, brutal truth. It was exactly what I wanted to say, but did not have the emotional energy to do so."[64]

Nondescriptive informal political representation may be permissible in contexts in which descriptive IPRs from subordinated groups face potential audiences of dominant group members who would not treat them well. Nondescriptive IPRs can help redistribute communicative labor from those who have historically been burdened with the demand that they perform it.

Third, consider *explicit request*. WNR uses an explicit request model—a white volunteer provides assistance only when WNR is tagged in a social media post by a person of color.[65] That nondescriptive informal political representation may be permissible in contexts of explicit request does not mean, however, that it is permissible any time there is an explicit request from a member of the group to be represented. There may be complications—for instance, other members of the same group may object to the explicit request, either on the general grounds that they do not want a nondescriptive representative or on the specific grounds that they do not want *this* party to be their nondescriptive representative. However, at least in those rare cases in which there is widespread (or even unanimous) agreement among the members of the represented group concerning the appropriateness of the explicit request, other things being equal, nondescriptive informal political representation by the explicitly requested party is permissible.

Fourth, consider *discounting*. As discussed in the previous section, "Arguments for the Descriptive Preference Principle," in some cases, audiences will either lower their credence in or outright reject the statements or actions of a descriptive IPR precisely because of the IPR's descriptive similarity to those they represent.[66] Audiences may engage in this kind of discounting for a variety of reasons, including prejudicial biases against a descriptive IPR or the view that descriptive IPRs, by virtue of their similarity to the represented group's members, stand to gain from representing the group's members in a particular way. Chenoa Alamu describes the phenomenon this way: "Honestly and unfortunately there are many white people who won't listen to a black person about race. . . . We are deemed whiny, complaining, we should have gotten over it by now, pull ourselves up by our bootstraps."[67] Autism scholar and activist M. Remi Yergeau describes the phenomenon this way:

> Something I tend to see explicitly—whether it is in a research setting, a clinic, a social skills group, or even in a book club that consists of autistic people—is that autistic people are less likely to be believed because they are perceived as being unable to intuit what other non-autistic people are thinking. If I disagree with a parent or colleague, I am the one who is read as having failure typically in these exchanges. Somehow having this diagnosis makes me less believable and it is intricately connected to cultural narratives around empathy. It is hard to know what to do with that. Like other forms of bias, it can be hard to pinpoint and people are less likely to see it as bias.[68]

Such audiences are, of course, criticizable for their errant discounting.[69] Even so, if it is predictable that an audience will discount in ways that forestall a descriptive IPR's effectiveness, that is a reason (though not necessarily a dispositive reason) to allow for IPRs immune to discounting. More precisely: if in some context (1) it is reasonably foreseeable that an audience will discount the representative statements or actions of a descriptive IPR, and (2) the inability to represent effectively will have reasonably foreseeable and serious consequences for the represented group, then in that context the represented group has a strategic reason to prefer nondescriptive IPRs. Alamu's reflection continues, "We need more white people to speak out, to hold other white people accountable to their innate racism. . . . [I]f a white person calls it out, tells it like it is, then a white person is more likely to listen."[70] In recounting her interaction with the "white dude follower," Michelle T. also expressed a version of this discounting justification for nondescriptive IPRs: "Interestingly enough, he did not have a retort to this white woman's words, whereas in the past, he continued to push back and completely reject my points, even though they're the same as hers. When white people speak to other white people to educate them and call them out AND in, it is more effective than if I, a WOC, does so. Sad, but true. This is why we need true allies, not just performative ones."[71]

Represented group members may thus prefer nondescriptive IPRs in contexts in which the group's members anticipate that the nondescriptive IPR will be immune to the discounting to which the descriptive IPR would foreseeably be subjected.

One may object: that an audience will foreseeably discount a descriptive IPR in some context does not counsel in favor of preferring nondescriptive IPRs in those contexts; to do so would be tantamount to capitulating to the objectionable epistemic shortcomings of the audience.

But there are at least two reasons to think that, when descriptive IPR discounting is reasonably foreseeable, nondescriptive IPRs should be permitted or even preferred. First, among the purposes of informal political representation—a purpose it shares with political representation generally—is effective communication of the values, interests, preferences, and perspectives of a given represented group. By stipulation, contexts in which descriptive IPR discounting is reasonably foreseeable are contexts in which the representation of a given group is likely to be less effective than it might otherwise have been. So, foreseeable representative ineffectiveness is a reason to allow nondescriptive IPRs to represent before discounting audiences. To allow this is not to forgive discounting audiences their epistemic or moral failings, but to attempt effective representative communication under markedly nonideal conditions. Second, descriptive IPRs should not be forced to face the harms and wrongs that come along with being subjected to foreseeably discounting audiences. It would be burdensome to expect them to do so. So, in some contexts, discounting and burden justifications converge: nondescriptive IPRs ought to speak or act before discounting audiences so that descriptive IPRs are not forced to choose between subjecting themselves to a discounting audience or leaving a group in need with no representative at all.

Yet, these reasons to permit or prefer nondescriptive IPRs in contexts of foreseeable discounting—effectiveness and burdensomeness—are not dispositive. Even when an audience's foreseeable discounting makes it the case that a nondescriptive IPR would be more effective and less burdened than a descriptive IPR, that does not settle the matter as to whether a nondescriptive IPR should be preferred or even permitted. Sometimes, countervailing considerations counsel against preferring or even permitting nondescriptive IPRs, even when nondescriptive IPRs would be less burdened and more effective at communicating on the represented group's members behalf than descriptive IPRs would be. To see this, consider a case in which audiences' discounting is foreseeable, burdensome, and disruptive of IPR effectiveness, but in which it seems not only ill advised but in fact objectionable to suggest that nondescriptive IPRs should be preferred or perhaps even permitted.

As Yergeau argues in *Authoring Autism: On Rhetoric and Neurological Queerness*, autistic people face widespread and pervasive discounting. The discounting they face is especially pernicious because it concerns not some one aspect of autistic people's interactions with nonautistic audiences but is instead in many cases global. Discussing their own experience, Yergeau reports that many people, including their own "colleagues and therapists," have told them "that autism precludes me from being rhetorical." Yergeau's statements generally are discounted on the ground that they are autistic: "Anything I claim here is held suspect on the basis of my very being— because . . . I lack a theory of my mind and the minds of others, anything I say is inherently unreliable, idiosyncratic, and special. My rhetorical moves are not rhetorical moves, but are rather symptoms of a problemed and involuntary body. . . . I have symptoms, and they [nonautistic people] have rhetoric."[72]

As Yergeau explains, the discounting autistic people face often results from the disclosure of an autistic spectrum disorder diagnosis, which may "precipitate a negative judgement of capacity involving permanent loss of credibility."[73] This loss of credibility can take a variety of forms. In some cases, the loss of credibility is specific to the topic of autism itself: "Autistic people are figured as lacking authority to speak on or from within autism." In other cases, the loss of credibility is more general: "autistics are considered liars" or "inherently unreliable." In still other cases, nonspeaking autistic people and those who do "not speak, read, write, type, point, or sign" may be completely communicatively excluded or disregarded.[74]

Furthermore, the widespread and pervasive discounting of autistic people's communications is influenced and reinforced by people who work closely with autistic people and devote their professional lives to understanding autism: researchers, clinicians, and special education curriculum developers. Many clinicians regard autistic people as "nonsymbolic and thereby non-rhetorical." Researchers "proclaim autistic speech acts and gestures [are] behaviors lacking in meaning, purpose, or social value."[75] For example, cognitive neuroscientist Francesca Happé writes: "Without mentalizing ability, the transparency of intentions that allows humans to use language in a truly flexible way is not open to autistic communicators."[76]

Yet, as Yergeau emphasizes, matters are even more complicated. When and insofar as autistic people are regarded as capable of speaking knowledgeably and believably about autism, their very identity as autistic is put into question: "Clinical constructions of autism frequently position expertise and self-knowledge as antithetical to autism itself" so that, for instance, "[t]he ability to say, 'I have autism' . . . is intuited as evidence that one does not have autism—or, at least, not real or severe autism." Yergeau reports that "part of the autistic experience is not being believed" and, in particular, that "diagnostic denials from laypersons and strangers are incredibly common." They recall a woman on a bus denying that Yergeau is autistic: "No . . . You have the Asperburgers."[77]

Reflecting on the bind faced by many autistic people—regarded as "too autistic to make claims about autism" or "not autistic enough to make claims about autism," or both—Yergeau describes the communicative situation of autistic people this way: "forever suspend[ed] . . . in places from which they cannot argue, cannot assert, cannot intend."[78]

In contexts of discounting like those described by Yergeau—where the members of the represented group are prejudicially regarded as incapable of speaking for themselves—the suggestion that nondescriptive IPRs should be permitted or preferred is especially fraught. Even the mere fact that the represented group has a nondescriptive IPR may reinforce the very prejudicial attitudes that gave rise to the audience's discounting in the first place. That is, the discounting audience may regard the fact that autistic people have a nondescriptive IPR as evidence that autistic people generally are, by virtue of their autism, unable to give voice to their own values, interests, preferences, and perspectives. So, even if, by virtue of their immunity to discounting, a nondescriptive IPR for autistic people would be more effective than a descriptive IPR in a particular instance and would ease the burdens of representation otherwise faced by a descriptive IPR, the fact that the group has a nondescriptive IPR may itself reinforce the prejudicial attitudes that gave rise to the audience's discounting in the first place.

An audience's discounting can foreseeably stymie a descriptive IPR's effectiveness, subject them to unjust communicative burdens, and have reasonably foreseeable and serious consequences for the represented group. These considerations jointly provide strategic reasons for represented groups to prefer nondescriptive IPRs in some contexts. But these strategic reasons are not dispositive. There will often be countervailing considerations that will count against nondescriptive informal political representation. Here, I have considered just one: the entrenchment of the very prejudicial attitudes that gave rise to the discounting in the first place.

Fifth, consider *risks of exposure*. Yet another context in which nondescriptive IPRs can be crucial are contexts in which it would be risky for any descriptively similar party to reveal themself to be either descriptively similar to or a member of the represented group. Such contexts are not difficult to imagine: discovered undocumented Americans face deportation, scholars in repressive societies face political imprisonment, registered sex offenders face widespread social stigmatization. And yet, members of these groups benefit from the public expression of their values, interests, preferences, and perspectives. In such contexts, nondescriptive IPRs can give voice to imperiled groups' concerns free from fear of the harms that would befall an exposed descriptive representative. Nondescriptive parties may even owe it to such groups' members to do so.[79]

In each of the aforementioned contexts—restricted access, burden, explicit request, discounting, and risk of exposure—there is some reason to think that nondescriptive IPRs are appropriate alternatives to descriptive IPRs. Are there commonalities among these contexts that allow us to have a principled understanding of when there is reason to allow nondescriptive IPRs or even to favor them over descriptive IPRs?

In contexts of restricted access and discounting, descriptive IPRs are stymied in their efforts to provide effective representation. In contexts of restricted access, this is so because descriptive IPRs lack the ability to enter fora where representation would take place. In contexts of discounting, although descriptive IPRs are not barred from the forum for representation or from engaging in representation, they are precluded from engaging in meaningful or effective representation because their representative statements or actions are simply not taken up or treated as serious by relevant audiences.

By contrast, in contexts of burden and risk of exposure, descriptive IPRs are not precluded from providing effective representation. They may have access to the relevant fora, and their representation may well be taken up and treated as serious by relevant audiences. Rather, what is common to such contexts is that the costs descriptive IPRs will be forced to pay in order to represent will often be so high that no one could be expected to pay them.

These descriptive IPRs face difficult choices between, on the one hand, providing effective representation and, on the other, protecting themselves from foreseeable and significant harm.

Contexts of explicit request stand apart—these are contexts in which the represented group itself, or some of its members, explicitly requests representation by nondescriptive parties. The reasons a represented group might engage in explicit request vary, but may emanate from concerns contemplated in the other four contexts: that a descriptive IPR would either be precluded from providing them effective representation (*restricted access, discounting*) or could only represent under conditions that would be too costly for them to reasonably be asked to bear (*burden, risk of exposure*).

The arguments advanced in this section jointly support the modest claim that there are contexts in which there is reason to allow for or perhaps even to prefer nondescriptive IPRs to represent certain groups, provided that (1) the groups need or would benefit from informal political representation but (2) descriptive informal political representation is unavailable or inadvisable. Note how modest this claim is: There is no presumption in favor of nondescriptive representation in the five contexts considered. Nor have I argued that the reasons in favor of nondescriptive informal political representation in these contexts are dispositive. These five contexts should be considered occasion to open, not close, the inquiry as to whether a particular nondescriptive IPR ought to be permitted or preferred in a particular case. Whether a nondescriptive IPR ought to be permitted or preferred is a context-sensitive matter, and must be tested against each of the arguments advanced in favor of descriptive representation. A salient point of contact between the arguments favoring descriptive representation and those concerning nondescriptive representation is the displacement concern: Even if a nondescriptive IPR may otherwise be preferable in a particular case, they may displace a descriptive IPR, particularly in settings like negotiations where, practically speaking, there is space for only one or a few IPRs. In such settings, one wants a representative who is not merely attuned to the group's stated concerns but who can imagine and anticipate new considerations (*understanding*), who is regarded as knowledgeable about the group (*credibility*), whom group members trust (*trust*). These aims seem to strongly favor descriptive representation in settings where there can only be one IPR; any nondescriptive party who takes up the role, however much they may offer the group, will still be displacing a descriptive IPR more likely to advance each of these aims. Moreover, as evidenced by several paradigmatic examples of informal political representation contemplated throughout this book—Rev. Dr. Martin Luther King Jr., Greta Thunberg, Booker T. Washington, and Malala Yousafzai—IPRs tend to become entrenched in their roles. Because that is so, allowing for a nondescriptive IPR is often not a mere passing, at-a-time consideration but can have repercussions for a group for some time after, as lament over Bono's ongoing nondescriptive IPR role illustrates.

Who May Be a Nondescriptive Informal Political Representative?

Even when there is good reason to permit or prefer nondescriptive informal political representation in a particular case, that does not mean that just any nondescriptive IPR will do. There will be further constraints on who should or even who may be a nondescriptive IPR for a given group—some substantive, others procedural; some context sensitive, others context independent. Some of these constraints follow from arguments advanced elsewhere in this book. Others follow from more general moral commitments concerning how we ought and ought not relate to one another. Developing a comprehensive account of who may and may not be nondescriptive IPRs for different groups in different contexts is a book-length undertaking in its own right; I will not offer such an account here. Moreover, because groups vary widely with respect to what representative needs they have, it may in any case be more useful to think about what reasons particular groups have to permit or prefer nondescriptive IPRs than to attempt to provide a one-size-fits-all account of these reasons. Still, it will be helpful to examine just one consideration that may help us to navigate the boundaries of nondescriptive representation.

Consider, as an example, a procedural constraint on who can become a nondescriptive IPR for a given group: widespread group disavowal. Widespread group disavowal should, in general, be viewed as a procedural constraint on who may become (or remain) an IPR for a given represented group. As discussed, both group authorization and group disavowal clarify how the members of a given represented group themselves understand their relationships to a given or would-be IPR (see Chapters 3 and 5).

Although there will rarely, if ever, be perfect accord among group members concerning who ought to be their IPR—and this productive contestation is valuable, as it can allow for the emergence of several IPRs who themselves must vie for support from the represented group's members—in some cases there will be apparent widespread disavowal of a given nondescriptive party. Widespread group disavowal of a given nondescriptive party should, in general, be regarded as giving both the nondescriptive party and any conferring audiences reasons to not put the nondescriptive party in the position of IPR in the first place and otherwise to revoke IPR status from the nondescriptive party if they already have it. What does this mean, concretely?

For the nondescriptive parties themselves: When a given nondescriptive party faces apparent widespread disavowal from the represented group, that nondescriptive party should not attempt to create conditions that make audience conferral more likely (see Chapter 1). If instead they have already received widespread audience conferral, then, generally, the nondescriptive IPR ought to take steps to disavow the role (see Chapter 1). Recall, however, that conscripted IPRs have grounds to reasonably reject the ascription of duties to disavow (see Chapter 2).

For audiences: When a given nondescriptive party is widely disavowed by a given group, an audience ought not confer IPR status on that party (see Chapter 2). Audiences that have already conferred IPR status on the party ought to revoke conferral in view of the widespread group disavowal.

These responsibilities are not distinctive to nondescriptive parties but generalize to any IPR or would-be IPR who receives widespread group disavowal. But the responsibility for the would-be or already representative party to disavow the role and for the audience to revoke the role is even stronger when the party is not descriptively similar for the very reasons that create a general background presumption against nondescriptive informal political representation.

Return to an earlier example. Imagine that there is some compelling reason to have a nondescriptive IPR speak for autistic people in a particular context. Even if that is so, there is reason to think that the advocacy organization Autism Speaks would be an especially contentious choice for the role, because so many members of such a wide variety of autistic communities have raised vigorous and constant objections against the organization. Autism Speaks faces widespread, persistent, and vociferous dissent for many of its advocacy decisions across several decades, including "portray[ing] autism as a silent and sinister killer" that tears families apart, portraying autism as equivalent to or worse than death, prioritizing research on and advocacy for seeking a cure for autism over other aims, and evidencing "a long and continued pattern of exclusion of Autistic voices from its work on autism."[80] The mere proliferation of opinion pieces asserting that Autism Speaks does not speak for, or indeed silences, autistic people may itself be adequate grounds to assume that the organization is the target of widespread group disavowal and for that reason would be an especially unfitting nondescriptive IPR for autistic people.[81]

Conclusion

In this chapter, I have provided preliminary answers to two questions essential to understanding the place of the descriptive preference principle in informal political representation.

First, I considered five arguments often advanced in favor of the descriptive preference principle that seem to apply, if with modification, to both formal and informal political representation: understanding, credibility, trust, self-determination, and displacement arguments. I cautioned that understanding arguments sometimes bring with them essentializing assumptions about the relationships between descriptive representatives and those they represent and that these assumptions can, in turn, objectify and instrumentalize the represented group members while both harming and burdening the descriptive representatives. I argued that credibility arguments lose their strength when audiences' prejudicial attitudes cause them either to discount or accord excessive credibility to descriptive representatives. I raised no concerns about trust arguments, concluding that when descriptive similarity enhances the trust between representative and represented, other things being equal, descriptive representatives should be preferred to nondescriptive representatives. I concluded that self-determination arguments clearly favor preferring member representation over nonmember representation, particularly for groups historically regarded as incapable of self-governance. However, I also pointed out that self-determination arguments do not support the broader claim that such groups need descriptive representatives. Rather, these arguments support the narrower claim that such groups ought to be able to select from among their own members. Finally, I considered displacement to be not a normative argument in favor of the descriptive preference principle in its own right, but instead an observation that can provide support for such a normative argument.

Second, I considered five contexts in which groups might have reasons to permit or prefer nondescriptive IPRs—restricted access, burden, explicit request, discounting, risk of exposure—and offered some reasons to think so.

A recurring theme in the above discussion is that being in the position of IPR can be burdensome, costly, harmful, or even dangerous. IPR is not a position that is always undertaken voluntarily (see Chapters 1 and 2).[82] When not undertaken voluntarily, the position of IPR is often foisted on members of subordinated groups by audiences comprising members of dominant groups. This discussion provides a framework for thinking about meaningful and permissible alternatives to the burdensome forms of descriptive informal political representation. Beyond identifying contexts that might allow for nondescriptive informal political representation, we must also consider the special responsibilities nondescriptive IPRs have to the groups for which they come to speak or act. In this book's Conclusion, I enumerate questions about nondescriptive IPRs' duties that would benefit from further exploration.

This chapter has treated the question: What difference does it make that my IPR is like me in a particular, politically salient respect? In Chapter 7, I turn to a complementary question: What difference does it make that my IPR is unlike me in a particular, politically salient respect—namely, in being an expert in some respect in which I am not?

7

Expertise and Representative Deference

On April 28, 2021, *Nature* published an editorial, "To Remedy Health Disparities, More Scientists Must 'Get Political,'" which observes that "the [COVID-19] pandemic has given scientists a more prominent voice in society" and advises scientists to use their newfound "voice in decision-making . . . to advocate for policies that would improve social determinants of better health, such as living wages, employment protections and high-quality educational opportunities." The editorial recommends not merely that scientists should turn their sights to social issues but that they should give voice to the interests of the worst off. It goes on to point out that academic scientists are better positioned to do this than state and county public health officials precisely because academic scientists are not hired by elected politicians and so their "budgets and jurisdictions" are not "determined by those politicians."[1] Freed from fear of reprisal by elected politicians, these scientists may give voice to the interests of disproportionately impacted communities. When scientists undertake these public-facing advocacy roles, they are sometimes treated by audiences to be not merely speaking about matters affecting the worst off but, further, to be speaking for the worst off. This has been the case for Dr. Mona Hanna-Attisha, whose research and public speaking on the drinking water crisis in Flint, Michigan, at first brought her to national attention as an expert on the matter, then later earned her the designation "spokeswoman for a tragedy."[2]

When informal political representatives (IPRs) are effective, it is often precisely because audiences regard them as knowledgeable, credible, trustworthy, even expert with respect to the represented or some set of issues with special bearing on the represented's interests. (The *Nature* editorial suggests that scientists would make valuable political representatives precisely because of their "research expertise."[3]) At the same time, represented groups whose members are marginalized or oppressed often come to rely on their IPRs for any political influence they hope to have, which can lead to relationships between IPRs and the represented that are objectionably inegalitarian (see Chapter 4). To ameliorate the inequality found in such relationships, one may argue that IPRs for oppressed or marginalized groups ought always to defer to that group and its members when deciding how to represent the group. Call this *the representative deference principle.*

To say that expert IPRs ought always to defer seems unduly prohibitive and, in some cases, dangerous to the represented group's members. Experts often have technical knowledge that the rest of us lack. But to say instead that expert IPRs ought never defer seems objectionably paternalistic and threatens to deepen rather than ameliorate extant relational inequality. So, when should expert IPRs defer to oppressed or marginalized represented groups regarding matters about which they are expert? Should they defer regarding even, say, dangerous and urgent threats to the represented group's members' health and safety and, if so, when and why? If the answer is "no" to either or both of these questions, what revisions can we make to the representative deference principle to make it action guiding for expert IPRs of oppressed or marginalized groups?

One of the most persuasive defenses of the representative deference principle (although he does not call it that) is advanced by Michael Walzer in his essay "The Obligations of Oppressed Minorities."[4] Although Walzer's account is compelling, I disagree with some of the conclusions he draws. Through explaining my disagreement, I provide an account of informal political representation by experts that is neither dominating nor unconditionally deferential.

I proceed in this chapter as follows: First, I present Walzer's motivations and argument for the principle, highlighting and critically examining two criteria on which he relies to advance his argument: the helpfulness criterion and the general consciousness criterion. Second, I respond by raising concerns about three key features of his argument: ambiguity in the helpfulness criterion, confusion as to when deference is required to promote relations of equality, and the assumption that the members of an oppressed or marginalized group tend to share a general consciousness. Third, with these concerns in view, I move on to a more general discussion of three related but distinct questions concerning representative deference: (1) whether

IPRs may ever make claims to special knowledge or expertise, (2) whether they may make such claims to justify decisions to not defer to the represented in particular cases, and (3) whether an IPR's justifying the decision to not defer to the represented by appeal to their special knowledge or expertise creates an impermissibly inegalitarian relationship between the representative and the represented. To aid in answering these questions, I consider contexts in which the members of a represented group have false consciousness or internalized damaging false beliefs about their circumstances. Fourth, and finally, I examine how the descriptive preference principle (see Chapter 6) and the representative deference principle interact. Specifically, I argue that, absent these principles, non-deferential nondescriptive IPRs may end up engaging in objectionable and degrading forms of paternalism.

Michael Walzer on Helpfulness and General Consciousness

Even in reasonably democratic societies, there are oppressed groups and marginalized groups whose members, though they may be counted or recognized as citizens of those societies in some ways, "for whatever reason, do not 'count' in the same way as everyone else," notes Walzer. He adds, "The pressure they can bring to bear within the political system is limited"—their abilities to participate politically stymied by a wide variety of unjust circumstances, including but not limited to economic inequality, "political dispersion, disunity, . . . and isolation—incapacities at which the whole society more or less openly conspires."[5]

About such groups, Walzer makes three claims that seem to me right and uncontroversial. First, he claims that because "oppressed minorities do not find participation easy . . . [IPRs] must act on their behalf" in many cases.[6] Second, he claims that struggles "being fought on behalf of the oppressed . . . must eventually broaden to include [the oppressed themselves]." (Throughout this book, I advocate actions more proximate in time than "eventually.") Third, and crucially for our purposes, Walzer claims that when IPRs "commit themselves to work on behalf of the oppressed, [they] also commit themselves to work as effectively as they can and actually to help the oppressed whenever they can."[7]

Yet Walzer doubts whether parties who act on behalf of oppressed or marginalized groups could both make "plausible claims to special knowledge . . . such as a doctor or a lawyer might make" and at the same time struggle effectively for the equal treatment or liberation of the members of those groups.[8] The arguments he makes in support of this doubt deserve critical scrutiny.

First, consider Walzer's characterization of what it means to help someone: "'Helping' someone usually means doing something for him that he regards or seems likely to regard (given his present state of mind) as helpful."[9] Call this *the helpfulness criterion*. Yet, there are many circumstances in which we think a person is helped, although they would, given their present state of mind, deny it. Consider the opioid addict who has just been involuntarily entered into a treatment program with high rates of successful rehabilitation or the intoxicated person at the bar who has had their car keys taken away by a friend. Both parties seem clearly to have been helped, although, given their present states of mind, they would likely deny this.[10] Next, consider an example in which the helped party's judgment is not impaired. Consider a person who is reasonably reluctant to be vaccinated against COVID-19 because they are a member of a group on which their government has historically engaged in medical experimentation.[11] Suppose that their employer will not allow them to continue at their job if they remain unvaccinated.[12] They love their job, yet they have avoided even making a cancelable medical appointment to be vaccinated. You, their spouse, notice that the deadline for them to make an appointment to be vaccinated is imminent, and you make an appointment for them, intending to discuss the decision with them later that day. You have not thereby committed them to being vaccinated; you have simply preserved for them an opportunity to do so, should they change their mind. You have helped them, even if, given their present state of mind, they would not say that you have.[13]

Walzer does not deny that there are justifiable exceptions to the helpfulness criterion, at least in certain circumstances. Yet such exceptions, he adds, usually require "some plausible claim to special knowledge on the part of the active persons—such as a doctor or a lawyer might make." Walzer denies, however, that an IPR could both make claims to special knowledge and struggle for the equality or liberation of the oppressed or marginalized group. In fact, he says that "this is an *especially implausible* claim for [IPRs] to make, so long as they wish to maintain that they are struggling for equality."[14] Walzer suggests that an IPR could not both make plausible claims to special knowledge and struggle for equality on behalf of the represented group. I examine this suggestion below.

Second, Walzer claims that the IPR must set their immediate goals in accordance with the "general consciousness of the oppressed group" and not in accordance with "their own ideology." According to Walzer, IPRs count as acting in the interests of the oppressed "only if they respond to the felt needs of their putative constituents and represent these to the larger community." This second claim is complementary to the helpfulness criterion. That is, Walzer claims not only that (1) the helpfulness of a particular action should be judged by the helped party at the time at which the action is performed, but further that (2) the higher-order principles in accordance with which the helper acts should concord with "the general consciousness" of the helped party, as well.[15] Call this second claim *the general consciousness criterion*.

Walzer is led by well-founded and serious concerns to endorse these two criteria. Oppressed or marginalized groups often lack community recognition in both senses discussed earlier: dominant groups in their societies tend neither to regard them as belonging nor to take their interests seriously. Recall that they "do not 'count' in the same way as everyone else." Further, they are prevented from effectively organizing by myriad "incapacities"— including economic inequality, "political dispersion, disunity, . . . and isolation." These difficulties, in turn, stymie their abilities to engage in effective political participation in their own right. Unrecognized, unorganized, and unable to participate, oppressed or marginalized groups are often not well situated to struggle for their own liberation or equality. By virtue of these conditions, the groups have trouble effectively speaking and acting for themselves. IPRs who can "speak or act on [their] behalf" may ease some of these difficulties. For these reasons, oppressed or marginalized groups often come to rely on their IPRs (see Chapter 4). Because this is so, Walzer is concerned about the consequences for oppressed and marginalized groups whose IPRs do not defer to their expressed interests: "They are a competing elite. They make similar claims to esoteric knowledge. They replace the general struggle for freedom and equality with their own struggle for recognition and power."[16]

Walzer's concerns have considerable force: If the IPR for an oppressed or marginalized group does not give voice to the group's expressed preferences or concerns, who will? And might IPRs not simply become additional oppressors of the group by wielding their special knowledge as justification to override the group's expressed preferences? One can easily imagine cases in which IPRs use claims of expertise to further political agendas that either do not directly advance or even actively endanger groups' members' interests.

Notwithstanding his apt diagnosis of the stakes, there are reasons to worry about the hidden commitments and limitations underlying Walzer's positive account. In the next section, I critically examine three aspects of this account: ambiguity in the helpfulness criterion, confusion as to when deference is required to promote relations of equality, and the assumption that the members of an oppressed or marginalized group tend to share a general consciousness.

Responding to Michael Walzer

First, consider again the helpfulness criterion. At what level of description ought we to evaluate helpfulness? Imagine the members of an oppressed group and their IPR both broadly agree that the group is living under conditions of considerable injustice that require immediate remediation. The group's members face difficulties that include widespread and pervasive illness that could be easily treated with access to better medical care. In addition, life expectancy within the group is considerably lower than life expectancy in the general population. Group members and their IPR agree that the present circumstances are markedly unjust and ought to be corrected. They agree that the higher-order aims of the IPR's actions are to combat the unjust circumstances that have harmed the health of the group's members. They agree that the represented group's members must have access to better and more reliable health care. The group's members also do, in some sense, share a general consciousness: they agree that it would help them if their IPR were to fight for access to better health care on their behalf.

With these goals in mind, the IPR decides to use their public platform to support a single-payer healthcare system, claiming that this is what would best serve the needs of the represented group's members in their quest to receive adequate health care. Based on careful study of the present political and economic climate, the IPR has expertise that justifies believing that supporting single-payer healthcare is the best way to ensure access to better health care for the represented group's members at this time. So, the IPR takes actions on behalf of the represented group in accordance with this belief. The members of the represented group, however, do not see it the same way. After decades of oppression and neglect, the members of the represented group largely do not trust the government and suspect that the health care that would be available to them under a single-payer system would not leave them much better off than they are right now.[17]

What would Walzer's theory recommend in this case? On the one hand, the group denies that their IPR's stumping for single-payer healthcare is helpful to them. On the other hand, they agree that the IPR should take steps on their behalf that will secure them access to better health care, and their IPR reasonably believes that single-payer healthcare is required in order to do that. It is certainly possible that the group's members misunderstand, are less than fully informed about, or fail to see the connection between pursuing single-payer healthcare and the promotion of access to better health care. Indeed, Walzer himself seems to want to countenance this possibility by pointing out the "incapacities" of oppressed group's members. Surely, when the issue under discussion requires understanding the intricacies of how to implement a single-payer healthcare system, that is an incapacity that many of us share. And so, saying that the represented group's members have this misunderstanding, lack information, or fail to see the connection between their sought ends and the proposed means does not require believing that the represented group's members somehow lack sophistication and insight regarding their circumstances. It just turns out that it is difficult for most people to understand why single-payer healthcare is the best option for the represented group.

The problem with Walzer's helpfulness criterion is that it does not provide a clear recommendation about how to proceed when the group's members deny that a particular action (supporting single-payer healthcare) is helpful but would not deny the action's helpfulness if they accepted the relationship between that action and their higher-order commitments (access to better health care). The IPR and the group can have a common view of the sought ends of the representation (health care access), but differ on the means the IPR ought to undertake to achieve it.

Some suggestions elsewhere in the account provide guidance on what means an IPR may pursue: Walzer does not counsel brute deference to the group on the question of the IPR's means; he advocates for efforts at consciousness-raising. Further, he maintains, as noted, that IPRs should "respond to the felt needs of their putative constituents and represent these to the larger community."[18] Taken together, these two recommendations suggest that an IPR may not take particular means to the represented's ends until the IPR has convinced the group that those means would respond to the group's felt needs. But limiting the IPR's actions to those of which the IPR can effectively convince the members of an oppressed or marginalized group faces many practical difficulties, since both group authorization (see Chapter 3) and consultation (see Chapter 4) are difficult to achieve in informal contexts generally, and particularly difficult to achieve in contexts of oppression or marginalization.

Second, setting these practical difficulties aside, there is a deeper problem in the argument that needs to be addressed directly—namely, the proposed relationship between the representative deference principle and equality. Walzer claims that IPRs who do not represent "the felt needs of their putative constituents . . . to the larger community . . . often stand to the oppressed group in rather the same relation as does the oppressor government. They are a competing elite. They make similar claims to esoteric knowledge. They replace the general struggle for freedom and equality with their own struggle for recognition and power."[19] This argument rests on an equivocation between two senses of *equality*. First, there is the sort of equal status that an IPR might help the represented group achieve in the broader society that has oppressed the group—that is, the sort of equality that *justice without* duties aim to secure. Second, there are the sorts of egalitarian relations that an IPR must take steps to promote in their own relationship with the members of the group they represent—that is, the sort of equality that *democracy within* duties aim to secure. Distinguishing between these two senses of *equality* helps us to better articulate the different considerations that bear on whether, when, and to what extent an IPR must represent the represented's felt needs.

As I argued in Chapter 4, IPRs are required to promote both types of equality for the oppressed or marginalized groups they represent. And, barring exceptional circumstances, IPRs may not sacrifice egalitarian relationships with the represented even in the interest of seeking equality for the represented in the broader oppressive society. But doesn't that mean that, in the single-payer healthcare case, the IPR must defer to the represented's expressed preference against single-payer healthcare on pain of otherwise violating their *democracy within* duties?

Not necessarily. Whether promoting egalitarian relations between representative and represented requires deference to the represented's felt needs depends on further, specific features of the IPR's relationship to the represented. As discussed, IPRs who are more trusted by the represented have greater latitude than IPRs who are less trusted. In the case at hand, although the represented's trust in their government and the broader society may be quite low, their trust in their IPR may be quite high. In nascent representative relationships or when trust is low, the IPR ought not stump for single-payer healthcare before or without consultation or attempts at consciousness-raising. By contrast, when trust is high between the IPR and the represented, and particularly when the IPR is group authorized, the IPR is permitted to make independent decisions in accordance with their own judgment concerning how to represent the group and to experiment on the group's behalf, provided that the IPR leaves themself open to criticism from the group's members and facilitates ex post consultation (see Chapter 4). Even so, a well-trusted or group-authorized IPR's decision to act in contravention of the represented group's felt needs is risky. The expert IPR who stumps for single-payer healthcare despite their awareness of the group's skepticism jeopardizes the trusting relationship they have cultivated with the represented group and may jeopardize any group authorization they have received. But this does not mean that they have thereby treated the represented in an inegalitarian or oppressive manner.

Furthermore, in some rare exceptional circumstances IPRs may be justified in diverging from *democracy within* duties, provided that the divergences are (1) narrowly tailored to compelling interests, and (2) justifiable to the represented. Supposing that the health care inequities faced by the group's members are especially dire and so meet this exceptionality condition, the IPR may temporarily diverge from *democracy within* duties in the interest of working to secure health care that would better the represented group's members circumstances, even if the group's members would not consider doing so helpful given their present states of mind. There sometimes are real disparities in knowledge between a represented group and its IPR. If the group's situation is sufficiently dire, the benefits of exploiting the IPR's special knowledge may justify a divergence from *democracy within* duties. Yet such a choice is not costless for an IPR; indeed, they must bet the continued existence of their relationship to the represented group against it. By acting on their special knowledge and against the expressed interests of the represented, the IPR opens themself up to the objection that they have acted paternalistically, risking injury to their relationship with the represented that they must subsequently take steps to repair.[20] If repair is impossible, they may instead need to leave the role altogether—through the path to resignation described in Chapter 4.

Naturally, concerns about relations of inequality between the IPR and the represented arise when the IPR substitutes their own judgment of what is best for the group for the group's judgment and acts on the basis of their own judgment. Yet such concerns may be assuaged provided the IPR takes steps to make themselves vulnerable to the represented's criticism (see Chapter 4). It does not straightforwardly follow from the fact that an IPR does not represent the felt needs of the represented in a particular case that that IPR becomes a "competing elite" or "replace[s] the general struggle for freedom and equality with their own struggle for recognition and power." Sensitivity to the particular features of both the representative-represented relationship (trust and group authorization, in particular) and the represented group's needs at the time can help us distinguish between contexts in which failures to defer are objectionable and inegalitarian and contexts in which deference is neither required nor expected.

Walzer in fact levels criticism at not one but two different types of actions in which IPRs might engage—actions that deserve separate treatment. One, just considered, concerns the permissibility of expert IPRs representing groups in ways that do not accord with the represented's felt needs when the IPR's expertise gives them special insight into what would best advance the represented group's members aims. In addition, Walzer criticizes as inegalitarian the very act of making "claims to esoteric knowledge." Yet it is not obvious why a claim to special knowledge or expertise in itself establishes a relationship of inequality between the IPR and the represented group. Neither knowing something that someone else does not know nor expressing that one has such knowledge automatically guarantees that one will establish an inegalitarian relationship with the party to whom or for whose benefit one expresses this claim to special knowledge. In fact, an IPR may in some cases use their special knowledge in the interest of "respond[ing] to the *felt needs* of their putative constituents."[21] Constituents (the represented) may have a clear, cogent, and unambiguous sense of what their needs are, but may still have no way of knowing what would be the best response to those felt needs. Responding to their felt needs may require ferreting out the underlying sources of those felt needs—a task that the IPR, by virtue of their special knowledge or expertise, may be in a better position to carry out than the group's members without the IPR's special knowledge or expertise. In the next section, I distinguish different types of special knowledge claims and discuss several contexts in which IPRs' making claims to special knowledge is not merely permissible but can be valuable to their relationship with the represented.

Third, return to the general consciousness criterion. Walzer states that the IPR's immediate goals "must be set by the general consciousness of the oppressed group." This prescription is based on the assumption that members of an oppressed group share a general consciousness and that this general consciousness will be accessible to the IPR, or even to the oppressed group's members themselves. But what if the group has no general consciousness? As Walzer himself acknowledges, members of oppressed groups commonly face numerous "incapacities," including "lack of education," "political dispersion, disunity, . . . and isolation"—circumstances that may well prevent a general consciousness from forming.[22] (Furthermore, assuming that a group shares a general consciousness seems to rely on the further assumption that groups are homogeneous with regard to their members' experiences of their own oppression, which I have questioned elsewhere in this book.) Yet if the group has no general consciousness, then an IPR does not violate the group's general consciousness by trying out one representative tactic or another based on the IPR's own special knowledge or expertise about how best to meet the group's felt needs. The IPR's experimentation may also spur in the represented group shared ideas about their values, commitments, and shared priorities. That is, the IPR's actions and words may in fact serve as a catalyst for the emergence of a group consciousness in the represented group's members.

An IPR might justifiably resist the representative deference principle for many reasons. Being required to always work within a framework set out by a represented group, even when that group is oppressed and its members do not have a sense of how to satisfy their interests (presuming those interests are unified and clear to group members), can leave an IPR with few practicable options. Moreover, the members of the group may lack a unified sense of their interests, they may not know themselves to be oppressed, and the circumstances they face may be sufficiently dire as to grant an IPR to act with greater latitude than would have been allowed by a model like Walzer's.

That said, Walzer's account reinforces concerns that motivate the central ethical challenge of this book—that IPRs have power with respect to those they represent and can wield this power unaccountably, making claims to special knowledge merely to justify refusals to defer to the group they are meant to serve. What place, if any, can there be for claims to special knowledge or expertise in the practice of informal political representation?

Expertise and the Limits of Deference

Ought IPRs not make claims to special knowledge or expertise? There are three distinct though related questions at issue here. First, there is the general question whether or not IPRs ought ever to make claims to special knowledge or expertise simpliciter. Second, there is the narrower question whether or not IPRs may make claims to special knowledge or expertise in order to justify their decisions to not defer to the represented on a particular matter. If they may not do so, then, third, there is the question whether the reason that IPRs may not draw on their special knowledge or expertise to justify decisions to not defer to the represented is because doing so creates an impermissibly inegalitarian relationship between the representative and the represented. I consider these distinct questions now.

The first prohibition—barring IPRs from making claims to special knowledge or expertise for any reason—is too general. There are at least two types of cases in which an IPR might make a claim to special knowledge or expertise where doing so would support, not jeopardize, their egalitarian relationship to the represented.

First, an IPR might point out to the represented that they have expertise, knowledge, or skills that group members lack but that would improve the group's circumstances not in order to position themself as superior to group members but instead to persuade group members that they are capable of serving as an IPR for the group and to garner group members' trust. For instance, an IPR might point to their training in economics or time spent as a healthcare policymaker when attempting to justify their recommendation that the represented pursue single-payer healthcare. Or they may point out that their fluency in multiple languages positions them well to communicate between a represented group and an audience that does not speak the same language. Rigoberta Menchú knew how to speak Spanish, "the language of her oppressors," while many of the Indigenous people of Guatemala for whom she spoke did not.[23] Or an IPR might have educational training or skill in community organizing that makes them especially well suited to the role of IPR. The IPR who claims special knowledge in order to convince the represented of their worthiness to serve as an IPR aims to express deference and recognition respect to the represented group: they make an appeal to the group that the group permit them to serve as the group's IPR. This is a way of attempting to make the relationship between representative and represented more democratic, an attempt to give reasons that the represented may or may not take up. At least in these sorts of cases, it does not seem that a claim to special knowledge or expertise is, by itself, necessarily wrongful.

Second, an IPR might instead make a different sort of claim to special knowledge, but one that also aims to express recognition respect to the represented: a descriptive similarity claim (see Chapter 6). Unlike claims to special knowledge by which IPRs claim to know things the represented do not, descriptive similarity claims concern knowledge, experience, or information shared between representative and represented. For instance, an IPR might claim to have firsthand knowledge of what it is like for the represented based on their own experiences, either as a member of the same group or in analogous circumstances. The appeal to first-person familiarity with the represented's circumstances can be a way for the IPR to communicate that they know enough to be useful to the represented, to assure the represented of their commitment to the represented's causes, or to gain the represented's trust. Such claims may also serve as appeals to receive group conferral, to gain group authorization, or to be trusted to make the right decisions about what the group would want or accept at the negotiating table.

In both of the contexts just considered, IPRs claim special knowledge in order to express deference or recognition respect, to seek approval, or to gain trust. The claims are expressed directly to the represented and issued as appeals, requests, or evidence of competence. They are not expressed as status distinctions between the IPR and the representative, nor are they expressed to justify an IPR's unwillingness to engage or listen to the represented. These examples attest that IPRs can make claims to special knowledge without thereby treating the represented in an oppressive or inegalitarian manner. Minimally, such claims are permissible in some cases—particularly when they are made in one of the manners characterized above, where the aim of the claim is deference to the represented group, an attempt to persuade the group of the claimant's suitability to serve as an IPR for the group. So, a general prohibition on IPRs making claims to special knowledge or expertise seems unwarranted.

We turn now to the remaining two questions: May IPRs ever make plausible claims to special knowledge or expertise to justify a decision to not defer to the represented on a particular matter? If not, is it because doing so creates an impermissibly inegalitarian relationship between the representative and the represented? To answer these questions, we consider contexts in which the members of a represented group have false consciousness or internalized damaging false beliefs about their circumstances.

What role can claims to special knowledge play when a group's members have false consciousness or internalized damaging false beliefs about their own circumstances? A person who grows up in a community where sexual assault or sexual violence is normalized or treated as a matter of course may have difficulty identifying a particular experience of rape as rape (even knowing all of the facts about what the term *rape* means and knowing all the facts about what their own experience was), or may internalize "damaging false beliefs about their responsibilities and the causes of their rapes."[24] Or a person may be a member of a group, none of whose members know the true, underlying causes of their shared oppressive conditions. Not knowing the causes, group members may feel that they have unmet needs but have only a vague sense of what those needs are. Such group members will be poorly situated to know how best to better their circumstances.

Given his commitment to the helpfulness criterion, Walzer's response to cases involving phenomena like false consciousness or internalized damaging false beliefs can seem unsatisfying: "'Helping' someone usually means doing something for him that he regards or seems likely to regard (given his present state of mind) as helpful." And although he nods toward some set of exceptions to this general rule, one gets the sense that the range of plausible claims to special knowledge that an IPR is permitted to make is vanishingly small. Walzer allows that IPRs "may and often should seek 'to raise the level of consciousness' among the oppressed through various sorts of educational and political work, even, sometimes, by setting an example of boldness and militancy."[25] Yet, even so, this suggestion leads one to believe that the IPR must first bring the group around to seeing the IPR's viewpoint and only then may proceed in a way the IPR considers necessary for combatting the group's oppression. But if the ultimate goal is to aid the represented group by liberating the group's members from their oppression, why think that IPRs must commit themselves to working within the parameters of values, interests, or preferences that are themselves the products of the group's members false consciousness or internalized damaging false beliefs? There is, of course, much to be said in favor of an IPR's taking their cues and guidance from those for whom they speak or act; doing so can exhibit recognition respect, build trust, and undermine extant relational inequality and relationships of domination (see Chapter 4). Yet it is difficult to ignore the dangers of doing so when the guidance provided by the represented is itself the product of external social forces, oppressive structures, or racist, classist, and sexist impositions that one takes up as one's own just by happenstance because one has grown up in a society that inculcates and prizes these attitudes.

Further, there are certain types of represented groups with respect to which the claim that one must first seek to raise the consciousness of the group's members seems inapposite. Consider the case of elderly people living with severe dementia, who are as susceptible to elder abuse as the rest of the elderly population, if not more so.[26] A distinguishing feature of those living with severe dementia is that, often, their circumstances leave them especially poorly situated to advocate for themselves or even speak for themselves at all. Sometimes, they have lost capacity or their judgment is impaired. At other times, they are simply not regarded as credible sources of information about their own experience. Elderly people living with severe dementia therefore need others who can articulate their needs for them and make demands on their behalf. The law authorizes proxies to speak and act on behalf of individual persons living with severe dementia.[27] Yet people living with severe dementia may well also need IPRs to speak to their shared political interests. We cannot in such cases condition the permissibility of the IPR's activities on deference to the group's members nor on attempts at consciousness-raising.[28]

Yet Walzer is right that an IPR cannot claim their own normative authority to represent a group as they see fit simply by virtue of having special knowledge about the group's oppressive circumstances. After all, it is possible for the group's oppressors to have this sort of knowledge. And, more generally, having special knowledge about the group's circumstances does not prevent a party from being dishonest or corrupt, and difficult to hold accountable. Accordingly, we need a model of informal political representation that countenances the indispensability of certain forms of special knowledge or expertise while also recognizing that the represented ought to have some say in how they are represented. Such a model will not discount the importance of IPRs' plausible claims to special knowledge or expertise (as Walzer's account seems to have done) but will also take seriously that certain protections and safeguards are required—in particular, a responsibility on the part of the IPR to satisfy their *democracy within* and *justice without* duties alongside a commitment to ongoing dialogue with the represented in which the legitimate complaints of the represented are taken seriously and engaged critically. When the group's members complain, those complaints must be taken seriously—credible good faith justifications should, when possible, be provided. In some cases, the IPR will get things wrong. If they do, they will have to acknowledge their error and change course. But this is different from saying that the IPR cannot try out an uncertain course of action in the first place.

As Walzer points out, and as I discussed in Chapter 4, some IPRs will have not only a role in representing a group to nongroup audiences but also a parallel role as a group leader, aiming to raise group members' consciousness about their circumstances and the underlying causes of those circumstances. The leader-representative must not merely speak or act on behalf of the group to other audiences—"stat[ing] plainly and unequivocally the legitimate demands of their people," as W. E. B. Du Bois puts it—but must also work to educate, to raise consciousness, and to provide clear justifications as to why the IPR makes the decisions that they do, when such justifications are demanded.[29] Facing outward, toward the audience, the IPR represents the group. The IPR stands in for the group where the group cannot itself be. The IPR states the legitimate demands of the people for whom they speak or act. Facing inward, toward the group, the IPR serves as interlocutor and reason giver—and may also in some cases attempt to serve as consciousness-raiser, educator, leader.

Concerns about Paternalism

In these final two chapters, I have aimed to critically examine two principles that receive widespread endorsement: the descriptive preference principle and the representative deference principle. In neither case has it been my aim to reject these principles, but to explore their hidden commitments and limitations. The need for some version of each principle is obvious and becomes even clearer when we consider what might happen in their joint absence: IPRs who are neither relevantly similar to nor defer-ential to those for whom they speak or act may end up engaging in objec-tionable and degrading forms of paternalism, even if they are epistemically well situated to speak or act for the represented group.

To motivate the dangers of rejecting both the descriptive preference principle and the representative deference principle, consider an example. Imagine a man who is neither a member of nor relevantly descriptively similar to members of the LGBTQIA+ community (call him "John") is an IPR for the LGBTQIA+ community in the United States. He has received audience conferral from a wide variety of audiences. He also has group con-ferral and group authorization. John has exhibited devotion and commit-ment to LGBTQIA+ causes throughout his life. Moreover, there is no ques-tion that John is deeply knowledgeable about LGBTQIA+ communities based on years of dialogue, community participation, study, and serious re-flection. He is widely regarded as an expert on LGBTQIA+ impact litiga-tion. He has brought many such cases himself, consulted on many others, engaged in research and scholarship on the topic. Recently, John has come to have serious and well-founded misgivings about how an impending im-pact litigation case is proceeding. He believes wholeheartedly on the basis of good evidence and decades of experience that bringing this case now will establish bad precedent. He is inclined to write an editorial on the topic to publicly give voice to this concern. Yet John knows that he is an IPR and expects that views he expresses publicly will be ascribed to the LGBTQIA+ community, or at least some part of it, even if he explicitly states, "I am speaking only for myself." And he has reason to believe that his doubts about the case are not shared by most of the people for whom he is treated as speaking; he has talked about it with a lot of people and read what others have written on the topic. In fact, many of the people with whom he has privately discussed this matter have advised him against publicly expressing his concerns about the case. Some substantively disagree with him about the dangers of bringing the case. Others, although they privately agree with him, worry that John's public skepticism will itself be detrimental to the case's chances of success. Still others advise him that there are certain discus-sions you have only within a group, among group members (the *in-confidence complaint*; see Chapter 5). Intuitively, it seems that, in deference to the ad-vice he has received, John should not publicly announce his views on the matter. There seems to be something deeply objectionable and impermissibly paternalistic about John deciding to communicate publicly on this contentious matter. Although John is knowledgeable, credible, widely trusted, and group authorized, he lacks standing.

Standing, in this sense, is not a status brought about by audience conferral, group conferral, group authorization, nor all of these together. I stipulated that John has all of these. Nor is standing in this sense merely the status of being a group member or descriptively similar to members of the represented group. As discussed, although group membership and descriptive similarity often serve as guarantors of other qualities we might want in a representative—understanding, credibility, trust—those do not seem to be at issue in this case. John understands the stakes of the case; he is regarded by represented and audience alike to be credible; he has the represented group's trust. John is deeply connected and committed to the LGBTQIA+ community. Rather, it is a particular aspect of group membership that is both important and absent in this case: because John is not a group member, and because the outcome of this legal case will only affect group members, he is not vulnerable to losing what group members might lose. To have standing is to be vulnerable to lose something oneself by virtue of the outcome of one's own attestations.

But what does this mean for our theory? Does it mean that in every case, at least one of the two, the descriptive preference principle or the representative deference principle, must be satisfied on pain of otherwise leaving a represented group susceptible to objectionable and degrading forms of paternalism? That cannot be right, because there will be cases about which it is true that both (1) a represented group would benefit greatly from having nonmember or even nondescriptive IPRs, and (2) the members of the represented group are not best situated (precisely because of what grounds their group membership) to be deferred to—recall the case of elderly people living with severe dementia. We may say that there is paternalism taking place when the nonmember or nondescriptive IPR speaks for elderly people living with severe dementia, but it is not clear that the paternalism is either degrading or objectionable.

There is an independent principle at work in some of these cases, but not others:

Nonmember deference: If a group's members (1) have historically faced oppressive conditions, and (2) the group's oppressors justified maintaining those oppressive conditions based on their view that the group's members were not capable of self-governance, then (3) there is a strong presumption against nonmembers (and an especially strong presumption against nonmembers who are themselves the group's oppressors or even part of a group that historically comprised the group's oppressors) speaking or acting for the oppressed group without deferring to the oppressed group.

The nonmember deference principle may help us distinguish between cases in which nonmember IPRs must defer to the represented and cases in which they need not. Cases in which nonmember IPR deference is required will often involve represented groups whose members are united by their disability, ethnicity, gender, race, religion, sex, or sexual orientation. The fact that, historically, many groups whose members had these features in common were treated as incapable of self-governance gives us good reason to ensure that members of these groups in particular be treated and regarded as capable of speaking and acting for themselves—meaning at least that, in these cases, at least one of the descriptive preference principle or the representative deference principle must be abided. Yet there will be exceptions. Cases in which nonmember IPR deference is not required will often involve groups whose members are united by severe impairments in their abilities to judge what would be best for themselves—for instance, people with substance abuse problems or people who are severely cognitively impaired. This is not, of course, to say that members of groups like these have not also historically been treated as though they are incapable of self-governance. And so, in cases like these, we would not say that the nonmember deference principle is inapplicable, but rather that the presumption against nonmember representation is rebutted by other, serious concerns about, for instance, the safety of group members.

The nonmember deference principle is also compatible with allowing that, in certain exceptional cases, an IPR who is not a member of the represented group could speak or act for the group without deferring to the members of that group in particular instances of representation, provided that they (1) had an especially robust sort of group authorization from the members of the oppressed group more generally and (2) are in conversation with the members of the oppressed group—thereby leaving themself open to criticism and complaint, as the *democracy within* duties require.

Conclusion

The question whether—and, if so, when—expert IPRs for oppressed or marginalized groups should defer to those they represent on matters about which the IPRs are themselves experts is an especially difficult one. In this chapter, I have aimed to open an examination of this question. To do so, I considered Michael Walzer's compelling argument in favor of the representative deference principle, in which he argues that IPRs should (1) help the represented, where this means doing something for the represented that the represented regard or seem "likely to regard . . . as helpful," (2) guide their actions to accord with the represented group's general consciousness, and (3) not attempt to justify failures to satisfy 1 or 2 by making appeals to special knowledge or expertise. According to Walzer, IPRs who do not abide by these responsibilities risk creating inegalitarian relations with those they represent and contributing to their oppression. I then appraised three limitations of Walzer's argument: first, the helpfulness criterion admits of ambiguity that prevents it from being action guiding in some cases; second, deference is not always required to promote relations of equality in representative-represented relationships; and third, it is not clear why we should believe that oppressed or marginalized groups will tend to share a general consciousness. With these concerns in mind, I then considered whether—and, if so, when—it may be permissible or even valuable for expert IPRs to make claims to special knowledge or expertise. I identified contexts in which IPRs do so not to justify refusals to defer, but instead to express deference or recognition respect, to seek approval, or to gain trust. I then considered whether IPRs may make appeals to expertise to justify not deferring when the represented have false consciousness or internalized damaging false beliefs about their circumstances—tentatively concluding that they sometimes may, but only if they satisfy their *democracy within* and *justice without* duties (see Chapter 4).

I close by considering how the lessons of Chapters 6 and this chapter interact. The aims of the two chapters have been to examine the strengths and explore the limitations of, respectively, the descriptive preference principle and the representative deference principle—to ask whether these principles really ought in all cases to place constraints on who a representative must be (descriptive preference principle) and how a representative must act (representative deference principle). The motivations for endorsing these principles are obvious and reasonable. When formal protections are, by definition, unavailable—IPRs being neither subject to voting nor fearful of impeachment or other procedural reprisals in any traditional sense—we can be tempted to ask other mechanisms to do the protective work that these procedural mechanisms otherwise might.

We may quite reasonably think that those who are like us will be better at representing us because they will know better what it is like for us—this is one justification for the descriptive preference principle. So, too, may we quite reasonably think that people know best what they themselves need, and so an IPR should whenever possible simply serve as their mouthpiece and stick to the script—this is one justification for the representative deference principle. Each of these demands is meant to serve as a proxy measure for some other good that we are not guaranteed when representation lacks the formal, structural protections available (at least in theory) in government, corporations, and civil society organizations.

Yet these proxy measures can sometimes be tools too blunt for the nuanced purposes they are meant to satisfy. People who are not at all like us may sometimes be our best representatives, and may in fact owe it to us to do that communicative labor in our steads. So, too, might we be best served if a representative takes on a leadership role and helps us to understand what would be best for us when our interests are "uncrystallized," when there is no "general consciousness" common to all the members of our group, or when we struggle even to know what needs we might have.[30] And so, we ought to reject theories that would require inflexible adherence to the descriptive preference principle and the representative deference principle in all cases, instead favoring more nuanced, context-sensitive accounts that help us understand when and why these principles serve represented groups' ends.

Of course, it can be difficult to know what such a nuanced, context-sensitive account might look like without knowing which contexts matter. So as to offer some guidance on this front, I have throughout this book provided resources for understanding the many components of informal political representation and for distinguishing between a wide variety of different manifestations of the phenomenon. Specifically, I have

1. developed the audience conferral account of IPR emergence, which enables us to distinguish between voluntary and conscripted IPRs (Chapters 1 and 2);

2. advanced an account of the ethics of audience conferral and detailed when and why conscripted IPRs need not fulfill the demands of the role (Chapter 2);

3. examined how group authorization grants IPRs greater independence to represent in accordance with their own visions of what justice requires (Chapter 3), including freedom from the requirement to defer to the represented on matters about which the representative is expert (Chapter 7);

4. detailed two sets of duties IPRs have to the oppressed or marginalized groups they represent—the *democracy within* and *justice without* duties—and explained how adherence to these duties may both undermine skeptical concerns about the permissibility of informal political representation (Chapter 4) and mitigate concerns about IPRs making claims to expertise (Chapter 7);

5. schematized different legitimate complaints that represented groups in particular may raise to their IPRs and examined how these complaints shape and constrain the deliberative, democratic relationship between representative and represented (Chapter 5);

6. considered when and why IPRs should be descriptively similar to or themselves members of the group they represent and when nondescriptive representation may be permissible or preferrable (Chapter 6); and, finally,

7. examined how several of the aforementioned considerations help us elaborate the representative deference principle (Chapter 7).

Conclusion

Informal political representation plays an outsized role in all our lives. People come to speak or act for us all the time. Their statements or actions are ascribed to us and, depending on what they have said or done, our lives can be changed quite profoundly as a result. Sometimes, it is we ourselves who are the informal political representatives (IPRs), whether for groups of which we are members or instead for groups whose interests we champion from the outside, to whose struggles we aim to give voice. At other times, we are audiences who—for better or, often, for worse—foist the role of IPR on unwitting or unwilling others, expecting them to give voice to large, heterogeneous communities whose members have widely disparate values, interests, preferences, and perspectives.

Yet despite its ubiquity and centrality to our lives, informal political representation has until recently been accorded only scant and passing attention. It is a phenomenon just familiar enough to be folded into ongoing debates about formal political representation and either treated as analogous or cast aside as deviant. But there is no substitute for treating informal political representation on its own terms—examining its many faces, exploring its unique promises and troubling flaws.

One may speculate that informal political representation has been overlooked or misunderstood for so long, in part, because of a background assumption that political philosophy has, properly, to do with institutions—what they are, how we rely on and otherwise interact with them, and how they ought to be arranged. If that is right, then perhaps informal political representation has not received more philosophical treatment because it appears to fall largely outside the scope of traditional, institutional forms of political participation. Yet, as we have seen throughout this book, informal political representation often takes place within formal political institutions, with audiences who are themselves institutional actors: Aalayah Eastmond at the U.S. Congress, Rev. Dr. Martin Luther King Jr. with the Montgomery City Council, Rigoberta Menchú with elected officials in Guatemala, Greta Thunberg and Malala Yousafzai at the United Nations, Booker T. Washington at the White House. So, informal political representation is a practice that has many homes—emerging in both public and private, both within and outside the bounds of institutional structures.

Even more surprisingly, informal political representation sometimes makes formal political institutions possible. Indeed, a foundational moment in the formation of the United States was an instance of informal political representation bringing about formal political representation:

> On the tenth of May 1775, a few hours after the surrender of Ticonderoga, the second continental congress met at Philadelphia. Among the delegates appeared Franklin and Samuel Adams; John Adams and Washington and Richard Henry Lee; soon joined by Patrick Henry, and by George Clinton, Jay, and the younger Robert R. Livingston of New York.
>
> They formed no confederacy; they were not an executive government; they were not even a legislative body; but only committees from twelve colonies, deputed to consult on measures of conciliation, with no means of resistance to oppression beyond a voluntary agreement to suspend importations from Great Britain. They owed the hall for their sessions to the courtesy of the carpenters of the city; there was not a foot of land over which they had jurisdiction; and they had not power to appoint one civil officer to execute their decisions. Nor was one soldier enlisted nor one officer commissioned in their name. They had no treasury, and no authority to lay a tax or to borrow money. They had been elected, in part at least, by bodies which had no recognised legal existence; they were intrusted with no powers but those of counsel; most of them were held back by explicit or implied instructions; and they represented nothing more solid than the unformed opinion of an unformed people. They were encountered by the decision of parliament to enforce its authority, by the king's refusal to act as a mediator, and the actual outbreak of civil war. The waters

had risen; the old roads were obliterated; and they must strike out a
new path for themselves and for the continent.

The exigency demanded the instant formation of one great com-
monwealth, and the declaration of independence.[1]

In addition to being a valuable historical example of a formal political
institution emerging from informal political representation, this Second
Continental Congress example illustrates two points central to the argument of this book.

The first point concerns the role of formalistic mechanisms in explaining
what political representation is. In *The Concept of Representation*, Hanna
Pitkin discusses the deficiencies of "formalistic" accounts that define *representative* as "someone who has been authorized to act" (authorization accounts) or "someone who is to be held to account, who will have to answer
to another for what he does" (accountability accounts).[2] Authorization accounts make representation seem like "a kind of 'black box' shaped by the
initial giving of authority, within which the representative can do whatever
he pleases. . . . There is no such thing as the activity of representing or the
duties of a representative; anything done after the right kind of authorization and within its limits is by definition representing." Likewise, accountability accounts define representation mostly in terms of how the activity
comes to an end. Per Pitkin, these formalistic accounts provide insufficient
explanations of what the activity of representation is—neither type "can
tell us anything about what goes on *during* representation."[3] In this book,
I have made a complementary point: that neither authorization nor accountability is necessary for representation to emerge. As the Second Continental Congress example illustrates, political representation can emerge
before—and therefore without—the formal authorization and accountability mechanisms with which it is so commonly associated.[4] Understood
quite generally, political representation is a practice whereby one party
(the representative) speaks or acts for another party (the represented) before some audience in a context concerning matters apt for broad public
discussion.[5] This basic case of political representation includes constitutive
features common to both formal and informal cases: a representative, a represented party, an audience, a context, and matters apt for broad public discussion. Absent from this enumeration are authorization and accountability.

There can be no doubt that authorization and accountability mechanisms can add important structural and normative features to the phenomenon. Structurally, both types of mechanisms can make political representation organized, reliable, and repeatable. Normatively, authorization can grant a representative license to act in accordance with their own discretion and, further, can imbue the representative with normative powers to bind the represented to certain actions, outcomes, and states of affairs. Accountability mechanisms can reflect and enforce the values in accordance with which a representative is expected to act. Yet neither, I have argued, is necessary for there to be political representation.

Second, the example illustrates several different sorts of phenomena that fall within what I have called *the space of political representation* (see Chapter 1), showing both (1) how informal political representation can emerge in the first place, and (2) how a given instance of political representation may shift from being informal to being formal: At first there may seem to be nothing but a rented hall and a few who have convened to deliberate in their individual capacities. Yet when an audience treats those convened parties as giving voice to the "unformed opinion of an unformed people," that audience confers on those convened parties the roles of IPRs for that unformed people, and a concomitant power to influence how that audience and other audiences understand the values, interests, and preferences of that unformed people. Then, the initially informal political representation may become more formal in one or more respects—authorization, accountability, group membership, norms. (Of course, in other cases, it might go the other way round: a formal political representative (FPR) relationship might become more informal in one or more of these respects.)

Informal political representation does not depend for its conceptual or normative foundations or its legitimacy as a political practice on the conceptual or normative foundations or the legitimacy of formal political representation. It is not formal political representation downgraded. Instead, both phenomena are parts of a vast space of political representation, some regions of which are much more theoretically developed than others. In this book, I have systematically examined a relatively underexplored region of that space.

In this Conclusion, I take the opportunity to look from our present moment both backward and forward in time to see what careful attention to informal political representation might teach us about where we have come from and where we are headed. How might our understanding of even our most foundational moral and political commitments be enriched by a sensitivity to the practice of informal political representation? In the next section, I identify some of the key insights of this book and highlight questions that would benefit from further theoretical and empirical exploration. Then, I close by exploring some areas of public and private life that may be better understood with the help of the theoretical apparatuses offered in this book.

Key Insights and Open Questions

Audience conferral (Chapters 1, 2, 3, and 6). Audiences confer the role of IPR on parties, often on unreasonable, specious, or objectionable grounds. Dominant audiences have considerable power to place heavy and unwelcome burdens on the shoulders of subordinated parties on whom they confer the role of IPR for fellow group members. A new appreciation of the power and burden of audience conferral should make audiences—including all of us—wary. When we treat a party as speaking or acting for others, we both empower and burden them. We make a claim on them that they represent others and, as audiences, we should take care to do so in ways both reasonable and permissible.

At the outset of this book, I cautioned that it is not my account that confers power on audiences to say who represents whom; to claim this would be to give my theory entirely too much influence over our extant social relations. Instead, my aim throughout this book has been to examine the role of the IPR in societies like ours. Doing so requires acknowledging that audiences confer this role for all sorts of reasons and with many different motivations—sometimes in ways that are deeply misguided or truly objectionable. Others are led by these misguided and objectionable instances of audience conferral to conclude that, in fact, no IPR emerges when audience conferral is epistemically or morally errant in some way.[6] But to conclude that errant audience conferral simply misfires (and therefore no IPR emerges) is, I think, unhelpful when trying to theorize about this phenomenon as it actually appears in societies like ours. Here, I recount a few different features of my account that help us understand both why it is important to include these misguided and objectionable cases within the ambit of our theorizing and how to ameliorate moral concerns that arise from thinking about the phenomenon this way.

First, to deny the power that audiences have to confer IPR status on unwitting and unwilling parties is, in a way, to miss the point. It is precisely because audiences can foist people into the position of IPR over their objections or without their knowledge that we should want to include these cases within the ambit of our theory. You are an audience, and so am I. Throughout the course of our lives, we all unreflectively treat people as speaking or acting for others—often, although not always, because they are descriptively similar to or even fellow group members with those others. (In some cases, powerful audiences whose interests are not aligned with a group will confer IPR status on a party more likely to represent the group in a manner sympathetic to the audiences' interests—a phenomenon I call *IPR capture*.) However innocent, well meaning, or unwitting these audiences may be, their conferral is often not merely harmful but often wrongful to both the conferred-upon party and the represented group.

In light of this, I outlined preliminary guidelines for thinking about how to be an audience member in Chapter 2: I argued that, given how burdensome the role of IPR can be and how easy it is to confer the role on others, there is an extraordinarily high bar on the permissible performance of audience conferral, and I provided the *audience conferral permissibility test,* a multipronged test for assessing whether audience conferral is permissible in a given case. I also emphasized how important it is that each of us, and particularly those of us who are members of our society's dominant groups, recognize that we commonly but often unwittingly inhabit the dubious role of conferring audience. As audiences, we are criticizable for burdening members of subordinated groups with pro tanto duties to represent fellow group members. Further, I claimed that audiences ought to actively avoid forming, and actively aim to revise, sincere but misguided attitudes and habits that lead to unreflective conferral.

Doubtless it will take us some time to start seeing ourselves as representatives and audiences in spite of ourselves. That project will be aided not only by revising our concepts and refining our theories but also by rethinking what falls within the ambit of civic education—namely, learning that often we serve in the role of representative or audience, often by mere happenstance. Accordingly, a question that deserves further exploration is this:

1. What sort of civic education could help us understand the roles we play in informal political representative relationships?[7]

Second, I have made clear that just because someone is conscripted into the role of IPR does not mean that they have any responsibility whatsoever to fulfill the role (see Chapter 2). I enumerate and discuss grounds on which IPRs can reasonably reject the ascription of pro tanto duties that would otherwise accrue to them by virtue of their power to influence, including (1) that the audience's conferral is based on objectionable interests or views, or is otherwise demeaning, degrading, or would require the IPR to violate their self-respect, and (2) that satisfying the duties would be unduly burdensome. I also clarify that, in many cases, IPRs can and perhaps should disavow, reject, or simply ignore objectionable or unduly burdensome audience conferral.

Third, I preserve a core insight common to my account and the accounts of those who would deny that audience conferral is sufficient for bringing about an IPR's emergence—namely, that there is a difference between a de facto IPR and an authorized IPR (see Chapters 1 and 3). Parties conferred IPR status only by an audience other than the group they represent are IPRs in a de facto sense. They have the power to influence, but they are not authorized IPRs. Authorized IPR status can be granted only by the group to be represented (see Chapter 3). We should not, however, conclude that all de facto IPRs (those who have not been informally authorized or ratified) are illegitimate. Informal authorization and ratification are difficult to effect and, so, relatively rare. Many if not most of the people who are IPRs are not in positions that would allow them to be authorized by the group they represent. So, we need to make distinctions of finer grain even among de facto IPRs by considering questions like these: Has the audience conferred IPR status for the right reasons and are their motivations for conferring the status of IPR on this particular party good ones? Does the conferred-upon party want to be in the role of IPR? Does the represented group want them in the role? Is there a rebuttable presumption against taking this party to speak or act for the group? The *audience conferral permissibility test* comprises these questions (see Chapter 2).

Fourth, I offer an ameliorative suggestion: I argue that, in some contexts, there is reason to permit or even prefer the emergence of nondescriptive IPRs for oppressed or marginalized groups precisely because, by taking up the role of IPR, these nondescriptive parties can alleviate some of the burdens faced by descriptively similar parties or fellow group members who will otherwise inevitably be called upon to serve as IPRs (see Chapter 6).

Although this suggestion may strike some as undesirable, those resistant to contemplating any contexts in which nondescriptive IPRs are permissible end up shifting the burden of representation squarely back onto descriptive parties and fellow group members.

There are outstanding theoretical and empirical research questions here, too, particularly concerning the heterogeneity of audience conferral:

2. What does audience conferral look like in real life?
3. What are audiences' various motivations for seeking out IPRs?
4. For what reasons do audiences confer IPR status on some people rather than others?

Conscription (Chapter 2). This book reconceptualizes informal political representation to accommodate both conscripted and voluntary IPRs. An IPR's desire to represent, intention to represent, or awareness that they represent may each play a role in helping us understand how the IPR came to be in their position and what their duties are once so positioned. Yet neither desire nor intention nor awareness is necessary for emerging as an IPR.

Recognizing and accommodating conscripted IPRs improves our theory in at least three ways. First, the theory helps us get the right analytical grip on informal political representation by identifying a core feature of the phenomenon obscured by other accounts: the power IPRs can have to influence how the represented are regarded by various audiences and how they come to have this power to influence. Second, the theory provides a more coherent and more complete account of both how IPRs come to have duties to those they represent and how their duties vary depending on, among other things, whether they volunteered or were conscripted. Many of an IPR's duties emerge by virtue of their power to influence audiences, not by virtue of choices that that IPR may have made to gain that power. Willingness plays no role in constituting a party as an IPR, but does make a difference as to what duties that party thereby acquires. Voluntarist accounts conflate what makes it the case that a party is an IPR with what makes it the case that an IPR has duties by virtue of being so positioned. Third, a theory of informal political representation that accommodates conscripted IPRs tells each of us what we may owe the represented because, as we have seen, any one of us may be an IPR or, for that matter, a conscripting audience. Understanding the phenomenon of conscripted informal political representation allows us to surface essential normative questions about informal political representation that are otherwise occluded.

In a way, being conscripted as an IPR is not at all unusual. Often, although we do not choose to be so, we find ourselves in positions that require us to act, to respond: the responsibility to offer rescue or succor, the duty to warn others of harm. Matters are similar, if usually less dire, when we are conferred the status of IPR: an audience makes a claim on us that we speak or act in another's stead. It may be that the audience has harmed or wronged us by making this claim on us, but that consideration makes it no less true that, by virtue of audience conferral, we may come to have considerable power to influence the lives of others—sometimes many others—through what we say or do on their behalf. Recognizing and understanding conscripted informal political representation allows us to build a more complete and coherent moral theory of informal political representation—one that seats informal political representation more seamlessly into the moral structure of our everyday lives.

All theories of informal political representation must have something to say about conscripted informal political representation. So, there is theoretical work to be done to fashion new theories of representation that are duly sensitive to the reality of IPR conscription, and attendant empirical questions:

5. What does IPR conscription actually look like in the world?
6. How has IPR conscription developed across societies and across time?

Representative Powers (Chapters 2 and 3). IPRs' powers—the power to influence that emerges from audience conferral and the discretionary and normative powers that can emerge from group authorization—are at the heart of what it is to be an IPR. We care about the role of the IPR at least in part because it imbues particular persons or groups with (1) the capacity, through the IPR's statements or actions, to shape an audience's doxastic attitudes about a represented group and its values, interests, or preferences (*power to influence*), and sometimes (2) greater latitude to represent in accordance with their own vision of what justice requires (*discretionary powers*) or (3) the ability to commit the represented to certain actions, outcomes, or states of affairs (*normative powers*). Questions about these powers include the following:

7. What do the exercises of these powers look like in real life?
8. Can one reject these powers and, if so, how?

Group Authorization (Chapter 3). Informal group authorization and informal group ratification give IPRs greater latitude than they might otherwise have had to represent in accordance with their own visions of what justice requires (*discretionary powers*) and, in some cases, the ability to make commitments on the represented's behalf (*normative powers*). Although I have provided characterizations of informal group authorization and informal group ratification, they deserve further empirical and theoretical attention:

9. How common and widespread are informal group authorization and informal group ratification?
10. Are there particular theories of group agency that are especially well suited to helping us understand group authorization?
11. How can attention to group authorization and informal political representation help us better understand the normative structure of tripartite relationships more generally?

Representative Duties to Oppressed and Marginalized Groups (Chapter 4). As discussed, our theory of informal political representation should be evaluated partly by how it handles cases of representation of oppressed and marginalized groups—those most in need of IPRs and those most vulnerable to the damaging effects of their IPRs' foibles, blunders, and vices. Accordingly, I structured the discussion of Chapter 4 as a response to skeptical challenges to the informal political representation of oppressed and marginalized groups. There are two questions that would benefit from further exploration:

12. Does this account capture all significant skeptical challenges to the informal political representation of oppressed and marginalized groups or are there further challenges that deserve our attention?
13. If further skeptical challenges are insurmountable, how, if at all, can societies curtail the practice of informal political representation of oppressed and marginalized groups?

Responding to skeptical challenges to informal political representation, I have argued that IPRs should satisfy two sets of duties: *democracy within* duties, which concern how the representative treats and relates to the represented, and *justice without* duties, which concern how, when, where, and before whom IPRs should speak or act on represented parties' behalf. To satisfy their *democracy within* duties, IPRs should promote deliberative, dialogical social practices in their relationships to the represented—consultation, transparency, welcoming criticism, tolerating dissent. Although some of the justifications for promoting these practices require no empirical defense—these practices just do partly constitute what it is to treat another as an equal and to show them recognition respect in the context at issue—I also suggested that these deliberative social practices could be instrumentally useful in helping IPRs to better understand the values, interests, preferences, and circumstances of their constituents. This suggestion needs to be borne out by empirical research. There are three questions that would be fruitful starting points for such research:

14. Do these deliberative social practices in fact ameliorate the dangers about which skeptics are concerned?
15. Do these practices improve IPRs' understanding of the values, interests, preferences, or circumstances of the groups they represent?
16. How, if at all, do IPRs already engage in these deliberative social practices?

The Legitimate Complaints of the Represented (Chapter 5). The legitimate complaints of the represented are essential to the deliberative, dialogical relationship between the represented, their IPRs, and third parties. I have provided a schema for thinking about some of the most important genera and species of complaints, but surely have not captured them all. One question for further research is as follows:

17. What further complaints should we incorporate into the schema provided, and who has standing to raise them?

As I have noted, W. E. B. Du Bois endorses the importance and permissibility of such complaints, proclaiming "honest and earnest criticism from those whose interests are most nearly touched" to be "the soul of democracy and the safeguard of modern society." Yet he also makes a stronger claim: "The black men of America have a duty to perform, a duty stern and delicate,—a forward movement to oppose a part of the work of their greatest leader. . . . [S]o far as Mr. [Booker T.] Washington apologizes for injustice, North or South, does not rightly value the privilege and duty of voting, belittles the emasculating effects of caste distinctions, and opposes the higher training and ambition of our brighter minds,—so far as he, the South, or the Nation, does this,—we must unceasingly and firmly oppose them." Here, Du Bois does not merely laud the value of criticism to a well-functioning democracy, but further claims that "those whose interests are most nearly touched" (that is, the represented) have a "duty" to "unceasingly and firmly oppose" errant representation.[8] Many represented groups are significantly burdened by the fact of having an IPR who has come to them unbidden, which can make the proposed duty to dissent seem especially onerous. A question for further research is as follows:

18. Do represented groups have a duty, rather than a mere permission, to dissent against their errant IPRs and, if so, what grounds this duty?

Descriptive Representation and Fellow Group Member Representation (Chapter 6). A central concern for any theory of informal political representation is how and why it accommodates or rejects the descriptive preference principle: for a given context of representation, other things being equal, there is good reason to prefer group representation by descriptive representatives to group representation by those who are not descriptive representatives (*nondescriptive representatives*).

I have distinguished between a variety of different arguments offered in favor of this principle in FPR and IPR contexts, respectively, and suggested that these distinctions depend, in part, on the fact that, although there are institutionally codified limits on how many FPRs there can be in a given representative body, there are no such hard limits on how many IPRs there can be. I have acknowledged, however, that there may be practical limits on how many IPRs can be given meaningful attention by an audience (the displacement concern). Whether this is so depends on empirical research into this pair of questions:

19. How many IPRs can be given meaningful attention by a given audience?
20. Are there de facto limits on how many IPRs there can be for a given group in a given context at a given time?

In addition to the displacement concern, I have also examined several other arguments in favor of the descriptive preference principle—understanding, credibility, trust, and self-determination. Although this provides a broad canvassing of many arguments employed in popular and scholarly contexts, surely other compelling arguments are or could be advanced in favor of the descriptive preference principle as it applies to informal political representation in particular. So, there is also more theoretical work to be done here:

21. What further arguments are there in favor of the descriptive preference principle as it applies to informal political representation and what objections do these further arguments face?

I have further considered several contexts in which there are compelling reasons to permit or even prefer nondescriptive IPRs—restricted access, burden, discounting, explicit request, risk of exposure. Surely there are others. So, another question ripe for future research is this:

22. For which further contexts are there compelling arguments for permitting or even preferring nondescriptive IPRs?

Nondescriptive Representation, Expertise, and the Looming Threat of Paternalism (Chapters 6 and 7). A consideration left open at the conclusion of Chapter 6 is what sorts of relationships nondescriptive IPRs must develop to those they represent. Unlike descriptive IPRs and member IPRs, nondescriptive IPRs are often, in certain important respects, farther from the concerns faced by those they represent. They may not share lived experience of what matters most to the group they represent. They may lack knowledge about the represented group's members' values, interests, and preferences. The represented groups' stakes may not be theirs. We may think of these as different types of "distance" between nondescriptive IPRs and those they represent—doxastic, conative, and otherwise. I concluded

Chapter 7 by suggesting that a principle called *nonmember deference*—which states that there is a presumption against nonmembers speaking or acting for an oppressed group without deferring to the group—is compatible with allowing that, in certain exceptional cases, an IPR for an oppressed group who is not a member of the group could speak or act for the group without deferring to the members of that group in particular instances of representation, provided that they (1) had an especially robust sort of group authorization from the members of the group more generally and (2) are in conversation with the members of the group. In view of these considerations, several important theoretical questions remain open for further discussion:

23. Under which exceptional circumstances, if any, might it be permissible for a nondescriptive IPR to not defer to the members of the oppressed or marginalized group they represent concerning the substance or form of the representation they provide?
24. How does expertise make a difference to these considerations? When, if ever, do nondescriptive expert IPRs have standing to speak or act for a group in ways that most of the group's members, given their present states of mind, would not endorse?
25. How can the nonmember deference principle help us to distinguish between cases in which nondescriptive expert IPRs must defer to the represented and cases in which they need not?

Overarching Questions. In addition to the aforementioned insights and questions, which emerge from specific chapters, there is another sort of question—the answer to which will, I believe, help us better understand how both representative institutions and individual representative relationships develop over time. As we saw in the Second Continental Congress example, FPR institutions can emerge directly from IPR practices. Historically informed theoretical research into cases like these can help us better understand when, how, and why FPR institutions emerge from IPR practices:

26. Are IPR practices necessary predecessors of FPR institutions in societies like ours?

Looking at this relationship from the other direction, it is common for people to serve contemporaneously as FPRs for one group while serving as

IPRs for another. A familiar example of this phenomenon is virtual representation, whereby people formally elected by their constituents end up also representing people who do not fall within their constituencies.[9] So, it is worth considering the following further question too:

27. When and why do FPR institutions give way to IPR practices?

Looking to our representative history will help us more fully develop our overall model of the space of political representation, in which a representative party can be more or less formal in any one of a variety of respects.[10]

Future Directions

Informal political representation is a powerful practice that informs every dimension of our political lives. Yet because it is an underexplored phenomenon, we have not yet had full opportunity to consider how it arises within and shapes our political or legal institutions, or even our less institutional, more proximate political relationships. How might our understanding of these institutions and relationships be enriched by thinking about informal political representation's role in shaping them? In this section, I briefly explore the role of informal political representation in the law, arts and scholarship, and the media.

Informal Political Representation in the Law. Paradigmatic accounts of legal and political representation diverge: Lawyers represent their individual clients. Although political representation also involves representing individuals, it usually and centrally involves representing groups and representing individuals as parts of these groups.[11] This received view is oversimplified in a variety of ways. Relevant for our purposes is that this received view ignores the reality that legal representation is often group representation and, in some cases, informal political representation in particular. Consider two areas of the law that make this challenge to the received view particularly salient—the doctrine of stare decisis and public interest lawyering.

Stare decisis is "the doctrine that courts will adhere to precedent in making their decisions."[12] Stare decisis makes each lawyer who goes before a judge on behalf of a particular client a potential informal representative for future, similarly situated parties in that "same court and all courts of lower rank in subsequent cases where the same legal issue is raised."[13] Consider: When a lawyer in a particular case argues on behalf of their individual client, they serve as their own client's formal legal representative. The lawyer represents that individual client before the court, and their arguments are meant to apply the relevant law to the facts of the instant case—that is, their client's particular circumstances. This does not mean, however, that those arguments will be applied only to the instant case and thereafter set aside. Lawyers do not get to dictate to courts how courts use their arguments going forward. Successful legal arguments are often taken up by a court and incorporated into the court's opinion as grounds for its holding. The lawyer's arguments thereby become part of that court's precedent and, given stare decisis, those incorporated arguments will inform legal determinations the court makes with respect to future parties similarly situated to the instant client. How can we understand the relationship between the lawyer in the original case and those future similarly situated parties? Having entered no agency relationship with these future parties, the lawyer is not their formal legal representative. Still, the lawyer does seem to be speaking for future similarly situated parties. Given the precedential nature of the legal system, lawyers know their successful arguments will apply to future similarly situated parties. So the lawyer in the original case may fairly be characterized as the potential informal representative of future similarly situated parties who come before that court or courts of lower rank.

Informal political representation arises even more obviously in public interest lawyering. Stephen Ellmann notes, "A great deal of what public interest lawyers do will be done on behalf of groups, either explicitly or implicitly."[14] Public interest lawyers, impact litigators, structural reform litigators, and movement lawyers may be the formal legal representatives of particular individual clients (or certified classes of clients), but it is no secret that they contemporaneously and often intentionally serve as IPRs of broader groups, movements, or causes. (I will use *public interest lawyering* and *public interest lawyer* as umbrella terms to cover, respectively, all of these related practice areas and their practitioners.) In some cases, they represent the interests not of already formed groups but rather of pluralities, and the success of their legal strategies "may hinge on the degree to which they transform this multiplicity of people into a group."[15]

Public interest lawyers, of necessity, bring individual lawsuits on behalf of particular named parties before courts. Yet these individual lawsuits are very often brought not simply (or even primarily) with the aim of redressing named parties' complaints but with the aim of changing laws and policies that affect much larger groups of people. In fact, in many public interest organizations, the issue to be litigated precedes in both consideration and time the client who will be named in the litigation. As Deborah Rhode writes, "In many organizations, if lawyers saw 'a problem that should be litigated,' they would search for an appropriate party. As one leader put it, 'we find issues, then we find a client.'"[16]

Because public interest litigation is aimed at improving the circumstances of many people and not just named parties, public interest lawyers must find "legal strategies that target broad situations rather than just individual circumstance."[17] This aim informs many of the strategic decisions public interest lawyers make: which cases to bring; when to bring them; which interests to include within the ambit of the litigation; and which clients should represent the broader interests of the group, class, or movement.[18] Given their concomitant roles as IPRs, it is unsurprising that public interest lawyers face difficult decisions of the same type as those faced by IPRs more generally. Case selection, for instance, involves challenges familiar to IPRs like deciding which conflicting group interests to prioritize and anticipating how various audiences (courts, media, the broader public) will regard the case—the so-called "optics" of the case.[19] Also like IPRs more generally, how public interest lawyers select and conduct their cases raises questions about whether they can be held accountable by the broader groups they represent. As Scott Cummings writes, "Because social movements, by definition, have conflicting interests and opposing claims to leadership and agenda-setting authority, how lawyers make client selection decisions invariably involves choosing sides in internal movement debates—implicating the very questions about accountability to broader movement constituencies that the movement lawyering model seeks to minimize."[20] And, just like IPRs more generally, public interest lawyers face practical difficulties consulting the broader groups they represent.

Some public interest lawyers also face further consultative difficulties specific to lawyering. As Ronald Edmonds writes,

> Practicing and potential civil rights attorneys . . . are not trained to respond to clients who do not pay their fees. A class action suit serving only those who pay the attorney fee has the effect of permitting the

fee paying minority to impose its will on the majority of the class on whose behalf suit is presumably brought. Thus, these attorneys do not consult representatives of the most numerous portion of citizens who comprise a "class" in a class action suit. Failure to consult with the numerical majority in a class action desegregation suit has the effect of making the attorney an instrument of autocracy and coercion.[21]

But, as was discussed in Chapter 4, the expectation that IPRs consult the represented before acting can seem unrealistic. As then chief litigation officer of the National Association for the Advancement of Colored People, Nathaniel Jones, wrote in a July 31, 1975, letter to Derrick Bell: "It would be absurd to expect that each and every black person should be polled before a lawsuit is filed, or a plan of desegregation is proposed. Certainly, school boards, who resist these suits, do not poll their patrons on their views before shaping a position."[22]

Finding themselves in the dual role of lawyer and IPR, public interest lawyers must balance the needs of particular clients with the interests of broader groups for whom they want to induce change. Unfortunately, the canons of legal ethics seem to complicate rather than illuminate what public interest lawyers ought to do in their capacities as IPRs. As Cummings points out, "Although traditional legal ethics treats the representation of organizations as a straightforward exercise in following the clearly defined instructions of an organization's 'duly authorized constituents,' scholars have persuasively shown how this view rests on the unhelpful fiction of organizational personhood that obscures underlying governance complexity and potential conflicts of interest. Particularly in a fluid environment of grassroots organizations with nascent or decentralized governance structures, deferring to 'authorized constituents' may risk accepting the views of more empowered voices within movement conversations."[23]

Then, even when all of those concerns are sorted through and resolved, there remains the ground-level consideration that actual individual clients have real and pressing interests at stake in these cases—individual interests whose satisfaction may imperil the group interests at stake.[24]

Informal Political Representation in the Arts, Scholarship, and Journalism. As noted in Chapter 2, many people who speak, write, or create artworks focused on the plights of particular social groups—including anthropologists, sociologists, documentarians, and journalists—recognize that they are expected, both by audiences and by the groups themselves, to speak and act for those groups as their IPRs.[25] It is not hard to see why this expectation emerges. Many such parties produce their work for broad public consumption, intending to give voice to the values, interests, preferences, and perspectives of the groups that are the subject matter of their work. And, unlike many of the unwitting parties considered in this book who find themselves (to their considerable surprise) thrust one day into the role of IPR for an entire community (often on objectionable or specious grounds), authors, artists, scholars, and journalists can (and, it seems to me, should) reasonably expect that work they produce for the express purpose of giving public voice to the experiences and circumstances of particular social groups' members will naturally lead audiences and the groups themselves to treat them as speaking or acting for those groups too. It should not surprise us that audiences treat knowledgeable parties who produce work expressly for public consumption as speaking or acting for the groups that are the underlying subject matter of that work.

Yet, as James Baldwin cautions, "the reality of man as a social being is not his only reality and that artist is strangled who is forced to deal with human beings solely in social terms; and who has, moreover, as [Richard] Wright had, the necessity thrust on him of being the representative of some thirteen million people. It is a false responsibility (since writers are not congressmen) and impossible, by its nature, of fulfillment."[26] Baldwin balks at the idea that an author or artist might be treated or expected to serve as an IPR. He suggests that authors and artists should not be subject to this expectation both because by that expectation they are "strangled" and because the role is a "burden."[27] Baldwin is right; the role of the IPR can be burdensome. More than that, however, the role's demands could have a chilling effect on the work that such parties produce.

Baldwin's concern raises two different sorts of questions, one of which is better thought of as a forward-looking, aspirational question concerning what we, collectively, want the roles of authors, artists, scholars, and journalists to be; the other of which is better thought of as a question about the individual political morality of these roles as they currently manifest in societies like ours.

As to the aspirational, collective question: We do, of course, already regard the roles of artist, author, scholar, and journalist as protected social roles in many respects. Preserving the values of artistic and intellectual freedom is a fundamental requirement in a free and open democratic society. So, it may be that we should all disfavor the expectation that these parties serve as IPRs insofar as the expectation will have a predictable, direct, and deleterious chilling effect on what these parties are willing to produce. We may all share an interest in strictly separating art, literature, scholarship, and reporting from informal political representation insofar as doing so grants their producers greater freedom "to be curious in public."[28] Treating these roles as protected from the representation expectation would ensure the roles' inhabitants more creative and intellectual autonomy to explore their ideas about the groups whose lives they discuss than if they were expected to contemporaneously represent those groups. On the other hand, if the account presented in this book has succeeded in persuading you that the role of the IPR is exceedingly common—that representatives are, indeed, everywhere—then the artist, author, researcher, or journalist may not be specially burdened by this role. They may even be better off than the rest of us at informally representing insofar as they actually know what they are talking about. I do not mean to understate the significance and weightiness of the role of IPR. Rather, I want to reveal it as an utterly ordinary social role—inevitable and quotidian. It is also an open question to what extent the representation expectation will lead to the chilling effect described.

Now, "leaving aside the considerable question of what relationship precisely the artist bears" to the IPR and, with it, the question whether we collectively have interest in strengthening social norms that more strictly separate the roles of artist, author, scholar, and journalist from the role of IPR, we turn to questions of individual political morality.[29] These are questions concerning what the moral situation is for artists, authors, scholars, and journalists right now, in societies like ours, given that such parties are often treated as speaking and acting for groups that are the subject matter of their work. These parties often receive considerable personal benefits for the work they produce about the groups that are the subject matter of their work: book deals, fellowships, residencies, prizes, lucrative speaking tours. And although in many cases the artists, authors, scholars, and journalists alone may benefit from the production of their works, they certainly do not produce the work alone. They produce this work in concert with the group members who are their sources, on whom they rely for information about and access to the group. We may well think that the fact that these parties (and often not the group members who are the subject matter of their work) receive personal benefits for their work gives them special responsibility to the group to serve as its IPR, at least in cases in which the group's members want them to serve in this role.

There is much more to be said about how to understand the overlapping relationships between these roles. Accordingly, I explore these questions elsewhere.[30] There is, however, no denying the value of framing these as questions about informal political representation and drawing on the resources of this concept to better understand the difficult moral position of the public-facing artist, author, scholar, or journalist whose work concerns a particular group.

Informal Political Representation in the Media. I have returned repeatedly to the role that audiences play in the emergence of IPRs and how audience conferral generates duties for both audiences and IPRs. Still, this is only a starting point in coming to understand what responsibilities we have as audience members. Our understanding of our roles as audiences (and what duties accrue to us by virtue of those roles) will be enriched by empirical research concerning when, how, and why audience conferral occurs across a wide variety of social contexts.

One question that will benefit from further ethical reflection is how we should think about the interaction effects between audiences. Although audience conferral itself is indexed to a particular audience, interaction effects often occur between audiences (see Chapter 1). That one audience treats a party as speaking or acting for a group can persuade or pressure another audience to do so. How this persuasion or pressure manifests will no doubt reflect the relationships of power between the interacting audiences. Further work needs to analyze the relationships of power between audiences that affect how one particularly powerful audience may persuade or compel another less powerful audience to follow its lead in conferring IPR status on a given party.

A particularly interesting specification of this general question concerns the interaction effects between audiences and the media. On the account provided in this book, when an editorialist or pundit, for instance, designates a given party to be a representative of a particular group, they are themselves a conferring audience. But the media is not just one more powerful audience among others that persuades (or compels) a less powerful audience to fall in line and confer IPR status on the same party they have. Media are intentionally produced so as to be consumed by further audiences, so it seems reasonable to say that the editorialist or pundit also plays an additional role as an intermediator between the conferred-upon party and further audiences. Media outlets are, in short, both audiences themselves and habitually (and intentionally) parties whose aims are to create conditions that make audience conferral more likely by persuading (or manipulating) their readerships, viewerships, and listenerships to take one party rather than another to be the IPR for a given group.[31] We should ask, then: What special, further responsibilities accrue to media's creators—journalists, editorialists, and editors—by virtue of this influential intermediator role?

It is my hope that, by developing a systematic theory of informal political representation, I have provided valuable resources for researchers who choose to explore any of the open questions above, or still others that I have not imagined. But more immediately, I hope to have illuminated the role of informal political representation in our everyday lives. Informal political representation is not merely a topic for scholarly research but a social practice that makes our relationships to our communities personal and proximate in ways that other sorts of political participation do not. Representation is not the exclusive province of those born politicians, who deftly, with ease, and gladly, speak or act for others. Rather, speaking and acting for others is a fundamental feature of everyday life.

Throughout our lives, we will find ourselves in the three positions that make up the IPR relationship—audience, represented group member, and IPR—sometimes in more than one of these positions at the same time. We should ask ourselves when this is so. How many times have I, in passing conversation or with a mindless question, treated someone as speaking or acting for a group? Through my conferral, I unwittingly foist on them the position of IPR, thereby both empowering and burdening them. On the other side of things, how often are my statements and actions imputed to others as expressions of their values, interests, or preferences? Whether we know it or not, what we say or do may be ascribed to others, influencing or even fundamentally shaping how they are regarded by a variety of audiences. We should consider these facts when we decide how to communicate with others. We should want to know what is required of us if it turns out that we are representatives in spite of ourselves.

Informal political representation, as a phenomenon that arises, in the first instance, out of audience conferral, gives us a new vantage point from which to understand both our relationships to others and our own positions as political actors and moral agents. We all need IPRs, whether internationally recognized movement leaders or just everyday people, to express in public the interests of the many groups to which we belong. Marginalized and oppressed groups particularly need informal political representation, as formal political representation is so often disproportionately low and sometimes entirely absent. IPRs emerge both within and beyond traditional political settings. Some testify before Congress, others on social media. Although unelected, IPRs can have significant power to influence how a wide variety of audiences regard those they represent. Such power generates unexpected duties for both IPRs and their audiences. Among neighbors and friends, in school or at the school board meeting, any one of us may at any time be called upon to be an IPR, speaking or acting for others whether we know it or not. We are not just speaking for ourselves.

Notes

Introduction

1. See Mónica Brito Vieira, "Founders and Re-founders: Struggles of Self-Authorized Representation," *Constellations* 22, no. 4 (2015): 500.

2. Some groups' marginalization is not unjust because, for instance, (1) their members choose self-segregation from mainstream society (e.g., insular religious communities), or (2) their marginalization results from their own morally objectionable shared ideologies (e.g., hate groups). The scope of the ensuing argument does not range over such groups. Going forward, I use the term *marginalized* as shorthand for *unjustly marginalized*.

3. Booker T. Washington, "The Standard Printed Version of the Atlanta Exposition Address," in W. E. B. Du Bois, *The Souls of Black Folk: Authoritative Text, Contexts, Criticism,* ed. Henry L. Gates Jr. and Terri H. Oliver (New York: W. W. Norton, 1999), 170.

4. For defenses of this claim, see Linda Martín Alcoff, "Feminism, Speaking for Others, and the Role of the Philosopher: An Interview with Linda Martín Alcoff," *Stance: An International Undergraduate Philosophy Journal* 9, no. 1 (2016): 92: "You can't entirely avoid speaking for others. Some have argued that there are so many problems with speaking for others that we should just stop doing it. But that's not always possible. There are refugees who don't have access to the media. There are animals who cannot speak directly. There is the environment that cannot speak. We cannot put a complete ban on speaking for others, but it's always preferable to be a conduit that makes it possible for others to speak, and to 'speak with' rather than 'speak for,' to get more voices heard." See also Robert A. Dahl, *Democracy and Its Critics* (New Haven, CT: Yale University Press, 1989), 225–231; Iris M. Young, *Inclusion and Democracy* (New York: Oxford University Press, 2000), 124–125; and Jane J. Mansbridge, *Beyond Adversary Democracy* (New York: Basic Books, 1980), 249–251.

5. Young, *Inclusion and Democracy,* 125.

6. W. E. B. Du Bois, "The Talented Tenth," in *The Negro Problem* (New York: James Pott, 1903), 31. I discuss Du Bois throughout this book; my interpretation of his writings has been influenced by a number of Du Bois scholars, but especially Lawrie Balfour, *Democracy's Reconstruction: Thinking Politically with W. E. B. Du Bois* (New York: Oxford University

Press, 2011); Elvira Basevich, *A Duboisian Democracy: On Method and Practice* (New York: Oxford University Press, forthcoming); Elvira Basevich, *W. E. B. Du Bois: The Lost and the Found* (Medford, MA: Polity Press, 2021); Derrick Darby, "Du Bois's Defense of Democracy," in "Democratic Failure," ed. Melissa Schwartzberg and Daniel Viehoff, *NOMOS* 63 (2020): 207–246; Derrick Darby, *A Realistic Blacktopia: Why We Must Unite to Fight* (Oxford: Oxford University Press, 2023), esp. 161–188; Robert Gooding-Williams, *In the Shadow of Du Bois: Afro-Modern Political Thought in America* (Cambridge, MA: Harvard University Press, 2009); Robert Gooding-Williams, "W. E. B. Du Bois," in *Stanford Encyclopedia of Philosophy,* Stanford University, 1997–, article published September 13, 2017, https://plato .stanford.edu/entries/dubois/; Adolph L. Reed Jr., *W. E. B. Du Bois and American Political Thought: Fabianism and the Color Line* (Oxford: Oxford University Press, 1997); Melvin L. Rogers, "The People, Rhetoric, and Affect: On the Political Force of Du Bois's *The Souls of Black Folk,*" *American Political Science Review* 106, no. 1 (2012): 188–203; Tommie Shelby, *We Who Are Dark: The Philosophical Foundations of Black Solidarity* (Cambridge, MA: Belknap Press of Harvard University Press, 2005); Paul C. Taylor, *Black Is Beautiful: A Philosophy of Black Aesthetics* (Hoboken, NJ: Wiley, 2016); and Paul C. Taylor, "W. E. B. Du Bois," *Philosophy Compass* 5, no. 11 (2010): 904–915. I also benefited greatly from participation in a graduate seminar, "Reading Du Bois," taught by Tommie Shelby and Walter Johnson at Harvard University in spring 2016; conversations with students in my seminar, "Du Bois and Democracy," at San Francisco State University in spring 2019 and Stanford University in winter 2021 and winter 2023; and many conversations with Kurt Nutting.

7. Tarana Burke, "#MeToo Was Started for Black and Brown Women and Girls. They're Still Being Ignored," *Washington Post,* November 9, 2017, https://www.washingtonpost.com /news/post-nation/wp/2017/11/09/the-waitress-who-works-in-the-diner-needs-to-know -that-the-issue-of-sexual-harassment-is-about-her-too/.

Although many examples in this book are drawn from the political context of the United States, I provide a general conceptual and normative framework for understanding informal political representation.

8. Alicia Garza, "A Herstory of the #BlackLivesMatter Movement," in *Are All the Women Still White? Rethinking Race, Expanding Feminisms,* ed. Janell Hobson (Albany: State University of New York Press, 2016), 23–28.

9. *Preventing Gun Violence: A Call to Action; Testimony before the Committee on the Judiciary,* House of Representatives, 116th Cong. (2019) (testimony of Aalayah Eastmond, senior at Marjory Stoneman Douglas High School), https://www.congress.gov/116/meeting/house/108 838/witnesses/HHRG-116-JU00-Wstate-EastmondA-20190206.pdf, emphasis in original.

10. See, e.g., Malala Yousafzai, "Malala Yousafzai UN Speech: Girl Shot in Attack by Taliban Gives Address | The New York Times," video, 16:21, YouTube, July 12, 2013, https:// www.youtube.com/watch?v=5SClmL43dTo; Greta Thunberg, "Transcript: Greta Thunberg's Speech at the U.N. Climate Action Summit," NPR, September 23, 2019, https://www.npr.org /2019/09/23/763452863/transcript-greta-thunbergs-speech-at-the-u-n-climate-action-summit.

11. Mansbridge, *Beyond Adversary Democracy,* 39–135, 251.

12. On symbolic representatives, see Hanna Fenichel Pitkin, *The Concept of Representation* (Berkeley: University of California Press, 1967), 92–111; on descriptive representatives, see the texts referenced in Chapter 6 of the present volume.

13. Although this is not a book on leaders or leadership, I hope to explore the relationships between informal political representation and leadership in future work. For an extremely helpful discussion of the normative relationships between representation and leadership, see Eric Beerbohm, "Is Democratic Leadership Possible?" *American Political Science Review* 109, no. 4 (2015): 639–652. See also Eric Beerbohm, *In Our Name: The Ethics of Democracy* (Princeton, NJ: Princeton University Press, 2012).

14. Throughout this book, I use *they, their,* and *them* as both third-person singular pronouns and third-person plural pronouns.

15. There has been notable and illuminating work on IPRs, self-appointed representatives, nonelectoral representatives, and other similar phenomena. See Linda Alcoff, "The Problem of Speaking for Others," *Cultural Critique*, no. 20 (1991): 5–32; Mónica Brito Vieira, ed., *Reclaiming Representation: Contemporary Advances in the Theory of Political Representation* (New York: Taylor and Francis, 2017); Mónica Brito Vieira, "Representing Silence in Politics," *American Political Science Review* 114, no. 4 (2020): 976–988; Mark Brown, "Deliberation and Representation," in *The Oxford Handbook of Deliberative Democracy,* ed. Andre Bächtiger, John S. Dryzek, Jane Mansbridge, and Mark Warren (Oxford: Oxford University Press, 2018), 171–186; Dario Castiglione and Mark E. Warren, "Rethinking Democratic Representation: Eight Theoretical Issues and a Post-script," in *The Constructivist Turn in Political Representation,* ed. Lisa Disch, Nadia Urbinati, and Mathijs van de Sande (Edinburgh: University of Edinburgh Press, 2019), 21–47; Joshua Cohen, Joel Rogers, and Erik Olin Wright, eds., *Associations and Democracy* (London: Verso Books, 1995); Lisa J. Disch, "The 'Constructivist Turn' in Democratic Representation: A Normative Dead-End?," *Constellations* 22, no. 4 (2015): 487–499; Lisa J. Disch, *Making Constituencies: Representation as Mobilization in Mass Democracy* (Chicago: University of Chicago Press, 2021); Lisa Disch, "Toward a Mobilization Conception of Democratic Representation," *American Political Science Review* 105, no. 1 (2001): 100–114; Suzanne Dovi, *The Good Representative* (Malden, MA: Blackwell, 2007); Suzanne Dovi, "Political Representation," in *Stanford Encyclopedia of Philosophy,* Stanford University, 1997–, article last revised August 29, 2018, https://plato.stanford.edu/archives/fall2018/entries/political-representation; John S. Dryzek and Simon Niemeyer, "Discursive Representation," *American Political Science Review* 102, no. 4 (2008): 481–493; Inigo Gonzalez-Ricoy and Felipe Rey, "Enfranchising the Future: Climate Justice and the Representation of Future Generations," *WIREs Climate Change* 10, no. 5 (2019): e598; Samuel Hayat, "Unrepresentative Claims: Speaking for Oneself in a Social Movement," *American Political Science Review* 116, no. 3 (2022): 1038–1105; Connor K. Kianpour, "The Minority Retort: In Defense of Defection in Marginalized Groups," *Public Affairs Quarterly* 36, no. 4 (2022): 280–308; Connor K. Kianpour, "The Political Speech Rights of the Tokenized," *Critical Review of International Social and Political Philosophy* (2023): 1–21; Jonathan W. Kuyper, "Systemic Representation: Democracy,

Deliberation, and Nonelectoral Representatives," *American Political Science Review* 110, no. 2 (2016): 308–324; Mansbridge, *Beyond Adversary Democracy,* 39–135, 251; Hélène Landemore, *Open Democracy: Reinventing Popular Rule for the Twenty-First Century* (Princeton, NJ: Princeton University Press, 2020); Jane Mansbridge, "Clarifying the Concept of Representation," *American Political Science Review* 105, no. 3 (2011): 621–630; Jane Mansbridge, "Recursive Representation," in *Creating Political Presence: The New Politics of Democratic Representation,* ed. Dario Castiglione and Johannes Pollak (Chicago: University of Chicago Press, 2018), 298–338; Jane Mansbridge, "Rethinking Representation," *American Political Science Review* 97, no. 4 (2003): 515–528; Jane Mansbridge, James Bohman, Simone Chambers, Thomas Christiano, Archon Fung, John Parkinson, Dennis F. Thompson, and Mark E. Warren, "A Systemic Approach to Deliberative Democracy," in *Deliberative Systems: Deliberative Democracy at the Large Scale,* ed. John Parkinson and Jane Mansbridge (Cambridge: Cambridge University Press, 2012), 1–26; Laura Montanaro, "The Democratic Legitimacy of Self-Appointed Representatives," *Journal of Politics* 74, no. 4 (2012): 1094–1107; Laura Montanaro, *Who Elected Oxfam? A Democratic Defense of Self-Appointed Representatives* (Cambridge: Cambridge University Press, 2017); Michele Moody-Adams, *Making Space for Justice: Social Movements, Collective Imagination, and Political Hope* (New York: Columbia University Press, 2022), esp. 1–113; Phillip Pettit, "Varieties of Public Representation," in *Political Representation,* ed. Ian Shapiro, Susan C. Stokes, Elisabeth Jean Wood, and Alexander S. Kirshner (Cambridge: Cambridge University Press, 2010), 61–89; Anne Phillips, *The Politics of Presence* (Oxford: Oxford University Press, 1995); Adolph L. Reed Jr., *The Jesse Jackson Phenomenon: The Crisis of Purpose in Afro-American Politics* (New Haven, CT: Yale University Press, 1986); Andrew Rehfeld, *The Concept of Constituency: Political Representation, Democratic Legitimacy, and Institutional Design* (Cambridge: Cambridge University Press, 2005); Andrew Rehfeld, "The Concepts of Representation," *American Political Science Review* 105, no. 3 (2011): 631–641; Andrew Rehfeld, "Representation Rethought: On Trustees, Delegates, and Gyroscopes in the Study of Political Representation and Democracy," *American Political Science Review* 103, no. 2 (2009): 214–230; Andrew Rehfeld, "Towards a General Theory of Political Representation," *Journal of Politics* 68 (2006): 1–21; Felipe Rey, "The Representative System," *Critical Review of International Social and Political Philosophy* 26, no. 6 (2020): 831–854; Felipe Rey, *El sistema representativo: Las representaciones políticas y la transformación de la democracia parlamentaria* (Barcelona: GEDISA, 2023); Jennifer C. Rubenstein, "The Misuse of Power, Not Bad Representation: Why It Is Beside the Point That No One Elected Oxfam," *Journal of Political Philosophy* 22, no. 2 (2014): 204–230; Michael Saward, "Authorisation and Authenticity: Representation and the Unelected," *Journal of Political Philosophy* 17, no. 1 (2009): 1–22; Michael Saward, *The Representative Claim* (Oxford: Oxford University Press, 2010); T. M. Scanlon, *The Difficulty of Tolerance* (Cambridge: Cambridge University Press, 2003), 3, 108–109, 190–192, 194, 197–201 (on informal politics); Dara Z. Strolovitch, *Affirmative Advocacy: Race, Class, and Gender in Interest Group Politics* (Chicago: University of Chicago Press, 2008); Nadia Urbinati, "Representation as Advocacy: A Study of Democratic Deliberation," *Political Theory* 28, no. 6 (2000): 758–786; Nadia Urbinati, *Representative Democracy: Principles and Genealogy* (Chicago: University of Chicago Press, 2006); Nadia Urbinati and Mark E. Warren, "The Concept of Representation in Contemporary Democratic Theory," *Annual Review of Political Science* 11 (2008): 387–412; Ashwini Vasanthakumar, *The Ethics of Exile: A Political Theory of Diaspora* (Oxford: Oxford University Press, 2021), esp. 141–160; Ashwini Vasanthakumar, "Exile Political Representation," *Journal of Political Philosophy* 24, no. 3 (2016): 277–296; Mark E. Warren, "Informal Representation: Who Speaks for Whom?," *Democracy and Society* 1, no. 1 (2004): 8–15; S. Laurel Weldon, *When Protest Makes Policy: How Social Movements Represent Disadvantaged Groups* (Ann Arbor: University of Michigan Press, 2011); Melissa S. Williams, *Voice, Trust, and Memory: Marginalized Groups and the Failings of Liberal Representation* (Princeton, NJ: Princeton University Press, 1998); Iris Marion Young, "Deferring Group Representation," in "Ethnicity and Group Rights," ed. Ian Shapiro and Will Kymlicka, *NOMOS* 39 (1997): 349–376; Iris Marion Young, *Inclusion and Democracy* (New York: Oxford University Press, 2000); and Iris Marion Young, *Justice and the Politics of Difference* (Princeton, NJ: Princeton University Press, 1990).

16. Alexander M. Bickel, "The Supreme Court and Reapportionment," in *Reapportionment in the 1970s,* ed. Nelson W. Polsby (Berkeley: University of California Press, 1971), 59, quoted in Lani Guinier, *The Tyranny of the Majority: Fundamental Fairness in Representative Democracy* (New York: Free Press, 1994), 268n21.

17. Young, "Deferring Group Representation," 353.

18. James Madison, "The Same Subject Continued: The Union as a Safeguard against Domestic Faction and Insurrection," *Federalist,* no. 10, November 23, 1787, https://guides .loc.gov/federalist-papers/text-1-10#s-lg-box-wrapper-25493273.

19. See, e.g., Malcolm X, "Malcolm Highlights the Problem with 'Negro' Leaders. Michigan State University, East Lansing, Michigan. 23 January 1963," in *The Autobiography of Malcolm X: Speeches and Interviews,* http://ccnmtl.columbia.edu/projects/mmt/mxp/speeches /mxt19.html; W. E. B. Du Bois, "Of Mr. Booker T. Washington and Others," in *The Souls of Black Folk,* ed. David W. Blight and Robert Gooding-Williams (Boston: Bedford Books, 1997), 67: "Nearly all the former ones had become leaders by the silent suffrage of their fellows, had sought to lead their own people alone, and were usually, save Douglass, little known outside their race. But Booker T. Washington arose as essentially the leader not of one race but of two,—a compromiser between the South, the North, and the Negro."

20. Social groups are groups whose members, by and large, regard themselves to be members of the group. Members may see themselves as having common interests or special affinity with other group members by virtue of shared circumstances, whether contemporary or historical; Young, *Justice and the Politics of Difference,* 43. A person's membership in the group may be obvious to outsiders by virtue of shared physical, social, cultural, or linguistic indicators, as when "race and gender mark the body," but this need not be so; Patricia Hill Collins, "Some Group Matters: Intersectionality, Situated Standpoints, and Black Feminist Thought," in *A Companion to African-American Philosophy,* ed. Tommy L. Lott and John P. Pittman (Malden, MA: Blackwell, 2006), 211.

Different social groups may be more or less socially cohesive, and members may be more or less likely to regard their own memberships as salient features of their identities. As Collins, "Some Group Matters," 211, puts the point, "Examining how race and class, on the one hand, and gender, on the other, have been historically organized in the United States suggests that they represent two divergent ways of constructing groups. . . . Because women are separated from one another by race and class, they face different challenges both in conceptualizing themselves as a group at all and in seeing themselves as a group similar to race-class groups."

How an IPR ought to represent a particular social group is a context-sensitive matter, guided both by what the group's members share (common underlying values, interests, and preferences) and what they do not share (divergent or conflicting interests). Accordingly, there is no easy generalization to be made about how IPRs ought to represent social groups. I return to the difficulty of generalization when I discuss IPRs' *justice without* duties in Chapter 4.

21. Young, "Deferring Group Representation," 352.

22. Young, "Deferring Group Representation," 352.

23. W. E. B. Du Bois, "Of the Training of Black Men," in *The Souls of Black Folk,* ed. Blight and Gooding-Williams, 101. On uncrystallized interests, see also Jane Mansbridge, "Should Blacks Represent Blacks and Women Represent Women? A Contingent 'Yes,'" *Journal of Politics* 61, no. 3 (1999): 643–648; and Jane Mansbridge, "The Future of Political Theory: Lippincott Lecture," *Contemporary Political Theory* 22, no. 2 (2023): 255–256.

24. Scott Strzelczyk, for instance, leads the Western Maryland Initiative and purports to speak for the people of Allegany, Carroll, Frederick, Garrett, and Washington Counties when he calls for secession of these counties from the existing state of Maryland. Citizens in the counties already have FPRs, making Strzelczyk a supplemental IPR (provided, of course, that he has in fact been conferred IPR status by an audience). Michael S. Rosenwald, "Western Maryland Secessionists Seek to Sever Ties with the Liberal Free State," *Washington Post,* September 8, 2013, https://www.washingtonpost.com/local/western-maryland-secessionists -seek-to-sever-ties-with-the-liberal-free-state/2013/09/08/15e97aa8-1651-11e3-804b-d3a1a 3a18f2c_story.html.

By contrast, many U.S. prisoners are prohibited from taking part in the election of FPRs, meaning that they cannot be said to have formal political representation (although one might argue that they have virtual representation). On virtual representation, see Joseph Fishkin, "Taking Virtual Representation Seriously," *William and Mary Law Review* 59, no. 5 (2017): 1681–1728. So when Kim Kardashian speaks for U.S. prisoners at the White House, her informal political representation of prisoners is not supplemental; "Kim Kardashian Visits White House with Prisoners She Helped Free," BBC, March 5, 2020, https://www.bbc.com /news/world-us-canada-51744918; NBC News, "Watch Kim Kardashian West's Full White House Speech on Prison Reform," video, 5:37, YouTube, June 13, 2019, https://www .youtube.com/watch?v=fz-oGxLVJpY.

25. See Erwin Chemerinsky, "In Defense of Judicial Supremacy," *William and Mary Law Review,* 58, no. 5 (2017): 1463: "prisoners, criminal defendants, or those who are not citizens . . . lack political power—they do not give money to political candidates; they are generally prohibited from voting; and they are unpopular and often unsympathetic. When is the last time a legislature acted to expand the rights of prisoners or criminal defendants?"

26. See, e.g., Fishkin, "Virtual Representation."

27. William Safire, "On Language: Third Rail," *New York Times Magazine,* February 18, 2007, http://www.nytimes.com/2007/02/18/magazine/18wwlnsafire.t.html.

28. See, e.g., Keri B. Burchfield and William Mingus, "Not in My Neighborhood: Assessing Registered Sex Offenders' Experiences with Local Social Capital and Social Control," *Criminal Justice and Behavior* 35, no. 3 (2008): 356–374; and Chemerinsky, "Judicial Supremacy," 1463.

29. Marjorie A. Shields, "Validity of Statutes Imposing Residency Restrictions on Registered Sex Offenders," 25 A.L.R. 6th 227 (2007).

30. See, e.g., Kari White, "Where Will They Go? Sex Offender Residency Restrictions as Modern-Day Banishment," *Case Western Reserve Law Review* 59, no. 1 (2008): 161–189; Maurice Chammah, "Making the Case against Banishing Sex Offenders," Marshall Project, October 5, 2016, https://www.themarshallproject.org/2016/10/05/making-the-case-against-banishing-sex-offenders.

31. Chammah, "Sex Offenders."

32. Robin van der Wall, quoted in Chammah, "Sex Offenders."

33. Registered sex offenders are informally politically represented by groups like Reform Sex Offender Laws and Texas Voices for Reason and Justice; Chammah, "Sex Offenders."

34. Louis Theroux, "A Place for Paedophiles," BBC, video, 45:00, April 2009, https://www.bbc.co.uk/programmes/b00k3ms6; Louis Theroux, "Where They Keep the Paedophiles," BBC, April 17, 2009, http://news.bbc.co.uk/2/hi/uk_news/magazine/8004064.stm.

35. Andy Duehren, "U.S. Supreme Court Ruling Could Imperil Texas Sex Offender Rules," *Texas Tribune,* June 19, 2017, https://www.texastribune.org/2017/06/19/supreme-court-ruling-could-imperil-texas-sex-offender-laws/.

36. Although IPRs do not face formal recall or other formal sanctions for representing unpopular groups, they may, of course, still face informal reprisals for their representative decisions. For instance, an IPR may represent a broader group comprising several subgroups. If members of the broader group object to the representation of an unpopular or stigmatized subgroup by the IPR, then the IPR who decides to represent this subgroup over the larger group's objections can be disauthorized or even pushed out by the larger group.

37. Rigoberta Menchú, *I, Rigoberta Menchú: An Indian Woman in Guatemala,* ed. Elisabeth Burgos-Debray, trans. Ann Wright (New York: Verso Books, 2010). On political representation as an act of making present, see Phillips, *The Politics of Presence.* On Menchú speaking for others, see Alcoff, "The Problem of Speaking for Others," 8, 18–19.

38. In Chapter 4, I discuss cases in which representation before certain audiences should be avoided.

39. In Chapter 5, I discuss the *in confidence* complaint, whereby a group objects that their IPR has violated the group's shared norm of nondisclosure concerning certain matters.

40. In some cases (like the case of gig workers), some interests cannot be met unless the members of the group work collectively to secure the satisfaction of those interests.

For some recent discussions on the creation of constituencies, the construction of the represented by the representative (or by their representative activities), as well as discussion of the "constructivist turn" in theories of political representation, see Dovi, "Political Representation"; Disch, "The 'Constructivist Turn'"; Disch, *Making Constituencies;* Thomas Fossen, "Constructivism and the Logic of Political Representation," *American Political Science Review* 113, no. 3 (2019): 824–837; Montanaro, *Who Elected Oxfam?,* 38; Saward, "Authorisation and Authenticity"; and Saward, *The Representative Claim.* For a discussion of the stages of development of the proletariat from "an incoherent mass" of "labourers" to their "organization . . . into a class, and consequently into a political party," see Karl Marx and Friedrich Engels, "Manifesto of the Communist Party," in *The Marx-Engels Reader,* 2nd ed., ed. Robert C. Tucker (New York: W. W. Norton, 1978), 480–481.

41. Kuyper, "Systemic Representation."

42. Menchú, *I, Rigoberta Menchú,* xi–xii.

43. Abahlali baseMjondolo Movement SA v. Premier of the Province of Kwazulu-Natal, CCT 12 / 09 (Constitutional Court of South Africa, 2009), https://collections.concourt.org .za/handle/20.500.12144/3576.

44. Martin Luther King Jr., *Stride toward Freedom: The Montgomery Story* (Boston: Beacon Press, 2010), 96–121; on the Montgomery Bus Boycott, see David J. Garrow, *Bearing the Cross: Martin Luther King, Jr., and the Southern Christian Leadership Conference* (New York: William Morrow, 2004), 11–82.

45. This group identification is to be distinguished from *people who identify as Muslims,* an identification generated by individual group members themselves. On the phenomenon of being perceived to "look Muslim," see, e.g., Sheryll Cashin, "To Be Muslim or Muslim-Looking in America: A Comparative Exploration of Racial and Religious Prejudice in the 21st Century," *Duke Forum for Law and Social Change* 2, no. 1 (2010): 125–140; Peter Hopkins, "Gendering Islamophobia, Racism and White Supremacy: Gendered Violence against Those Who Look Muslim," *Dialogues in Human Geography* 6, no. 2 (July 2016): 186–189; Peter Hopkins, Katherine Botterill, Gurchathen Sanghera, and Rowena Arshad, "Encountering Misrecognition: Being Mistaken for Being Muslim," *Annals of the American Association of Geographers* 107, no. 4 (2017): 934–948; Mei-Po Kwan, "From Oral Histories to Visual Narratives: Re-presenting the Post–September 11 Experiences of the Muslim Women in the USA," *Social and Cultural Geography* 9, no. 6 (2008): 653–669; Reza Shaker, Annika Jungmann, Philipp Zimmermann, Lotta Häkkinen, and Tauri Tuvikene, "Embodied Othering

Encounters with Muslim(-Looking) Passengers: Riding across Amsterdam, Tallinn, Leipzig, and Turku1," *Sociological Forum* 37, no. 2 (2022): 486–509.

46. The term *power* can pick out a variety of different phenomena, including two types of coercive power (the threat of sanction and the use of force), persuasive power (genuine persuasion on the merits), and capacity. See Jane Mansbridge, "Using Power / Fighting Power," *Constellations* 1, no. 1 (1994): 56, 69nn1–2. Unless otherwise noted, I use the term *power to influence* to pick out a party's capacity to influence, which is sometimes but not always also persuasive power.

47. On secondary marginalization, see Cathy J. Cohen, *The Boundaries of Blackness: AIDS and the Breakdown of Black Politics* (Chicago: University of Chicago Press, 1999), esp. 70–76; on what she calls "the problem of intra-group conflict," see Dovi, *The Good Representative*, 35–36, 46–47, 51.

48. See Wendy Salkin, "The Conscription of Informal Political Representatives," *Journal of Political Philosophy* 29, no. 4 (2021): 429–455.

49. Isabel Kershner, "Speech by Netanyahu Opens Political Divisions in Israel, Too," *New York Times,* March 1, 2015, https://www.nytimes.com/2015/03/02/world/middleeast /netanyahus-speech-opens-political-divisions-in-israel-too.html.

50. Teresa Welsh, "Netanyahu Calls on American Jews to Oppose Nuclear Deal with Iran," *U.S. News and World Report,* August 4, 2015, http://www.usnews.com/news/articles /2015/08/04/israeli-prime-minister-netanyahu-makes-direct-appeal-to-american-jews -over-iran-deal.

51. Welsh, "Netanyahu Calls on American Jews."

52. David Harris Gershon, "Senator Feinstein on 'Arrogant' Netanyahu's Claim to Represent All Jews: 'He Doesn't Speak for Me,'" *Daily Kos,* March 1, 2015, http://www.dailykos .com/story/2015/03/02/1367889/-Senator-Feinstein-on-arrogant-Netanyahu-s-claim-to -represent-all-Jews-He-doesn-t-speak-for-me.

53. Barbara Ransby, *Ella Baker and the Black Freedom Movement: A Radical Democratic Vision* (Chapel Hill: University of North Carolina Press, 2003), 176.

54. See Cohen, *Boundaries of Blackness,* esp. 70–76; and Dovi, *The Good Representative*, 35–36, 46–47, 51.

55. George Monbiot, "Bono Can't Help Africans by Stealing Their Voice," *Guardian,* June 17, 2013, http://www.theguardian.com/commentisfree/2013/jun/17/bono-africans -stealing-voice-poor.

56. Max Bankole Jarrett, quoted in Barry Malone, "Are Bono and Bob Geldof Good for Africa?," *Reuters,* May 13, 2009, https://www.reuters.com/article/us-ethiopia-geldof/are -bono-and-bob-geldof-good-for-africa-idUSTRE54C3KO20090513.

57. See also Cohen, *Boundaries of Blackness,* 70–76.

58. In thinking through the ethics of representation, I have found guidance from many sources, which I reference throughout the book. See Alcoff, "The Problem of Speaking for

Others"; Beerbohm, *In Our Name;* Eric Beerbohm, "The Ethics of Electioneering," *Journal of Political Philosophy* 24, no. 4 (2016): 381–405; Dovi, *The Good Representative,* esp. 52–200; Suzanne Dovi, "Good Representatives Foster Autonomy," *PS: Political Science and Politics* 51, no. 2 (2018): 323–326; Suzanne Dovi and Jesse McCain, "The Ethics of Representation," in *Political Ethics: A Handbook,* ed. Edward Hall and Andrew Sabl (Princeton, NJ: Princeton University Press, 2022), 82–103; Du Bois, "Mr. Booker T. Washington"; Alexander A. Guerrero, "The Paradox of Voting and the Ethics of Political Representation," *Philosophy and Public Affairs* 38, no. 3 (2010): 272–306; Niko Kolodny, *The Pecking Order: Social Hierarchy as a Philosophical Problem* (Cambridge, MA: Harvard University Press, 2023), esp. 345–401; Niko Kolodny, "Rule over None II: Social Equality and the Justification of Democracy," *Philosophy and Public Affairs* 42, no. 4 (2014): 317–320; David Plotke, "Representation Is Democracy," *Constellations* 4, no. 1 (1997): 19–34; Andrew Sabl, *Ruling Passions: Political Offices and Democratic Ethics* (Princeton, NJ: Princeton University Press, 2002); Russell Hardin, "Representing Ignorance," *Social Philosophy and Policy* 21, no. 1 (2004): 76–99; Montanaro, "The Democratic Legitimacy"; Montanaro, *Who Elected Oxfam?;* Sofia Näsström, "Democratic Representation beyond Election," *Constellations* 22, no. 1 (2015): 1–12; Eline Severs and Suzanne Dovi, "Why We Need to Return to the Ethics of Political Representation," *PS: Political Science and Politics* 51, no. 2 (2018): 309–313; Seana Shiffrin, "Democracy Representation as Duty Delegation," *Proceedings and Addresses of the American Philosophical Association* 96 (2022): 90–116; Dennis F. Thompson, "The Ethics of Representation," *Hastings Center Report* 11, no. 1 (1981): 10–14; Melissa S. Williams, *Voice, Trust, and Memory: Marginalized Groups and the Failings of Liberal Representation* (Princeton, NJ: Princeton University Press, 1998).

59. In previous work I labeled this phenomenon "audience uptake." See Salkin, "The Conscription of Informal Political Representatives"; and Wendy Salkin, "Democracy Within, Justice Without: The Duties of Informal Political Representatives," *Noûs* 56, no. 4 (2022): 940–971. The label misled some to think that I meant to suggest that audiences were discovering that certain parties were already IPRs, independent of those audiences' conferral of the status. But audiences do not find people who are already IPRs (although they may find people on whom others have already conferred the status); they make people into IPRs by conferring the status on them. To allay confusion, I have opted to use the term *audience conferral* in this book.

60. T. M. Scanlon, *What We Owe to Each Other* (Cambridge, MA: Belknap Press of Harvard University Press, 1998), 295–327.

61. For example, Leo Townsend and Dina Lupin, "Representation and Epistemic Violence," *International Journal of Philosophical Studies* 29, no. 4 (2021): 585, make such a claim: "The problem with Salkin's conscriptionist account of representation, in our view, is that it hands too much power to audiences, making their uptake not just necessary but *sufficient* for conferring the status of spokesperson or representative" (responding to Salkin, "The Conscription of Informal Political Representatives").

62. Malcolm X, "Malcolm Highlights the Problem with 'Negro' Leaders."

63. In previous work, I labeled this phenomenon "group uptake"; see Salkin, "The Conscription of Informal Political Representatives"; Salkin, "Democracy Within, Justice Without." The label misled some to think that I meant to suggest that groups were discovering that certain parties were already authorized IPRs, independent of those groups themselves authorizing the IPRs. But represented groups do not find authorized IPRs (although they may find people who other groups have already authorized)—they themselves authorize their own IPRs. To allay confusion, I have opted to use the term *group authorization* in this book.

64. On the vulnerability of the represented to their representatives, see Dovi, *The Good Representative*, 22, 28, 33, 35–36, 63, 131, 136–137, 142–143, 172, 187, and 189; and Dovi, "Good Representatives Foster Autonomy."

65. S. Andrew Schroeder, "Diversifying Science: Comparing the Benefits of Citizen Science with the Benefits of Bringing More Women into Science," *Synthese* 200, no. 4 (2022): 11n16, helpfully discusses the role of informal political representation in citizen science.

66. See Dorothy Schwartz's comments in the minutes of Hackensack City Council meetings at which she spoke: City of Hackensack, New Jersey, legislation database, accessed July 28, 2022, https://ecode360.com/HA0454/search?query=%22dorothy%20schwartz%22&scope=all&sortOrder=relevance&selections=.

Chapter 1. Audience Conferral

1. Martin Luther King Jr., *Stride toward Freedom: The Montgomery Story* (Boston: Beacon Press, 2010), 34–36, 50–52, 97–101.

2. King, *Stride toward Freedom*, 89, 41, 60, 96, 98.

3. See Michael Saward, *The Representative Claim* (Oxford: Oxford University Press, 2010), 48.

4. In this book, I use "spokesperson" and its variants interchangeably with "representative" and its variants.

5. See Linda Alcoff, "The Problem of Speaking for Others," *Cultural Critique*, no. 20 (1991): 8–9, 30n7; Saward, *The Representative Claim*, 49.

6. *Oxford English Dictionary*, s.v. "speak for," accessed October 25, 2023, https://www.oed.com/search/dictionary/?scope=Entries&q=speak+for. In this book, I use *speak for* and its variants interchangeably with *speak on behalf of* and its variants.

7. Alcoff, "The Problem of Speaking for Others," 9.

8. Alcoff, "The Problem of Speaking for Others," 9.

9. Jane Mansbridge, "Clarifying the Concept of Representation," *American Political Science Review* 105, no. 3 (2011): 628, points out that "those who attend a town meeting and make binding collective decisions that affect those who are absent do in some way stand in for the absentees, even if that is not their intent."

10. Similarly, I understand *acting for* to pick out a spectrum of phenomena on which some instance of acting for another are authorized while others are not; some instances of acting for another are intentional while others are not.

11. Although I am not, in this book, offering an account of group assertion or group speech acts, I have found research on the topic helpful. See Jennifer Lackey, "Group Assertion," *Erkenntnis* 83, no. 1 (2018): 21–42; Kirk Ludwig, "What Are Group Speech Acts?" *Language and Communication* 70 (2020): 46–58; and Grace Paterson, "Group Speakers," *Language and Communication* 70 (2020): 59–66.

12. Elsewhere I have discussed the many different ways judges are representatives; see Wendy Salkin, "Speaking for Others from the Bench," *Legal Theory* 29, no. 2 (2023): 151–184.

13. Mansbridge, "Clarifying the Concept of Representation," 628, calls for such an analysis of the relationship between formal and informal political representation:

> Normatively, it is worth parsing out more fully the spectrum between formal and informal representation, the attendant strong through weak claims that "constituents" can make on their "representatives," and the judgments that third parties can make on the system. An articulated spectrum of this sort might capture both the intuitive force of [Andrew] Rehfeld's statement, "In the case of a direct democracy, citizens are not political representatives because they are not standing in for anyone but acting as themselves" . . . and also the ways in which those who attend a town meeting and make binding collective decisions that affect those who are absent do in some way stand in for the absentees, even if that is not their intent.

In many ways, this book is an attempt to do the parsing that Mansbridge recommends.

14. Audience conferral is not a form of authorization. Authorization requires the conscious, if not intentional, granting of discretionary and sometimes normative power to the authorized party. By contrast, audience conferral is a fact that makes it the case that a party comes to have the power to influence an audience—a fact that can be realized in a variety of ways, some conscious and others not, some intentional and others not. A subsequent section of this chapter is devoted to characterizing audience conferral in some detail.

15. For other treatments of authorization in nonelectoral contexts, see Alcoff, "The Problem of Speaking for Others," 10; Lisa J. Disch, "The 'Constructivist Turn' in Democratic Representation: A Normative Dead-End?," *Constellations* 22, no. 4 (2015): 487–499; Lisa J. Disch, *Making Constituencies: Representation as Mobilization in Mass Democracy* (Chicago: University of Chicago Press, 2021), 34, 43, 153–154n5; Suzanne Dovi, *The Good Representative* (Malden, MA: Blackwell, 2007), 8, 18, 53–55, 60–65; Laura Montanaro, *Who Elected Oxfam? A Democratic Defense of Self-Appointed Representatives* (Cambridge: Cambridge University Press, 2017), 83–85; Michael Saward, "Authorisation and Authenticity: Representation and the Unelected," *Journal of Political Philosophy* 17, no. 1 (2009): 1–22; and Saward,

The Representative Claim, 102–110. On representative authorization generally, see especially Thomas Hobbes, *Leviathan* (New York: Oxford University Press, 1996); and Hanna Fenichel Pitkin, *The Concept of Representation* (Berkeley: University of California Press, 1967), 38–59.

16. Of course, generalizations admit of exceptions. The group *future generations* has an ill-defined membership but can be formally represented in law. On the representation of future generations, see, e.g., Inigo Gonzalez-Ricoy and Felipe Rey, "Enfranchising the Future: Climate Justice and the Representation of Future Generations," *WIREs Climate Change* 10, no. 5 (2019): e598.

17. See National Association for the Advancement of Colored People, Constitution of the National Association for the Advancement of Colored People, 2019, article 4, "Membership," and article 10, "Expulsion, Suspension or Removal of Officers and Members," https://naacp.org/resources/naacp-constitution.

18. On the normative dimensions of elections, see Eric Beerbohm, *In Our Name: The Ethics of Democracy* (Princeton, NJ: Princeton University Press, 2012); Emilee Booth Chapman, *Election Day: How We Vote and What It Means for Democracy* (Princeton, NJ: Princeton University Press, 2022); and Alexander A. Guerrero, "The Paradox of Voting and the Ethics of Political Representation," *Philosophy and Public Affairs* 38, no. 3 (2010): 272–306.

19. For other treatments of representative accountability, see Disch, *Making Constituencies,* 40, 137; Dovi, *The Good Representative,* 51–52, 61–62, 65–68, 95–96, 139–140; Ruth W. Grant and Robert O. Keohane, "Accountability and Abuses of Power in World Politics," *American Political Science Review* 99, no. 1 (2005): 29–43; Mansbridge, "Clarifying the Concept of Representation," 621, 625, 628; Jane Mansbridge, "A 'Selection Model' of Political Representation," *Journal of Political Philosophy* 17, no. 4 (2009): 369–398; Montanaro, *Who Elected Oxfam?,* 85–90; Pitkin, *The Concept of Representation,* 55–59; and Saward, *The Representative Claim,* 82–110.

20. Wendy Salkin, "The Conscription of Informal Political Representatives," *Journal of Political Philosophy* 29, no. 4 (2021): 437.

21. Movement for Black Lives, "Black Power Rising: Our Five-Year Plan," accessed September 19, 2023, https://m4bl.org/black-power-rising/.

22. See King, *Stride toward Freedom:* "At a special session of the MIA executive board a negotiating committee of twelve was appointed and I was chosen to serve as their spokesman" (96–97). "That afternoon, I returned to Atlanta to make at least an appearance at the meeting of Negro leaders. There I found an enthusiastic group of almost a hundred men from all over the South, committed to the idea of a Southern movement to implement the Supreme Court's decision against bus segregation through nonviolent means. Before adjourning they voted to form a permanent organization, the Southern Christian Leadership Conference, and elected me president, a position I still hold" (168).

23. To say that an audience treats a party as speaking or acting for another individual or group in a context is to say that the audience engages in one or more of a complex of actions

with respect to the party in that context (*conferral actions*). I discuss these actions in the next section of this chapter.

24. Two points are worth noting here. First, audience conferral admits of three subtypes: group conferral, nongroup conferral, and mixed conferral (that is, conferral by audiences comprising both group members and nonmembers). Second, there is a distinction between *group conferral* and *group authorization*. The Booker T. Washington example discussed in this chapter illustrates this conceptual cleavage, and Chapter 3 is devoted to discussing *informal group authorization*. See also Saward, *The Representative Claim*, 48. I return to this distinction again in this chapter and in Chapter 3.

25. I have developed this definition of *political* from the definition in Jane Mansbridge, "Everyday Talk in the Deliberative System," in *Deliberative Politics: Essays on Democracy and Disagreement*, ed. Stephen Macedo (Oxford: Oxford University Press, 1999), 214–215: "'that which the public ought to discuss,' when that discussion forms part of some, perhaps highly informal, version of a collective 'decision,'" where "decisions" are, in turn, defined as "collective choices."

26. Jane Mansbridge, "Everyday Talk," 215.

27. Greta Thunberg, "Transcript: Greta Thunberg's Speech at the UN Climate Action Summit," NPR, September 23, 2019, https://www.npr.org/2019/09/23/76345 2863/tran script-greta-thunbergs-speech-at-the-u-n-climate-action-summit.

28. King, *Stride toward Freedom*, 97–101.

29. See Town of Greece, NY v. Galloway, 572 U.S. 565 (2014).

30. In this case, you happen to be a member of the group for which you have become an IPR, although as we shall see in Chapter 6, nonmembers may be IPRs too.

31. Mansbridge, "Clarifying the Concept of Representation," 628 makes a similar point, although she describes it as a matter of audience "taking" rather than a matter of audience treatment: "In the largest social sense we represent others, often unintentionally, any time a third party takes some feature of our existence or self-presentation as a guide to others' intentions, capacities, preferences, or other characteristics."

32. As discussed, I understand *speak for* and *act for* to pick out a spectrum of phenomena. Thus, what it means to say that "an audience believes that a given party speaks or acts for a given group" will depend on the concept of *speak for* or *act for* with which the audience is working.

33. See Saward, *The Representative Claim*, 37–38: "an audience . . . might consist of a large or small, proximate or dispersed, or self-aware or disparate set of people; indeed, it might only consist of me."

34. Jacqueline M. Moore, *Booker T. Washington, W. E. B. Du Bois, and the Struggle for Racial Uplift* (Lanham, MD: Rowman and Littlefield, 2003), 32.

35. Booker T. Washington, *Up from Slavery: An Autobiography* (New York: Doubleday, Page, 1907), 217.

36. Mark Bauerlein, "Booker T. Washington and W. E. B. Du Bois: The Origins of a Bitter Intellectual Battle," *Journal of Blacks in Higher Education* 46 (2004): 107.

37. "Teddy Roosevelt's 'Shocking' Dinner with Washington," NPR, May 14, 2012, https://www.npr.org/2012/05/14/152684575/teddy-roosevelts-shocking-dinner-with-washington; National Park Service, "Booker T. Washington," Theodore Roosevelt Inaugural National Historic Site, last modified April 25, 2012, https://www.nps.gov/thri/bookertwashington.htm. I say "arguably" here because it may be that President William McKinley conferred the status of IPR on Booker T. Washington in 1898, a consideration I discuss later in this chapter.

38. National Park Service, "Booker T. Washington."

39. National Park Service, "Booker T. Washington." On Washington's relationship to Roosevelt, see also Robert J. Norrell, *Up from History: The Life of Booker T. Washington* (Cambridge, MA: Belknap Press of Harvard University Press, 2009), 1–5, 8, 9–12, 203, 238–262, 288–310, 312, 324, 330–331, 342, 346–347, 349–357, 361, 363, 373, 374, 384–389, 401, 404, 414, 437, and 439.

40. W. E. B. Du Bois, "The Social Significance of Booker T. Washington," *Du Bois Review: Social Science Research on Race* 8, no. 2 (2011): 374.

41. Norrell, *Up from History,* 384–85, 389, 396, 401, 404.

42. Washington, *Up from Slavery,* 167.

43. Du Bois, "Mr. Booker T. Washington," 63, 67–72. For a helpful discussion of Du Bois's evaluation of Washington as a spokesman and "nongovernmental leader," see Chike Jeffers, "Du Bois on Government and Democratic Leadership," *Monist* 107, no. 1 (2024): 1–12.

44. Du Bois, "Mr. Booker T. Washington," 64.

45. See Saward, *The Representative Claim,* 48: "Representative claims can only work, or even exist, if audiences acknowledge them in some way, and are able to absorb, reject, or accept them, or otherwise engage with them."

46. Du Bois, "The Social Significance," 374. For evidence that Du Bois wrote this essay in 1935, see Robert Brown, "Introduction to 'The Social Significance of Booker T. Washington' by W. E. B. Du Bois," *Du Bois Review: Social Science Research on Race* 8, no. 2 (2011): 360–362.

47. Du Bois, "The Social Significance," 374.

48. Washington, *Up from Slavery,* 167.

49. In thinking through this aspect of audience conferral, I have found guidance in Michael E. Bratman, *Shared Agency: A Planning Theory of Acting Together* (New York: Oxford University Press, 2014); and Michael E. Bratman, *Shared and Institutional Agency: Toward a Planning Theory of Human Practical Organization* (New York: Oxford University Press, 2022), 32n57, 33–41.

50. Although a represented group member's disavowal ("They don't speak for me!") cannot revoke de facto IPR status conferred by a different audience, a represented group member's avowal ("They *do* speak for me!") confers de facto IPR status, as it is a form of group conferral.

51. King, *Stride toward Freedom,* 89.

52. David J. Garrow, *Bearing the Cross: Martin Luther King, Jr., and the Southern Christian Leadership Conference* (New York: William Morrow, 2004), 54.

53. King, *Stride toward Freedom,* 98.

54. See Garrow, *Bearing the Cross,* 54–55.

55. On self-appointment, see Montanaro, *Who Elected Oxfam?,* esp. 42–62; see also Laura Montanaro, "The Democratic Legitimacy of Self-Appointed Representatives," *Journal of Politics* 74, no. 4 (2012): 1094–1107.

56. Isabel Kershner, "Speech by Netanyahu Opens Political Divisions in Israel, Too," *New York Times,* March 1, 2015, https://www.nytimes.com/2015/03/02/world/middleeast/netanyahus-speech-opens-political-divisions-in-israel-too.html.

57. Washington, *Up from Slavery,* 167.

58. Moore, *Booker T. Washington,* 32.

59. "Mr. McKinley at Tuskegee: Visits the Educational Institution for Colored People under Booker T. Washington's Direction," *New York Times,* December 17, 1898, https://www.nytimes.com/1898/12/17/archives/mr-mckinley-at-tuskegee-visits-the-educational-institution-for.html. See also Norrell, *Up from History,* 168–169, 330.

60. "Mr. McKinley at Tuskegee."

61. Washington, *Up from Slavery,* 217; Bauerlein, "Booker T. Washington," 107.

62. See, e.g., Andrew Rehfeld, "Towards a General Theory of Political Representation," *Journal of Politics* 68, no. 1 (2006): 13.

63. For a similar classroom example, see Emmalon Davis, "Typecasts, Tokens, and Spokespersons: A Case for Credibility Excess as Testimonial Injustice," *Hypatia* 31, no. 3 (2016): 491–492. See also Lawrence Blum, *High Schools, Race, and America's Future: What Students Can Teach Us about Morality, Diversity, and Community* (Cambridge, MA: Harvard Education Press, 2012), 54–55, 162; and Caitlin Murphy Brust and Rebecca M. Taylor, "Resisting Epistemic Injustice: The Responsibilities of College Educators at Historically and Predominantly White Institutions," *Educational Theory* 73, no. 4 (2023): 551–571.

64. While an informal representative may, of course, also impact an audience's understanding of the group's circumstances, this would in the first instance be to speak about the represented group and only in some cases amount to speaking for the represented group.

65. Lauren McGuill, "CME Panel Features Black Voices," *Northern Iowan,* February 17, 2020, https://www.northerniowan.com/12333/showcase/cme-panel-features-black-voices/.

66. See, e.g., Rehfeld, "Towards a General Theory," 5–7, 9, 11–17, 19.

67. Sharon Kiraly, "Improve 8–30 (g)," email to State Housing Committee of Connecticut General Assembly, February 15, 2017, https://www.cga.ct.gov/2017/HSGdata/Tmy/2017HB-07057-R000216-Kiraly,%20Sharon,%20Resident-Fairfield,%20CT-TMY.PDF.

68. But this does not mean that Kiraly is not a representative at all. There are many different concepts of representative, and some of them may apply to her. Consider the concept of *descriptive representative*: a party who is a token of a type by virtue of being similar

in a relevant respect to other tokens of that type. If Kiraly is herself elderly or has a disability and crosses the road in the relevant area, then she might appropriately be considered a descriptive representative of that group whether or not the committee treats her as speaking or acting for them. If one must be ascribed the role of descriptive representative by an audience, then Kiraly would be a descriptive representative of the elderly or those living with a disability only if some audience designated her as one. I do not assume that the role of descriptive representative requires audience designation, but will not argue for that claim here. I discuss descriptive representation in Chapter 6.

69. Du Bois, "Mr. Booker T. Washington"; Du Bois, "The Social Significance."

70. There is a separate question here concerning whether a party could be conferred or otherwise come to have the moral authority to speak or act for a group by means other than informal group authorization. For instance, one might think that group membership or demonstrated commitment to the group's interests grants a party the requisite sort of moral authority. I shall set this question aside.

Chapter 2. Conscription and the Power to Influence

1. I draw on the account of the principles of *due care* and *loss prevention* set out in T. M. Scanlon, *What We Owe to Each Other* (Cambridge, MA: Belknap Press of Harvard University Press, 1998), 295–327.

2. Jane Mansbridge, "Clarifying the Concept of Representation," *American Political Science Review* 105, no. 3 (2011): 628, makes a similar point, referring to a town meeting as one setting in which we might "make binding collective decisions for others without seeing ourselves as representatives or having formal relations of accountability to others." See also Jane J. Mansbridge, *Beyond Adversary Democracy* (New York: Basic Books, 1980), 251.

3. Ta-Nehisi Coates, "Ta-Nehisi Coates Looks Back at 8 Years of Writing in the Obama Era," interview by Robin Young, *Here and Now,* WBUR, September 28, 2017, https://www .wbur.org/hereandnow/2017/09/28/ta-nehisi-coates-eight-years-in-power.

4. Ta-Nehisi Coates, "Imagining a New America," interview by Krista Tippett, *On Being,* October 16, 2017, https://onbeing.org/programs/ta-nehisi-coates-imagining-a-new -america/; Jennifer Senior, "Through the Lens of the Obama Years, Ta-Nehisi Coates Reckons with Race, Identity and Trump," *New York Times,* October 1, 2017, https://www .nytimes.com/2017/10/01/books/review-ta-nehisi-coates-we-were-eight-years-in-power .html; David Smith, "Ta-Nehisi Coates: The Laureate of Black Lives," *Guardian,* October 8, 2017, https://www.theguardian.com/books/ 2017 / oct / 08 / ta-nehisi-coates-our-story-is- a-tragedy-but-doesnt-depress-me-we-were-eight-years-in-power-interview; Cornel West, "Ta-Nehisi Coates Is the Neoliberal Face of the Black Freedom Struggle," *Guardian,* December 17, 2017, https://www.theguardian.com/commentisfree/2017/dec/17/ta-nehisi-coates-neoliberal -black-struggle-cornel-west.

5. As discussed in Chapter 1, audience conferral is indexed to the audience that brings it about, so these instances of audience conferral are each, individually, adequate to make it the case that Coates is an IPR for Black Americans by the lights of the conferring audience.

6. Coates, "Ta-Nehisi Coates Looks Back."

7. Taylor Garron, "Aïsha Unceremoniously Elected Spokesperson for All Black Women," *Reductress,* November 21, 2017, https://reductress.com/post/aisha-unceremoniously-elected -spokesperson-for-all-black-women; Clancy Overell, "Aboriginal Coworker Asked to Speak on Behalf of 700,000 People in Passing Conversation," *Betoota Advocate,* https://www .betootaadvocate.com/uncategorized/aboriginal-coworker-asked-to-speak-on-behalf-of -700000-people-in-passing-conversation/.

8. On assumptions about doxastic or conative homogeneity, see Emmalon Davis, "Typecasts, Tokens, and Spokespersons: A Case for Credibility Excess as Testimonial Injustice," *Hypatia* 31, no. 3 (2016): 485–501; and Nora Berenstain, "Epistemic Exploitation," *Ergo* 3 (2016): 569–590.

9. Samuel Hayat, "Unrepresentative Claims: Speaking for Oneself in a Social Movement," *American Political Science Review* 116, no. 3 (2022): 1038, identifies and examines a nearby phenomenon, whereby parties that "actively refuse to be seen as speaking for anyone but themselves" may still, by so claiming, come to represent the group for which they deny speaking. Davis, "Typecasts, Tokens, and Spokespersons," 490–493, identifies and examines a phenomenon similar to IPR conscription: "compulsory representation." Kwame Anthony Appiah, "Go Ahead, Speak for Yourself," *New York Times,* August 10, 2018, https://www .nytimes.com/2018/08/10/opinion/sunday/speak-for-yourself.html, points out that "sometimes the representative is conjured into being."

10. Laura Montanaro, *Who Elected Oxfam? A Democratic Defense of Self-Appointed Representatives* (Cambridge: Cambridge University Press, 2017), 44.

11. Michael Saward, *The Representative Claim* (Oxford: Oxford University Press, 2010), 36–37. Saward offers a brief example of a nonvoluntary IPR, but neither treats the phenomenon in depth nor explores its implications for informal political representation more generally (61–62, 187n17).

12. Andrew Rehfeld, "Towards a General Theory of Political Representation," *Journal of Politics* 68, no. 1 (2006): 6, 12.

13. Montanaro, *Who Elected Oxfam?,* 42–44, 45; Saward, *The Representative Claim,* 36–38, 95–102; Rehfeld, "Towards a General Theory," 6, 12–13. While these theories could possibly accommodate conscripted IPRs, none sufficiently acknowledges the distinction between voluntary and conscripted IPRs nor appreciates the importance of the distinction.

14. Wendy Salkin, "The Conscription of Informal Political Representatives," *Journal of Political Philosophy* 29, no. 4 (2021): 429–455. On "the harm of compulsory representation," see Davis, "Typecasts, Tokens, and Spokespersons," 490–493. See also Berenstain, "Epistemic Exploitation."

15. See, e.g., Mark B. Brown, "Survey Article: Citizen Panels and the Concept of Representation," *Journal of Political Philosophy* 14, no. 2 (2006): 203–225; Alexander A. Guerrero, "Against Elections: The Lottocratic Alternative," *Philosophy and Public Affairs* 42, no. 2 (2014): 135–178; Alexander Guerrero, "The Epistemic Pathologies of Elections and the Epistemic Promise of Lottocracy," in *Political Epistemology,* ed. Elizabeth Edenberg and Michael Hannon (Oxford: Oxford University Press, 2021), 156–179; Eduardo J. Martinez, "Realizing the Value of Public Input: Mini-public Consultation on Agency Rulemaking," *Philosophical Issues* 31, no. 1 (2021): 240–257; and Doreen Tembo, Gary Hickey, Cristian Montenegro, David Chandler, Erica Nelson, Katie Porter, Lisa Dikomitis, et al., "Effective Engagement and Involvement with Community Stakeholders in the Co-production of Global Health Research," *BMJ* 372, no. 178 (2021): 1–6.

16. Malcolm X, "Malcolm Highlights the Problem with 'Negro' Leaders. Michigan State University, East Lansing, Michigan. 23 January 1963," in *The Autobiography of Malcolm X: Speeches and Interviews,* http://ccnmtl.columbia.edu/projects/mmt/mxp/speeches/mxt19.html.

17. See W. E. B. Du Bois, *The Philadelphia Negro: A Social Study* (New York: Oxford University Press, 2017).

18. Martin Luther King, Jr., *Stride toward Freedom: The Montgomery Story* (Boston: Beacon Press, 2010), 98.

19. See Ida B. Wells, *A Red Record: Tabulated Statistics and Alleged Causes of Lynchings in the United States, 1892–1893–1894* (Chicago: privately published, 1894); Ida B. Wells, *Southern Horrors: Lynch Law in All Its Phases* (New York: New York Age Print, 1982); and Ida B. Wells and Alfreda M. Duster, *Crusade for Justice: The Autobiography of Ida B. Wells,* 2nd ed. (Chicago: University of Chicago Press, 2020).

20. Wells and Duster, *Crusade for Justice.*

21. On the objectionable inability or unwillingness of audiences to regard members of a subordinated group as individuals, see, e.g., Douglas Flamming, *Bound for Freedom: Black Los Angeles in Jim Crow America* (Berkeley: University of California Press, 2005), 12: "When white people looked at other white people, they saw individuals, but when they looked at black people, they went into group-think mode, imposing blanket characterizations on any Negro in front of them."

22. For pointed satire on the latter objectionable inference, see Paul Beatty, *The Sellout* (New York: Farrar, Straus and Giroux, 2015), 11–12.

23. See, e.g., Wells and Duster, *Crusade for Justice,* 57, 105, 149, 179, 209, 226, 227, 231, 241, 313.

24. Stephanie C. Palmer, "Wells-Barnett, Ida B.," in *Encyclopedia of African American History 1896 to the Present,* ed. Paul Finkelman (Oxford: Oxford University Press, 2009), vol. 5, 105–108.

25. Laito Zarkpah, quoted in Lauren McGuill, "CME Panel Features Black Voices," *Northern Iowan,* February 17, 2020, https://www.northerniowan.com/12333/showcase/cme-panel-features-black-voices/.

26. See Booker T. Washington, "The Standard Printed Version of the Atlanta Exposition Address," in *The Souls of Black Folk: Authoritative Text, Contexts, Criticism,* ed. Henry Louis Gates Jr. and Terri Hume Oliver, (New York: W. W. Norton, 1999), 169; W. E. B. Du Bois, "Of Mr. Booker T. Washington and Others," in *The Souls of Black Folk,* ed. David W. Blight and Robert Gooding-Williams (Boston: Bedford Books, 1997), 62–72; and National Park Service, "Booker T. Washington," Theodore Roosevelt Inaugural, National Park Service, last modified April 25, 2012, https://www.nps.gov/thri/bookertwashington .htm. See, generally, Robert J. Norrell, *Up from History: The Life of Booker T. Washington* (Cambridge, MA: Belknap Press of Harvard University Press, 2009).

27. King, *Stride toward Freedom,* 98: "The mayor then turned to the Negro delegation and demanded: 'Who is the spokesman?' When all eyes turned toward me, the mayor said: 'All right, come forward and make your statement'"; David J. Garrow, *Bearing the Cross: Martin Luther King, Jr., and the Southern Christian Leadership Conference* (New York: William Morrow, 2004), 308: "On December 3, King met with Johnson and presidential civil rights advisor Lee White for forty-five minutes."

28. Jennifer Crothers, "Bono and George W Bush Ignite a Beautiful Bromance—But Who Knew They Were Even Mates?," *Mirror,* May 27, 2017, https://www.mirror.co.uk/3am /celebrity-news/bono-george-w-bush-ignite-10509445; George W. Bush, "George W. Bush: PEPFAR Saves Millions of Lives in Africa. Keep it Fully Funded," *Washington Post,* April 7, 2017, https://www.washingtonpost.com/opinions/george-w-bush-pepfar-saves-millions-of -lives-in-africa-keep-it-fully-funded/2017/04/07/2089fa46-1ba7-11e7-9887 -1a5314b56a08_story.html; Colin Stutz, "Bono Shares Photo with George W. Bush, Praising His Commitment to Fighting AIDS," *Billboard,* May 26, 2017, https://www.billboard.com /articles/columns/rock/7809579/bono-george-w-bush-photo-fighting-aids-trump.

29. Malala Yousafzai, "Malala: Her Meeting with Obama," interview by Jodi Kantor, video, *New York Times,* October 10, 2014, https://www.nytimes.com/video/world/asia /100000003169045/malala-her-meeting-with-obama.html.

30. "Kim Kardashian Visits White House with Prisoners She Helped Free," BBC, March 5, 2020, https://www.bbc.com/news/world-us-canada-51744918; NBC News, "Watch Kim Kardashian West's Full White House Speech on Prison Reform," video, YouTube, June 13, 2019, https://www.youtube.com/watch?v=fz-oGxLVJpY.

31. Noah Bierman and Tracy Wilkinson, "In Guatemala, Harris Tells Would-Be Migrants to U.S., 'You Will Be Turned Back,'" *Los Angeles Times,* June 7, 2021, https://www.latimes .com/politics/story/2021-06-07/vice-president-harris-meets-with-guatemalan-leader-on -migration-issues.

32. When the memberships of an audience and a represented group are completely coextensive (as when an IPR is representing the group to itself), the IPRs' pro tanto duties are generated by a group comprising the same numerical individuals as the group to whom their satisfaction is owed. Still, the groups they form—audience and represented, respectively— will be distinct.

33. King, *Stride toward Freedom,* 99.

34. See Scanlon, *What We Owe to Each Other*, 295–327.

35. Scanlon, *What We Owe to Each Other,* 300–301.

36. One need not agree with Scanlon's view to accept this example for the purpose of understanding the structure of an IPR's pro tanto duties.

37. See, generally, Montanaro, *Who Elected Oxfam?,* but esp. 42–62. See also Laura Montanaro, "The Democratic Legitimacy of Self-Appointed Representatives," *Journal of Politics* 74, no. 4 (2012): 1094–1107.

38. The form of this modified principle follows the format of Scanlon's original principle of *due care*; Scanlon, *What We Owe to Each Other,* 300. I have presented it in the text without quotation marks or brackets to make it readable.

39. The form of this modified principle follows the format of Scanlon's original principle of *loss prevention*; Scanlon, *What We Owe to Each Other,* 300–301. I have presented it in the text without quotation marks or brackets to make it readable.

It may be that these modified forms of the principles of *due care* and *loss prevention* apply any time there is a tripartite relationship where one party (like the represented, here) is dependent on a middleman party (here, the IPR) for their relationship to the third party (here, the audience). Establishing this more general application of the modified principles, however, is outside the scope of the present discussion.

40. But, as I have mentioned above, it may be that in some cases the representative also owes it to the audience to show the audience due care and to prevent the audience's losses—this is so at least when the representative intentionally holds themself forth as an IPR for the group or when the audience is relatively disempowered vis-à-vis the represented.

41. Scanlon, *What We Owe to Each Other,* 300–301.

42. On conflicts between IPR duties, see Chapter 4 of the present volume. On FPRs facing competing norms, see Alexander A. Guerrero, "The Paradox of Voting and the Ethics of Political Representation," *Philosophy and Public Affairs* 38, no. 3 (2016): 281–283.

43. James Baldwin, "Many Thousands Gone," in *Notes of a Native Son* (Boston: Beacon Press, 1984), 32–33.

44. I develop my discussion of the interactions between these roles in Wendy Salkin, "'Writers Are Not Congressmen'" (unpublished manuscript, December 31, 2023), Microsoft Word file.

Chapter 3. Group Authorization

1. This complaint is discussed in greater detail in Chapter 5.

2. Malcolm X, "Malcolm Highlights the Problem with 'Negro' Leaders. Michigan State University, East Lansing, Michigan. 23 January 1963," in *The Autobiography of Malcolm X: Speeches and Interviews,* http://ccnmtl.columbia.edu/projects/mmt/mxp/speeches/mxt19 .html.

3. David J. Garrow, *Bearing the Cross: Martin Luther King, Jr., and the Southern Christian Leadership Conference* (New York: William Morrow, 2004), 23.

4. Martin Luther King, Jr., *Stride toward Freedom: The Montgomery Story* (Boston: Beacon Press, 2010), 41–43.

5. American Law Institute, "Agency Defined," *Restatement (Third) of Agency,* § 1.01 (2006), https://www.westlaw.com/Document/Iebdeef61da4911e295e30000833f9e5b/View /FullText.html?transitionType=Default&contextData=(sc.Default)&VR=3.0&RS=cblt1.0.

6. "[Ratification] In General," *Williston on Contracts,* 4th ed., § 35:22 (1993), https://www.westlaw.com/Document/Ie2725152d21111d9a974bad5e31cfc15/View /FullText.html?transitionType=Default&contextData=(sc.Default)&VR=3.0&RS=cblt1 .0: "Ratification may be defined generally as the adoption or confirmation of a prior act purportedly performed on the principal's behalf by an agent without the agent obtaining prior authority"; American Law Institute, "Ratification Defined," *Restatement (Third) of Agency,* § 4.01 (2006), https://www.westlaw.com/Document/Iebdfd9c5da4911e295e3000 0833f9e5b/View/FullText.html?transitionType=Default&contextData=(sc.Default)&VR =3.0&RS=cblt1.0: "Ratification is the affirmance of a prior act done by another, whereby the act is given effect as if done by an agent acting with actual authority."

Of course, there are exceptions in some cases, as when a principal (a defendant, say) is appointed an attorney by the court, which attorney has the agential power to commit the principal to certain courses of action or states of affairs although not selected in the first instance by the defendant themself. Here the defendant, like other principals, retains the retrospective power of dismissal.

7. American Law Institute, "Agency Defined," § 1.01.

8. American Law Institute, "Agency Defined," § 1.01.

9. Elizabeth S. Anderson, "What Is the Point of Equality?," *Ethics* 109, no. 2 (1999): 313. On the principle of equal consideration of interest, see Thomas Christiano, *The Rule of the Many: Fundamental Issues in Democratic Theory* (Boulder, CO: Westview, 1996), 59–60.

10. On informal authorization and informal ratification, see Wendy Salkin, "Democracy Within, Justice Without: The Duties of Informal Political Representatives," *Noûs* 56, no. 4 (2022): 940–971; and Wendy Salkin, "You Say I Want a Revolution," *Monist* 107, no. 1 (2024): 39–56. For other treatments of authorization in nonelectoral contexts, see Lisa J. Disch, "The 'Constructivist Turn' in Democratic Representation: a Normative Dead-End?," *Constellations* 22, no. 4 (2015): 487–499; Lisa J. Disch, *Making Constituencies: Representation as Mobilization in Mass Democracy* (Chicago: University of Chicago Press, 2021), 34, 43, 153–154n5; Suzanne Dovi, *The Good Representative* (Malden, MA: Blackwell, 2007), 8, 18, 53–55, 60–65; Laura Montanaro, *Who Elected Oxfam? A Democratic Defense of Self-Appointed Representatives* (Cambridge: Cambridge University Press, 2017), 83–85; Michael Saward, "Authorisation and Authenticity: Representation and the Unelected," *Journal of Political Philosophy* 17, no. 1 (2009): 1–22; and Michael Saward, *The Representative Claim* (Oxford: Oxford University Press, 2010), 102–110. On representative authorization generally, see especially

Thomas Hobbes, *Leviathan* (New York: Oxford University Press, 1996); and Hanna Fenichel Pitkin, *The Concept of Representation* (Berkeley: University of California Press, 1967), 38–59.

11. One may, on similar grounds, be inclined to doubt whether there is even such a thing as informal authorization. In the next section, I use the example of King in Montgomery during the bus boycott to illustrate what informal authorization might look like. However, even considering this example, one may yet be inclined to either (1) deny that what took place in Montgomery amounts to authorization, or (2) argue that authorization procedures by their enactment transform informal representation into formal representation. Regarding the first point, I leave it to the reader to assess for themself whether what is described in the next section amounts to authorization. Regarding the second point, I describe a "space of political representation" within which representation can be more or less formal by virtue of a number of different features—one of which is authorization (see Chapter 1). So a more precise way to describe what took place in Montgomery is that King was authorized by bus boycotters and, when this happened, his representation became *more* authorizationally formal than it had been before this authorizational moment but remained informal (or more informal) in other respects—for instance, insofar as he represented a group whose boundaries were not clear, was subject only to loosely defined social norms rather than codified and institutionalized rules, and could not have been effectively or reliably held accountable for his representative activities.

12. See Mónica Brito Vieira, "Founders and Re-founders: Struggles of Self-Authorized Representation," *Constellations* 22, no. 4 (2015): 510: "We should beware . . . of assuming consent from a lack of objection."

13. On representatives as delegates, see Pitkin, *The Concept of Representation*, 112–143.

14. In Pitkin, *The Concept of Representation,* Pitkin characterizes the trustee as "acting for the sake of" another (126). They are entrusted with acting in the group's interest and are "under no obligation to consult [their] beneficiaries or obey their wishes" (128). The trustee is obligated to promote the welfare of the entrusted, regardless of whether the entrusting party acknowledges that this is what they are doing (128). They must do what they think best. For Pitkin, trustees are not representatives. What I am suggesting, contra Pitkin, is that given either informal group authorization or informal group ratification, it may be that it is permissible for an informal political representative to take on a more trustee-like relationship to the group and to act with greater independence by virtue of having garnered the trust and support of the represented.

Those not inclined to preserve the delegate-trustee distinction may think of the IPR granted greater independence as engaged in *gyroscopic representation,* wherein, according to Jane Mansbridge, "Rethinking Representation," *American Political Science Review* 97, no. 4 (2003): 520–522, "the representative looks within, for guidance in taking action, to a contextually derived understanding of interests, interpretive schemes ('common sense'), conscience, and principles. . . . In this form of representation, the representative does not have to conceive of him or herself . . . as 'acting for' [the represented]. . . . Gyroscopic representation stresses the representative's own principles and beliefs." See also Andrew Rehfeld, "Representation

Rethought: On Trustees, Delegates, and Gyroscopes in the Study of Political Representation and Democracy," *American Political Science Review* 103, no. 2 (2009): 214–230.

15. King, *Stride toward Freedom*, 32.

16. King, *Stride toward Freedom*, 33–35. See also Garrow, *Bearing the Cross*, 18.

17. Garrow, *Bearing the Cross*, 19.

18. King, *Stride toward Freedom*, 40. See also Garrow, *Bearing the Cross*, 19.

19. Garrow, *Bearing the Cross*, 21.

20. King, *Stride toward Freedom*, 42.

21. King, *Stride toward Freedom*, 49.

22. Ratification, generally, is "the adoption or confirmation of a prior act purportedly performed on the principal's behalf by an agent without the agent obtaining prior authority. When an agent lacks actual authority to agree on behalf of the principal, the principal may still be bound if it acquiesces in the agent's action, or fails promptly to disavow the unauthorized conduct after acquiring knowledge of the material facts. The subsequent affirmance by a principal of a contract made on its behalf by one who had at the time neither actual nor apparent authority constitutes a ratification, which relates back and supplies original authority to execute the contract." "[Ratification] In General," § 35:22.

23. On self-appointing representatives, see Laura Montanaro, "The Democratic Legitimacy of Self-Appointed Representatives," *Journal of Politics* 74, no. 4 (2012): 1094–1107; and Montanaro, *Who Elected Oxfam?*

24. Garrow, *Bearing the Cross*, 15.

25. Garrow, *Bearing the Cross*, 26n12.

26. King, *Stride toward Freedom*, 97.

27. T. M. Scanlon, *What We Owe to Each Other* (Cambridge, MA: Belknap Press of Harvard University Press, 1998), 303.

28. As I discuss in Chapters 4 and 6, in many cases IPRs will enter into negotiation or decision-making fora without advanced knowledge about the range of possible agreements, outcomes, or even topics. In these cases, it will be important for the IPR to have discretion to make decisions in these fora without having to consult the group first. Group consultation ex post becomes correspondingly more important as a check on the IPR's ex ante discretion.

29. There will be some cases in which it may be reasonable for an IPR to raise expectations in a negotiating counterpart concerning what the represented will do even if they do not have a clear indication that the represented group will go along with what the IPR agrees to on the group's behalf. For instance, a union's bargaining team might reasonably decide to bluff and claim that the union's membership will go on strike if the negotiating counterpart (an employer) does not meet some key demand, even if the bargaining team knows or has reason to believe that the membership would not go on strike. Although the bargaining team's bluff might raise expectations in the employer that the represented group would not meet, it seems like a permissible strategy, and might even be welcomed by the union's membership. (A union's bargaining team will, of course, usually be FPRs. But the point holds

for IPRs, too.) However, doing so can be risky, as the employer may call the bargaining team's bluff, and when the union's membership declines to strike, this could make the employer less likely to rely on the bargaining team's claims going forward.

30. King, *Stride toward Freedom,* 42.

31. Booker T. Washington, "The Standard Printed Version of the Atlanta Exposition Address," in *The Souls of Black Folk: Authoritative Text, Contexts, Criticism,* ed. Henry Louis Gates Jr. and Terri Hume Oliver (New York: W. W. Norton, 1999), 167–170.

32. Mark Bauerlein, "Booker T. Washington and W. E. B. Du Bois: The Origins of a Bitter Intellectual Battle," *Journal of Blacks in Higher Education* 46 (2004): 107; W. E. B. Du Bois, "Of Mr. Booker T. Washington and Others," in *The Souls of Black Folk,* ed. David W. Blight and Robert Gooding-Williams (Boston: Bedford Books, 1997), 63; Robert J. Norrell, *Up from History: The Life of Booker T. Washington* (Cambridge, MA: Belknap Press of Harvard University Press, 2009); Booker T. Washington, *Up from Slavery: An Autobiography* (New York: Doubleday, Page, 1907), 217.

33. Du Bois, "Mr. Booker T. Washington," 67–70.

34. Du Bois, "Mr. Booker T. Washington," 64.

35. Du Bois, "Mr. Booker T. Washington"; Norrell, *Up from History,* 4.

36. On strategic defenses of Washington's "Atlanta Compromise" and his economy-first strategy more generally, see, e.g., Bauerlein, "Booker T. Washington"; Melbourne Cummings, "Historical Setting for Booker T. Washington and the Rhetoric of Compromise, 1895," *Journal of Black Studies* 8, no. 1 (1977): 80–81; Louis R. Harlan, *Booker T. Washington,* vol. 2, *The Wizard Of Tuskegee, 1901–1915* (New York: Oxford University Press, 1986), 202–237; Louis R. Harlan, "Booker T. Washington in Biographical Perspective," *American Historical Review* 75, no. 6 (1970): 1581–1585; Desmond Jagmohan, "Booker T. Washington and the Politics of Deception," in *African American Political Thought: A Collected History,* ed. Melvin L. Rogers and Jack Turner (Chicago: University of Chicago Press, 2021), 167–191; Desmond Jagmohan, *Dark Virtues: Booker T. Washington's Tragic Realism* (Princeton, NJ: Princeton University Press, forthcoming); Desmond Jagmohan, "Making Bricks without Straw: Booker T. Washington and the Politics of the Disenfranchised" (PhD diss., Cornell University, 2015), 315–379, https://ecommons.cornell.edu/bitstream/handle/1813 /39321/dj89.pdf; Robert J. Norrell, "Booker T. Washington: Understanding the Wizard of Tuskegee," *Journal of Blacks in Higher Education* 42 (2003): 96–109; and Paul Stob, "Booker T. Washington, 'Atlanta Exposition Address' (18 September 1895)," *Voices of Democracy* 16 (2021): 1–15.

37. See, e.g., Giles v. Harris, 189 U.S. 475 (1903); Louis R. Harlan, "The Secret Life of Booker T. Washington," *Journal of Southern History* 37, no. 3 (1971): 397–399; Harlan, *Booker T. Washington,* 244–248; Harlan, "Booker T. Washington in Biographical Perspective," 1585; Jagmohan, "Making Bricks," 34; August Meier, "Toward a Reinterpretation of Booker T. Washington," *Journal of Southern History* 23, no. 2 (1957): 225; Richard H. Pildes, "Democracy, Anti-democracy, and the Canon," *Constitutional Commentary* 17 (2000): 295.

38. Malcolm X, "Malcolm Highlights the Problem with 'Negro' Leaders." See also Liam Kofi Bright, "White Psychodrama," *Journal of Political Philosophy* 31, no. 2 (2023): 198–221.

39. There is no limit on how many people can simultaneously serve as IPRs for a given group. This is another distinction between formal and informal political representation. It may be, however, that one IPR gets the lion's share of audience attention, and so in this sense one IPR's emergence could preclude another's.

40. National Park Service, "Booker T. Washington," Theodore Roosevelt Inaugural, National Park Service, last modified April 25, 2012, https://www.nps.gov/thri/bookertwashington .htm. On Roosevelt's relationship to Washington, see Norrell, *Up from History,* 1–5, 8, 9–12, 203, 238–262, 288–310, 312, 324, 330–331, 342, 346–347, 349–357, 361, 363, 373, 374, 384–389, 401, 404, 414, 437, 439; on Taft's relationship to Washington, see Norrell, *Up from History,* 4, 384–385, 389, 396, 401, 404.

41. Du Bois, "Mr. Booker T. Washington," 64–67.

42. Huma Yusuf, "About the Malala Backlash," *New York Times,* July 18, 2013, http:// latitude.blogs.nytimes.com/2013/07/18/the-malala-backlash/; Humaira Awais Shahid, quoted in Nico Hines, "Has Malala Become a Puppet of the West?," *Daily Beast,* April 12, 2014, https://www.thedailybeast.com/has-malala-become-a-puppet-of-the-west; Omer Farooq Khan, "Malala Faces Pak Backlash for Questioning Need to Marry," *Times of India,* June 6, 2021, https://timesofindia.indiatimes.com/world/pakistan/malala-faces-pak -backlash-for-questioning-need-to-marry/articleshow/83267776.cms. The person quoted in the Hines article, Humaira Awais Shahid, is a Pakistani journalist, human rights activist, and former legislator; see Humaira Shahid (@HumairaAShahid), "Journalist, Human Rights activist & former MPA Punjab Assembly. Author of 'Devotion & Defiance.' Awarded Honoris Causa. A Seeker of Truth," Twitter biography, May 2, 2018, https://twitter.com /HumairaAShahid.

43. Naila Inayat, "Malala Yousafzai Is Adored around the World, but Many in Pakistan Have Come to Hate Her," *USA Today,* April 18, 2018, https://www.usatoday.com/story /news/world/2018/04/18/malala-nobel-laureate-pakistan-backlash/518752002/.

44. Fouzia Saeed, quoted in Inayat, "Malala Yousafzai."

45. Taiba Ikhlas, quoted in Inayat, "Malala Yousafzai."

Chapter 4. The Duties of Informal Political Representatives

1. On IPRs being unauthorized, see, e.g., Malcolm X, "Malcolm Highlights the Problem with 'Negro' Leaders. Michigan State University, East Lansing, Michigan. 23 January 1963," in *The Autobiography of Malcolm X: Speeches & Interviews,* http://ccnmtl.columbia.edu /projects/mmt/mxp/speeches/mxt19.html. On IPRs being unaccountable, see Adolph L. Reed Jr., *The Jesse Jackson Phenomenon: The Crisis of Purpose in Afro-American Politics* (New Haven, CT: Yale University Press, 1986). On IPRs being inaccurate, see, e.g., Samuel Cornish

and John Russwurm, "To Our Patrons," *Freedom's Journal,* March 16, 1827, https://infoweb
.newsbank.com/apps/readex/doc?p=EANX&docref=image/v2%3A132FB88A169
69E1C%40EANX-132FC89EEDB64928%402388432-132FC0E68E066888%400.   On
IPRs being elitist, see Jennifer Morton, "The Miseducation of the Elite," *Journal of Political
Philosophy* 29, no. 1 (2021): 3–24; and Reed, *The Jesse Jackson Phenomenon,* 35. On IPRs being
homogenizing, see, e.g., George Cook, "Al Sharpton Does Not Speak for All African Americans," *Daily Kos,* October 17, 2009, http://www.dailykos.com/story/2009/10/18/794463/
-Al-Sharpton-does-not-speak-for-all-African-Americans; on representation and homogeneity,
see also Kwame Anthony Appiah, *The Ethics of Identity* (Princeton, NJ: Princeton University
Press, 2005), 151–154, 336–337n59. On IPRs being overpowering and concessive, see
W. E. B. Du Bois, "Of Mr. Booker T. Washington and Others," in *The Souls of Black Folk,*
ed. David W. Blight and Robert Gooding-Williams (Boston: Bedford Books, 1997), 63–70.
On IPRs being overcommitting, see, e.g., Martin Luther King Jr., *Stride toward Freedom:
The Montgomery Story* (Boston: Beacon Press, 2010), 97. On IPRs being occlusive, see Linda
Alcoff, "The Problem of Speaking for Others," *Cultural Critique,* no. 20 (1991): 5–32; and
George Monbiot, "Bono Can't Help Africans by Stealing Their Voice," *Guardian,* June 17,
2013, http://www.theguardian.com/commentisfree/2013/jun/17/bono-africans-stealing
-voice-poor. On IPRs being oppressive, see Alcoff, "The Problem of Speaking for Others";
and Michael Walzer, "The Obligations of Oppressed Minorities," in *Obligations: Essays on
Disobedience, War, and Citizenship* (Cambridge, MA: Harvard University Press, 1970), 46–73.
As I argue in Wendy Salkin, "Democracy Within, Justice Without: The Duties of Informal
Political Representatives," *Noûs* 56, no. 4 (2022): 940–971, and explain further here, the
concern that IPRs are inegalitarian arises from the convergence of several of the aforementioned skeptical concerns in the particular context of oppression or marginalization.

2. On the vulnerability of the represented to their representatives, see Suzanne Dovi, *The
Good Representative* (Malden, MA: Blackwell, 2007), 22, 28, 33, 35–36, 63, 131, 136–137,
142–143, 172, 187, 189; Suzanne Dovi, "Good Representatives Foster Autonomy," *PS:
Political Science and Politics* 51, no. 2 (2018): 323–326.

3. Malcolm X, "The Problem with 'Negro' Leaders."

4. Reed, *The Jesse Jackson Phenomenon,* 123–127.

5. Alcoff, "The Problem of Speaking for Others," 9.

6. Cornish and Russwurm, "To Our Patrons," 1.

7. Larry M. Bartels, *Unequal Democracy: The Political Economy of the New Gilded Age*
(Princeton, NJ: Princeton University Press, 2008), 281; Morton, "The Miseducation of the
Elite"; Keeanga-Yamahtta Taylor, "Joe Biden, Kamala Harris, and the Limits of Representation," *New Yorker,* August 24, 2020, https://www.newyorker.com/news/our-columnists/joe
-biden-kamala-harris-and-the-limits-of-representation; Olúfẹ́mi O. Táíwò, *Elite Capture:
How the Powerful Took Over Identity Politics (and Everything Else)* (Chicago: Haymarket Books,
2022), esp. 15–24.

8. Reed, *The Jesse Jackson Phenomenon,* 35. See also Richard F. Fenno Jr., *Home Style: House Members in Their Districts* (London: Scott, Foresman, 1978), 115, quoted in Jane Mansbridge, "Should Blacks Represent Blacks and Women Represent Women? A Contingent 'Yes,'" *Journal of Politics* 61, no. 3 (1999): 645; Olúfẹ́mi Táíwò, "Identity Politics and Elite Capture," *Boston Review,* May 7, 2020, http://bostonreview.net/race/olufemi-o-taiwo -identity-politics-and-elite-capture.

9. Barbara Ransby, *Ella Baker and the Black Freedom Movement: A Radical Democratic Vision* (Chapel Hill: University of North Carolina Press, 2003), 176.

10. Cook, "Al Sharpton."

11. Matthew S. McCoy, Emily Y. Liu, Amy S. F. Lutz, and Dominic Sisti, "Ethical Advocacy across the Autism Spectrum: Beyond Partial Representation," *American Journal of Bioethics* 20, no. 4 (2020): 14, discuss a related phenomenon, which they call "partial representation," that "occurs when an actor claims to represent the whole of a certain group but appropriately engages with only a subset of that group."

12. Du Bois, "Of Mr. Booker T. Washington," 63.

13. W. E. B. Du Bois, "The Social Significance of Booker T. Washington," *Du Bois Review: Social Science Research on Race* 8, no. 2 (2011): 374.

14. As PON Staff, "The Anchoring Effect and How It Can Impact Your Negotiation," *Daily Blog, Program on Negotiation—Harvard Law School,* August 8, 2023, https://www.pon .harvard.edu/daily/negotiation-skills-daily/the-drawbacks-of-goals/, notes, "The anchoring effect is a cognitive bias that describes the . . . tendency to rely too heavily on the first piece of information offered (the 'anchor') when making decisions. . . . Once an anchor is set, other judgments are made by adjusting away from that anchor, and there is a bias toward interpreting other information around the anchor"; see also Stephanie Jung and Peter Krebs, *The Essentials of Contract Negotiation* (Cham, Switzerland: Springer, 2019), 28–32.

15. Du Bois, "Of Mr. Booker T. Washington," 64.

16. King, *Stride toward Freedom,* 97.

17. Alcoff, "The Problem of Speaking for Others," 7; Monbiot, "Bono Can't Help Africans." Another form of occlusion, whereby an IPR prioritizes some group members' interests over other group members' interests, is an often unavoidable feature of group representation. I discuss this other form of occlusion in Chapter 5.

18. Carl Jorgensen, "Booker T. Washington and the Sociology of Black Deficit," in *The Racial Politics of Booker T. Washington,* ed. Donald Cunnigen, Rutledge M. Dennis, and Myrtle Gonza Glascoe (Amsterdam: Elsevier JAI, 2006), 117. See also Du Bois, "Of Mr. Booker T. Washington," 36–37.

19. Alcoff, "The Problem of Speaking for Others," 7; Monbiot, "Bono Can't Help Africans." See also, generally, Walzer, "The Obligations of Oppressed Minorities," 53–55.

20. See, e.g., Lucile Montgomery, *SNCC Violence in Selma Report,* 1965, Lucile Montgomery Papers, Wisconsin Historical Society, https://content.wisconsinhistory.org/digital /collection/p15932coll2/id/35358; and Angela Davis, "Political Prisoners, Prisons and Black

Liberation," in *If They Come in the Morning: Voices of Resistance,* ed. Angela Davis (New York: Third Press, 1971), 21–38.

21. See Elizabeth S. Anderson, "What Is the Point of Equality?," *Ethics* 109, no. 2 (1999): 287–337; Thomas Christiano, *The Rule of the Many: Fundamental Issues in Democratic Theory* (Boulder, CO: Westview, 1996), 59–60; and Samuel Scheffler, "The Practice of Equality," in *Social Equality: On What It Means to Be Equals,* ed. Carina Fourie, Fabian Schuppert, and Ivo Wallimann-Helmer (New York: Oxford University Press, 2015), 21–44. On relational equality, democracy, and representation, I have also found guidance from Eric Beerbohm, *In Our Name: The Ethics of Democracy* (Princeton, NJ: Princeton University Press, 2012); Niko Kolodny, *The Pecking Order: Social Hierarchy as a Philosophical Problem* (Cambridge, MA: Harvard University Press, 2023); Niko Kolodny, "Rule over None II: Social Equality and the Justification of Democracy," *Philosophy and Public Affairs* 42, no. 4 (2014): 287–336; Samuel Scheffler, "Choice, Circumstance, and the Value of Equality," *Politics, Philosophy and Economics* 4, no. 1 (2005): 5–28; Samuel Scheffler, "What Is Egalitarianism?," *Philosophy and Public Affairs* 31, no. 1 (2003): 5–39; and Jonathan Wolff, "Fairness, Respect, and the Egalitarian Ethos," *Philosophy and Public Affairs* 27, no. 2 (1998): 97–122.

In saying that IPRs should refrain from dominating the represented, I mean that IPRs should take steps to avoid dominating the represented insofar as it is possible for them to do so. I am mindful that some are of the view that it is not always up to those who dominate whether they dominate or not; that the mere capacity to interfere with another is sufficient to make one a dominator. See, e.g., Frank Lovett, *A General Theory of Domination and Justice* (Oxford: Oxford University Press, 2010); and Philip Pettit, *Republicanism: A Theory of Freedom and Government* (New York: Oxford University Press, 2002). I am not arguing that IPRs have the responsibility to refrain from having a capacity that they are unable to avoid having.

22. Alcoff, "The Problem of Speaking for Others," 7; Walzer, "The Obligations of Oppressed Minorities," 53–54.

23. On recognition respect, see Stephen L. Darwall, "Two Kinds of Respect," *Ethics* 88, no. 1 (1977): 36–49, 38. On the relation between equality and domination, see Anderson, "What Is the Point of Equality?," 313–315.

24. Darwall, "Two Kinds of Respect," 46.

25. Consider the argument in Edmund Burke, "Speech to the Electors of Bristol," in *The Founders' Constitution,* ed. Philip B. Kurland and Ralph Lerner (Chicago: University of Chicago Press, 1987), vol. 1, chap. 13, doc. 7, http://press-pubs.uchicago.edu/founders /documents/v1ch13s7.html, that the representative ought to give "great weight" to the "wishes" of the represented and "high respect" to "their opinion," and "above all, ever, and in all cases, to prefer their interest to his own," but is not expected to "sacrifice to [the represented]" "his unbiassed opinion, his mature judgment, his enlightened conscience." For Burke, the representative "owes" the represented "not his industry only, but his judgment."

26. On the relationships between trust and political representation, see Dovi, *The Good Representative,* 125–144; Jane Mansbridge, "Rethinking Representation," *American Political Science Review* 97, no. 4 (2003): 515–528; Mansbridge, "Should Blacks Represent Blacks?," 628, 635, 639, 641–643, 652, 654; and Melissa S. Williams, *Voice, Trust, and Memory: Marginalized Groups and the Failings of Liberal Representation* (Princeton, NJ: Princeton University Press, 1998), 30–33, 149–175.

27. On the relationship between trust and consultation, see Mansbridge, "Rethinking Representation."

28. On uncrystallized interests, see Mansbridge, "Should Blacks Represent Blacks?"; and Jane Mansbridge, "The Future of Political Theory: Lippincott Lecture," *Contemporary Political Theory* 22 (2023): 255–256.

29. See, e.g., James N. Druckman, "A Framework for the Study of Persuasion," *Annual Review of Political Science* 25, no. 1 (2022): 70–71, 81; and Gabriel S. Lenz, *Follow the Leader? How Voters Respond to Politicians' Policies and Performance* (Chicago: University of Chicago Press, 2012), esp. chaps. 3 and 4. For a study of how partisan elites shape partisans' perception of the economy, see Martin Bisgaard and Rune Slothuus, "Partisan Elites as Culprits? How Party Cues Shape Partisan Perceptual Gaps," *American Journal of Political Science* 62, no. 2 (2018): 456–469. For discussion of the normative relationships between representation and leadership, see Eric Beerbohm, "Is Democratic Leadership Possible?," *American Political Science Review* 109, no. 4 (2015): 639–652. See also Eric Beerbohm, *In Our Name: The Ethics of Democracy* (Princeton, NJ: Princeton University Press, 2012).

30. See Elizabeth Anderson, "The Epistemology of Democracy," *Episteme: A Journal of Social Epistemology* 3, no. 1 (2006).

31. Panel on Measuring Rape and Sexual Assault in Bureau of Justice Statistics Household Surveys, Committee on National Statistics; Division on Behavioral and Social Sciences and Education, and National Research Council, *Estimating the Incidence of Rape and Sexual Assault,* ed. Candace Kruttschnitt, William D. Kalsbeek, and Carol C. House (Washington, DC: National Academies Press, 2014).

32. Randall Kennedy, "Martin Luther King's Constitution: A Legal History of the Montgomery Bus Boycott," *Yale Law Journal* 98, no. 6 (1989): 1022: "Upwards of ninety percent of the black, bus-riding population—some 40,000 Negroes—honored the plea to stay off the buses."

33. King, *Stride toward Freedom,* 33.

34. King, *Stride toward Freedom,* 42.

35. See, generally, Danielle Allen and Jennifer S. Light, eds., *From Voice to Influence: Understanding Citizenship in a Digital Age* (Chicago: University of Chicago Press, 2015).

36. See, e.g., Axel Bruns and Jean Burgess, "Twitter Hashtags from Ad Hoc to Calculated Publics," in *Hashtag Publics: The Power and Politics of Discursive Networks,* ed. Nathan

Rambukkana (New York: Peter Lang, 2015), 13–27; and Karissa McKelvey, Joseph Di-Grazia, and Fabio Rojas, "Twitter Publics: How Online Political Communities Signaled Electoral Outcomes in the 2010 US House Election," *Information, Communication and Society* 17, no. 4 (2014): 436–450.

37. See Joshua Cohen, "Deliberation and Democratic Legitimacy," in *Deliberative Democracy: Essays on Reason and Politics* (Cambridge, MA: MIT Press, 1997), 74n12: "Deliberation is reasoned in that the parties to it are required to state their reasons for advancing proposals, supporting them, or criticizing them. They give reasons with the expectation that those reasons (and not, for example, their power) will settle the fate of their proposal." See also Amy Gutmann and Dennis Thompson, *Democracy and Disagreement* (Cambridge, MA: Belknap Press of Harvard University Press, 1996), 128–164; and Iris Marion Young, *Inclusion and Democracy* (New York: Oxford University Press, 2000), 131.

38. King held meetings; see King, *Stride toward Freedom,* 47–53. See also Ta-Nehisi Coates, "I Left Twitter," *Atlantic,* July 5, 2012, https://www.theatlantic.com/personal/archive/2012/07/i-left-twitter/259451/.

39. King, *Stride toward Freedom,* 33.

40. King, *Stride toward Freedom,* 100.

41. Pettit, *Republicanism,* 31; on domination, see also Anderson, "What Is the Point of Equality?"; Ian Shapiro, *Politics against Domination* (Cambridge, MA: Belknap Press of Harvard University Press, 2016); Ian Shapiro, "On Non-domination," *University of Toronto Law Journal* 62, no. 3 (2012): 293–336.

42. See, e.g., King, *Stride toward Freedom,* 47–53; Jane J. Mansbridge, *Beyond Adversary Democracy* (New York: Basic Books, 1980), 39–135; Derek Thompson, "The Political Question of the Future: But Are They Real? What Happens When Live-Streams Become the New Fireside Chats?," *Atlantic,* January 7, 2019, https://www.theatlantic.com/ideas/archive/2019/01/politicians-are-live-streaming-videos-instagram/579490/.

43. On the relationship between egalitarianism and nondomination, see Anderson, "What Is the Point of Equality?," 313–315.

44. Anderson, "What Is the Point of Equality?," 313.

45. Jorgensen, "Booker T. Washington," 117.

46. Du Bois, "Of Mr. Booker T. Washington," 64.

47. An IPR may rely on the represented for ancillary benefits they receive from being in the position of IPR—perhaps their public acclaim, relevance, sense of purpose, or even pecuniary benefits (see Chapter 2). Those shall not concern us here, however.

48. Wendy Salkin, "The Conscription of Informal Political Representatives," *Journal of Political Philosophy* 29, no. 4 (2021): 429–455.

49. Du Bois, "Of Mr. Booker T. Washington," 63–64, 67–70. It is outside the scope of this book to consider whether Washington's concessions were warranted.

50. As discussed in Chapter 2, in many cases the IPR will not have this discretion. See also Salkin, "The Conscription of Informal Political Representatives."

51. One version of this question is tackled in Chapter 6.

52. Mark Feeney, "Globe Wins Pulitzer Gold Medal for Coverage of Clergy Sex Abuse," *Boston Globe,* April 8, 2003, https://archive.boston.com/globe/spotlight/abuse/extras /pulitzers.htm.

53. See Laura Montanaro, *Who Elected Oxfam? A Democratic Defense of Self-Appointed Representatives* (Cambridge: Cambridge University Press, 2017), 38: "a group does not necessarily exist as a politically relevant entity—to itself or to others—prior to representation."

54. See Michael Saward, *The Representative Claim* (Oxford: Oxford University Press, 2010), 35–56.

55. See Melissa S. Williams, *Voice, Trust, and Memory: Marginalized Groups and the Failings of Liberal Representation* (Princeton, NJ: Princeton University Press, 1998), 198.

56. See, e.g., Arabella Kyprianides, Clifford Stott, and Ben Bradford, "'Playing the Game': Power, Authority and Procedural Justice in Interactions between Police and Homeless People in London," *British Journal of Criminology* 61, no. 3 (2021): 670–689; Barry Friedman, "Are Police the Key to Public Safety? The Case of the Unhoused," *American Criminal Law Review* 59, no. 4 (2022): 1597–1642; and Adora Svitak, "Why You Should Think Twice about Calling the Police on Homeless People," *Bold Italic,* October 22, 2018, https:// thebolditalic.com/why-you-should-think-twice-about-calling-the-police-on-homeless -people-bfec223444f9.

57. I do not mean to suggest that FPRs ought not engage in the self-evaluation here prescribed for IPRs. They should.

58. Here I rely on the notion of political influence found in Ronald Dworkin, "What Is Equality? Part 4: Political Equality," *University of San Francisco Law Review* 22, no. 1 (1987): 9, which he contrasts with political impact: "Someone's impact in politics is the difference he can make, just on his own, by voting for or choosing one decision rather than another. Someone's influence . . . is the difference he can make not just on his own but also by leading or inducing others to believe or vote or choose as he does."

59. Dworkin, "What Is Equality?," 21.

60. Alexander M. Bickel, "The Supreme Court and Reapportionment," in *Reapportionment in the 1970s,* ed. Nelson W. Polsby (Berkeley: University of California Press, 1971), 59, quoted in Lani Guinier, *The Tyranny of the Majority: Fundamental Fairness in Representative Democracy* (New York: Free Press, 1994), 268n21.

61. Thomas Christiano, "Democracy as Equality," in *Democracy,* ed. David Estlund (Malden, MA: Blackwell, 2002), 46–47.

62. See, e.g., Andrea Castillo, "Trump Is Stripping Immigrant Children of Protections, Critics Say. Supporters Say He's Closing Loopholes," *Los Angeles Times,* September 2, 2019, https://www.latimes.com/california/story/2019-08-16/la-me-immigrant-children -protections; Alex Connor, "'The Actual Thing Is Way, Way Worse Than We Were Depicting,'

Says Photographer Behind Viral Photo of Caged Kid," *USA Today,* June 19, 2018, https://www .usatoday.com/story/news/nation-now/2018/06/18/viral-photo-toddler-crying -miscaptioned-not-ice-custody/710396002/; Camila Domonoske and Richard Gonzales, "What We Know: Family Separation and 'Zero Tolerance' at the Border," NPR, June 19, 2018, https://www.npr.org/2018/06/19/621065383/what-we-know-family-separation -and-zero-tolerance-at-the-border; César Cuauhtémoc García Hernández, "Abolish Immigration Prisons," *New York Times,* December 2, 2019, https://www.nytimes.com/2019 /12/02/opinion/immigration-detention-prison.html; David A. Graham, "Are Children Being Kept in 'Cages' at the Border?," *Atlantic,* June 18, 2018, https://www.theatlantic .com/politics/archive/2018/06/ceci-nest-pas-une-cage/563072/; Amanda Holpuch, "US to Remove Limit on How Long Immigrant Children Can Be Detained," *Guardian,* August 21, 2019, https://www.theguardian.com/us-news/2019/aug/21/us-to-remove-limit-on-how -long-immigrant-children-can-be-detained; Tal Kopan, "The Simple Reason More Immigrant Kids Are in Custody Than Ever Before," CNN, September 14, 2018, https://www .cnn.com/2018/09/14/politics/immigrant-children-kept-detention/index.html; Gianluca Mezzofiore, "The Truth behind This Photo of an 'Immigrant Child' Crying Inside a Cage," CNN, June 18, 2018, https://www.cnn.com/2018/06/18/us/photo-migrant-child-cage -trnd/index.html; Joan Walsh, "What Senator Jeff Merkley Saw at an Immigrant Detention Center for Children," *Nation,* June 6, 2018, https://www.thenation.com/article/archive /senator-jeff-merkley-saw-immigrant-detention-center-children/; and Alexandra Yoon-Hendricks and Zoe Greenberg, "Protests across U.S. Call for End to Migrant Family Separations," *New York Times,* June 30, 2018, https://www.nytimes.com/2018/06/30/us /politics/trump-protests-family-separation.html.

63. Elizabeth Anderson, "Democracy: Instrumental vs. Non-instrumental Value," in *Contemporary Debates in Political Philosophy,* ed. Thomas Christiano and John Christman (Malden, MA: Wiley-Blackwell, 2009), 219.

64. King, *Stride toward Freedom,* 100–101.

65. These negotiations in fact broke down due to standing segregation laws and the bus company's racist commitments; King, *Stride toward Freedom,* 101.

66. Rev. L. Roy Bennett, quoted in King, *Stride toward Freedom,* 34.

67. See Walzer, "The Obligations of Oppressed Minorities," 53–55.

68. See Walzer, "The Obligations of Oppressed Minorities," 53–55.

69. Elizabeth S. Anderson and Richard H. Pildes, "Expressive Theories of Law: A General Restatement," *University of Pennsylvania Law Review* 148, no. 5 (2000): 1529.

Chapter 5. The Legitimate Complaints of the Represented

1. W. E. B. Du Bois, "Of Mr. Booker T. Washington and Others," in *The Souls of Black Folk,* ed. David W. Blight and Robert Gooding-Williams (Boston: Bedford Books, 1997), 64–65. On this passage and what he calls Du Bois's "democratic criticism model of

legitimate leadership" (55), see Robert Gooding-Williams, *In the Shadow of Du Bois: Afro-Modern Political Thought in America* (Cambridge, MA: Harvard University Press, 2009), 54–58, 152.

2. George Cook, "Al Sharpton Does Not Speak for All African Americans," *Daily Kos,* October 17, 2009, http://www.dailykos.com/story/2009/10/18/794463/-Al-Sharpton-does-not-speak-for-all-African-Americans.

3. Isabel Kershner, "Speech by Netanyahu Opens Political Divisions in Israel, Too," *New York Times,* March 1, 2015, https://www.nytimes.com/2015/03/02/world/middleeast/netanyahus-speech-opens-political-divisions-in-israel-too.html.

4. Sam Levine, "Dianne Feinstein: Benjamin Netanyahu 'Arrogant' for Claiming to Speak for Jews," *Huffington Post,* March 1, 2015.

5. There may be exceptional cases in which an ally, activist, or other concerned third party might reasonably raise the complaint on behalf of the represented. When such a third party does so, they may themself be conferred de facto IPR status by another audience, making them an intermediate IPR of the represented group on whose behalf they raise the complaint.

6. Although IPRs are particularly susceptible to these procedural and power complaints, they are not distinctly susceptible to them. Many of the complaints that can be raised against IPRs can also be raised against formal political representatives.

7. H. L. A. Hart, *The Concept of Law,* 2nd ed. (New York: Oxford University Press, 1994), 56–57, 88–91.

8. See, e.g., Ida B. Wells, *Southern Horrors: Lynch Law in All Its Phases* (New York: New York Age Print, 1982), https://search.alexanderstreet.com/view/work/bibliographic_entity%7Cbibliographic_details%7C4402564?account_id=14026&usage_group_id=97196; and Ida B. Wells, *A Red Record: Tabulated Statistics and Alleged Causes of Lynchings in the United States, 1892–1893–1894* (Chicago: privately published, 1894).

9. Nicole Russell, "What Women Really Want Is the Patriarchy," *Federalist,* April 13, 2016, http://thefederalist.com/2016/04/13/what-women-really-want-is-the-patriarchy/.

10. Condition 2 distinguishes cases in which the misdescription complaint is apt from mere honest mistakes: when a party makes a reasonable and good faith effort to find out whether their claim is true before making it ("Group *G* wants *p*") but makes an honest mistake (*G* in fact wants *q*, which is easily mistaken for *p*), that party stands open to correction for having erred, but not to complaint.

11. See, e.g., Tara Katrusiak Baran, "Why the Next U.S. President Should Be a Woman," *Huffington Post,* February 10, 2017, http://www.huffingtonpost.ca/tara-katrusiak-baran/why-the-next-president-sh_b_14677840.html; Shanice Barnes, "5 Reasons Why Women Would Make Great Presidents," *Her Campus,* October 23, 2015, https://www.hercampus.com/school/valdosta/5-reasons-why-women-would-make-great-presidents; Angie Kim, "Why America Needs a Female President," *New York Times,* November 2, 2016, https://www

.nytimes.com/2016/11/03/opinion/why-america-needs-a-female-president.html; Kristina Marusic, "7 Reasons to Want a Woman as Your President," *Women's Health,* April 26, 2016, https://www.womenshealthmag.com/life/awesome-woman-president; Marie O'Reilly, "The Real Impact of a Female President? More Women in Politics," PRI, October 25, 2016, https://www.pri.org/stories/2016-10-24/real-impact-female-president-more-women -politics; and Thomas Scheff, "5 Reasons Why Women Should Be Presidents," *Psychology Today,* June 27, 2014, https://www.psychologytoday.com/blog/lets-connect/201406/5 -reasons-why-women-should-be-presidents.

12. "Male Supremacy," Extremist Files, Southern Poverty Law Center, accessed September 13, 2023, https://www.splcenter.org/fighting-hate/extremist-files/ideology/male -supremacy.

13. Du Bois, "Of Mr. Booker T. Washington," 67.

14. Malcolm X, "Malcolm Highlights the Problem with 'Negro' Leaders. Michigan State University, East Lansing, Michigan. 23 January 1963," in *The Autobiography of Malcolm X: Speeches and Interviews,* http://ccnmtl.columbia.edu/projects/mmt/mxp/speeches /mxt19.html.

15. David J. Garrow, *Bearing the Cross: Martin Luther King, Jr., and the Southern Christian Leadership Conference* (New York: William Morrow, 2004), 54.

16. Barry Malone, "Are Bono and Bob Geldof Good for Africa?," Reuters, May 13, 2009, https://uk.reuters.com/article/uk-ethiopia-geldof/are-bono-and-bob-geldof-good-for -africa-idUKTRE54C3LT20090513.

17. Du Bois, "Of Mr. Booker T. Washington," 67.

18. Although Du Bois's critique of Washington provides a helpful articulation of the *partiality* complaint, I do not mean to take a position on the substantive question as to whether Du Bois had it right that Washington's willingness to compromise was in fact evidence of Washington's failure to be loyal or partisan toward the interests of those for whom he spoke or acted. One might think Washington believed his accommodationist / incrementalist approach to promoting the rights and interests of Black southerners to be a way of being loyal to them under conditions of extreme racial injustice and oppression— where Washington's background political realism convinced him that this approach was the only one that would be given any real hearing in that political climate. I take no position here on whether this is so. On Booker T. Washington's political thought, see Desmond Jagmohan, *Dark Virtues: Booker T. Washington's Tragic Realism* (Princeton, NJ: Princeton University Press, forthcoming); and Desmond Jagmohan, "Making Bricks without Straw: Booker T. Washington and the Politics of the Disenfranchised" (PhD diss., Cornell University, 2015), https://ecommons.cornell.edu/bitstream/handle/1813/39321 /dj89.pdf.

19. Rigoberta Menchú, *I, Rigoberta Menchú: An Indian Woman in Guatemala,* ed. Elisabeth Burgos-Debray, trans. Ann Wright (New York: Verso Books, 2010), 9.

20. Menchú, *I, Rigoberta Menchú,* 9 ("This is because many religious people have come among us and drawn a false impression of the Indian world."), 13, 22 ("We know we must hide so much in order to preserve our Indian culture and prevent it being taken away from us.").

21. Martin Luther King Jr., *Stride toward Freedom: The Montgomery Story* (Boston: Beacon Press, 2010), 169; on the bombings, see 166–172.

22. Barbara Ransby, *Ella Baker and the Black Freedom Movement: A Radical Democratic Vision* (Chapel Hill: University of North Carolina Press, 2003), 176.

23. Suzanne Dovi, *The Good Representative* (Malden, MA: Blackwell, 2007), 51.

24. For a discussion of the treatment of gay Black men by other sectors of the Black community during the beginning of the AIDS epidemic, see Cathy J. Cohen, *The Boundaries of Blackness: AIDS and the Breakdown of Black Politics* (Chicago: University of Chicago Press, 1999).

25. See, e.g., Gabriel Arkles, Pooja Gehi, and Elana Redfield, "The Role of Lawyers in Trans Liberation: Building a Transformative Movement for Social Change," *Seattle Journal for Social Justice* 8, no. 2 (2010): 579, 583–594; Leonore F. Carpenter, "Getting Queer Priorities Straight: How Direct Legal Services Can Democratize Issue Prioritization in the LGBT Rights Movement," *Journal of Law and Social Change* 17, no. 2 (2014): 110–122; and Thomas B. Stoddard, "Why Gay People Should Seek the Right to Marry," *Out/Look: National Lesbian and Gay Quarterly* 6 (1989): 9–13.

26. See, e.g., Arkles, Gehi, and Redfield, "Trans Liberation," 579, 588; Carpenter, "Getting Queer Priorities Straight," 107; Keith Cunningham-Parmeter, "Marriage Equality, Workplace Inequality: The Next Gay Rights Battle," *Florida Law Review* 67 (2015): 1112; Paula Ettelbrick, "Since When Is Marriage a Path to Liberation?" *Out/Look: National Lesbian and Gay Quarterly* 6 (1989): 9, 14–17; Jann Ingmire, "Young People Support LGBT Rights but Disagree on Priorities," *UChicago News,* August 5, 2014, https://news.uchicago .edu/story/young-people-support-lgbt-rights-disagree-priorities; Osamudia James, "Superior Status: Relational Obstacles in the Law to Racial Justice and LGBTQ Equality," *Boston College Law Review* 63 (2022): 246; John F. Kowal, "The Improbable Victory of Marriage Equality," Brennan Center for Justice, September 20, 2015, https://www.brennancenter.org /our-work/analysis-opinion/improbable-victory-marriage-equality; Jens Manuel Krogstad, "What LGBT Americans Think of Same-Sex Marriage," Pew Research Center, January 27, 2015, https://www.pewresearch.org/fact-tank/2015/01/27/what-lgbt-americans-think-of -same-sex-marriage/; Danielle Kurtzleben, "The Story of Marriage Equality Is More Complicated—and Costly—Than You Remember," NPR, December 31, 2021, https://www.npr .org/2021/12/31/1068894397/the-story-of-marriage-equality-is-more-complicated-and -costly-than-you-remember; C. Shawn McGuffey, "Intersectionality, Cognition, Disclosure and Black LGBT Views on Civil Rights and Marriage Equality," *Du Bois Review: Social Science Research on Race* 15, no. 2 (2018): 441–465; Aisha C. Moodie-Mills, *Jumping beyond the Broom: Why Black Gay and Transgender Americans Need More Than Marriage Equality,*

Center for American Progress, January 2012, 14, https://cdn.americanprogress.org/wp
-content/uploads/issues/2012/01/pdf/black_lgbt.pdf; Jackson Wright Shultz and Kristopher
Shultz, "Queer and Trans after *Obergefell v. Hodges:* An Autoethnographic Oral History,"
Humboldt Journal of Social Relations 38 (2016): 46, 51; and Dean Spade, "Keynote Address:
Trans Law Reform Strategies, Co-optation, and the Potential for Transformative Change,"
Women's Rights Law Review 30 (2009): 288, 305.

27. Libby Adler, "The Gay Agenda," *Michigan Journal of Gender and Law* 16, no. 1
(2009): 164, 168, 197; Amy Brandzel, "Queering Citizenship? Same-Sex Marriage and the
State," *GLQ: A Journal of Lesbian and Gay Studies* 11, no. 2 (2005): 196; Cunningham-
Parmeter, "Marriage Equality," 1103; Nancy D. Polikoff, "We Will Get What We Ask for:
Why Legalizing Gay and Lesbian Marriage Will Not 'Dismantle the Legal Structure of
Gender in Every Marriage,'" *Virginia Law Review* 79, no. 7 (1993): 1549–1550.

28. William N. Eskridge Jr., "Comparative Law and the Same-Sex Marriage Debate: A
Step-by-Step Approach toward State Recognition," *McGeorge Law Review* 31, no. 3 (2000):
648, 650–653.

29. See, e.g., Tessa E. S. Charlesworth and Mahzarin R. Banaji, "Patterns of Implicit and
Explicit Attitudes: I. Long-Term Change and Stability from 2007 to 2016," *Psychological
Science* 30, no. 2 (2019): 174–192; Tina Fetner, "U.S. Attitudes toward Lesbian and Gay
People Are Better than Ever," *Contexts* 15, no. 2 2016): 20–27; Gayle Kaufman and D'Lane
Compton, "Attitudes toward LGBT Marriage and Legal Protections Post-Obergefell," *Sex-
uality Research and Social Policy* 18, no. 2 (2021): 321–330; German Lopez, "Public
Opinion Had Swung Strongly in Favor of Same-Sex Marriage," *Vox,* last updated March 31,
2016, https://www.vox.com/2015/6/26/17937616/same-sex-gay-marriage-public-opinion
-supreme-court; Gallup, "Marriage," accessed July 31, 2022, https://news.gallup.com/poll
/117328/marriage.aspx; Pew Research Center, "Attitudes on Same-Sex Marriage: Public
Opinion on Same-Sex Marriage," May 14, 2019, https://www.pewresearch.org/religion/fact
-sheet/changing-attitudes-on-gay-marriage/; Samantha Schmidt, "Americans' Views Flipped
on Gay Rights. How Did Minds Change So Quickly?," *Washington Post,* June 7, 2019,
https://www.washingtonpost.com/local/social-issues/americans-views-flipped-on-gay
-rights-how-did-minds-change-so-quickly/2019/06/07/ae256016-8720-11e9-98c1
-e945ae5db8fb_story.html; and Margaret E. Tankard and Elizabeth Levy Paluck, "The Effect of a Supreme Court Decision Regarding Gay Marriage on Social Norms and Personal
Attitudes," *Psychological Science* 28, no. 9 (September 2017): 1336.

30. Andrew R. Flores, Christy Mallory, and Kerith J. Conron, "The Impact of *Obergefell v. Hodges* on the Well-Being of LGBT Adults," Williams Institute, University of
California–Los Angeles, June 2020, 1, https://williamsinstitute.law.ucla.edu/publications
/happiness-after-obergefell/; Eugene K. Ofosu, Michelle K. Chambers, Jacqueline M. Chen,
and Eric Hehman, "Same-Sex Marriage Legalization Associated with Reduced Implicit and
Explicit Antigay Bias," *Proceedings of the National Academy of Sciences* 116, no. 18 (2019):
8846–8851.

31. See, e, g., D. Dangaran, "Abolition as Lodestar: Rethinking Prison Reform from a Trans Perspective," *Harvard Journal of Law and Gender* 44, no. 1 (2021): 174–75, 177; Marie-Amélie George, "Expanding LGBT," *Florida Law Review* 73, no. 2 (2021): 250; Marie-Amélie George, "The LGBT Disconnect: Politics and Perils of Legal Movement Formation," *Wisconsin Law Review* 2018 (2018): 567; James, "Superior Status," 246–47; Sonia Katyal and Ilona Turner, "Transparenthood," *Michigan Law Review* 117, no. 8 (2019): 1593; and Courtney Vinopal, "LGBTQ Activists on What Progress Looks Like 5 Years after Same-Sex Marriage Ruling," PBS, June 29, 2020, https://www.pbs.org/newshour/nation/lgbtq-activists-on-what -progress-looks-like-5-years-after-same-sex-marriage-ruling. See also, generally, Marie-Amélie George, "Framing Trans Rights," *Northwestern University Law Review* 114, no. 3 (2019): 627.

32. Yuvraj Joshi, "Respectable Queerness," *Columbia Human Rights Law Review* 43, no. 2 (2012): 436.

33. See, e.g, Arkles, Gehi, and Redfield, "Trans Liberation," 583–594; Carpenter, "Getting Queer Priorities Straight"; and George, "The LGBT Disconnect."

34. George Monbiot, "Bono Can't Help Africans by Stealing Their Voice," *Guardian,* June 17, 2013, http://www.theguardian.com/commentisfree/2013/jun/17/bono-africans -stealing-voice-poor.

35. On anchoring, see PON Staff, "The Anchoring Effect and How It Can Impact Your Negotiation," *Daily Blog, Program on Negotiation—Harvard Law School,* August 8, 2023, https://www.pon.harvard.edu/daily/negotiation-skills-daily/the-drawbacks-of-goals/. See also Stephanie Jung and Peter Krebs, *The Essentials of Contract Negotiation* (Cham, Switzerland: Springer, 2019), 28–32.

36. Booker T. Washington, "The Standard Printed Version of the Atlanta Exposition Address," in *The Souls of Black Folk: Authoritative Text, Contexts, Criticism,* ed. Henry Louis Gates Jr. and Terri Hume Oliver (New York: W. W. Norton, 1999), 170.

37. Du Bois, "Of Mr. Booker T. Washington," 64.

38. Du Bois is also raising a different sort of critique of Washington: that one should, as a condition of one's self-respect, ask for more even if one will not get it. I will not pursue that further critique here.

Chapter 6. Descriptive and Nondescriptive
Informal Political Representation

1. Representation theorists have offered various characterizations of descriptive representatives. A. Phillips Griffiths, in A. Phillips Griffiths and Richard Wollheim, "Symposium: How Can One Person Represent Another?," *Proceedings of the Aristotelian Society*, supplementary vol. 34 (1960): 188, characterizes descriptive representation as follows:

This sense of representation, in which one person represents another by being sufficiently like him, I shall call *descriptive representation.* I am a descriptive representative of my generation—a sample, specimen, or analogue—when I am sufficiently like my fellows for someone to be reasonably safe in drawing conclusions about the other members of my generation from what they know about me. I cannot, of course, be *made* such a representative; I can only properly be thought to be one if I am in fact already like my contemporaries. For one thing descriptively to represent another it is both necessary and sufficient that it is similar in some respects to what it is supposed to represent.

According to Hanna Fenichel Pitkin, *The Concept of Representation* (Berkeley: University of California Press, 1967), 61, descriptive representation "depends on the representative's characteristics, on what he is or is like. . . . The representative does not act for others; he 'stands for' them, by virtue of a correspondence or connection between them, a resemblance or reflection."
Jane Mansbridge, "Should Blacks Represent Blacks and Women Represent Women? A Contingent 'Yes,'" *Journal of Politics* 61, no. 3 (1999): 628, 629, characterizes descriptive representatives as "individuals who in their own backgrounds mirror some of the more frequent experiences and outward manifestations of belonging to the group," adding, "In 'descriptive' representation, representatives are in their own persons and lives in some sense typical of the larger class of persons whom they represent. Black legislators represent Black constituents, women legislators represent women constituents, and so on."
For a recent challenge to traditional accounts of what descriptive representation is, see Danielle Casarez Lemi, "What Is a Descriptive Representative?" *PS: Political Science and Politics* 55, no. 2 (2022): 290–292.
2. Mansbridge, "Should Blacks Represent Blacks?," 629.
3. On social groups and affinity groups, see Iris Marion Young, *Justice and the Politics of Difference* (Princeton, NJ: Princeton University Press, 1990), 172–173, 186–187.
4. Mansbridge, "Should Blacks Represent Blacks?," 635.
5. See, e.g., Mark Harrison, "Let Disabled People Speak for Themselves," *Guardian*, December 2, 2013, https://www.theguardian.com/society/2013/dec/02/disabled-people-speak -for-themselves; Jeana Jorgensen, "What If We Let People Speak for Themselves?" *Foxy Folklorist*, April 7, 2017, https://web.archive.org/web/20170628080941/http://www.patheos.com /blogs/foxyfolklorist/let-people-speak/; Aden Friday, "Let Trans People Speak for Themselves," *Establishment*, January 5, 2016, https://medium.com/the-establishment/let-trans-people-speak -for-themselves-c6b42b21fd09; Nelson Mandela, "Verwoerd's Tribalism," in *No Easy Walk to Freedom* (Portsmouth, NH: Heinemann, 1990), 77; Julie Ruvolo, "Letting Brazil's Homeless Speak for Themselves," *CityLab*, November 12, 2014, https://www.citylab.com/equity/2014 /11/making-homelessness-visible-in-brazil/382621/; and Olúfẹ́mi Táíwò, "Being-in-the-Room Privilege: Elite Capture and Epistemic Deference," *The Philosopher* 108, no. 4 (2020), https:// www.thephilosopher1923.org/post/being-in-the-room-privilege-elite-capture-and-epistemic -deference.
6. For helpful discussions of many different arguments for descriptive representation (particularly in FPR contexts) and criticisms of those arguments, see Linda Alcoff, "The

Problem of Speaking for Others," *Cultural Critique*, no. 20 (1991): 5–32; Suzanne Dovi, *The Good Representative* (Malden, MA: Blackwell, 2007), 27–51, 185–189; Suzanne Dovi, "Preferable Descriptive Representatives: Will Just Any Woman, Black, or Latino Do?" *American Political Science Review* 96, no. 4 (2002): 729–743; Irene Diamond and Nancy Hartsock, "Beyond Interests in Politics: A Comment on Virginia Sapiro's 'When Are Interests Interesting? The Problem of Political Representation of Women,'" *American Political Science Review* 75, no. 3 (1981): 717–721; Carol Gould, "Diversity and Democracy: Representing Differences," in *Democracy and Difference: Contesting the Boundaries of the Political*, ed. Seyla Benhabib (Princeton, NJ: Princeton University Press, 1996), 171–186; Lani Guinier, *The Tyranny of the Majority: Fundamental Fairness in Representative Democracy* (New York: Free Press, 1994), 41–156; Mala Htun, "Is Gender Like Ethnicity? The Political Representation of Identity Groups," *Perspectives on Politics* 2, no. 3 (2004): 439–458; Michael Rabinder James, "The Priority of Racial Constituency over Descriptive Representation," *Journal of Politics* 73, no. 3 (2011), 899–914; Mansbridge, "Should Blacks Represent Blacks?"; Anne Phillips, "Democracy and Representation: Or, Why Should It Matter Who Our Representatives Are?," in *Feminism and Politics*, ed. Anne Phillips (Oxford: Oxford University Press, 1998), 224–40; Anne Phillips, *Engendering Democracy* (Cambridge: Polity Press, 1991), esp. 60–91, Kindle; Anne Phillips, *The Politics of Presence* (Oxford: Oxford University Press, 1995); Pitkin, *The Concept of Representation*, 60–91; Virginia Sapiro, "When Are Interests Interesting? The Problem of Political Representation of Women," *American Political Science Review* 75, no. 3 (1981): 701–21; Dara Z. Strolovitch, *Affirmative Advocacy: Race, Class, and Gender in Interest Group Politics* (Chicago: University of Chicago Press, 2008); Melissa S. Williams, *Voice, Trust, and Memory: Marginalized Groups and the Failings of Liberal Representation* (Princeton, NJ: Princeton University Press, 1998); Iris Marion Young, "Deferring Group Representation," *NOMOS* 39 (1997): 349–376; Iris Marion Young, *Inclusion and Democracy* (New York: Oxford University Press, 2000), esp. 121–153; and Young, *Justice and the Politics of Difference*.

7. Mansbridge, "Should Blacks Represent Blacks?," 628.

8. Williams, *Voice, Trust, and Memory*, 116–148, 176–202.

9. See Mansbridge, "Should Blacks Represent Blacks?"; Phillips, *The Politics of Presence*; and Williams, *Voice, Trust, and Memory*, 198: "the scarce resource of political representation."

10. For discussions of evaluating political representatives in terms of their functions, see Dovi, *The Good Representative*, 61–89; Suzanne Dovi, "Political Representation," in *Stanford Encyclopedia of Philosophy*, Stanford University, 1997–, article last revised August 29, 2018, https://plato.stanford.edu/archives/fall2018/entries/political-representation; Russell Hardin, "Representing Ignorance," *Social Philosophy and Policy* 21, no. 1 (2004): 76–99; Mansbridge, "Should Blacks Represent Blacks?"; and Andrew Sabl, *Ruling Passions: Political Offices and Democratic Ethics* (Princeton, NJ: Princeton University Press, 2002).

11. On allies, I have found guidance from Lidal Dror, "Lived Experience, Theoretical Knowledge, and the Role of Allies in Social Movements" (unpublished manuscript, March 2023), Microsoft Word file.

12. Alcoff, "The Problem of Speaking for Others," explores the impact of one's social location on one's ability (and responsibility) to speak for others.

13. As mentioned, I do not explore the relationship between descriptive informal political representation and standpoint epistemology in this book, although I think there is much to be said on this front (see the Introduction). Some resources I have found especially helpful include Linda Martín Alcoff, "Epistemologies of Ignorance: Three Types," in *Race and Epistemologies of Ignorance*, ed. Shannon Sullivan and Nancy Tuana (Albany: State University of New York Press, 2007), 39–57; Linda Martín Alcoff, "On Judging Epistemic Credibility: Is Social Identity Relevant?," *Philosophical Exchange* 29, no. 1 (1999), 73–93; Elizabeth Anderson, "Feminist Epistemology and Philosophy of Science," in *Stanford Encyclopedia of Philosophy*, Stanford University, 1997–, article last revised February 13, 2020, https://plato.stanford.edu/entries/feminism-epistemology/#standpoint; Sandra Lee Bartky, "Toward a Phenomenology of Feminist Consciousness," *Social Theory and Practice* 3, no. 4 (1975): 425–439; Liam Kofi Bright, "Duboisian Leadership through Standpoint Epistemology," *Monist* 107, no. 1 (2024): 82–97; Patricia Hill Collins, "Black Feminist Epistemology," in *Black Feminist Thought: Knowledge, Consciousness, and the Politics of Empowerment*, 2nd ed. (New York: Routledge, 2000), 251–271; Lidal Dror, "Is There an Epistemic Advantage to Being Oppressed?," *Noûs* 57, no. 3 (2022): 618–640; Heidi Grasswick, "Feminist Social Epistemology," in *Stanford Encyclopedia of Philosophy*, Stanford University, 1997–, article last revised July 24, 2018, https://plato.stanford.edu/archives/fall2018/entries/feminist-social-epistemology/; Donna Haraway, "Situated Knowledges: The Science Question in Feminism and the Privilege of Partial Perspective," *Feminist Studies* 14, no. 3 (1988): 575–599; Sandra Harding, "Introduction: Standpoint Theory as a Site of Political, Philosophical, and Scientific Debate," in *The Feminist Standpoint Theory Reader: Intellectual and Political Controversies*, ed. Sandra Harding (New York: Routledge, 2004), 1–15; Sandra Harding, "Rethinking Standpoint Epistemology: What is 'Strong Objectivity'?," *Centennial Review* 36, no. 3 (1992): 437–470; Sandra Harding, "Standpoint Theories: Productively Controversial," *Hypatia* 24, no. 4 (2009): 192–200; Nancy C. M. Hartsock, "The Feminist Standpoint: Developing the Ground for a Specifically Feminist Historical Materialism," in *Discovering Reality: Feminist Perspectives on Epistemology, Metaphysics, Methodology, and Philosophy of Science*, ed. Sandra Harding and Merrill B. Hintikka (Dordrecht, Netherlands: Reidel, 1983), 283–310; bell hooks, *Feminist Theory: From Margin to Center* (London: Taylor and Francis, 2014), 43–67; Quill Kukla, "Objectivity and Perspective in Empirical Knowledge," *Episteme* 3, nos. 1–2 (2006): 80–95; Charles W. Mills, "White Ignorance," in *Race and Epistemologies of Ignorance*, ed. Shannon Sullivan and Nancy Tuana (Albany: State University of New York Press, 2007), 13–38; Sally J. Scholz, *Political Solidarity* (University Park: Penn State University Press, 2008), 151–187; Táíwò, "Being-in-the-Room Privilege"; Alessandra Tanesini, "Standpoint Theory Then and Now," in *The Routledge Handbook of Social Epistemology*, ed. Miranda Fricker, Peter J. Graham, David Henderson, and Nikolaj J. L. L. Pedersen (New York: Routledge, 2019), 335–343; Briana Toole, "Recent Work in Standpoint Epistemology," *Analysis* 81, no. 2 (2021):

338–350; Briana Toole, "From Standpoint Epistemology to Epistemic Oppression," *Hypatia* 34, no. 4 (2019): 598–618; Briana Toole, "Standpoint Epistemology and Epistemic Peerhood: A Defense of Epistemic Privilege," *Journal of the American Philosophical Association*, first view (2023) 1–18; and Alison Wylie, "Feminist Philosophy of Science: Standpoint Matters," *Proceedings and Addresses of the American Philosophical Association* 86, no. 2 (2012): 47–76.

14. Williams, *Voice, Trust, and Memory*, 131–133.

15. Statement of the Reverend Antoinette L. Brown at the Syracuse National Convention, 1852, quoted in Williams, *Voice, Trust, and Memory*, 133.

16. Williams, *Voice, Trust, and Memory*, 133.

17. Williams, *Voice, Trust, and Memory*, 133.

18. Williams, *Voice, Trust, and Memory*, 163. See also Thomas Dale Cowan and Jack Maguire, *Timelines of African-American History: 500 Years of Black Achievement* (New York: Berkley Pub. Group, 1994).

19. Williams, *Voice, Trust, and Memory*, 163.

20. On substantive representation, see Pitkin, *The Concept of Representation*, 112–143. See also Dovi, "Political Representation."

21. Michael Walzer, "The Obligations of Oppressed Minorities," in *Obligations: Essays on Disobedience, War, and Citizenship* (Cambridge, MA: Harvard University Press, 1970), 51.

22. There may well be intermediate positions between what I have here characterized as the moderate position and the strong position. I will not be able to articulate all such possible intermediate positions. Fortunately, the argument I am advancing does not require us to consider all of them, as the only feature of these various positions we are interested in tracking is whether or not they include a commitment to the claim that "first-person access is required to understand a given group's members values, interests, preferences, and perspectives." For our purposes, all positions that have that characteristic can be categorized as strong positions and all others as moderate.

23. On a related point concerning the value of descriptive representation when representatives are acting with greater discretion and with less direction information from the represented group, see Dovi, *The Good Representative*, 38; Mansbridge, "Should Blacks Represent Blacks," 630; Phillips, *Engendering Democracy*, 76; and Phillips, *The Politics of Presence*, 78, 80, 83.

24. Although, as mentioned, a descriptive representative may still be preferable insofar as they can credibly communicate to a descriptively dissimilar audience that the audience should not be able to understand and so should defer to the descriptive representative and group members as to how to satisfy group members' values, interests, and preferences.

25. Mansbridge, "Should Blacks Represent Blacks?," 637. See also Dovi, *The Good Representative*, 37; and Williams, *Voice, Trust, and Memory*, 5–6, 16, 147, 227–231.

26. Mansbridge, "Should Blacks Represent Blacks?," 638.

27. See e.g., Dovi, *The Good Representative*, 30–31, 34 (although Dovi provides an account that applies to both formal and informal representation); Phillips, *The Politics of Presence*, 62–66; and Williams, *Voice, Trust, and Memory*.

28. See, e.g., Adolph L. Reed Jr., *The Jesse Jackson Phenomenon: The Crisis of Purpose in Afro-American Politics* (New Haven, CT: Yale University Press, 1986), esp. 7 (on what Reed calls "an *organic* political relation"), 32–35, 123–36.

29. On "epistemic objectification," see Miranda Fricker, *Epistemic Injustice: Power and the Ethics of Knowing* (New York: Oxford University Press, 2007), 6, 133–139, 142; and Emmalon Davis, "Typecasts, Tokens, and Spokespersons: A Case for Credibility Excess as Testimonial Injustice," *Hypatia* 31, no. 3 (2016): 488.

30. On compulsory representation, see Davis, "Typecasts, Tokens, and Spokespersons," 490–493. See also Wendy Salkin, "The Conscription of Informal Political Representatives," *Journal of Political Philosophy* 29, no. 4 (2021): 429–455.

31. On this point, see Davis, "Typecasts, Tokens, and Spokespersons," 490. On epistemic dehumanization, see Fricker, *Epistemic Injustice*, 44, 133, 140.

32. On distancing, see Jennifer Morton, "The Miseducation of the Elite," *Journal of Political Philosophy* 29, no. 1 (2021): 8–9. See also Phillips, *Politics of Presence*, 171–178; Darien Pollock, "Political Action, Epistemic Detachment, and the Problem of White-Mindedness," *Philosophical Issues* 31, no. 1 (2021): 299–314; Reed, *The Jesse Jackson Phenomenon*; Olúfémi O. Táíwò, *Elite Capture: How the Powerful Took Over Identity Politics (and Everything Else)* (Chicago: Haymarket Books, 2022); Olúfémi O. Táíwò, "Identity Politics and Elite Capture," *Boston Review*, May 7, 2020, https://bostonreview.net/race/olufemi-o-taiwo-identity -politics-and-elite-capture; Táíwò, "Being-in-the-Room Privilege"; and Keeanga-Yamahtta Taylor, "Joe Biden, Kamala Harris, and the Limits of Representation," *New Yorker*, August 24, 2020, https://www.newyorker.com/news/our-columnists/joe-biden-kamala-harris -and-the-limits-of-representation.

33. One can continue to be a descriptive representative for a group even if one's epistemic ties to those with whom one shares descriptive similarity are eroded, provided that one is descriptively similar to the members of the represented group in some other relevant respect. But if a party is a descriptive representative at one time only by virtue of sharing epistemic ties to a group, should those epistemic ties erode, the party's descriptive similarity also falters.

34. Richard Fenno, *Home Style: House Members in Their Districts* (Boston: Little, Brown, 1978), 115, quoted in Mansbridge, "Should Blacks Represent Blacks?," 645.

35. See Nora Berenstain, "Epistemic Exploitation," *Ergo* 3 (2016): 569–590.

36. On what she calls "the 'retreat' response," see Alcoff, "The Problem of Speaking for Others," 8, 17–24. See also Dror, "Is There an Epistemic Advantage to Being Oppressed?," 637–638.

37. I return to these concerns below in my discussion of the fair distribution of communicative labor. On communicative labor, see Rachel McKinney, "Communication, Labor, and Communicative Labor" (PhD diss., City University of New York, 2015), https:// academicworks.cuny.edu/gc_etds/1047.

38. On what she calls "testimonial quieting," see Kristie Dotson, "Tracking Epistemic Violence, Tracking Practices of Silencing," *Hypatia* 26, no. 2 (2011): 236–257.

39. It may be that any sincere representative of women, descriptive or not, would face this problem. Those prejudiced against women may tend to be skeptical of anyone advancing women's interests. If so, descriptive representation would simply make this problem worse.

40. Davis, "Typecasts, Tokens, and Spokespersons," 486. On credibility excess and testimonial injustice, see José Medina, *The Epistemology of Resistance: Gender and Racial Oppression, Epistemic Injustice, and Resistant Imaginations* (New York: Oxford University Press, 2013); and José Medina, "The Relevance of Credibility Excess in a Proportional View of Epistemic Injustice: Differential Epistemic Authority and the Social Imaginary," *Social Epistemology* 25, no. 1 (2011): 15–35.

41. See Davis, "Typecasts, Tokens, and Spokespersons," 490–493; and Salkin, "The Conscription of Informal Political Representatives."

42. Mansbridge, "Should Blacks Represent Blacks?," 641. On trust in representative relationships, see Williams, *Voice, Trust, and Memory*, 12–14, 22, 149–175, 176, 193. On what she calls "critical trust building," see Dovi, *The Good Representative*, 124–144.

43. Mansbridge, "Should Blacks Represent Blacks?," 641 (discussing Claudine Gay, "Spirals of Trust? The Effect of Descriptive Representation on the Relationship between Citizens and Their Government," *American Journal of Political Science* 46, no. 4 [2002]: 717–732). As Mansbridge argues, "the shared experience imperfectly captured by descriptive representation facilitates vertical communication between representatives and [the represented]." That is, "Representatives and [represented parties] who share some version of a set of common experiences and outward signs of having lived through those experiences can often read one another's signals relatively easily and engage in relatively accurate forms of shorthand communication" (641).

44. Martin Luther King Jr., *Where Do We Go from Here: Chaos or Community?* (Boston: Beacon Press, 2010), 99.

45. Julius Lester, *Look Out, Whitey! Black Power's Gon' Get Your Mama!* (New York: Dial Press, 1968), 44.

46. On self-representation, see Williams, *Voice, Trust, and Memory*, 8, 11–14, 20, 119, 137, 141, 161–175.

47. The question how many IPRs can be given meaningful attention by various audiences would benefit from empirical research.

48. George W. Bush (@georgewbush), "Bono is the real deal. He has a huge heart and a selfless soul, not to mention a decent voice. @laurawbush and I are grateful he came to the ranch to talk about the work of @thebushcenter, @onecampaign, @PEPFAR, and our shared commitment to saving lives in Africa," Instagram post, May 26, 2017, https://www.instagram.com/p/BUkZ3WKBfXD/; George W. Bush, "George W. Bush: PEPFAR Saves Millions of Lives in Africa. Keep It Fully Funded," *Washington Post*, April 7, 2017, https://www.washingtonpost.com/opinions/george-w-bush-pepfar-saves-millions-of-lives-in-africa-keep-it-fully-funded/2017/04/07/2089fa46-1ba7-11e7-9887-1a5314b56a08_story.html; Jennifer Crothers, "Bono and George W Bush Ignite a Beautiful Bromance—but Who Knew They Were Even

Mates?," *Mirror*, May 27, 2017, https://www.mirror.co.uk/3am/celebrity-news/bono-george
-w-bush-ignite-10509445; Colin Stutz, "Bono Shares Photo with George W. Bush, Praising
His Commitment to Fighting AIDS," *Billboard*, May 26, 2017, https://www.billboard.com
/articles/columns/rock/7809579/bono-george-w-bush-photo-fighting-aids-trump.

For detailed discussions of Bono as an IPR, see Laura Montanaro, *Who Elected Oxfam?
A Democratic Defense of Self-Appointed Representatives* (New York: Cambridge University
Press, 2017), 2, 3, 6, 9, 10, 36, 42–46, 61, 70–71, 96–105. See also John S. Dryzek and
Simon Niemeyer, "Discursive Representation," *American Political Science Review* 102, no. 4
(2008): 481–493; and Michael Saward, *The Representative Claim* (New York: Oxford Uni-
versity Press, 2010), 61, 82, 99, 148–150.

49. George Monbiot, "Bono Can't Help Africans by Stealing Their Voice," *Guardian*,
June 17, 2013, http://www.theguardian.com/commentisfree/2013/jun/17/bono-africans
-stealing-voice-poor.

50. Max Bankole Jarrett, quoted in Barry Malone, "Are Bono and Bob Geldof Good for
Africa?," Reuters, May 13, 2009, https://www.reuters.com/article/us-ethiopia-geldof/are
-bono-and-bob-geldof-good-for-africa-idUSTRE54C3KO20090513.

51. Andrew Kaufmann, "You Don't Have to Be a Rock Star to Have a Voice," *Catalyst*,
Spring 2018, https://www.bushcenter.org/catalyst/are-we-ready/kaufmann-the-scope-of-leader
ship.html; George W. Bush Presidential Center, "Forum on Leadership: A Conversation with
President Bush and Bono," April 19, 2018, video, YouTube, https://www.youtube.com/watch
?v=6FHuzGaOfuM. See also "About Us—PEPFAR," The United States President's Emergency
Plan for AIDS Relief, U.S. Department of State, accessed February 12, 2024, https://www.state
.gov/about-us-pepfar/; Anthony S. Fauci and Robert W. Eisinger, "PEPFAR—15 Years and
Counting the Lives Saved," *New England Journal of Medicine* 378, no. 4 (2018): 314–316.

52. King, *Where Do We Go From Here?*, 99.

53. Shaun R. Harper, "Many Men Talk Like Donald Trump in Private. And Only Other
Men Can Stop Them," *Washington Post*, October 8, 2016, https://www.washingtonpost.com
/posteverything/wp/2016/10/08/many-men-talk-like-donald-trump-in-private-and-only
-other-men-can-stop-them/.

54. See Young, "Deferring Group Representation," 352.

55. See, e.g., Sarah McCammon, "Want to Have Better Conversations about Racism
with Your Parents? Here's How," NPR, June 15, 2020, https://www.npr.org/2020/06/09
/873054935/want-to-have-better-conversations-about-racism-with-your-parents-heres
-how; Ijeoma Oluo, *So You Want to Talk about Race* (New York: Seal Press, 2018).

56. For a description of the harms of what she calls "compulsory representation," see
Davis, "Typecasts, Tokens, and Spokespersons," 490–493. See also Berenstain, "Epistemic
Exploitation"; and Salkin, "The Conscription of Informal Political Representatives."

57. Davis, "Typecasts, Tokens, and Spokespersons," 490–493; Berenstain, "Epistemic
Exploitation."

58. On communicative labor, see McKinney, "Communicative Labor."

59. Reni Eddo-Lodge, "Why I'm No Longer Talking to White People about Race," *Guardian,* May 30, 2017, https://www.theguardian.com/world/2017/may/30/why-im-no -longer-talking-to-white-people-about-race. See also Reni Eddo-Lodge, *Why I'm No Longer Talking to White People about Race* (London: Bloomsbury Circus, 2017). On self-silencing and what she calls "testimonial smothering," see Dotson, "Tracking Epistemic Violence."

60. Michelle T., quoted in Ann Friedman, "Blinded by the Light," *Ann Friedman Weekly* (blog), August 25, 2017, https://mailchi.mp/ladyswagger/blinded-by-the-light.

61. Eddo-Lodge, "No Longer Talking."

62. Michelle T., quoted in Friedman, "Blinded by the Light."

63. Sarah Ruiz-Grossman, "These White People Will Respond to Your Racist Trolls So You Don't Have To," *Huffington Post,* September 19, 2017, https://www.huffingtonpost .com/entry/white-nonsense-roundup-racism-white-privilege_us_59c1811ae4b0186c220 69390.

64. Michelle T., quoted in Friedman, "Blinded by the Light."

65. "How It Works," White Nonsense Roundup, accessed August 12, 2022, https:// whitenonsenseroundup.com/how-it-works/.

66. This may be a form of identity-prejudicial credibility deficit. On credibility deficit, see Fricker, *Epistemic Injustice,* 17–29.

67. Chenoa Alamu, quoted in Ruiz-Grossman, "These White People."

68. M. Remi Yergeau, in Christina Nicolaidis, Damian Milton, Noah J. Sasson, Elizabeth (Lizzy) Sheppard, and M. Remi Yergeau, "An Expert Discussion on Autism and Empathy," roundtable, *Autism in Adulthood* 1, no. 1 (2019): 7.

69. See Fricker, *Epistemic Injustice,* 21–22.

70. Alamu, quoted in Ruiz-Grossman, "These White People."

71. Michelle T., quoted in Friedman, "Blinded by the Light."

72. M. Remi Yergeau, *Authoring Autism: On Rhetoric and Neurological Queerness* (Durham, NC: Duke University Press, 2018), 5, 31, Kindle.

73. Dinah Murray, "Introduction," in *Coming Out Asperger: Diagnosis, Disclosure, and Self-Confidence,* ed. Dinah Murray (London: Jessica Kingsley, 2006), 13, quoted in Yergeau, *Authoring Autism,* 138–139.

74. Yergeau, *Authoring Autism,* 138–139, 151, 51, 83–84, 55.

75. Yergeau, *Authoring Autism,* 15. As Yergeau notes, "Clinicians wield many justifica- tions for claiming autistics are nonsymbolic and thereby non-rhetorical. Autistic people struggle with metaphor; autistic people do not speak and / or have speech patterns that bear evidence of neurodivergence; autistic people lack empathy, an ultimate kind of social sym- bolism; autistic people's bodies move involuntarily, void of goal direction; autistic people fail to imitate prosocial others or make social inferences; and so on" (53).

76. Francesca G. E. Happé, "Understanding Minds and Metaphors: Insights from the Study of Figurative Language in Autism," *Metaphor and Symbol* 10, no. 4 (1995): 282, quoted in Yergeau, *Authoring Autism,* 15.

77. Yergeau, *Authoring Autism*, 140, 139, 167, 136.

78. Yergeau, *Authoring Autism*, 50–51.

79. On what she calls "the 'retreat' response," see Alcoff, "The Problem of Speaking for Others," 8, 17–24. See also Dror, "Is There an Epistemic Advantage to Being Oppressed?," 637–38.

80. Sara Luterman, "The Biggest Autism Advocacy Group is Still Failing Too Many Autistic People," *Washington Post*, February 14, 2020, https://www.washingtonpost.com /outlook/2020/02/14/biggest-autism-advocacy-group-is-still-failing-too-many-autistic -people/; Cristina Zapata, "Autism Speaks Silences Autistic Individuals," *Daily Titan*, April 7, 2021, https://dailytitan.com/opinion/autism-speaks-silences-autistic-individuals/article _8e840b0c-972e-11eb-bb13-37e1247edb74.html; Virginia Hughes, "Autistic People Spark Twitter Fight against Autism Speaks," *BuzzFeed News*, February 23, 2015, https://www .buzzfeednews.com/article/virginiahughes/autistic-people-spark-twitter-fight-against -autism-speaks; John Elder Robison, "My Time with Autism Speaks," in *Autistic Community and the Neurodiversity Movement: Stories from the Frontline*, ed. Steven K. Kapp (Singapore: Springer Singapore, 2020), 221–232; David Perry, "Speaking Out against Autism Speaks, Even If It Means No Ice Cream," *New York Times*, June 4, 2015, https://parenting .blogs.nytimes.com/2015/06/04/speaking-out-against-autism-speaks-even-if-it-means-no -ice-cream/; Suzanne Wright, "Autism Changes Everything," *Parade*, January 27, 2008, https://web.archive.org/web/20081202080054/ http://www.parade.com/articles/editions /2008/edition_01-27–2008/Autism_Changes_Everything; Yergeau, *Authoring Autism*, 73, 147; "ASAN-AAC Statement on Autism Speaks' DC 'Policy Summit,'" Autistic Self Advocacy Network, November 12, 2013, https://autisticadvocacy.org/2013/11/asan-aac -statement-on-autism-speaks-dc-policy-summit/.

81. See, e.g., Nick Hughes, "Autism Speaks Doesn't Speak for Everyone with Autism," *LancasterOnline*, February 2, 2020, https://lancasteronline.com/opinion/columnists/autism -speaks-doesn-t-speak-for-everyone-with-autism/article_d0c6a982-4362-11ea-af7c -ef0c1fc2ec22.html; Lisa Lilianstrom, "Autism Speaks Does Not Speak for Autistic People," *Study Breaks*, May 22, 2020, https://studybreaks.com/thoughts/autism-speaks/; Kai Lockwood, "Why Autism Speaks Does Not Speak for the Autistic Community," *Exonian*, April 2, 2020, https://theexonian.net/opinions/why-autism-speaks-does-not-speak-for-the-autistic -community; Luterman, "The Biggest Autism Advocacy Group"; C. L. Lynch, "It's April, So It's Time to Argue about Autism Speaks," NeuroClastic, March 29, 2019, https:// neuroclastic.com/autism-speaks-just-no/; Isabelle Ouyang, "Autism Speaks Doesn't Speak for Autism," *Pitt News*, April 1, 2016, https://pittnews.com/article/70201/opinions/autism -speaks-doesnt-speak-for-autism/; John Elder Robinson, "I Resign My Roles at Autism Speaks," *Look Me in the Eye* (blog), November 13, 2013, http://jerobison.blogspot.com/2013 /11/i-resign-my-roles-at-autism-speaks.html; Kori Tomelden, "Autism Speaks (and Jenny McCarthy) Do Not Speak for Me and My Family," *Kori at Home* (blog), September 22, 2021, https://koriathome.com/autism-speaks-jenny-mccarthy-not-speak/; Emily Willingham,

"Why Autism Speaks Doesn't Speak For Me," *Forbes*, November 13, 2013, https://www
.forbes.com/sites/emilywillingham/2013/11/13/why-autism-speaks-doesnt-speak-for-me/
?sh=1f050f023152; Zapata, "Autism Speaks Silences"; Jeffrey Zide, "Autism Speaks Does
Not Represent the Voices of Autistic People," *Daily Sundial*, April 23, 2012, https://sundial
.csun.edu/51953/opinions/autism-speaks-does-not-represent-the-voices-of-autistic-people/.

82. Salkin, "The Conscription of Informal Political Representatives."

Chapter 7. Expertise and Representative Deference

1. "To Remedy Health Disparities, More Scientists Must 'Get Political,'" editorial, *Nature* 592 (2021): 660.

2. Rochelle Riley, "Dr. Mona Hanna-Attisha Goes from Doctor to Global Hero," *Detroit Free Press,* April 29, 2016, https://www.freep.com/story/news/columnists/rochelle-riley
/2016/02/06/dr-mona-hanna-attisha-goes-doctor-global-hero/79772514/. See also Mona
Hanna-Attisha, Jenny LaChance, Richard Casey Sadler, and Allison Champney Schnepp,
"Elevated Blood Lead Levels in Children Associated with the Flint Drinking Water Crisis:
A Spatial Analysis of Risk and Public Health Response," *American Journal of Public Health*
106, no. 2 (2016): 283–290.

3. "Remedy Health Disparities."

4. Michael Walzer, "The Obligations of Oppressed Minorities," in *Obligations: Essays on
Disobedience, War, and Citizenship* (Cambridge, MA: Harvard University Press, 1970), 46–73.

5. Walzer, "Oppressed Minorities," 48, 58.

6. Walzer, "Oppressed Minorities," 58. Although he focuses on activists, his arguments
are most concerned with the fact that activists tend to act on behalf of others, and he treats
his arguments as relevant to discussions of political representatives. See Walzer, "Oppressed
Minorities," 54n7, where he discusses Hanna Fenichel Pitkin on representatives. For both
of these reasons, I believe that his arguments apply to IPRs for oppressed or marginalized
groups, whether or not they are activists. Going forward, I shall simply discuss IPRs.

7. Walzer, "Oppressed Minorities," 58, 53.

8. Walzer, "Oppressed Minorities," 53.

9. Walzer, "Oppressed Minorities," 53.

10. These parties may later revise their opinions, determining that they had been helped
at that earlier time, even if they denied it then. Of such cases we would not say that the
parties had not been helped until they themselves avowed that they had. We would instead
say that they reflected on their former circumstances and realized that they had been helped
to begin with.

11. See, e.g., Manuel E. Jimenez, Zorimar Rivera-Núñez, Benjamin F. Crabtree,
Diane Hill, Maria B. Pellerano, Donita Devance, Myneka Macenat, et al., "Black and Latinx
Community Perspectives on COVID-19 Mitigation Behaviors, Testing, and Vaccines,"
JAMA Network Open 4, no. 7 (2021): e2117074, 2.

12. See, e.g., Sarah Maslin Nir, "Their Jobs Made Them Get Vaccinated. They Refused." *New York Times,* October 24, 2021, https://www.nytimes.com/2021/10/24/nyregion/new -york-workers-refuse-vaccine.html.

13. Yet even if you have helped them by preserving an option for them, you have done so in a manner that, on some accounts, would be characterized as paternalistic. See Seana Valentine Shiffrin, "Paternalism, Unconscionability Doctrine, and Accommodation," *Philosophy and Public Affairs* 29, no. 3 (2000): 214:

> Even some freedom-enhancing behavior can be paternalist. Suppose A creates opportunities or presents choices for B, with B's welfare in mind, that B has explicitly declared he would prefer not to have. B finds too much choice overwhelming or worries about yielding to temptation. A provides these opportunities in ways, however, that are perfectly legitimate exercises of A's freedom and that do not infringe any of B's autonomy rights or personal boundaries. If A provides these opportunities solely because she believes that B has mistakenly cabined himself off or would develop a better character if he were tested, then I think A's behavior is paternalist even though it enhances B's freedom, at least in one sense, by expanding her range of choices. Here again, A forcibly substitutes her judgment about the right way for B to exercise and develop her agency.

14. Walzer, "Oppressed Minorities," 53, emphasis added.

15. Walzer, "Oppressed Minorities," 53, 54.

16. Walzer, "Oppressed Minorities," 52, 54.

17. We can contrast this case with one in which the group's members instead object to single-payer healthcare at least partly because they regard it as an impermissible constraint on their freedom of choice. To the extent that the group opposes single-payer healthcare in the name of individual freedom, there is a value dispute and not just a disagreement over facts on which the expert IPR can reasonably claim theoretical authority.

18. Walzer, "Oppressed Minorities," 54.

19. Walzer, "Oppressed Minorities," 54.

20. Here, I rely on the notion of paternalism set forth in Shiffrin, "Paternalism," 211–220.

21. Walzer, "Oppressed Minorities," 54, emphasis added.

22. Walzer, "Oppressed Minorities," 53, 58.

23. Elisabeth Burgos-Debray, "Introduction," in Rigoberta Menchú, *I, Rigoberta Menchú: An Indian Woman in Guatemala,* ed. Elisabeth Burgos-Debray, trans. Ann Wright (New York: Verso Books, 2010), xi–xii: "The voice of Rigoberta Menchú allows the defeated to speak. . . . That is why she resolved to learn Spanish and break out of the linguistic isolation into which the Indians retreated in order to preserve their culture. Rigoberta learned the language of her oppressors in order to use it against them. . . . She decided to speak in order to tell of the oppression her people have been suffering for almost five hundred years, so that the sacrifices

made by her community and her family will not have been made in vain." See also Linda Alcoff, "The Problem of Speaking for Others," *Cultural Critique*, no. 20 (1991): 18–19.

24. Heidi Grasswick, "Feminist Social Epistemology," in *Stanford Encyclopedia of Philosophy*, Stanford University, 1997–, article last revised February 15, 2013, https://plato .stanford.edu/archives/win2016/entries/feminist-social-epistemology/.

25. Walzer, "Oppressed Minorities," 53–54.

26. See, e.g., Andrew C. Coyne, William E. Reichman, and Lisa J. Berbig, "The Relationship between Dementia and Elder Abuse," *American Journal of Psychiatry* 150, no. 4 (1993): 643–646; and Colm Owens and Claudia Cooper, "The Relationship between Dementia and Elder Abuse," *Working with Older People* 14, no. 1 (2010): 19–21.

27. See Sally J. T. Necheles, "Statutes Providing for Health-care Powers of Attorney and Proxies," in *Corpus Juris Secundum* 77, August 2023 update, Right to Die § 7, https://www .westlaw.com/Document/Idf2d7b26b67c11d9a49dec8cdbddd959/View/FullText.html ?transitionType=Default&contextData=(sc.Default)&VR=3.0&RS=cblt1.0; and Sally J. T. Necheles, "Particular Medical Conditions for Which Withdrawal of Treatment May Be Available," in *Corpus Juris Secundum* 77, August 2023 update, Right to Die § 18, https://www .westlaw.com/Document/I91e3fbb4a93111da8c99fcfa17adde4c/View/FullText.html ?transitionType=Default&contextData=(sc.Default)&VR=3.0&RS=cblt1.0.

28. A question worth consideration, but which I cannot treat here, is whether there is good reason, in general, to prefer that people living with severe dementia have IPRs who are themselves the legally appointed proxies of particular people living with severe dementia. This is a specification of a more general question concerning whether proxies ought to serve as IPRs. For recent discussions of this question in the context of autism, see Elle Benjamin, Bethany E. Ziss, and B. R. George, "Representation Is Never Perfect, But Are Parents Even Representatives?" *American Journal of Bioethics* 20, no. 4 (2020): 51–53; and Matthew S. McCoy, Emily Y. Liu, Amy S. F. Lutz, and Dominic Sisti, "Ethical Advocacy across the Autism Spectrum: Beyond Partial Representation," *American Journal of Bioethics* 20, no. 4 (2020): 13–24.

29. W. E. B. Du Bois, "Of Mr. Booker T. Washington and Others," in *The Souls of Black Folk*, ed. David W. Blight and Robert Gooding-Williams (Boston: Bedford Books, 1997), 70.

30. On uncrystallized interests, see Jane Mansbridge, "Should Blacks Represent Blacks and Women Represent Women? A Contingent 'Yes,'" *Journal of Politics* 61, no. 3 (1999): 643. On general consciousness, see Walzer, "Oppressed Minorities," 53.

Conclusion

1. George Bancroft, *History of the United States of America,* vol. 6, *From the Discovery of the Continent [to 1789]* (New York: D. Appleton, 1895), 190–191.

2. Hanna Fenichel Pitkin, *The Concept of Representation* (Berkeley: University of California Press, 1967), 38, 48, 55.

3. Pitkin, *Concept of Representation,* 39, 58, emphasis in the original.

4. On the conceptual shortcomings of formalistic accounts of political representation that define political representation in terms of ex ante authorization or ex post accountability, see Pitkin, *Concept of Representation,* 38–59.

5. This definition of *political representation* owes much to definitions offered elsewhere, and especially Suzanne Dovi, "Political Representation," in *Stanford Encyclopedia of Philosophy,* Stanford University, 1997–, article last revised August 29, 2018, https://plato.stanford .edu/archives/fall2018/entries/political-representation; and Michael Saward, *The Representative Claim* (New York: Oxford University Press, 2010), 48. The definition of *political* draws on Jane Mansbridge, "Everyday Talk in the Deliberative System," in *Deliberative Politics: Essays on Democracy and Disagreement,* ed. Stephen Macedo (Oxford: Oxford University Press, 1999), 214–215.

6. See, e.g., Leo Townsend and Dina Lupin, "Representation and Epistemic Violence," *International Journal of Philosophical Studies* 29, no. 4 (2021): 577–594.

7. See, e.g., Caitlin Murphy Brust and Hannah Widmaier, "U.S. Higher Education's Civic Responsibility to Educate for Informal Political Representation," *Educational Theory* (forthcoming).

8. W. E. B. Du Bois, "Of Mr. Booker T. Washington and Others," in *The Souls of Black Folk,* ed. David W. Blight and Robert Gooding-Williams (Boston: Bedford Books, 1997) 65, 64, 72.

9. Joseph Fishkin, "Taking Virtual Representation Seriously," *William and Mary Law Review* 59, no. 5 (2017): 1681–1728.

10. See, e.g., Daniela Cammack, "Representation in Ancient Greek Democracy," *History of Political Thought* 42, no. 4 (2021): 567–601. See also Daniela Cammack, *Demos: How the People Ruled Athens* (Princeton, NJ: Princeton University Press, forthcoming).

11. Alexander M. Bickel, "The Supreme Court and Reapportionment," in *Reapportionment in the 1970s,* ed. Nelson W. Polsby (Berkeley: University of California Press, 1971), 59, quoted in Lani Guinier, *The Tyranny of the Majority: Fundamental Fairness in Representative Democracy* (New York: Free Press, 1994), 268n21.

12. Legal Information Institute, "Stare Decisis," Cornell University, last updated December 2021, https://www.law.cornell.edu/wex/stare_decisis. There are different subtypes of stare decisis: *vertical stare decisis* is "the obligation of lower courts to follow the decisions of higher courts," while *horizontal stare decisis* is "the obligation of courts to follow their own prior decisions." Thomas Healy, "Stare Decisis and the Constitution: Four Questions and Answers," *Notre Dame Law Review* 83, no. 697 (2008): 1176n10. See also John Bourdeau; Paul M. Coltoff; Gary C. Fredenburg, of the staff of the National Legal Research Group, Inc.; John A. Gebauer; Karl Oakes; Karen L. Schultz; and Barbara J. Van Arsdale, "Effect of Stare Decisis on Appellate Determinations, Generally," in *American Jurisprudence, Appellate Review,* 2nd ed., October 2023 update, § 516, https://www.westlaw.com/Document/I 3f03dea6b27b11d9815db1c9d88f7df2/View/FullText.html?transitionType=Default &contextData=(sc.Default)&VR=3.0&RS=cblt1.0; Joseph W. Mead, "Stare Decisis in

the Inferior Courts of the United States," *Nevada Law Journal* 12, no. 3 (2012): 787–830; and Frederick Schauer, "Stare Decisis—Rhetoric and Reality in the Supreme Court," *Supreme Court Review* 2018 (2018): 121, 122.

13. Bourdeau et al., "Effect of Stare Decisis."

14. Stephen J. Ellmann, "Client-Centeredness Multiplied: Individual Autonomy and Collective Mobilization in Public Interest Lawyers' Representation of Groups," *Virginia Law Review* 78 (1992): 1106.

15. Ellmann, "Client-Centeredness Multiplied," 1106.

16. Deborah L. Rhode, "Public Interest Law: The Movement at Midlife," *Stanford Law Review* 60, no. 6 (2008): 2063.

17. Ellmann, "Client-Centeredness Multiplied," 1106.

18. Ellmann, "Client-Centeredness Multiplied," 1105–1106; Rhode, "Public Interest Law," 2063.

19. Scott L. Cummings, "Movement Lawyering," *University of Illinois Law Review* 2017 (2017): 1693. As Lucie E. White, "Mobilization on the Margins of the Lawsuit: Making Space for Clients to Speak," *New York University Review of Law and Social Change* 16, no. 4 (1998): 545, notes, welfare litigators "choose their plaintiffs strategically. The main criterion is how good the story will look to the court, how closely it will comply with a 'fact pattern' that will compel the desired legal remedy."

As Martha L. Gómez, "The Culture of Non-Profit Impact Litigation," *Clinical Law Review* 23, no. 2 (2017): 648–649, notes, nonprofit impact litigation organizations pick "media-appealing cases"—"the more splash the better."

Financial contributors' opinions influenced the selection of clients in school desegregation cases brought by civil rights attorneys. As Derrick A. Bell, Jr., "Serving Two Masters: Integration Ideals and Client Interests in School Desegregation Litigation," *Yale Law Journal* 85, no. 4 (1976): 490, recounts, "Jack Greenberg, LDF Director-Counsel, acknowledges that fundraising concerns may play a small role in the selection of cases." Leroy Clark, "The Lawyer in the Civil Rights Movement—Catalytic Agent or Counter-Revolutionary?," *University of Kansas Law Review* 19, no. 3 (1971): 469, contends that "too often the litigation undertaken was modulated by that which was 'salable' to the paying clientele who, in the radical view, had interests threatened by true social change." The clientele were "those liberals (usually white) who make financial contributions."

This is an issue we considered in the Chapter 5 discussion of the strategic occlusion complaint and the marriage equality cases.

20. Cummings, "Movement Lawyering," 1693.

21. Ronald R. Edmonds, "Advocating Inequity: A Critique of the Civil Rights Attorney in Class Action Desegregation Suits," *National Black Law Journal* 3, no. 2 (1974): 179.

22. Nathaniel R. Jones, quoted in Bell, "Serving Two Masters," 516n64.

23. Cummings, "Movement Lawyering," 1693. See also American Bar Association, *Model Rules of Professional Conduct* (Chicago: American Bar Association, 2020), rule 1.13, "Organization as Client."

24. See, generally, Ellmann, "Client-Centeredness Multiplied."

25. See, e.g., James Clifford, "On Ethnographic Authority," *Representations* 2 (1983): 118–146; Ta-Nehisi Coates, "Ta-Nehisi Coates Looks Back at 8 Years of Writing in the Obama Era," interview by Robin Young, *Here and Now,* WBUR, September 28, 2017, https://www.wbur.org/hereandnow/2017/09/28/ta-nehisi-coates-eight-years-in-power; Elise Hu, *Flawless: Lessons in Looks and Culture from the K-Beauty Capital* (Penguin Random House, 2023), 6; Nick Lee, "Towards an Immature Sociology," *Sociological Review* 46, no. 3 (August 1998): 458–482; Wesley Lowery, "Wes Lowery: A Reckoning on Race and Objectivity in Journalism," Fall 2021, Northeastern College of Arts, Media and Design, video, YouTube, https://www.youtube.com/watch?v=KRK_hueIodA; Wesley Lowery, *They Can't Kill Us All: Ferguson, Baltimore, and a New Era in America's Racial Justice Movement* (New York: Little, Brown, 2016); Kalonji Nzinga, David N. Rapp, Christopher Leatherwood, Matthew Easterday, Leoandra Onnie Rogers, Natalie Gallagher, and Douglas L. Medin, "Should Social Scientists Be Distanced from or Engaged with the People They Study?," *Proceedings of the National Academy of Sciences* 115, no. 45 (2018): 11435–11441; Paul Rabinow, "Discourse and Power: On the Limits of Ethnographic Texts," *Dialectical Anthropology* 10, no. 1 (1985): 1–13; Laurel Richardson, "Narrative and Sociology," *Journal of Contemporary Ethnography* 19, no. 1 (1990): 116–135; Laurel Richardson, "The Collective Story: Postmodernism and the Writing of Sociology," *Sociological Focus* 21, no. 3 (1988): 199–208; Eddie Rodrigues and John Game, "Anthropology and the Politics of Representation," *Economic and Political Weekly* 33, nos. 42–43 (1998): 2709–2714; Jay Ruby, "Speaking for, Speaking about, Speaking with, or Speaking Alongside: An Anthropological and Documentary Dilemma," *Visual Anthropology Review* 7, no. 2 (1991): 50–67; Joyce Trebilcot, "Dyke Methods: Principles for the Discovery / Creation of the Withstanding," *Hypatia* 3, no. 2 (1988): 1–13; Nancy N. Chen, "'Speaking Nearby': A Conversation with Trinh T. Minh-Ha," *Visual Anthropology Review* 8, no. 1 (1992): 82–91; and Dorothy Willner, "For Whom the Bell Tolls: Anthropologists Advising on Public Policy," *American Anthropologist* 82, no. 1 (1980): 79–94. See also, generally, Gabriela Vargas-Cetina, ed., *Anthropology and the Politics of Representation* (Tuscaloosa: University of Alabama Press, 2013); and Ida B. Wells and Alfreda M. Duster, *Crusade for Justice: The Autobiography of Ida B. Wells,* 2nd ed. (Chicago: University of Chicago Press, 2020), 226. Linda Alcoff, "The Problem of Speaking for Others," *Cultural Critique,* no. 20 (1991): 6, points out scholarly discussions of these questions as they have arisen in anthropology. For a discussion of the roles that celebrities sometimes play as both documentarians and representatives, see Alexandra Cosima Budabin, "Documentarian, Witness, and Organizer: Exploring Celebrity Roles in Human Rights Media Advocacy," in

The Social Practice of Human Rights, ed. Joel R. Pruce (New York: Palgrave Macmillan, 2015), 63–78.

26. James Baldwin, "Many Thousands Gone," in *Notes of a Native Son* (Boston: Beacon Press, 1984), 33.

27. I will set aside the question whether it is impossible to fulfill the role of IPR. I imagine that, by this, Baldwin means that a party who is speaking for a group cannot fully articulate the values, interests, preferences, and perspectives of, say, all thirteen million people in the group for whom one is expected to speak. As I have expressed throughout this book, this is not the standard IPRs are expected to meet.

28. Ta-Nehisi Coates, "Ta-Nehisi Coates Looks Back."

29. Baldwin, "Many Thousands Gone," 33.

30. Wendy Salkin, "'Writers Are Not Congressmen'" (unpublished manuscript, December 31, 2023), Microsoft Word file.

31. See, e.g., Todd Gitlin, *The Whole World Is Watching: Mass Media in the Making and Unmaking of the New Left* (Berkeley, CA: University of California Press, 2003).

Acknowledgments

So many people have been generous with me, offering their time, energy, ideas, and encouragement.

For extensive feedback and guidance on the entire manuscript, I am enormously grateful to Elizabeth Anderson, Juliana Bidadanure, Michael Bratman, Emilee Booth Chapman, Jorah Dannenberg, David Estlund, David Hills, Ty Larrabee, Jane Mansbridge, Alison McQueen, Bernadette Meyler, Rob Reich, Debra Satz, Leif Wenar, and several anonymous reviewers.

For thoughtful and generous feedback on parts of the manuscript, I thank especially R. Lanier Anderson, Olivia Bailey, Adam Burgos, Daniela Cammack, Rosa Cao, Thomas Christiano, Nico Cornell, Derrick Darby, Jamie Dow, Lidal Dror, Johann Frick, Mikkel Gerken, Jonathan Gingerich, David Glick, Sally Haslanger, Yarran Hominh, Dana Howard, Miikka Jaarte, Robin Jeshion, Karen Jones, Kalewold Hailu Kalewold, Andrew Kirton, Niko Kolodny, Christine Korsgaard, Krista Lawlor, Helen Longino, Meica Magnani, Barry Maguire, Eduardo J. Martinez, Eliot Michaelson, Jennifer Morton, Véronique Munoz-Dardé, Jonathan Parry, Luca Passi, Dee Payton, Govind Persad, David Plunkett, Gina Schouten, S. Andrew Schroeder, Molly Scudder, Seana Valentine Shiffrin, Lucas Stanczyk, Shruta Swarup, Olúfẹ́mi O. Táíwò, Robert Talisse, Pars Tarighy, Kenneth A. Taylor, Whitney K. Taylor, Lisa Miracchi Titus, César Valenzuela, Kate Vredenburgh, and R. Jay Wallace.

I am fortunate to have mentors whose guidance has made all the difference. Thank you to Sally Haslanger for all her support over the years, and for helping me find the feminist philosophers of Cambridge, Massachusetts, including Nancy Bauer and Naomi Scheman, who offered much support to this project. I am deeply grateful to Leif Wenar for many, many valuable and supportive conversations, and for all the time and care he has shown to me and to my work. I have benefited enormously from my conversations with Michael Bratman over the years—he has generously offered many insights and challenges that have made this project better. David Hills has engaged so thoughtfully and generously with this project and has helped me see more clearly its many nuances and intricacies. I remember one of my first trail runs with David Plunkett in Oslo. My goal was to explain the main arguments of this book without breaking my ankle. On top of teaching me how to run and talk shop at the same time, David has been a caring mentor and friend, and somehow always checks in at just the right time. In addition to reading and providing handwritten feedback on the entire manuscript, Jane Mansbridge has been a mentor and guide to me for the past several years—introducing me to fellow junior scholars, sending me notes whenever she thinks of new aspects of the project, and giving me guidance on how to balance the demands of finishing a book with the reality of grieving my father's death. Ned Markosian taught me to punt when we first met in (the other) Cambridge and has continued to show me the same kindness, support, and encouragement ever since. Candice Delmas has provided me endless guidance throughout graduate school and since, generously sharing valuable insights on life as a junior scholar. Gina Schouten has always, always made time for my many questions and given me a ton of valuable advice.

This book grew out of my doctoral studies. I was and am fortunate to have been encouraged and guided by a tremendously supportive dissertation committee, to whom I am immensely grateful: Tommie Shelby, T. M. Scanlon, Richard Moran, and Eric Beerbohm.

Tim Scanlon has offered tremendous support to both me and to this project, when I was his student and in the years since. He impressed upon me the importance of making enough distinctions and making the right distinctions. There are some questions that Tim asked me early on in this project that I had to sit with for a good many years before knowing even roughly what I wanted to say. A good advisor, I think, asks good questions, and Tim has asked me some of the most central and most challenging.

Dick Moran has always approached my work with support, enthusiasm, and encouragement. In every conversation, he encouraged me to explore the project's many branching themes and not to be afraid to make bold

Acknowledgments
341

claims. I am immensely grateful for all the time, care, and attention Dick has offered in sitting with me and thinking through this project together.

Eric Beerbohm has helped me understand how my work fits into the landscapes of both philosophy and political theory. He has encouraged me to think about how the framework I am developing provides new resources for handling perennial questions in moral and political philosophy. Also, he has read everything; his depth and breadth of knowledge across fields, and his generosity in discussing it all with me, have been invaluable.

There is nothing I can say here that will give adequate expression to my gratitude to Tommie Shelby, my dissertation chair. He has supported this project since before I knew what it was or what it could be. A caring, compassionate, engaged, supportive, and intellectually generous mentor, Tommie has left an indelible impression on how I think about both the discipline and the canon of philosophy—what they are and what they can become. The first time we met, I explained that I wanted to write about speaking for others and Tommie asked me if I had ever read W. E. B. Du Bois's *The Souls of Black Folk.* I had not, so I read it. As will be obvious to readers of this book, it left a deep and lasting impression on me. Tommie taught me the value of reading widely both within philosophy and across disciplines—learning from arguments wherever they arise and thinking through them methodically and seriously. He has encouraged me to develop my own voice or, as he often puts it, "Just say the thing." That has been a hallmark of my experience of working with and learning from Tommie: as much as he offers his own insights and guidance, he has also, in so many ways, encouraged me to trust myself and trust my own judgment about my work, to simply work through my ideas to see where they might lead. He has fundamentally shaped my understanding of what it is that philosophers do.

I have presented ideas and arguments from this book at colloquia, workshops, and conferences in many different places: several American Philosophical Association meetings; the American Political Science Association's annual meeting; the California Philosophy Workshop; a Caribbean Philosophical Association conference; Claremont McKenna College; the ConceptLab at the University of Oslo; the Economics and Philosophy Conference; the Feminist Ethics and Social Theory annual meeting; the Harvard Moral and Political Philosophy Workshop, the Institute of Philosophy–London; the Massachusetts Institute of Technology; New York University;

Northwestern University; the North American Society for Social Philosophy annual meeting; the Philosophers' Cocoon Philosophy Conference; the Philosophy Desert Workshop; the Philosophy, Politics, and Economics Society annual meeting; Pompeu Fabra University; Princeton University; Rutgers University; San Francisco State University; Stanford University; the University of Barcelona; the University of California–Berkeley; the University of California–Davis; the University of California–Los Angeles; the University of California–Merced; the University of California–San Diego; the University of Chicago; the University of Cincinnati; the University of Lausanne; the University of Leeds; the University of Melbourne; the University of Oxford; the Vancouver Summer Philosophy Conference; and Yale Law School. I thank the convenors of these events for their invitations and for all the work they put into making these events happen. I also thank all those present on these occasions for their generous engagement with this project.

I would also like to acknowledge with gratitude the financial and institutional support of the American Council of Learned Societies; the Clayman Institute for Gender Research, the Cultivating Humanities and Social Sciences Grant, the Department of Philosophy, the McCoy Family Center for Ethics in Society, and the Stanford Humanities Center at Stanford University; the ConceptLab at the University of Oslo; the Department of Philosophy, the Edmond & Lily Safra Center for Ethics, and the Harvard Horizons Scholars Program at Harvard University; and the Department of Philosophy at San Francisco State University.

Portions of Chapters 1 and 2 were first published as "The Conscription of Informal Political Representatives," *Journal of Political Philosophy* 29, no. 4 (2021): 429–455. Chapter 4 incorporates text first published as "Democracy Within, Justice Without: The Duties of Informal Political Representatives," *Noûs* 56, no. 4 (2022): 940–971.

To those at Harvard University Press, thank you for bringing this book into the world. Thanks especially to Sharmila Sen, editorial director, who asked me when I was still a graduate student whether I was thinking of writing a book, and who has guided me and championed my project ever since. Sam Stark, my extraordinary editor, provided detailed feedback and guidance on each chapter, and patient guidance throughout the entire process of bringing this book to fruition. Jillian Quigley and Katrina Vassallo have provided enormously helpful editorial assistance. I thank Brian Bendlin and Mary Ribesky for copyediting and manuscript preparation.

This work has been strengthened and developed through the care and attention of research assistants and students, to whom I will always be grateful. For meticulous proofreading, note-taking, and citation wrangling, I thank César Valenzuela, a tremendous democratic theorist. For thorough proofreading and thoughtful indexing, I thank Miikka Jaarte, an outstanding political philosopher. For research assistance, I thank Ashwin Pillai, a serious legal scholar. I owe special thanks, also, to students in my seminars "Representation: Race, Law, and Politics" and "Speaking for Others."

I am fortunate to have the care and support of several wonderful scholarly and personal communities.

Graduate school and law school were happy times, thanks to dear friends: Lauren Ashwell, Lucia Ballard, Colin Bossen, Lidal Dror, Jonathan Gingerich, Christopher Hu, Abby Jaques, Céline Leboeuf, R. J. Leland, Christopher Lewis, S. M. Love, Rebecca Mason, Rachel Ann McKinney, Emily McWilliams, Julie Miller, Tomer Perry, Govind Persad, Moira Pulitzer-Kennedy, Ronni Gura Sadovsky, Jiewuh Song, Rebecca Taylor, Kate Vredenburgh, and Alexander Westerfield. Myisha Cherry and Rose Lenehan regularly sat with me on weekend afternoons to write together at Forge Baking Company in Somerville, Massachusetts. Thank you all for so many kindnesses and so much care.

I am deeply grateful for the mentorship and support I received from my colleagues in the Department of Philosophy at San Francisco State University. I am especially grateful to Ásta and the late Anita Silvers, who have supported and championed my projects since I was a graduate student. I also made several wonderful friends there: Rebecca Eissler has taught me how to celebrate small victories and how to press the Submit button. I am grateful for her friendship and our quality time spent watching sports together over the years. Robert Bonner, one of the most widely read people I know, has generously explored the ideas in this book with me many times over the years, and is always brimming with interesting examples and generative questions. Many of the arguments in this book were first tested out on long hikes with Whitney K. Taylor and our dogs, Birdie and Jackson. Fortunately, Whitney asked me the hardest questions when we were walking uphill, which allowed me to pretend I was unable to answer simply because I was winded. Thanks also to Kurt Nutting and Stephanie Kay for opening their home up to all of us (dogs included) on many weekend afternoons so that we could share stories, joke around, and relax in the sunshine;

and thanks to both Kurt and Stephanie for many fruitful and illuminating conversations about the ideas in this book.

I have been fortunate to have the support of a writing accountability group with whom I have met most weekdays for the past five years. Thank you to this group's participants, and special thanks to Emilee Booth Chapman, Tamar Green, Matthew Kohrman, Lisa Ouellette, and Aruna Ranganathan. I am grateful to both Kim Bain and Erin Lin, fellow participants in the Creative Connections Writing Retreat, for regular check-ins, boundless encouragement, and stunning portraits of their four-legged friends, Lord Baron of Bumblebee, Esq.; Mister Mistoffelees, M.D.; and Rubble "Lord Butterscotch" Lin. I thank Colin Bossen for encouraging me to pursue this project since graduate school, for hosting our writing retreat in Houston, and for many years of friendship.

Thank you to my neighbors and friends, who make life at Stanford University particularly sweet: Juliana Bidadanure, Anna Bigelow, Rosa Cao, Gregor Carrigan, Emilee Booth Chapman, Jorah Dannenberg, Thomas Icard, Hakeem Jefferson, Hayden Kantor, Roanne Kantor, Xiaochang Li, Alison McQueen, Antonia Peacocke, Solé Prillaman, Steven Roberts, Isaac Sorkin, Leif Wenar, and Mary Wootters. I am grateful to you for early morning runs, doggy play dates, long walks to talk through new ideas, board games, snacks, laughter, spending time with your wonderful families, and endless good advice and encouragement.

Julienne Grey has shown so much attention to and care about my research. She sends me "The Wendy Digest" every day, a compilation of articles and social media posts related to informal political representation, along with cheerful animal pictures. M. Rebekah Otto and Raphi Gottesman have encouraged this project, and me, for many years and on two coasts.

I dedicate this book to the memory of my grandmother, Joann Dziegiel, who encouraged me to read, be curious, and ask questions.

I finished writing this book the summer my father died. I had to be away from home for long periods of time and wrote on planes, and in airports, hospital rooms, and the homes of family and friends.

To my dear lifelong friends, thank you. Caseen Gaines and Johanna Calle, and their dogs Penny and Zira, opened their home to me, fed me, provided me dedicated writing space, brainstormed with me about this book, and supported me during an unpredictable and challenging time. Thank you also to Daniel Carola, Angela DeGregorio, Ashley Frabizzio,

Holly Martins, Kathleen Mish, Katie O'Connell, Mara Picca, Brian Roy, Fiona Sarne, Pars Tarighy, and the Townes family for your presence and outpouring of love and support during this time, and always. You all make home home.

Thank you to my parents-in-law, Angela and Tim Larrabee, for welcoming me into your family, taking me into your home, and letting me hide out in your backyard all summer, revising; to my siblings-in-law, Alex, Alyse, and Sydney Larrabee, for your love and compassion, and to the family dogs (Chubbs, Dublin, Remy, Rommi, and Taffy) for a lot of much-needed companionship. Thank you to the Larrabees, and to Jake Chamberlain, for taking care of our dog, Birdie, when we could not be with her.

Thank you to my aunt Ambor Elliott, my cousin Alyson Mitchel, her husband Nicholas Mitchel, my niblings Nixon and Sage, and their dog, Royal, for checking in on me, feeding me, and welcoming me into their homes over the past many years. My visits with them are invariably joyful—filled with laughter, fun, and so much food. Their unwavering love, support, generosity, and guidance have always helped me find a clear path.

Thank you to my husband, Ty Larrabee, and our dog, Birdie, for uprooting their lives to be everywhere I was while I balanced revising and grieving. Ty and Birdie joined me for many long walks into canyons in the unrelenting Utah summer heat just because I asked and I love them both so very much. Ty reads everything I write, often on short notice. He attends to every detail and leaves no question unasked. We have spent many mornings working through the ideas in this book together (and many afternoons and evenings too). His guidance, encouragement, love, support, and strongly held opinions on matters of grammar have been invaluable to me as I have written and rewritten this book. I also thank him for his endless patience in allowing this project to shape our lives in so many ways over the past several years. His sense of humor and overall optimism keep our home happy even as deadlines approach.

Thank you to my sister, Kerry J. Salkin, my brother-in-law David Futterman, my niblings Joshua and Anna, and their dog, Schmutz. Kerry and David took our father in, managed his affairs, and made the final months of his life as good as they could possibly have been. They did so while raising two small children and working full-time. On top of all that, they took me in, fed me, and comforted me as we all grieved. They made their home my home, and some of my best writing happened in their living room. As sad as these past many months have been, our time together has deepened our bonds, and I hope they know just how central they were to the completion of this book. (Thanks, also, to Josh and Anna for sharing their pizza and fries with me, and for always being sources of silliness and joy.)

Thank you to my mom, Linda B. Celauro, and her husband, Richard Regan, for making sure I was well fed. I learned from my mother what hard work looks like. (Even after retiring from her long and distinguished career as a lawyer, she still puts in way too many hours.) My whole life, she has worked tirelessly to make other people's lives, and especially mine, better. She frequently takes on difficult and complex projects for the people in her life—managing their health care, helping them find housing, settling their affairs upon their passing—just because these projects need doing. She is the person I turn to when I need to learn how to do something, because she knows how to do everything. She has sacrificed so much so that her daughter could become a philosopher, of all things. Thank you, Mom, for everything, always. I love you. This book is for you.

I began writing these acknowledgments while my dad, Richard E. Salkin, slept in his hospital room in Hackensack, New Jersey, the city where I grew up and where he was involved in local politics for many years. As his health declined, I felt the pull of home, where I spent my childhood putting up lawn signs and attending city council meetings. And although, perhaps to his credit, my dad did not call it *informal political representation,* he was the first to point out to me how important unelected spokespersons are to both the everyday function and long-term progress of a political community. I spoke with my dad most days for most of my life, and during our conversations, he offered patient encouragement and guidance, reassuring me often: "You'll get it done. You always have, you always will." I finished writing this book after he died and, so, before he got to read it. But he already knew everything in it from years of devoted public service. This book is for him.

Index

Abahlali baseMjondolo (movement), 8

Abernathy, Ralph, 119–120, 122

accountability, 11–12, 39–42, 114, 141, 145, 151; formal mechanisms for, 39; informal mechanisms for, 39–40; as unnecessary for informal political representation to emerge, 263–264

acting for, 322–323n1; conceived as a spectrum of phenomena, 296n10, 298n32; the sake of another, 307n14. *See also* speaking for

activists, 186

Africans, 14–15, 190, 221–222

AIDS. *See* HIV / AIDS

Alamu, Chenoa, 227–228

Alcoff, Linda, 35–36, 285n4

allyship, 206. *See also* nondescriptive representation

American Indians. *See* Indigenous people

anchoring effects, 142, 184, 198, 312n14

Anderson, Elizabeth, 170

apparent authority. *See* de facto informal political representatives: exhibiting apparent authority

art. *See* artistic freedom; artists

artistic freedom, 279–281

artists, 102–103, 277–280

ascription, 36, 46, 47, 50, 52, 54, 56, 75, 130; preemptive ascription, 50. *See also* conferral actions

audience conferral, 25, 33–34, 36–37, 43, 46–49, 109, 264, 294n59; aggregative, 57–58; backward-looking, 54; collective, 57–59; creating conditions that make audience conferral more likely, 60–62, 82, 101, 189–190, 235, 282; criticizable, 68–69, 265; defined, 46; derivative, 82, 85, 87; diachronic, 51–53; different types of, 298n24; distinguished from group authorization, 109–111, 296n14; by

disempowered audiences, 97–98; by empowered audiences, 96–97, 137; due to epistemic error, 65–69, 74; forward-looking, 54; key features of, 47–49; as necessary condition for informal representation, 43, 69–70; outstanding questions regarding, 265, 267; permissibility of, 85–92, 103; powers, permissions, and duties bestowed through, 111; and the power to influence, 47, 93; reasonableness of, 84–85, 87, 103; in the Second Continental Congress, 262–264; synchronic, 51–54; types of, 298n24; ubiquity of, 83, 90; and Booker T. Washington, 49–63, 129–130; widespread, 57, 59. *See also* audience conferral permissibility test; conferral actions; conferring audiences

audience conferral account, 46, 64–76; advantages of, 66–69, 72–76; concerns with, 73–74, 294n61

audience conferral permissibility test, 86–91, 103, 266–267

audiences. *See* conferring audiences

authorization. *See* group authorization; informal authorization

authorized informal political representatives, 19, 26, 72, 75, 123–124, 127; criticism of, 185, 199; distinguished from de facto informal political representatives, 19, 26, 72, 75–76, 110–111, 267; and principal-agent relationships, 112–115. *See also* discretionary and normative powers of authorized informal political representatives; group authorization; informal authorization; informal ratification

authors, 102–103, 277–280

autism, 228, 230–231, 235–236, 330n75

Autism Speaks (organization), 235–236

Ellman, Stephen, 275
emotional labor. *See* communicative labor
epistemic authority. *See* expertise
epistemic objectification, 213, 216
eradication (principle), 20, 21, 146–148, 165, 167, 171, 173, 198. See also *justice without* duties
Eskridge, William, 195–196
essentialism, 212–213, 222, 236
expertise, 22, 82, 216, 231, 238–240, 249–251; in health care policy, 243–246, 249; as justification for non-deference, 251–253; outstanding questions regarding, 273; and paternalism, 239, 246, 253–257, 273–274; and relational equality, 239, 245–247, 259; and value disputes, 333n17; Michael Walzer on, 239–245, 247–249, 251–253. *See also* representative deference principle
explicit request. *See* nondescriptive representation
expressive-wrong complaints, 184, 185, 186, 188, 190
external point of view, 182–183

failure-to-consult complaints, 184, 188–189, 192, 199, 277–278
false consciousness, 22–23, 240, 251–252, 257
Feinstein, Dianne, 181
Flint water crisis, 238
formalistic accounts of representation, 262
formalizing informal political representation, 41, 162–164, 263; desirability of, 162–163; feasibility of, 162; outstanding questions regarding, 274–275
formal political representation, 1, 163; defined, 37; distinguished from informal political representation, 1, 37–41; exclusion of oppressed and marginalized groups from, 9–10, 137, 143, 165, 282
formal political representatives, 1; as agents of their constituents, 114–115; authorization of, 38, 42, 114, 116; in backsliding or defective democracies, 140, 144, 145; legitimate complaints against, 146, 318n6; normative powers of, 114; simultaneously acting as informal political representatives, 41, 88, 102, 146, 274–275, 276
Freedom's Journal (publication), 141

Gay, Claudine, 217
Gayle, W. A., 33, 44, 60–62, 82, 92, 124–125, 171, 189–190. *See also* audience conferral: creating conditions that make audience con-

ferral more likely; King, Martin Luther, Jr.; Montgomery Bus Boycott
Geldof, Bob, 15, 190, 221
general consciousness criterion, 239, 242, 243, 248, 257, 258
Gershon, David Harris, 12
Griffiths, A. Phillips, 322–323n1
group authorization, 19, 38, 42, 74, 75, 76, 108, 109–112, 115–122, 132, 140, 145, 189–190, 234, 267, 269, 295n63, 301n70; as condition for the permissibility of audience conferral, 85–86, 88–90, 103; defined, 115; and *democracy within* duties, 21, 23, 138, 148, 153, 154, 171–172, 177–178, 192; distinguished from audience conferral, 26, 109–112; distinguished from group conferral, 43, 55, 109, 111, 131–134, 298n24; effects of, 122–131; and expert deference, 246, 247, 250, 254–256, 274; feasibility of, 71–72, 76, 171, 245, 266; formal and informal, 38, 42; outstanding questions regarding, 269; powers, permissions, and duties bestowed through, 111, 122–131, 142–143, 172, 259, 269, 307n14; as putative condition for informal representation, 26, 65, 70–73; types of, 115–122; as unnecessary for informal political representation to emerge, 71–74, 263–264. *See also* de facto informal political representatives: exhibiting apparent authority; informal authorization; informal ratification
group conferral, 43, 44, 55, 109, 111, 131–132, 250, 254, 255, 298n24, 299n50. *See also* audience conferral; group authorization
group consciousness, 4–5, 6, 7–8, 15, 137, 166, 248. *See also* general consciousness criterion
group homogeneity, 248; false assumption of, 12–13, 20, 79, 106, 212–213, 248, 303n21; informal representatives encouraging false assumption of, 137, 141, 144–145, 146, 151
group representation, 4–5, 169, 208, 213, 312n17; legal representation as, 275–278. *See also* represented groups
group speech acts, 296n11
group testimony, 23
gun violence, 2
gyroscopic representation, 307n14

Hanna-Attisha, Mona, 238
Happé, Francesca, 230
Harper, Shaun R., 225
Harris, Kamala, 92–93
Hart, H. L. A., 182, 189

Monbiot, George, 14, 197, 221
Montanaro, Laura, 79, 96, 302n13
Montgomery Advertiser (publication), 61
Montgomery Bus Boycott, 2, 19, 33, 44, 61–62, 82, 119–128, 157, 190, 194, 317n65; and en masse consultation, 156; as example of conflict between *democracy within* and *justice without* duties, 171–173, 176; as example of group authorization, 76, 110, 112, 115, 121, 306–307n11; and overcommitment, 142–143; and occlusion, 194; and proxy consultation, 155, 157
Montgomery Improvement Association (MIA), 33, 41, 61, 102, 124, 171, 190
Morton, Jennifer, 214
Mosely, Benjamin F., 61, 82, 189–190
Movement for Black Lives. *See* Black Lives Matter (movement)

National Association for the Advancement of Colored People (NAACP), 18, 39, 278
Native Americans. *See* Indigenous people
Nature (publication), 238
negotiation, 4, 123–128, 172–173, 199–200, 204, 210–211, 212, 220–221, 233, 308n28, 308–309n29
Netanyahu, Benjamin, 12, 41, 62, 181
New Orleans Tribune, The (publication), 207
Nixon, E. D., 119, 122
no conferral needed alternative, 64–65, 69–70
noncontribution (principle), 20, 21, 146–147, 148, 149, 171, 173. *See also democracy within* duties
nondescriptive representation, 18, 22, 23, 91–92, 201, 203, 205–206, 214, 215, 216, 218, 221, 219, 223–235, 267–278; of autistic people, 228, 230–231, 235–236; of Black Americans, 223–224; of LGBTQIA+ people, 254–256; outstanding questions regarding, 273–274; as permissible due to audience discounting, 227–232; as permissible due to burdens on descriptive representatives, 226–227, 229, 232; as permissible due to explicit request of group members, 227, 233; as permissible due to group's risks of exposure, 232; as permissible due to restricted access, 222, 224–226, 232; and widespread group disavowal, 234–236; of women, 225. *See also* descriptive preference principle; discounting; restricted access
non-ideal theory, 27–28. *See also* ideal theory

nonmember deference principle, 255–257, 273–274
normatively neutral approach, the, 24–27, 55, 67
norms: formal and informal, 40–42

Obama, Barack, 12, 92
objectification, 213, 214, 216, 222, 236
objective interests. *See* interests
occlusion, 11, 14, 143, 144, 145, 149, 150, 151; complaints, 184, 193–194, 199; of differences within a group, 208, 211, 213–214; to highlight the interests of a subset of the group, 11, 194–197, 312n17; to self-aggrandize, 11, 193–194; strategic, 195–197
oppressed and marginalized groups, 9–11; and community recognition, 169; and exclusion from formal political representation, 9–10, 137, 143, 165, 170, 283; as focus of non-ideal theory, 28; representatives' duties to, 20–21, 28, 138–139, 269. *See also democracy within* duties; *justice without* duties; reliance on informal political representatives: of oppressed and marginalized groups
oppression, 9–10; by informal political representatives, 11–12, 144–145, 149, 173–174, 242; the silencing effect of, 122, 156
overcommitment, 20, 137, 142–143, 145, 151; and group authorization, 172
Oxfam (organization), 79

pandemic. *See* COVID-19
partiality complaints, 184, 188–189, 190, 199, 319n18
partial representation, 312n11
paternalism, 23, 221–222, 239, 240, 246, 253–256, 273–274, 333n13
Pitkin, Hanna Fenichel, 263, 307n14, 322–323n1
political agency, 10, 139, 168–169, 170
political apathy, 169
political influence, 10, 137, 139, 168, 170, 178, 239, 316n58
political representation (in general), 5–6, 43–46, 262–263; space of, 38–42, 263, 275, 306–307n11. *See also* politics (subject matter)
politics (subject matter), 43–46, 298n25. *See also* informal nonpolitical representation
power, 293n46
power to influence, 11, 17–18, 19–20, 25, 26, 27, 33, 36, 47, 48, 66–69, 72, 77, 92–93, 111, 266; as a capacity to create expectations in audiences, 95–96; conferred by audiences, 97; of